VISUAL STUDIO HACKS™

Other resources from O'Reilly

Related titles	Excel Hacks™	Programming C#
	Windows Server Hacks™	C# Cookbook
	Windows XP Hacks™	Programming ASP.NET
	XML Hacks™	ASP.NET Cookbook

Hacks Series Home   *hacks.oreilly.com* is a community site for developers and power users of all stripes. Readers learn from each other as they share their favorite tips and tools for Mac OS X, Linux, Google, Windows XP, and more.

oreilly.com   *oreilly.com* is more than a complete catalog of O'Reilly books. You'll also find links to news, events, articles, weblogs, sample chapters, and code examples.

oreillynet.com is the essential portal for developers interested in open and emerging technologies, including new platforms, programming languages, and operating systems.

Conferences   O'Reilly brings diverse innovators together to nurture the ideas that spark revolutionary industries. We specialize in documenting the latest tools and systems, translating the innovator's knowledge into useful skills for those in the trenches. Visit *conferences.oreilly.com* for our upcoming events.

Safari Bookshelf (*safari.oreilly.com*) is the premier online reference library for programmers and IT professionals. Conduct searches across thousands of electronic books simultaneously, and zero in on the information you need in seconds. Read the books on your Bookshelf from cover to cover or simply flip to the page you need. Try it today for free.

VISUAL STUDIO HACKS™

James Avery

O'REILLY®

Beijing · Cambridge · Farnham · Köln · Paris · Sebastopol · Taipei · Tokyo

Visual Studio Hacks™
by James Avery

Copyright © 2005 O'Reilly Media, Inc. All rights reserved.
Printed in the United States of America.

Published by O'Reilly Media, Inc., 1005 Gravenstein Highway North,
Sebastopol, CA 95472.

O'Reilly books may be purchased for educational, business, or sales promotional use. Online editions are also available for most titles (*safari.oreilly.com*). For more information, contact our corporate/institutional sales department: (800) 998-9938 or *corporate@oreilly.com*.

Editor:	Brian Jepson	**Production Editor:**	Mary Brady
Series Editor:	Rael Dornfest	**Cover Designer:**	Hanna Dyer
Executive Editor:	Dale Dougherty	**Interior Designer:**	David Futato

Printing History:

March 2005:	First Edition.

 This book uses RepKover™, a durable and flexible lay-flat binding.

ISBN: 0-596-00847-3
[C]

Contents

Credits

About the Author

James Avery is an accomplished author and .NET architect. In addition to this book, James has written books for Microsoft Press and Wrox as well as publishing articles with *MSDN Magazine* and *ASPToday*.

After working for a number of large corporations and consulting companies, James recently left his job to go out on his own and formed his own company, Infozerk, Inc. (*http://www.infozerk.com*). James also founded and is the current president of the Cincinnati .NET User Group.

James lives in Cincinnati, Ohio, with his wonderful wife Tammy and their three cats. When he is not working on the laptop, you can find him fiddling with his digital cameras, reading, or playing Xbox.

James is a frequent blogger, and you can find his blog at *http://www.dotavery.com/blog*. James can also be contacted by email at *javery@infozerk.com*.

Contributors

I was very lucky that so many of the great people I asked to contribute to this book decided to do so. The list of contributors for this book runs the gamut from professional authors to individual, add-in developers. They did an incredible job, and this book would not be the same without them.

- Jamie Cansdale (*jamie.cansdale@testdriven.net*) is a London-based consultant programmer. In previous lives, he wrote computer games for Ocean and was a Java consultant for Sun Microsystems. More recently, he has been specializing in test-driven development and continuous integration on the .NET platform. He is the author of the TestDriven.NET add-in for Visual Studio and maintains a web log at *http://www.testdriven.net/weblog*.

- Jayme Davis is an enterprise application developer in Nashville, Tennessee. He has been working with Microsoft technologies for seven years, including .NET since the second beta release. You can reach Jayme at *jaymedav@yahoo.com.*

- Steven DeWalt is a Systems Architect living and working in the Columbus, Ohio, area. He began his career in computers at the ripe old age of 12, primarily with the now classic Commodore 64. Steven has a bachelor's degree in Computer and Information Science from Ohio State University. Steven was involved in the .NET Enterprise Early Adopter Program in 2001. He currently works for a large midwestern insurance company. As of late, Steven's been working a lot with .NET Interop with WinDNA/COM and J2EE.

- Dave Donaldson is an independent consultant specializing in application architecture and development for the Microsoft .NET platform. As an independent consultant, Dave spends much of his time working with his customers' technology leaders to ensure they implement .NET solutions appropriately. Before going independent, Dave spent five and a half years at Nationwide Insurance implementing large-scale web applications, in particular leading the effort to build the billing web application for managing customer bills. In addition to his consultant work, Dave is very active in the .NET community (online and offline) and is also a part-time author. He maintains a .NET software development blog at *http://www.arcware.net* and has been published in leading industry publications such as *MSDN Magazine* and *VB2TheMax.*

- As editor and main contributor to 4GuysFromRolla.com, a popular ASP/ASP.NET resource web site, Scott Mitchell has authored literally hundreds of articles on Microsoft web technologies since 1998. In addition to his vast collection of online articles, Scott has authored five books on ASP/ASP.NET. Scott has also written a number of print magazine articles, including articles for Microsoft's MSDN Magazine and asp.netPRO, as well as online content for Microsoft's MSDN web site. Scott's nonwriting accomplishments include public speaking, training, and software development. Scott holds a master's degree in Computer Science from the University of California, San Diego and is married to the beautiful Jisun. He can be reached at *mitchell@4guysfromrolla.com* or through his blog at *http://ScottOnWriting.NET.*

- Darrell Norton is a Senior Consultant for CapTech Ventures, a regional consulting firm in Richmond, Virginia. When he's not programming .NET, he spends his free time working out, snowboarding, and reading. His blog can be found at *http://www.codebetter.com/blogs/darrell.*

- Chris Nurse was born in Bradford, England, in 1964 and was given his first introduction to computers at the age of 12. Since then, hardly a day has gone by when he has not touched a computer. In 2002, Chris moved to Perth, Australia, where he spent two years writing patents until moving to a position developing software for the Department of Justice in Perth. There he is part of a team working on one of the largest .NET projects in Australia. In December 2002, Chris married Bobbie; the two were the first people in history to marry at the end of the world famous Bussleton Jetty. When not at the computer, Chris is either playing guitar or enjoying his recently discovered passion for fishing on the West Coast of Australia.

- Alex Papadimoulis lives in Berea, Ohio, and has lived in the Cleveland area his entire life. Currently employed by Ohio Savings Bank, he's been involved in information technology development for nearly a decade. Alex was awarded a bachelor of Computer Science from Baldwin Wallace College in 2002. Alex can usually be found answering questions in various Microsoft .NET newsgroups and posting some rather interesting real-life examples of how not to program on his blog, TheDailyWTF.com. You can contact Alex directly via email at *alex@papadimoulis.com*.

- Brian Sherwin is the Principal Member of SureWin Solutions, LLC, a consulting and training company focused on bringing companies back to making decisions on value, not a particular technology. As a consultant for nine years, he has worked with a number of technologies but has pitched his tent in the Microsoft camp with SQL Server and the .NET platform. Brian has been training developers in VB and C# since .NET was released into public beta in 2002. In his spare time, he enjoys being creative and playing games with his three children, Stephen, Anna, and JohnMark.

- Ben Von Handorf has been working with the .NET Framework since the beta in 2001. He currently works for Business Integration Group in Cincinnati, Ohio, where he also pursues his expensive hobbies including aviation and elderly felines.

- Roland Weigelt (whose blog can be found at *http://weblogs.asp.net/ rweigelt*) has been writing software since 1983, developing for PCs since 1988. His experience includes programming in C/C++, Java, JavaScript, Visual Basic, XSL, and C#. He is currently employed as a software developer at Comma Soft AG in Bonn, Germany, where he is working on frontend technologies, development tools, and framework API design in general.

- Michael Wood is a .NET developer and has been working with .NET since before Beta 2 in 2001. He lives in northern Kentucky and works across the river in Ohio as a developer and solution designer. His blog and contact information can be found at *http://www.mvwood.com/blog*.

Acknowledgments

My dad was a hacker before the term *hacker* was ever coined. Just about everything he has ever purchased or acquired has been taken apart, enhanced, gooped, or duct taped. Thanks, Dad, for showing me that just about anything can be improved (or broken).

A book is possible only with incredible effort from so many people. First, I would like to thank the people at O'Reilly, especially my editor Brian Jepson. I was lucky to have an editor who not only knows the technology but also is passionate about it. Brian did an incredible job throughout the entire process, and I greatly appreciate all of his great advice and hard work. I also want to thank John Osborn for working with me for more than a year to get this book out of the proposal phase and into actual writing.

I want to thank the following Microsofties for answering my emails and questions: Jim Blizzard, Mark Cliggett, Dan Fernandez, Sara Ford, Catherine Heller, James Lau, Adam Nathan, Scott Nonnenberg, Andy Pennell, Harry Pierson, Jason Salas, and Scott Swanson.

I would especially like to thank Josh Ledgard who helped me all the way from the proposal stage to being one of the technical reviewers for this book. I wish everyone at Microsoft had the same community passion that he does.

I want to thank all of my contributors and technical reviewers; they all went above and beyond the call of duty to ensure that this book was the best it could be. Ben Von Handorf, Dave Donaldson, and Jamie Cansdale all pulled double duty and were both contributors and technical reviewers. All three of these gentlemen contributed greatly to this book and deserve many thanks.

I also want to thank all the add-in and macro authors who gave me permission to talk about their add-ins or include their macros in this book. I hope they enjoy seeing their work in print.

I want to thank my mom for reading through an entire chapter of something she didn't understand just so she could remind me what correct grammar is (and take out all my commas).

Most of all, I want to thank my beautiful wife Tammy for her support during all the late nights and long weekends it took to write this book.

Preface

"Developers, developers, developers, developers, developers, developers," Steve Ballmer can be heard chanting while bouncing around on stage in a popular movie clip that circulated the Internet a while back. This movie is pretty recent, but this has really been the mantra of Microsoft since the very beginning. One thing Microsoft has always understood is that the platform that developers love is the platform that will have the most applications. Naturally the platform with the most applications is the platform that will be popular with users.

Because Microsoft has always focused on developers, providing high quality documentation and high-quality development tools has been a high priority for them from the beginning. Visual Studio is the culmination of more than 20 years of development tools. Visual Studio is one of the best development environments available anywhere and has long been considered one of the best reasons to use Microsoft development languages.

Visual Studio includes an incredible number of features, is very customizable, has a complete automation model, and much more. On top of the normal features in Visual Studio are hosts of free add-ins, macros, and power toys that can further enhance the functionality of Visual Studio. This book is all about exploring those features, add-ins, macros, and power toys and, through that, helping you become a better and more efficient developer.

Why Visual Studio Hacks?

The term *hacking* has a bad reputation in the media. They use it to refer to people who break into systems or wreak havoc with computers as their weapons. Among people who write code, though, the term *hack* refers to a "quick-and-dirty" solution to a problem or a clever way to get something done. And the term *hacker* is taken very much as a compliment, referring to someone as being *creative*—having the technical chops to get things done.

The Hacks series is an attempt to reclaim the word, document the good ways people are hacking, and pass on the hacker ethic of creative participation to the uninitiated. Seeing how others approach systems and problems is often the quickest way to learn about a new technology.

Visual Studio is an application that was ripe to have a Hacks book written about it. When I first got a copy of *Google Hacks* (the first Hacks book), I knew that this book had to be written. There are tons of tips and tricks, add-ins, and extensions for Visual Studio. I have watched presentations on a completely different topic when the presenter suddenly had to show off some cool trick figured out in Visual Studio. Trading Visual Studio tips and tricks has always been a favorite pastime of developers at conferences, in user groups, and at geek dinners. I wanted to capture those tips, tricks, add-ins, and extensions and compile them all together in one book.

When I first started thinking about writing this book, I knew I would be faced with a big decision on how to approach it. I could have written a book for the people who write add-ins, macros, and VSIP projects. While I think that book would have been a great deal of fun to write, I also think it would have left 99% of the developers out there in the dark.

Instead, I decided to write a book for every developer who uses Visual Studio. This book includes hacks that should benefit developers of all types, not just developers interested in extending Visual Studio. Although some of the hacks are about extending Visual Studio, that is not the focus of this book. Rather, the focus is learning how to better use this powerful application.

How to Use This Book

You can read this book from cover to cover if you like, but each hack stands on its own. So feel free to browse and jump to the sections that interest you most. If there's a prerequisite you need to know about, a cross-reference will guide you to the right hack.

An Important Note About Keyboard Shortcuts

Keyboard shortcuts can be used to save time when working with an application. Instead of taking your hands off the keyboard and reaching for the mouse, you can use a shortcut key and keep your hands on the keyboard. Throughout this book, we reference keyboard shortcuts for a number of different functions, but since Visual Studio includes a number of different keyboard mapping schemes and also allows you to customize keyboard shortcuts, it is difficult to say what keyboard shortcut will be valid for the scheme you are using. To resolve this issue, we specify the keyboard shortcut for the default Visual Studio keyboard mapping scheme, but we also include the name of the command for the shortcut.

Visual Studio uses commands to do everything: each menu button, toolbar button, or keyboard shortcut is really just a reference to a command. If you know the command, you can find the keyboard shortcut in your scheme using Tools → Options → Keyboard, assign a keyboard shortcut to that command [Hack #24], or just use the command through the command window [Hack #46]. Whenever we refer to a keyboard shortcut, you will see the name of the command either in the same sentence or in parentheses after the shortcut. The format of commands is normally two words separated by a period, for instance View.ClassView.

How This Book Is Organized

The book is divided into 13 chapters, organized by subject:

Chapter 1, *Master Projects and Solutions*
> Projects and solutions are used to organize files, executables, class libraries, and anything else that makes up your application. Consequently, learning how to get the most out of projects and solutions can greatly improve your experience with Visual Studio. This chapter covers how to get the most out of projects and solutions, including getting down and dirty with the undocumented format of project and solution files.

Chapter 2, *Master the Editor*
> At its heart, Visual Studio is just an editor, but it is quite a powerful editor. The Visual Studio editor includes features like IntelliSense, Syntax Coloring, Outlining, and much more. Visual Studio 2005 adds refactoring and code snippet functionality to the already-feature-rich editor of Visual Studio. This chapter covers how to get the most out of the editor by showing how to use these features to the fullest, as well as adding additional functionality to the editor through the use of third-party add-ins.

Chapter 3, *Navigating Visual Studio*
> Visual Studio includes a staggering number of windows, toolbars, commands, and editors. Visual Studio also includes an impressive number of ways to easily navigate both the application and your source code. This chapter covers how to easily move around the Visual Studio application as well as how to navigate your own source code.

Chapter 4, *Customizing Visual Studio*
> When writing code, it is nice to have things just the way you like them, and Visual Studio gives you plenty of opportunities to customize the application just the way you want it. This chapter covers how to customize shortcut keys, toolbars, menus, the toolbox, and much more. There is nothing better than getting it just the way you want it.

Chapter 5, *Debugging*

A large part of developing an application is finding and removing all the bugs in that application, which is where debugging comes in. Visual Studio provides an excellent debugging experience, making it easier than ever to find and fix bugs in your applications. This chapter covers how to get the most out of the debugger including how to debug not only your source code, but also T-SQL and scripting languages.

Chapter 6, *Speed Hacks*

Developers are constantly looking for ways to write code faster and more efficiently. This chapter covers a number of ways to write code more efficiently, including a number of macros to help automatically create connection strings, sign assemblies, update references, and more. This chapter also covers how to use the command window, as well as how to write and use custom tools to automatically generate code like collections and configuration sections.

Chapter 7, *Help and Research*

As a modern developer, you need to be able to quickly find answers to things you don't know, because it is simply impossible to know everything any more. This chapter covers various ways to get answers to your questions from within Visual Studio using the default help system or using add-ins to add more options. Another important part of development is being able to research how the internals of your application function. This chapter covers a number of applications that can be used to research how your application functions, including what IL it generates, statistics on your code, and what objects your application creates.

Chapter 8, *Comments and Documentation*

Code comments and documentation are very important parts of any application. When developers are maintaining an application or writing the next version of it, good comments and documentation are an invaluable resource. Writing this documentation is not always a pleasant experience though, since it is time consuming and sometimes tedious. This chapter covers how to use XML comments in .NET to make the creation of documentation easier, including a number of timesaving add-ins and applications.

Chapter 9, *Server Explorer Hacks*

The Server Explorer is one of the more neglected portions of Visual Studio. This chapter attempts to remedy that fact by covering how the Server Explorer can be used to interface with databases, services, and performance counters, as well as WMI.

Chapter 10, *Work with Visual Studio Tools*

Visual Studio includes a number of different tools that are not part of the normal IDE. This chapter covers how you can access a special command prompt, stress test applications, and generate code and UML, as well as obfuscate code with the various tools included with Visual Studio.

Chapter 11, *Visual Studio Tools for Office*

Visual Studio Tools for Office give you the opportunity to extend Office applications using the .NET language of your choice. This chapter covers the basics of using these tools, including a sample Word application and a sample Excel application.

Chapter 12, *Extending Visual Studio*

The nice thing about an application like Visual Studio is that, because its target audience is developers, the application authors know that those developers will want to write code that extends the functionality of the application. Visual Studio provides a number of different ways that you can extend its functionality. This chapter covers the Visual Studio extensibility model and how to create Visual Studio add-ins, as well as how to extend Visual Studio through normal Windows applications.

Chapter 13, *Enhancing Visual Studio*

A large number of add-ins and applications that enhance the functionality of Visual Studio are available. This chapter covers some of the better add-ins and applications that have not already been covered in other chapters. Some of the add-ins covered give you the ability to unit-test applications inside of Visual Studio, help with writing Web Services, blog from Visual Studio, spellcheck your code, and much more.

Conventions

The following is a list of the typographical conventions used in this book:

Italics

Used to indicate URLs, filenames, filename extensions, directory names, and folder names. For example, a path in the filesystem will appear as *C:\Program Files*.

Constant width

Used to show code examples, the contents of files, and console output, as well as the names of variables, commands, and other code excerpts.

Constant width bold

> Used to highlight portions of code, typically new additions to old code, as well as to show text that should be typed literally.

Constant width italic

> Used in code examples and tables to show sample text to be replaced with your own values.

Color

> The second color is used to indicate a cross-reference within the text.

You should pay special attention to notes set apart from the text with the following icons:

> This is a tip, suggestion, or general note. It contains useful supplementary information about the topic at hand.

> This is a warning or note of caution, often indicating that your money or your privacy might be at risk.

The thermometer icons, found next to each hack, indicate the relative complexity of the hack:

 beginner   moderate   expert

Using Code Examples

This book is here to help you get your job done. In general, you may use the code in this book in your programs and documentation. You do not need to contact us for permission unless you're reproducing a significant portion of the code. For example, writing a program that uses several chunks of code from this book does not require permission. Selling or distributing a CD-ROM of examples from O'Reilly books *does* require permission. Answering a question by citing this book and quoting example code does not require permission. Incorporating a significant amount of example code from this book into your product's documentation *does* require permission.

We appreciate, but do not require, attribution. An attribution usually includes the title, author, publisher, and ISBN; for example, "*Visual Studio Hacks* by James Avery. Copyright 2005 O'Reilly Media, Inc., 0596008473."

If you feel your use of code examples falls outside fair use or the preceding permission, feel free to contact us at *permissions@oreilly.com*.

Safari Enabled

 When you see a Safari® Enabled icon on the cover of your favorite technology book, it means the book is available online through the O'Reilly Network Safari Bookshelf.

Safari offers a solution that's better than e-books. It's a virtual library that lets you easily search thousands of top tech books, cut and paste code samples, download chapters, and find quick answers when you need the most accurate, current information. Try it for free at *http://safari.oreilly.com*.

How to Contact Us

We have tested and verified the information in this book to the best of our ability, but you may find that features have changed (or even that we have made mistakes!). As a reader of this book, you can help us to improve future editions by sending us your feedback. Please let us know about any errors, inaccuracies, bugs, misleading or confusing statements, and typos that you find anywhere in this book.

Please also let us know what we can do to make this book more useful to you. We take your comments seriously and will try to incorporate reasonable suggestions into future editions. You can write to us at:

O'Reilly Media, Inc.
1005 Gravenstein Highway North
Sebastopol, CA 95472
(800) 998-9938 (in the U.S. or Canada)
(707) 829-0515 (international/local)
(707) 829-0104 (fax)

To ask technical questions or to comment on the book, send email to:

bookquestions@oreilly.com

The web site for *Visual Studio Hacks* lists examples, errata, and plans for future editions. You can find this page at:

http://www.oreilly.com/catalog/visualstudiohks

The author maintains a web site where you can find updates to hacks and new information on Visual Studio, as well as errata and examples. You can find this page at:

http://www.visualstudiohacks.com

For more information about this book and others, see the O'Reilly web site:

http://www.oreilly.com

Got a Hack?

To explore Hacks books online or to contribute a hack for future titles, visit:

http://hacks.oreilly.com

CHAPTER ONE

Master Projects and Solutions
Hacks 1–5

The majority of the time you spend working with Visual Studio will be spent inside of a project or a solution. You might edit the odd file that is not attached to a project or solution, but most files you work with will be in the context of a project or solution.

Projects can be used for many purposes, but primarily they are used to organize source code that will be compiled into a library or application.

Solutions collect a number of projects together under a single structure. The metaphor of solution works because it collects all the projects that make up your *business solution*. You may have five projects that make up various parts of your overall business solution. For example, you might have a data access project, business layer project, service interface layer project, presentation layer project, and web controls project. The solution groups all of these projects together and allows you to quickly move between projects and manage references between them.

The hacks in this chapter show you how to create and manage projects and solutions, manage assembly references, and dissect the formats of project and solution files. If you're not already familiar with how to work with projects and solutions, this chapter will better prepare you to get the most out of the other hacks in this book.

HACK #1 Manage Projects and Solutions

Visual Studio is all about projects and solutions. It's essential that you understand the differences between them, and get comfortable with using them.

A large part of working with Visual Studio is the management of solutions and projects. Nothing can hamper a project more than a poorly designed solution or project structure. In this hack, you will learn how to work with and configure solutions and projects.

This hack applies to all versions of Visual Studio, but the dialogs and screens will vary slightly between versions. The screenshots in this hack are all taken from Visual Studio .NET 2003 unless noted otherwise.

Solutions

Solutions are Visual Studio's highest level of organization. They collect any number of projects together under one manageable structure. Solutions store information about the contained projects, including project dependencies and build order, and can also contain miscellaneous solution items. Solution files have a few limitations. Only a single solution can be opened in an instance of Visual Studio at a time, and solution files cannot contain other solution files. Projects, however, can be members of multiple solutions. This allows you to create a number of solutions for different purposes that make use of the same projects. (An example of this is business entities or interfaces that you need to share across client and server solutions.)

Solutions are the best way to keep projects under source control. If you add the solution to source control, every developer on the project can use the same solution and is guaranteed to use the same project and file structure.

Creating a solution. A solution is automatically created when you create a new project, but you can also create a blank solution without creating a project. To create a new blank solution, click on File → New → Blank Solution. You can then add whatever projects you need to the blank solution.

Solution settings. There are two types of solution settings: settings that are saved in the solution file (*.sln* extension) **[Hack #4]** and apply to all users of the solution, and settings that are saved in the solution user options file (*.suo* extension). The user options file is not shared between users and will apply only to the user who sets them. You can control a number of configuration settings at the solution level, including the startup project, project dependencies/build order, and build configuration:

The startup project
> The only purpose of the startup project settings is to configure what project Visual Studio should execute when you start the debugger. This setting has no impact on your actual application. The startup project will usually be one of the following kinds of projects:

Web project
> Starts an instance of Internet Explorer and loads your web project

Windows Forms project
> Launches an instance of your Windows Forms application

Console application project
> Launches your application in the console

You cannot set a class library, or any project without an executable output, to be the startup project. The startup project setting is stored at the user level in the solution user options file, which gives different users the ability to set up different startup projects. This also means that the startup project setting will not be transferred between users.

Visual Studio 2005 adds the ability to create multiple startup projects and lets you configure whether each project should be started in debug mode. The Visual Studio 2005 Startup Project property page, accessed by right-clicking on the solution in the Solution Explorer and choosing Set Startup Projects from the menu, is shown in Figure 1-1.

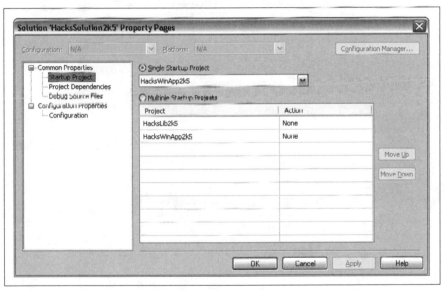

Figure 1-1. Visual Studio 2005 Startup Project property page

Project dependencies
> Project dependencies dictate the build order of your projects. Project dependencies are normally inferred from project references. If Project A references Project B, then Visual Studio knows that Project B must be built before Project A can be built. There are times when you will need

to manually set project dependencies; for such cases, use the Project Dependencies dialog to set which projects are dependent on other projects:

1. First, right-click on the solution and click the Project Dependencies item. You will see this option only if you have more than one project in your solution.

2. Next, choose the project you want to create a dependency for and check the box next to the project that this project is dependent on. In Figure 1-2, I have specified that the *HacksWinApp* project depends on the *HacksLib* project.

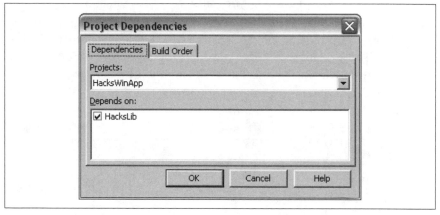

Figure 1-2. Project dependencies dialog

As you can see in Figure 1-3, Visual Studio appropriately sets the build order to build *HacksLib* first and then build *HacksWinApp*.

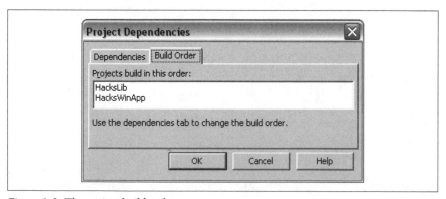

Figure 1-3. The project build order

Build configuration

Build settings are stored at both the project and solution level. The build settings for an individual project are stored in that project file. These settings define what the debug or release mode for a project should do. The build settings that are defined at the solution level simply define in what mode each of the projects in a solution should be built. By default, each project and solution contains a debug and release configuration. By selecting either the debug or release configuration at the solution level, the solution will build each of the projects with the corresponding project configurations. All of these settings are configured through the Configuration Manager, which can be seen in Figure 1-4.

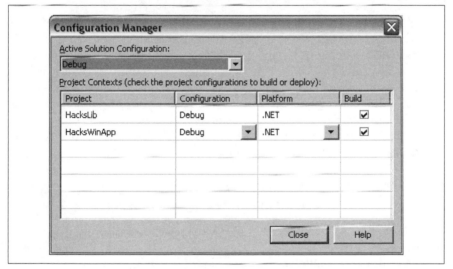

Figure 1-4. The Configuration Manager

The drop-down at the top is the solution configuration. In Figure 1-4, the selected solution configuration is Debug. You can see that, for this configuration, Visual Studio will build both of the projects with their respective debug configurations.

You can also create new configuration modes from the Configuration Manager. You might want to create a configuration that builds the *HacksLib* project in release mode but builds *HacksWinApp* in debug mode. To do this, you first need to select New from the drop-down at the top of the Configuration Manager. Next, you need to name your new solution configuration in the New Solution Configuration dialog shown in Figure 1-5.

After specifying your new configuration name, select which current configuration to copy the current settings from. This is a timesaving feature

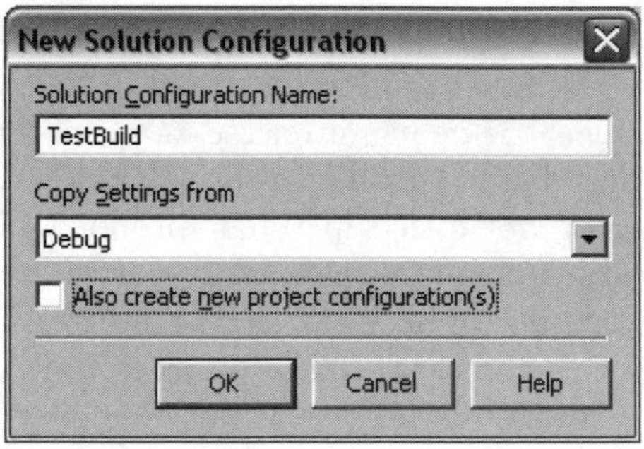

Figure 1-5. New Solution Configuration dialog

that allows you to avoid starting from scratch. The checkbox specifies whether you want to also create new project configurations. In this example, you are going to use the default debug and release configurations, so you don't need to create any new project configurations, which will be discussed under "Project settings," later in this hack. Uncheck this checkbox. After clicking the OK button, you will see your new configuration in the Configuration Manager. You can then configure the *HacksLib* project to be built in release mode and the *HacksWinApp* project to be built in debug mode or any other combination that you wish.

Solution Items

Solutions normally contain only projects, but you can also add miscellaneous items to your solutions. These items must be files that you don't want to be compiled. This could be project documentation, Visio documents, stylesheets, or any other documents that might not be directly linked to a particular project but relevant to the entire solution. You can even include code files (*.vb*, *.cs*, etc.). They won't be compiled, but if you wanted to include examples, this would be a perfect place.

To add a solution item, you simply need to right-click on the solution file and choose Add → Add New Item or Add → Add Existing Item. After creating a new file or selecting an already existing file, it will be added to a special folder in the solution titled Solution Items.

Projects

Projects are one of the most important parts of working with Visual Studio. Projects contain any number of source files that are compiled into some kind of output. The output could be a Windows Forms executable, console application, class library, or any number of various outputs. There are different projects for different languages including C++, C#, VB.NET, and more. There are also special purpose projects like the setup project and the database project [Hack #74]. Overall, Visual Studio contains more than 90 different project types. This number varies based on your installation settings and increases if you install add-ins or language services because they often create even more project types.

Create a project. When creating a project, you will either be creating a new project from scratch or adding a project to an existing solution. To create a new project from scratch, click on File ▸ New → Project and you will see the New Project dialog, which is shown in Figure 1-6. To add a project to an already existing solution, click on File → Add Project → New Project and you will see the same New Project dialog.

 If you plan on having more than one project, it is a good idea to first create a blank solution and then add projects to that blank solution [Hack #3].

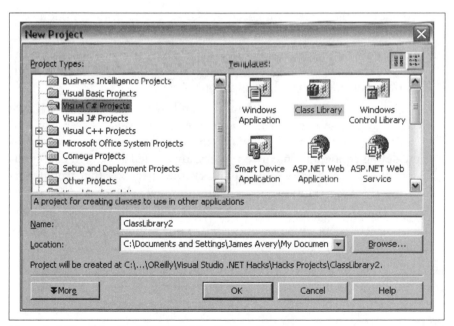

Figure 1-6. Visual Studio .NET 2003 New Project dialog

From this dialog, you can select the type of project that you would like to create. You can also name your project and specify where the project and project files should be stored. Once you have created a project, you can then configure that project.

Visual Studio 2005 adds additional functionality to this dialog by way of an option that allows you to download templates from the Internet. Using this functionality, you can download project templates, item templates, code snippets, and samples from the Internet and quickly add them to your copy of Visual Studio.

Project settings. A number of settings can be configured at the project level. I will continue with the example from the solution configurations section in which I created a *TestBuild* solution configuration that built one project in release mode and the other project in debug mode. My requirements might change, and instead of building the *HacksLib* project in release mode, I want to create a custom configuration for the project that optimizes the code but also includes debug information. There is no default configuration that optimizes code and includes debug information, so you will need to create a custom configuration. To do this:

1. Go back to the same Configuration Manager used in the solution configuration section and shown in Figure 1-4.

2. To create a new project configuration, select New from the list of existing project configurations. You are then shown the New Project Configuration dialog, which is shown in Figure 1-7.

3. Name your new project configuration and then select from which current configuration you want to copy the settings. In this case, you can name your configuration *TestBuild* and copy the current settings from the debug configuration. Since you already created a solution configuration called *TestBuild*, you can uncheck the checkbox that would normally create this solution configuration automatically for you.

4. After the project configuration is created, you can access it in the normal project property pages and adjust your settings. Figure 1-8 shows this property page for C# Projects.

I am not going to go into each of the individual properties here. You can select properties in the Configuration Manager and see a brief description of the property in the bottom of the pane as well as what compiler option that property corresponds to.

Figure 1-9 shows the property page for VB.NET Projects, which is a little different than the property page for C#.

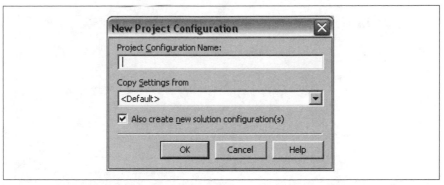

Figure 1-7. New Project Configuration dialog

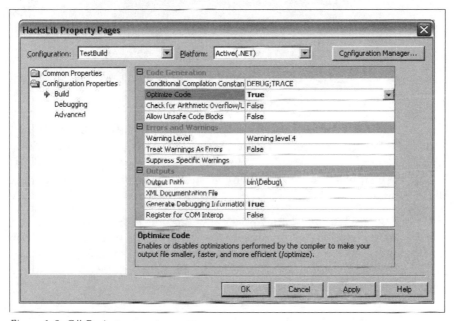

Figure 1-8. C# Project property pages

Temporary Projects

Visual Studio 2005 introduces the idea of temporary projects for *managed language projects* in which the IDE does not save any project files until you tell it to save the files. This is different than Visual Studio .NET 2002 and 2003 in which the project files are saved as soon as you create a new project. (This probably led you to creating lots of little projects that you never touched again, just to try out something. This is known as the *WindowApplication21 syndrome*.)

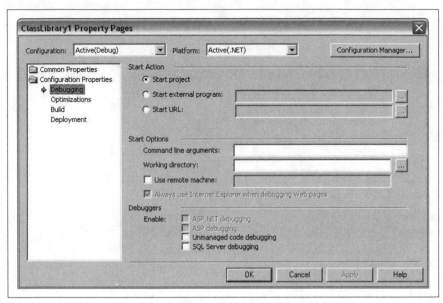

Figure 1-9. VB.NET project property pages

To enable this feature, you will need to ensure that the checkbox titled "Save new projects when created" in Tools → Options → Projects and Solutions → General is unchecked. When you first close a new project in Visual Studio 2005, it will ask you whether you want to save or discard the project and the project files.

Visual Studio 2005 keeps the project and solution files as temporary files while you are working with the unsaved project. As of this writing, the Visual Studio 2005 beta uses the *C:\Documents and Settings\<Username>\ Local Settings\Application Data\Zero Impact Projects* directory to hold these files, but this is subject to change.

AutoSave and AutoRecover

Visual Studio 2005 includes another new feature that allows you to configure Visual Studio to automatically save your projects and solutions and then recover them in the event of a crash of the IDE. To configure this functionality, go to Tools → Options → AutoRecover. This dialog is shown in Figure 1-10.

Using this dialog, you can configure how often your information should be saved and how long that recovery information should be stored. If Visual Studio crashes, you will be prompted to have Visual Studio automatically restore your project or solution when the IDE is restarted.

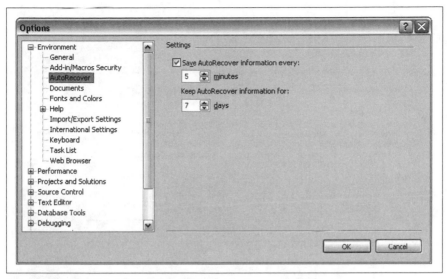

Figure 1-10. Visual Studio 2005 AutoRecover options

Master Assembly and Project References

Visual Studio uses references to identify the external assemblies that your project relies on. How these references are used depends on the type of reference as well as a number of other factors.

Adding a reference to a project is a simple matter of right-clicking on the references folder of a project and selecting Add Reference. (Add Web Reference is a completely different feature that is used for creating a reference to a web service and won't be covered here.)

The Add Reference dialog contains a number of tabs, three in Visual Studio .NET 2002 and 2003 and five in Visual Studio 2005. Figure 1-11 shows the Visual Studio .NET 2003 Add Reference dialog.

The .NET tab contains a list of .NET assemblies. You can select any of these assemblies and create a reference to that assembly. The COM tab contains a list of all the registered COM objects that you can reference. The Projects tab contains a list of all the projects in your solution, and by selecting one, you can create a reference directly to that project.

Visual Studio 2005's Add Reference dialog is shown with its extra tabs (Browse and Recent) in Figure 1-12.

The Browse tab is used to browse for an assembly from the filesystem—the same as the Browse button from the Add Reference dialog of older versions of Visual Studio. The other new tab is the Recent tab, which shows any assemblies you have recently used.

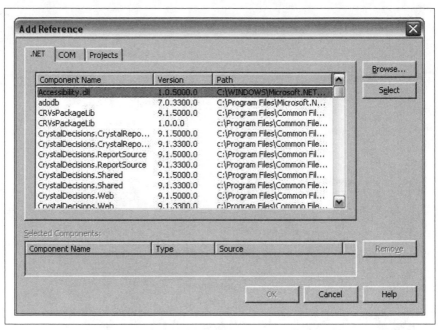

Figure 1-11. Visual Studio .NET 2003 Add Reference dialog

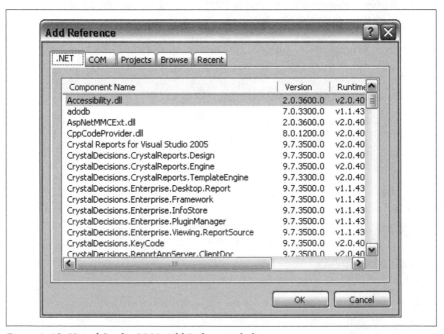

Figure 1-12. Visual Studio 2005 Add Reference dialog

The majority of the time this process is as simple as selecting what you want to reference and then clicking the OK button. However, a better understanding of how references work will help avoid headaches when sharing projects between users and when working with projects under source control. One of the most frequent issues that developers encounter when working with shared solutions and projects is broken references.

Assembly References

The first tab that you see in the Add Reference dialog is the .NET tab, which lists .NET assemblies you can reference in your application. You can add a reference to any of these assemblies by simply clicking on the assembly and then the Select button. You can also use the Browse tab or Browse button to manually browse the filesystem for an assembly.

How the list is created. The list of assemblies displayed in the .NET tab is based on a set of directories that is configured through the registry. Visual Studio generates this list by iterating through the .NET Framework directory as well as any directories configured in the registry. You can add your own assembly to this list by adding a key to the registry with the directory your assembly is located in:

1. Open *regedit* (click Start → Run, then type **regedit**).
2. Navigate to HKEY_LOCAL_MACHINE if you want to add the directory for all users on your machine or HKEY_CURRENT_USER if you want to add the directory just for yourself.
3. Navigate to *Software/Microsoft/.NETFramework/AssemblyFolders*. Under this folder, you will see all the currently configured entries. (If you are configuring this under HKEY_CURRENT_USER, you may need to create the *.NETFramework* and *AssemblyFolders* keys.)
4. Right-click on *AssemblyFolders*, choose New → Key, and name your key.
5. Double-click on the (Default) value of your new key and specify the directory you want to add.

Any assemblies in that directory will now appear in the list of assemblies listed in the .NET tab. You can also add a directory for a specific version of Visual Studio by following the preceding procedure but using the *Assembly-Folders* key, which can be found at *Software/Microsoft/VisualStudio/7.1/AssemblyFolders*.

How references are resolved. Items that appear in a project's references folder are more than simple references to files. The assembly that is ultimately linked into the project is resolved using a complex set of rules. If a referenced assembly exists in the project directory but is not visible in the project, there is no guarantee it will be used. (This is a common misconception and can lead to a lot of confusion.)

The rules Visual Studio uses to resolve references are as follows:

1. Assemblies that are visible in the project as project items or links are considered. If Visual Studio .NET 2005 with MSBuild is being used, these must have a Build Action of Content or None.

2. Assemblies in Reference Path directories are considered. These are stored in *.user* files and are visible under project properties.

3. The *HintPath* of the reference is considered. This is a path to the referenced assembly (relative to the project). It is stored when the reference is originally created.

4. Assemblies in the native framework directory are considered (e.g., *\Windows\Microsoft.NET\Framework\v1.1.4322* for Visual Studio .NET 2003).

5. Assemblies in the registered assembly folders are considered. These are the directories discussed in the last section about adding assemblies to the list of .NET assemblies. If Visual Studio .NET 2005 with MSBuild is being used, *HKLM\Software\Microsoft\.NETFramework\v2.x.xxxxx\ AssemblyFoldersEx* will be considered first.

6. If Visual Studio .NET 2005 with MSBuild is being used and the assembly has a strong name, Visual Studio will look in the GAC for the assembly.

It is important to note that this is the resolution process that Visual Studio goes through when determining what assembly to link to a project when building the solution, not the process that .NET goes through when finding the assembly to use when running the application.

Managing .NET references. References can become a problem if your project needs to be opened by another user who quite possibly won't have a copy of the assembly you are referencing. You can solve this problem in a number of ways. The easiest way is to make a copy of the assembly and include that assembly in your project. You cannot simply copy it to your project directory; you also need to ensure that it is a part of your project in Visual Studio. That way, you know that whoever opens the project will have access to this file. The major downside to this solution is that anytime this assembly changes, you will need to make a copy of the assembly and copy it into your project before you get the changes.

A good solution to the file reference issue is to create a single folder that contains all of the assemblies that are referenced through file references. This way, all the developers on a project can retrieve the latest versions of these assemblies from the same location, whether through a common shared directory or source control.

Project References

A project reference refers to another project in your solution; for instance, you might have a Windows Forms project that references a class library project. When the Windows Forms project is built, it will create a copy of the class library assembly and move it to your output directory.

What makes a project reference superior to an assembly reference is that Visual Studio will watch for any changes to the other project. When there are changes, you will automatically get a new copy of the assembly in your build directory. Visual Studio will also use project references to infer project dependencies. In the case of a Windows Forms project referencing a class library project, Visual Studio will determine that the class library project needs to be built before the Windows Forms project since the Windows Forms project depends on the output of the class library.

Project references also avoid problems when sharing the project between systems or when working with projects under source control.

The main thing to remember when working with references is to think not only about how the reference will work for you, but also how it will work for other developers working with your solution.

—James Avery and Jamie Cansdale

Organize Projects and Solutions

HACK
#3

Most development projects consist of more than one project and are grouped under a single solution file. How this solution file is created is the first thing to consider when organizing your projects and solutions.

Visual Studio creates a solution for you when you create a new project. The problem with this is that the solution will be named after your project and will be in the same directory as your new project. If you later add an additional project to your solution, your file structure will look something like this:

```
Folder A\
    Solution File
    Project File A
Folder B\
    Project File B
```

The problem with this structure is that it is not easy to work with since the solution file is nested inside one of the project directories and references a project file that is contained in a different directory. If you were to move Folder A to a different location, the solution would end up with a broken reference to Project File B. A better way to handle solution files is to *always* start with a blank solution and then add project files to this solution over time. To start with a blank solution, you simply need to click on File → New → Blank Solution. You can create a directory for this blank solution and add projects to this solution. Your file structure will now look more like this:

```
Solution Directory\
    Solution File
    Folder A\
        Project File A
    Folder B\
        Project File B
```

This file structure is much more manageable. You can check the entire solution into SourceSafe, you can safely move the solution directory, and you can even zip up the entire directory structure.

Working with Multiple Solutions

Whenever possible, you should stick to a single solution for your development project. But when you get above a certain number of projects in a solution, it starts to become unwieldy for you to manage. It is also inconvenient to have multiple executables or web projects in a single solution, as you will constantly be switching the startup project when you want to run or debug one of the other executables. There are a number of different strategies for working with multiple solutions:

Partitioned solutions under a master solution

Often, the number of projects in a solution becomes cumbersome and you need a new method of organization. The best way to deal with this is to create multiple subsolutions that contain the projects for a small section of the overall solution and keep a master solution that contains all of the projects. The reason this is possible is that projects can belong to any number of solutions, whereas solutions cannot belong to other solutions. Figure 1-13 shows an example of partitioned solutions with a master solution file.

This method of solution division is ideal when working with large projects because individual developers can work with a more manageable subset of projects. A master solution still exists that can be used by the build process and source control. This organization also allows you to continue to use project references, which are preferable to assembly references [Hack #2].

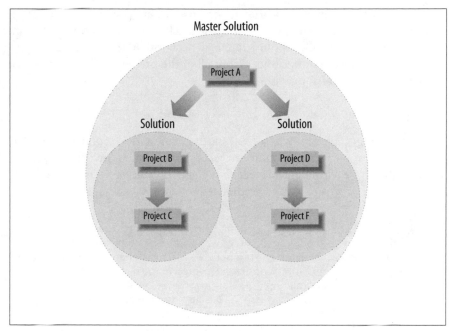

Figure 1-13. Partitioned solutions with master solution

Partitioned solutions without a master

You can also divide development projects into different solutions without using a master solution. The disadvantage of this method is that you won't have one place to build your project from. Figure 1-14 shows an example of partitioned solutions without the use of a master solution file.

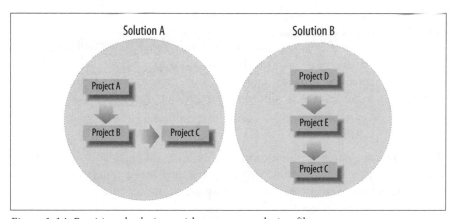

Figure 1-14. Partitioned solutions without master solution file

This organization makes the most sense when you are developing a client-server solution. Your client-side application can be one solution, and your server-side application can be another solution. Both solutions will share certain projects, but all of the projects will not be part of any single master solution.

Project Division

One of the big decisions when first starting a new development project is how to divide it into Visual Studio projects. This division into projects is different for each development project, but a general rule of thumb is to divide projects based on *layers* and dependencies.

Layers are the logical boundaries of your application. They may sometimes coincide with physical boundaries, like between two servers, but not always. The common three-layered application consists of a presentation layer that displays information to the user (ASP.NET web forms, Windows Forms, etc.), a business layer that includes the actual business logic for your application, and last, a data access layer that facilitates the interaction between your application and your database. The number and type of layers can vary greatly between applications. In some instances, the three-layer model is overkill; in other instances, it is woefully inadequate.

If you decide to divide your project into a façade layer, business layer, and data access layer, it is a good idea to have a project for each of those layers. This will enforce your decision by allowing layers to interface with only the public properties and methods of the other layers. You also have to consider dependencies. If you are using custom entities as your method of data transport, then you have to consider the fact that every layer will need to reference your custom entities. You therefore need to separate the custom entities into a separate project. Dividing your projects based on layer also provides a certain level of flexibility when you deploy your application.

Enterprise Templates

Enterprise Templates are a method of providing guidance and setting policy for the structure of a solution. Visual Studio includes a number of prefabricated Enterprise Templates for various general architectures. You can also create custom Enterprise Templates.

Enterprise Templates are available only to users of the Enterprise Developer and Enterprise Architect versions of Visual Studio.

To use Enterprise Templates, you first need to access the Create New Project dialog by navigating to File → New → Project. On this dialog is a folder titled Other Projects, which includes a folder titled Enterprise Template Projects. This folder contains a number of different templates for sample solution and project structures. You could select one of the predefined projects listed here, and Visual Studio would create a solution with a number of different projects. If you select "Visual C# simple distributed application," Visual Studio will create the following projects automatically:

- BusinessFacade
- BusinessRules
- DataAccess
- SystemFrameworks
- WebService
- WebUI
- WinUI

Chances are that you don't need all of these projects for your solution, or perhaps you need some of these and some other projects that weren't created automatically. The best solution is usually to start with a blank Enterprise Templates Solution and add your own projects.

You might wonder how this is different from just creating a normal solution. Enterprise Templates provide a number of features that are not available in normal Visual Studio solutions. Enterprise Templates allow you to set policies between projects; you can specify whether certain projects are allowed to reference other projects. For instance, you could forbid the BusinessFacade layer from directly referencing the DataAccess layer.

Enterprise Templates not only provide guidance for your solution and project organization and structure, they also enable a very cool feature in Visual Studio .NET 2002 and 2003; they give you the ability to use folders in your solutions. This feature is enabled by default in Visual Studio 2005, but Enterprise Templates are the only way to enable this functionality in Visual Studio .NET 2002 and 2003. It may not seem like much, but when you have a large number of projects in your solution, it is nice to be able to group them into logical folders. This way, if you are working on the data access layer, you can collapse all of your UI or business projects.

By using Enterprise Templates, you can also take advantage of some prefabricated projects called *building blocks* that are located under the Enterprise Template Project folder in the New Project dialog. An architect could create a number of Enterprise Templates to dictate how solutions should be built and organized inside his organization. Instead of starting from scratch, developers would use the template to dictate their general architecture.

Hack the Project and Solution Files

Discover the format of these two Visual Studio files and learn about a tool to convert these files between versions of Visual Studio.

Solution and project files are an essential part of working with Visual Studio. You will almost always work with the solution and project files through the IDE, whether adding projects to your solution or configuring your project. The purpose of this hack is to describe the format of these files for two reasons. If your project or solution files become corrupted, knowing the structure of these files might help you fix the file without having to re-create the entire project or solution. Also, knowing the structure of these files will help you if you want to convert these files or write a tool that works directly with these files.

> You must edit these files with extreme care. The format of these files is not published or documented and could change drastically in future versions. You should normally need to work with these files only through the IDE, and unless you find a compelling reason to, I would not directly edit these files. If you are interested only in converting the version of these files, then you may want to look toward the end of this hack under "Project and Solution File Conversion" to read about a tool that will do the conversion for you.

Solution Files

Visual Studio creates two separate files when you create a new solution in Visual Studio. The first file is the *.suo* (solution user options) file, which stores user settings such as the location of your breakpoints. This file is stored in binary format, which does not lend itself to easy editing. Since there are no compelling reasons to edit this file, I am not going to document the format of it here. If you think that this file is preventing your solution from opening, you can actually delete the file and Visual Studio will create a new one when you open the solution and save it when you close the IDE. By deleting the file, you will lose any of your user-specific settings like breakpoints, but this is a small price to pay for saving your solution. The *.suo* file is a hidden file, so you will need to make sure Windows Explorer is configured to show hidden files (this can be set through Tools → Folder Options → View in any Explorer window).

The second file that Visual Studio creates is the *.sln* file. This file stores information about the projects that make up this solution, source control settings, and other global settings that apply to all of the projects in the solution.

The first line of the solution file contains a declaration including the version of Visual Studio that this solution is built for:

```
Microsoft Visual Studio Solution File, Format Version 8.0
```

The version number used in the solution file is a little different than the version number you are used to seeing in the Visual Studio product name. Visual Studio .NET 2002 solution files have a version number of 7.0. Visual Studio .NET 2003 solution files have a version number of 8.0 (as opposed to the 7.1 number you are used to), and Visual Studio 2005 solutions files have a version number of 9.0. Visual Studio 2005 Beta 1 contains an additional line under this first line, which contains just the following:

```
# Visual Studio 2005
```

This line causes the icon of the file to be changed to a Visual Studio 2005-specific icon, and if removed, will prevent Visual Studio from opening this file when you double-click on it.

The next portion of the solution file contains a section for each of the projects that are contained in this solution:

```
Project("{FAE04EC0-301F-11D3-BF4B-00C04F79EFBC}") = "HacksWinApp",
"HacksWinApp\HacksWinApp.csproj",
"{75B7D1AE-1896-409D-B717-64D9AFCF0F59}"
    ProjectSection(ProjectDependencies) = postProject
        {89EE0E8E-C5C6-4772-A5EE-D347E40FB0E4} =
        {89EE0E8E-C5C6 4772-A5FF-D347E40FB0E4}
    EndProjectSection
EndProject
Project("{FAE04EC0-301F-11D3-BF4B-00C04F79EFBC}") = "HacksLib",
"HacksLib\HacksLib.csproj", "{89EE0E8E-C5C6-4772-A5EE-D347E40FB0E4}"
    ProjectSection(ProjectDependencies) = postProject
    EndProjectSection
EndProject
```

You can see that the syntax of the file is somewhat similar to Visual Basic. Each project has a Project and EndProject tag as well as a ProjectSection tag to track the dependencies for the project. The first GUID in the project tag is used to identify what type of project this is. In this instance, the GUIDs for both a C# Windows Forms project and a C# library project are the same, since these project types are really the same except for the output type setting. The strings on the right side of the equals sign include the name of the project, its path relative to the solution root, and the unique GUID for this project. This GUID is used for a number of things including tracking dependencies.

> You can view a list of all the project GUIDS by opening *regedit* (Start → Run, then type **regedit**) and navigating to *HKEY_ LOCAL_MACHINE\SOFTWARE\Microsoft\VisualStudio\7.1\ Projects*.
>
> Under this key are all the GUIDs for the project available on your machine; the name and the extension of the project are listed as well.

In Visual Studio .NET 2003 and Visual Studio 2005, project dependencies are also tracked here. These are not the implicit dependences that are created by project references. When Project A references Project B, there is an implicit dependency. Project B must be built before Project A since it references the other project's output. Since this type of dependency is project-specific information, it is stored in the project file. (In this example, it would be stored in Project A's project file since it is referencing Project B, rather than the solution file we are looking at here.) Project files and dependencies are described in the next section.

The dependences stored in the `ProjectSection` tag are configured at the solution level. They define when a project must be built before another project, but they may not directly reference each other. This is stored in the `ProjectSection` tag of the project that is dependent on the other project. In this example, the *HacksWinApp* project is dependent on the *HacksLib* project and thus includes a reference to the GUID of the other project. This dependency is normally configured by right-clicking on the solution file, selecting Properties from the context menu, and navigating to Project Dependencies in the property page that appears.

Visual Studio .NET 2003 includes a `ProjectSection` tag even if there is no dependency (you can see this in the `HacksLib` project tag). Visual Studio 2005 completely omits the `ProjectSection` tag if there are no dependencies for the project. Visual Studio .NET 2002 stores the dependency information in a completely different section of the solution file, which we will cover next.

The next section in the solution file is the `Global` section, which begins with a `Global` tag and ends with an `EndGlobal` tag. Inside these tags are a number of `GlobalSection` tags that store an array of different pieces of information, including the configuration settings for various projects as well as source control information. Here is a look at the Global section of this example solution file from Visual Studio .NET 2003:

```
Global
    GlobalSection(SolutionConfiguration) = preSolution
        Debug = Debug
        Release = Release
    EndGlobalSection
    GlobalSection(ProjectConfiguration) = postSolution
        {75B7D1AE-1896-409D-B717-64D9AFCF0F59}.Debug.ActiveCfg
        = Debug|.NET
        {75B7D1AE-1896-409D-B717-64D9AFCF0F59}.Debug.Build.0
        = Debug|.NET
        {75B7D1AE-1896-409D B717 64D9AFCF0F59}.Release.ActiveCfg
        = Release|.NET
        {75B7D1AE-1896-409D-B717-64D9AFCF0F59}.Release.Build.0
        = Release|.NET
        {89EE0E8E-C5C6-4772-A5EE-D347E40FB0E4}.Debug.ActiveCfg
        = Debug|.NET
        {89EE0E8E-C5C6-4772-A5EE-D347E40FB0E4}.Debug.Build.0
        = Debug|.NET
        {89EE0E8E-C5C6-4772-A5EE-D347E40FB0E4}.Release.ActiveCfg
        = Release|.NET
        {89EE0E8E-C5C6-4772-A5EE-D347E40FB0E4}.Release.Build.0
        = Release|.NET
    EndGlobalSection
    GlobalSection(ExtensibilityGlobals) = postSolution
    EndGlobalSection
    GlobalSection(ExtensibilityAddIns) = postSolution
    EndGlobalSection
EndGlobal
```

The SolutionConfiguration and ProjectConfiguration sections contain the build configuration settings for the solution and its projects. The ExtensibilityGlobals and ExtensibilityAddIns sections are included for the benefit of add-in authors. The ExtensibilityGlobals section can be used to store global information about the solution, and the ExtensibilityAddIns section lists all the add-ins that are used in this solution.

Visual Studio .NET 2002 also uses the Global section to store information about project dependences. Here is an example of that configuration section:

```
GlobalSection(ProjectDependencies) = postSolution
    {1C19F285-69AF-409E-8D5B-A354B68B41FF}.0
    = {CBBAD9B0-CB56-44CA-8312-A9258F2061E2}
EndGlobalSection
```

This section simply specifies that the project identified by its GUID on the left of the equals sign depends on the project identified by its GUID on the right side of the equals sign.

Visual Studio 2005 includes an additional section that is not present in any of the older versions of Visual Studio; it's shown here:

```
GlobalSection(SolutionProperties) = preSolution
    HideSolutionNode = FALSE
EndGlobalSection
```

If the FALSE is switched to TRUE, then the solution node is hidden in the IDE.

Project Files

Each project creates a number of files to store information about itself. This includes a project file and a user settings file. The extension for the project file is based on the language type; for example, a C# Project is saved with the extension *.csproj* and a VB.NET Project is stored with the extension *.vbproj*. Thankfully, the internal formats of these various files are based on the same XML schema. The beginning of each project file includes some basic information about the project, including the version of Visual Studio that it was created for as well as the GUID for this project. Here is an example of this section:

```
<VisualStudioProject>
<CSHARP
        ProjectType = "Local"
        ProductVersion = "7.10.3077"
        SchemaVersion = "2.0"
        ProjectGuid = "{89EE0E8E-C5C6-4772-A5EE-D347E40FB0E4}"
    >
```

This is from a Visual Studio .NET 2003 project file, which is why the ProductVersion is set to 7.1 and the SchemaVersion is set to 2.0. In Visual Studio .NET 2002, the ProductVersion would be 7.0 and the SchemaVersion would be 1.0. These settings are no longer relevant in Visual Studio 2005 as project files are now MSBuild files.

 Notice that the version number used for Visual Studio .NET 2003 is 7.1 in the project file and 8.0 in the Solution file.

The next section of the project file is the Build section, which includes build settings and configuration settings as well as references information. Here is the Build settings section:

```
<Build>
    <Settings
        ApplicationIcon = ""
        AssemblyKeyContainerName = ""
```

```
       AssemblyName = "HacksLib"
       AssemblyOriginatorKeyFile = ""
       DefaultClientScript = "JScript"
       DefaultHTMLPageLayout = "Grid"
       DefaultTargetSchema = "IE50"
       DelaySign = "false"
       OutputType = "Library"
       PreBuildEvent = ""
       PostBuildEvent = ""
       RootNamespace = "HacksLib"
       RunPostBuildEvent = "OnBuildSuccess"
       StartupObject = "">
```

As you can see, this section includes information like the AssemblyName and OutputType of the project. The next part of the Build section is for the various build configurations:

```
<Config
    Name = "Debug"
    AllowUnsafeBlocks = "false"
    BaseAddress = "285212672"
    CheckForOverflowUnderflow = "false"
    ConfigurationOverrideFile = ""
    DefineConstants = "DEBUG;TRACE"
    DocumentationFile = ""
    DebugSymbols = "true"
    FileAlignment = "4096"
    IncrementalBuild = "false"
    NoStdLib = "false"
    NoWarn = ""
    Optimize = "false"
    OutputPath = "bin\Debug\"
    RegisterForComInterop = "false"
    RemoveIntegerChecks = "false"
    TreatWarningsAsErrors = "false"
    WarningLevel = "4"/>
```

This section includes configuration-specific build settings. The project file will usually contain at least a Debug and Release section. The next part of the Build section contains all of the references for this project. Here is an abbreviated example of this section:

```
<References>
    <Reference
      Name = "System"
      AssemblyName = "System"
      HintPath = "..\..\..\..\..\..\..\..\..\WINDOWS\Microsoft.NET\
                 Framework\v1.1.4322\System.dll"
</References></Build>
```

The References section contains a reference tag for each assembly referenced by the project. Starting with Visual Studio 2005, you can create a reference to either an assembly or an executable, which comes in very handy when you are trying to unit-test a Windows application, since this lets you directly reference your application. To get this same functionality in Visual Studio .NET 2003, you can actually hack the project file to create a reference to an executable—you simply need to manually enter a reference tag in the references element pointing to your executable. Your new reference tag would look exactly like this example, except it would be pointed to an *.exe* file instead of a *.dll* file.

After the Build section is the Files section of the project file, which can be seen here:

```
<Files>
        <Include>
            <File
                RelPath = "AssemblyInfo.cs"
                SubType = "Code"
                BuildAction = "Compile"
            />
            <File
                RelPath = "Class1.cs"
                SubType = "Code"
                BuildAction = "Compile"
            />
        </Include>
    </Files>
</CSHARP>
</VisualStudioProject>
```

This section simply tracks all of the files that are included in this project. The schema of the project file is pretty straightforward in case you need to edit it directly.

Visual Studio also creates a user-specific project file much like the *.suo* file created for the solution file except with an extension of *<projectextension>. user*, so if you were using VB.NET, it would be *vbproj.user*. Similarly, this user-specific file does not contain anything pertinent enough to cover here, and is also hidden by default, so you will need configure Windows Explorer to show hidden files through Tools → Folder Options → View.

Visual Studio 2005 has not been mentioned up until this point because the project files in Visual Studio 2005 are completely different than the project files in Visual Studio .NET 2002 and 2003. The project files in Visual Studio 2005 are MSBuild XML files. MSBuild is the new build tool used in Visual Studio 2005 and is a completely different, complex topic that is not going to be covered here. It is similar to NAnt in that is uses XML files to describe how the project should be built.

Project and Solution File Conversion

Visual Studio does an excellent job of converting files from older versions to newer versions. For instance, if you open a Visual Studio .NET 2002 solution in Visual Studio .NET 2003, it will first ask if you want to convert the solution. After you say yes, it will convert all of your solution and project files to the new version of Visual Studio .NET. Now what if you accidentally converted those files and didn't have a backup? Or perhaps you are writing a solution in Visual Studio .NET 2003 and find out that your client has only Visual Studio .NET 2002? One method would be to create a new solution in the old version, create an identical project structure, and then copy all the files over and add them to their respective projects. Thankfully, there is a better solution. There is a tool available that will automatically convert the project and solution files for you as well as the *.resx* files if you are using Windows Forms.

The tool is called Visual Studio Converter 2.0 and can be downloaded from *http://www.codeproject.com/macro/vsconvert.asp*.

This tool is simple to use. Figure 1-15 shows an example of this conversion tool's user interface.

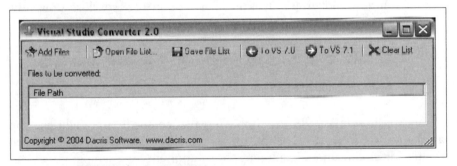

Figure 1-15. Visual Studio Converter 2.0

To convert files, you first need to click the Add Files button and select all the solution, projects, and *.resx* files for your solution. For a simple, one-form C# Windows Forms application, you would need to include the *.sln*, *.csproj*, *.csproj.user*, and *Form1.resx*. You will have an additional *.resx* file for each form in your application. Next, you need to click one of the two conversion buttons to convert the files to either Visual Studio 7.0 (2002) or Visual Studio 7.1 (2003). When initially converting a 2002 project to the 2003 format, it is best to use the Visual Studio conversion process. After this initial process, this tool is a great way to convert the files back and forth as needed.

Currently, it converts only between Visual Studio .NET 2002 and Visual Studio .NET 2003.

Remove SourceSafe Bindings

HACK #5

Visual SourceSafe comes bundled with Visual Studio for free, so it is one of the most popular source code control programs for Visual Studio developers. However, it will leave cruft in your source tree that you might want to get rid of if you send your code elsewhere.

In order to do its job, SourceSafe adds some XML elements to the Visual Studio solution and project files and adds some source control files to each project directory. These changes are transparent when using SourceSafe, but cause problems when sharing the solution with someone who does not use SourceSafe or someone who does not have access to your SourceSafe database. It could also cause problems if you are attempting to change your source code control provider from SourceSafe to something else, like CVS or Subversion.

Removing Bindings

You must change two things to remove all SourceSafe bindings. The solution file and all project files must have any source control information removed, and any files ending in *.scc* must be deleted. To do this, the Visual Studio solution and project files must not be in use, so close down the Visual Studio IDE.

> It is best to make a copy of the entire Visual Studio solution before hacking any files. If something goes wrong, you should have a backup.

Visual Studio solution files are simple text files ending in *.sln*. Right-click on a solution file, select the Open With... option, then choose Notepad to open the file for modification. Examining the solution file for a sample Visual Studio application called SourceSafeBindingRemover yields this code:

```
Microsoft Visual Studio Solution File, Format Version 8.00
Project("{FAE04EC0-301F-11D3-BF4B-00C04F79EFBC}") =
"SourceSafeBindingRemover",
"SourceSafeBindingRemover\SourceSafeBindingRemover.csproj",
"{C7687560-4B36-47E3-AF33-748E76411259}"
    ProjectSection(ProjectDependencies) = postProject
    EndProjectSection
EndProject
```

```
Global
    GlobalSection(SourceCodeControl) = preSolution
        SccNumberOfProjects = 2
        SccLocalPath0 = .
        CanCheckoutShared = false
        SolutionUniqueID = {634C866F-3CEB-43A1-9C7F-D34A03F0A044}
        SccProjectUniqueName1 =
        SourceSafeBindingRemover\\SourceSafeBindingRemover.csproj
        SccLocalPath1 = .
        CanCheckoutShared = false
        SccProjectFilePathRelativizedFromConnection1 =
            SourceSafeBindingRemover\\
    EndGlobalSection
    GlobalSection(SolutionConfiguration) = preSolution
        Debug = Debug
        Release = Release
    EndGlobalSection
    GlobalSection(ProjectConfiguration) = postSolution
      {C7687560-4B36-47E3-AF33-748E76411259}.Debug.ActiveCfg
        = Debug|.NET
      {C7687560-4B36-47E3-AF33-748E76411259}.Debug.Build.0
        = Debug|.NET
      {C7687560-4B36-47E3-AF33-748E76411259}.Release.ActiveCfg
        = Release|.NET
      {C7687560-4B36-47E3-AF33-748E76411259}.Release.Build.0
        = Release|.NET
    EndGlobalSection
    GlobalSection(ExtensibilityGlobals) = postSolution
    EndGlobalSection
    GlobalSection(ExtensibilityAddIns) = postSolution
    EndGlobalSection
EndGlobal
```

The first line is the solution file version declaration. The first element is the
Project section that begins on the second line and continues to the
EndProject line. The second element is the Global section. The Global section contains things such as the active solution configuration and source
control, and inside it are individual GlobalSections that contain the various
settings. The GlobalSection(SourceCodeControl) contains the SourceSafe
bindings. To remove the SourceSafe bindings from the solution file, remove
the entire section from the line with GlobalSection(SourceCodeControl) until
the first EndGlobalSection. Save the solution file before closing Notepad.

Each project file needs to be modified in a similar manner, but the project
files are easier to modify. Using Notepad to look at a sample project file
shows this format:

```
<VisualStudioProject>
    <CSHARP
        ProjectType = "Local"
        ProductVersion = "7.10.3077"
```

```
            SchemaVersion = "2.0"
            ProjectGuid = "{C7687560-4B36-47E3-AF33-748E76411259}"
            SccProjectName = "SAK"
            SccLocalPath = "SAK"
            SccAuxPath = "SAK"
            SccProvider = "SAK"
    >
        <Build>
            <Settings
                ApplicationIcon = "App.ico"
                AssemblyKeyContainerName = ""
                AssemblyName = "SourceSafeBindingRemover"
                AssemblyOriginatorKeyFile = ""
                DefaultClientScript = "JScript"
                DefaultHTMLPageLayout = "Grid"
                DefaultTargetSchema = "IE50"
                DelaySign = "false"
                OutputType = "WinExe"
                PreBuildEvent = ""
                PostBuildEvent = ""
                RootNamespace = "SourceSafeBindingRemover"
                RunPostBuildEvent = "OnBuildSuccess"
                StartupObject = ""
            >
                <Config
                    Name = "Debug"
                    AllowUnsafeBlocks = "false"
                    BaseAddress = "285212672"
                    CheckForOverflowUnderflow = "false"
                    ConfigurationOverrideFile = ""
                    DefineConstants = "DEBUG;TRACE"
                    DocumentationFile = ""
                    DebugSymbols = "true"
                    FileAlignment = "4096"
                    IncrementalBuild = "false"
                    NoStdLib = "false"
                    NoWarn = ""
                    Optimize = "false"
                    OutputPath = "bin\Debug\"
                    RegisterForComInterop = "false"
                    RemoveIntegerChecks = "false"
                    TreatWarningsAsErrors = "false"
                    WarningLevel = "4"
                />
... sections deleted
        </CSHARP>
</VisualStudioProject>
```

The lines that need to be deleted are all within the <CSHARP> XML tag. If it is a
VB project, the tag will be VisualBasic instead. Delete all lines that begin with

SCC within the opening CSHARP or VisualBasic XML tag. In the preceding sample file, the four lines starting with SccProjectName, SccLocalPath, SccAuxPath, and SccProvider would all need to be deleted. Save the file and close Notepad. You will need to do this for each project file in your application.

With Visual Studio 2005, the project file is a completely different format (it is now based on MSBuild), but the data you will need to delete is very similar. Here is the relevant section of the project file:

```
<PropertyGroup>
    <Configuration Condition=" '$(Configuration)' == '' ">Debug</
Configuration>
    <Platform Condition=" '$(Platform)' == '' ">AnyCPU</Platform>
    <ProductVersion>8.0.40903</ProductVersion>
    <SchemaVersion>2.0</SchemaVersion>
    <ProjectGuid>{951EBC65-CA21-4C24-B501-DFF2A03A03F1}</ProjectGuid>
    <OutputType>Library</OutputType>
    <StartupObject>
    </StartupObject>
    <AssemblyName>SourceSafeBindingRemover</AssemblyName>
    <RootNamespace>SourceSafeBindingRemover</RootNamespace>
    <SccProjectName>SAK</SccProjectName>
    <SccLocalPath>SAK</SccLocalPath>
    <SccAuxPath>SAK</SccAuxPath>
    <SccProvider>SAK</SccProvider>
</PropertyGroup>
```

In this example, the elements named SccProjectName, SccLocalPath, SccAuxPath, and SccProvider would all need to be deleted.

The last thing to do is remove all the files that SourceSafe creates with the *.scc* extension. Every directory will contain a file called *vssver.scc*. Folders with project files will have an associated *mssccprj.scc* file. There are also files ending with *<Project Name>.csproj.vspscc* (*vbproj* if it is a Visual Basic Project) or *<Solution Name>.etp.vspscc*. All of these files should be deleted, and with that, your application will have all the SourceSafe bindings removed.

Hacking the Hack

I have written a simple Windows application that automates the removal of SourceSafe bindings using the previous steps. You can download the latest version from *http://workspaces.gotdotnet.com/SourceSafeBindingRemover*.

You can see this application in Figure 1-16.

Using it is simple. Select the solution root folder using the Choose Folder button and click the Remove SourceSafe Bindings button. If the Remove Bindings? checkbox is unchecked, then the window will show you a preview of all the files that will be deleted. This will help you make sure that

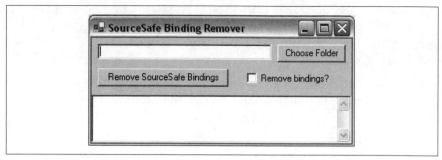

Figure 1-16. SourceSafe Binding Remover

none of your source code files are accidentally included in the delete list. If the checkbox is checked, clicking the Remove SourceSafe Bindings button will remove all SourceSafe bindings from the selected root folder and any subfolder, recursively.

Currently this tool works only for Visual Studio .NET 2002 and Visual Studio .NET 2003.

—Darrell Norton

Master the Editor
Hacks 6–15

Visual Studio is, above all else, a code editor. Before getting into some of the more advanced hacks like creating and using add-ins, customizing Visual Studio, or speeding up how quickly you write code, you must first learn how to best take advantage of the editor that is at the heart of Visual Studio.

The editor is where you probably spend most of your time in Visual Studio—after all, the editor is where you write and edit your code. The editor is also probably a key reason that you have decided to use Visual Studio as opposed to a simple text editor like Notepad. The editor offers enhancements like syntax coloring, IntelliSense, code formatting, and much more.

This chapter includes hacks on how to best take advantage of the clipboard, including an add-in that can be used to easily paste long strings into the editor. This chapter also include hacks that look at how to get the most out of IntelliSense and how to master the use of regions. Last, you will learn how to choose the right editor and learn how to use a couple new editor features in Visual Studio 2005.

Throughout this book, we will cover a lot of keyboard shortcuts, but since keyboard shortcuts differ between developer profiles, we will also include the name of the command for that keystroke. For example, when referring to the Ctrl-C shortcut, we will also include the name of the command in parentheses (Edit.Copy). If you know the command, you can always use the Keyboard Settings screen to either find the keystroke for that command in your profile, or you can create a new shortcut for that command. For more information on creating and managing your keyboard shortcuts, please refer to "Create Your Own Shortcuts" [Hack #24].

Master the Clipboard

#6

In theory, a clipboard should be simple: copy, cut, or paste. But that's no fun! You can learn how to really supercharge these operations.

Visual Studio contains a number of different features pertaining to cutting and pasting and the clipboard. Some of these features are old text editor favorites that are finally making it into Visual Studio, and some are new innovations from the Visual Studio team. These might seem like small features in a program that is as feature-packed as Visual Studio, but the clipboard will affect your day-to-day programming more than most other features.

Clipboard Ring

When you copy and paste text in any application, you are usually limited to copying and pasting one item at a time. If you want to copy two separate sentences, you have to copy the first one, paste it, then come back and repeat this for the next sentence. This can become tedious when you have 10 different things to copy and they reside in 10 different places in the document. You end up switching back and forth between the two documents 10 times, once for each sentence you want to copy.

The clipboard ring eliminates this limitation. The clipboard ring allows you to cut or copy up to 20 selections and access them using a keyboard shortcut. Here is the process for using the clipboard ring:

1. Copy (Ctrl-C, Edit.Copy) or Cut (Ctrl-X, Edit.Cut) up to 20 text selections, one after the other. These selections are organized as a last-in-first-out (LIFO) stack. That is, the last item you cut or copy will be the top item on the clipboard ring.

2. Press Ctrl-Shift-V to paste the first selection (the item on the top) from the clipboard ring into your document.

3. If you don't want to paste the first selection, press Ctrl-Shift-V (Edit. CycleClipboardRing) again, and the first thing you pasted will be replaced with the next selection from the clipboard ring. For example, if you wanted to paste the fourth item in the clipboard ring, you would simply press Ctrl-Shift-V four times. If you want to paste the same item more than once, simply pressing Ctrl-V (Edit.Paste) after the first time will work, since it will now be the current item on the clipboard.

Instead of moving between two documents a number of times, copying and pasting different selections, you can first copy all of the selections from the first document, then go to the second document and, using the clipboard ring, paste all of those selections. The clipboard ring also comes in handy when you have two or more separate things that you need to paste multiple times; using the clipboard ring, you can switch back and forth between these items easily.

You can also view the current contents of the clipboard ring by selecting the Clipboard Ring tab in the Toolbox dialog. This tab, shown in Figure 2-1, displays all of the selections currently living in the clipboard ring and allows you to drag the selections to paste them into your document.

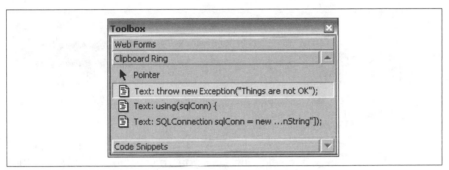

Figure 2-1. Clipboard Ring tab in Toolbox dialog

While the Clipboard Ring tab is a good way to get a better understanding of the clipboard ring, it is not as efficient as the shortcut keys. Visual Studio .NET 2003 users will find that the Clipboard Ring tab is absent in Visual Studio 2005, so it is best to use the shortcut keys instead of the Toolbox tab.

Line-Based Cut and Paste

The clipboard ring is not the only copy and paste feature in Visual Studio; a number of shortcut keys allow you to copy and paste code even faster.

Most applications rely on you selecting which text you want to cut, copy, or delete. Visual Studio makes the very simple assumption that if you have not selected any text that you want to cut, copy, or delete, *the editing action will be performed on the entire current line*. If you wanted to move one line below another line, you could move the cursor to the first line, press Ctrl-X (Edit. Cut) to cut the line, press the down arrow to move to the next line down, and then press Ctrl-V (Edit.Paste) to paste the entire line. Other shortcuts like Ctrl-C (Edit.Copy) and Ctrl-L (Edit.LineCut) follow this same rule and allow you to copy or delete the current line by simply pressing the shortcut keys without selecting any text. Any time you can avoid reaching for the mouse to select text is time saved.

Block Selection

Normal text selection is done on a line-by-line basis; it is impossible to select parts of multiple lines with normal text selection. Figure 2-2 shows how it is not possible to select just the right side of the equals sign using normal text selection. This is a drawback that most of us have become accustomed to.

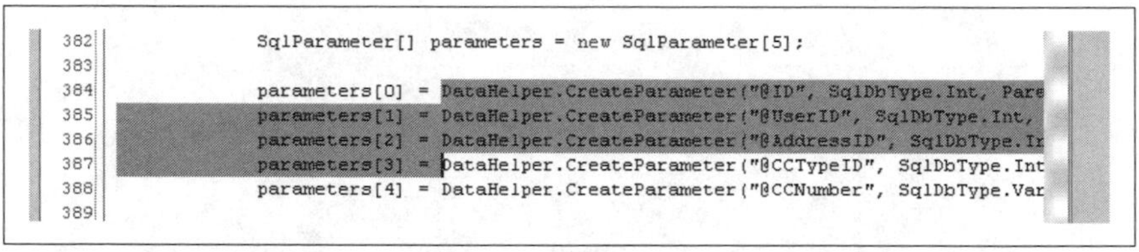

```
382     SqlParameter[] parameters = new SqlParameter[5];
383
384       parameters[0] = DataHelper.CreateParameter("@ID", SqlDbType.Int, Pare
385       parameters[1] = DataHelper.CreateParameter("@UserID", SqlDbType.Int,
386       parameters[2] = DataHelper.CreateParameter("@AddressID", SqlDbType.Ir
387       parameters[3] = DataHelper.CreateParameter("@CCTypeID", SqlDbType.Int
388       parameters[4] = DataHelper.CreateParameter("@CCNumber", SqlDbType.Var
389
```

Figure 2-2. Normal text selection

Visual Studio has a feature that allows you to get around this limitation. By holding the Alt key while selecting text, you trigger *block selection*, which allows you to select text regardless of what line it is on. Figure 2-3 shows how block selection can be used to select only text to the right of the equals sign.

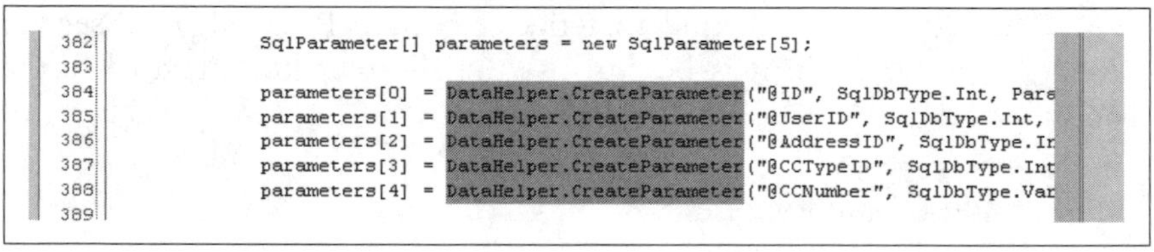

```
382     SqlParameter[] parameters = new SqlParameter[5];
383
384       parameters[0] = DataHelper.CreateParameter("@ID", SqlDbType.Int, Pare
385       parameters[1] = DataHelper.CreateParameter("@UserID", SqlDbType.Int,
386       parameters[2] = DataHelper.CreateParameter("@AddressID", SqlDbType.Ir
387       parameters[3] = DataHelper.CreateParameter("@CCTypeID", SqlDbType.Int
388       parameters[4] = DataHelper.CreateParameter("@CCNumber", SqlDbType.Var
389
```

Figure 2-3. Block text selection

Block selection can be used to select any amount of text in a block, as opposed to line by line. You can use block selection whether you select text with the mouse or the keyboard (hold down Alt and Shift, and press the arrow keys to perform a block selection with the keyboard).

When pasting block selections, Visual Studio will insert each line of the block onto a subsequent existing line, unlike normal selections where new lines will be inserted. Thus, it is important to be sure that the destination for your block selection is the same number of lines as the source.

Make Pasting into Visual Studio Easier

Don't be limited to plain text. You can paste strings into Visual Studio as comments, string, StringBuilders, and more.

SmartPaster is a plug-in for Visual Studio .NET 2003 that allows text on the clipboard to be pasted in a format compatible with C# and Visual Basic code. SmartPaster can be downloaded from *http://www.papadimoulis.com/alex/SmartPaster1.1.zip*. After downloading and installing SmartPaster, you will see a new item on the right-click (context) menu, which is shown in Figure 2-4.

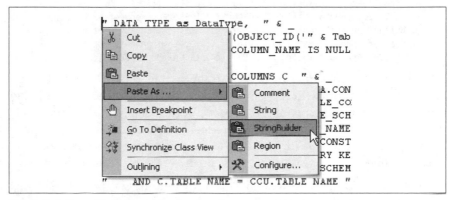

Figure 2-4. SmartPaster menu

Paste as String/StringBuilder

I find myself most frequently pasting text as a string or a StringBuilder. You can copy any sort of text from another application, then when you paste that text into Visual Studio, you can choose to paste it as a string or as a StringBuilder.

Many developers like to build a SQL statement using a tool such as Query Analyzer, for easy testing and debugging, or Microsoft Access, for quick, visual development. As simple as it is to build queries externally, putting them into code can often be a challenge, especially when the queries span multiple lines. SmartPaster eases the task of bringing external queries to code: simply copy your query to the clipboard and paste as a string or String-Builder. For example, if you copied the following SQL to your clipboard:

```
SET ROWCOUNT 10
SELECT ProductName
FROM Products
ORDER BY Products.UnitPrice DESC
```

then paste the code into Visual Studio using Paste As → String, you would
see the following code:

```
@"SET ROWCOUNT 10" + Environment.NewLine +
@"SELECT ProductName" + Environment.NewLine +
@"FROM Products" + Environment.NewLine +
@"ORDER BY Products.UnitPrice DESC" + Environment.NewLine +
@""
```

You could also paste this code using Paste As → StringBuilder and specify a
StringBuilder name of "sqlBuilder," and this would result in the following
code:

```
StringBuilder sqlBuilder = new StringBuilder(141);
sqlBuilder.AppendFormat(@"SET ROWCOUNT 10{0}", Environment.NewLine);
sqlBuilder.AppendFormat(@"SELECT ProductName{0}", Environment.NewLine);
sqlBuilder.AppendFormat(@"FROM Products{0}", Environment.NewLine);
sqlBuilder.AppendFormat(@"ORDER BY Products.UnitPrice DESC");
```

Like SQL statements, text displayed to the user is often developed externally, either by a copywriter, business analyst, or coder (such as myself), and
requires the spellchecker within Microsoft Word. Usually, pasting such code
would require going character by character, escaping quotes, and manually
adding in line breaks. With SmartPaster, a quick right-click, paste-as, and
your external copy is now internal without any of the normal hassle.

In an ideal world, all messages and dialogs would be stored in an external
resource file and all SQL statements would be in views and stored procedures. But in a world of deadlines and disposable microapplications, doing
it the right way is often trumped by "make sure it works."

As we've seen, SmartPaster offers the option of pasting your text as a string
or a StringBuilder. While the difference may seem cosmetic, there are actually appropriate times to use one over the other. The reasoning behind this is
that string literals (i.e., strings explicitly declared in your code, as opposed
to those input by the user) are immutable. This means that every operation
on a string, such as a concatenation or replacement, involves creating an in-
memory buffer, performing the operation, creating a new string, and finally
passing the old one to garbage collection.

Knowing that, it's fairly easy to decide whether to use a string or a String-
Builder. If the text will always be static, such as a tool tip, there will be no
advantage to using a StringBuilder (even if string literals are concatenated
across lines, the compiler joins them in memory). However, if the text will
vary on conditions, such as a runtime error message, then there will definitely be a performance hit using a string as opposed to a StringBuilder.

Paste as Comment

Just as with strings, any text on the clipboard may be pasted as a block of comments. I've found this very helpful in many cases. Having instant blocks of comments makes development much easier because of the following reasons:

- Business rule requirements may be pasted directly into the code for easier translation and to explain what is being done.
- Documentation from MSDN or other sources may be pasted in, avoiding the need to switch between the code and a browser window.
- When upgrading code from another platform, the legacy code can be pasted as a comment, making it easier to ensure the logic is the same.

To paste text as a comment, you simply need to copy text to your clipboard and then choose Paste As → Comment. For example, if you copied the following piece of text to your clipboard:

```
Call the test method to walk through this scenario and test every part.
```

and then pasted it into your document using Paste As → Comment, you would see the following comment added:

```
//Call the test method to walk through this scenario and test every part.
```

Paste as Region

When pasting as a region, the clipboard text will simply appear between #region and #endregion tags with a region name of your choice. This feature is often helpful when organizing code within your application or pasting regions of code developed by someone else.

First, copy a piece of code like this one to your clipboard:

```
private void DoSomething( )
{
    //Write Code Here
}
```

Then select Paste As → Region, and you will see the dialog shown in Figure 2-5.

From this dialog, you specify the name of the region that you want to use; after you click OK, this code will be pasted into your document:

```
#region DoSomething Method
private void DoSomething( )
{
    //Write Code Here
}
#endregion
```

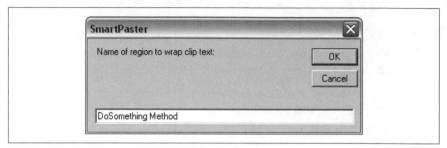

Figure 2-5. Region dialog

Configuration

SmartPaster offers a number of configuration options to make the add-in work best for you. The SmartPaster configuration dialog is shown in Figure 2-6 and can be accessed through Paste As → Configure.

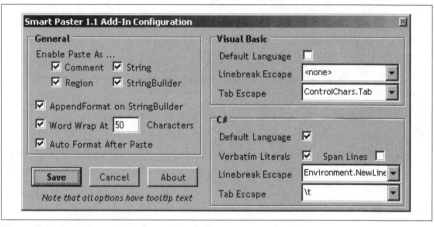

Figure 2-6. SmartPaster Configuration dialog

A bit of explanatory text is available as a tool tip for all of the options, and most options are self-explanatory.

Line breaks. There are quite a few ways to specify line breaks: ControlChars. NewLine, Environment.NewLine, Char(13), and depending on your language, vbCrLf, \n, and \r\n. Most of these accomplish the same thing: insert the special ASCII characters CR (carriage return), LF (line feed), or both.

The recommended way of adding line breaks is with Environment.NewLine. Unlike the other methods, this will insert the appropriate ASCII representation of a line break: an LF for Unix, a CR for Apple, and a combination of the two for Windows.

However, practicality often supersedes portability, and for most cases, escaped carriage returns (i.e., \r and \n) are the absolute simplest to use. SmartPaster allows you to easily configure which option to use.

AppendFormat on StringBuilder. The AppendFormat checkbox determines how control characters should be handled within a string pasted as a String-Builder. While this is mostly a matter of preference, one factor to consider may be performance. A string literal concatenated with another constant (such as "Hello World" & vbCrLf), will be combined at compile time, thus creating only one interned string. The AppendFormat method uses a formatter to parse the string and arguments such as "Hello World{0}", vbCrLf at runtime, incurring a slight overhead.

Key Bindings

When installed, SmartPaster adds five configurable environment commands, one for each method of pasting, and the final to open the configuration dialog. These commands can be bound to a key combination [Hack #24] or placed easily on a taskbar to make the options work best for you.

—Alex Papadimoulis

Master IntelliSense

#8

Visual Studio can read your mind. Learn how to have Visual Studio's IntelliSense feature do lots of the typing for you.

Even if you have used Visual Studio only a couple times, I am sure you have noticed one of its trademark features: IntelliSense. The most popular form of IntelliSense assists you as you code by providing a list of the members for each class immediately after you finish typing the class name (and the following period). This is not the only form of IntelliSense though; this feature finds its way into a multitude of different areas of Visual Studio.

Complete Word

The first, and most useful, IntelliSense feature is actually just a shortcut: Ctrl-Space (Edit.CompleteWord). By using the Ctrl-Space shortcut, you can summon IntelliSense at any point during your coding session, not just when you finish typing a class name. This is one of the few shortcuts that can really change the way that you write code.

If you have already starting typing when you press Ctrl-Space, Visual Studio will take one of two actions. If there is only one object that matches what you have typed in so far, it will automatically complete the object name; for instance, if you typed in **HttpR**, it would automatically complete the rest of the object name (HttpRequest). If there are a number of objects that match what you have typed in, it will display the full list of members with the first match highlighted. Figure 2-7 shows what the listbox would look like if you only typed in the letter *P*.

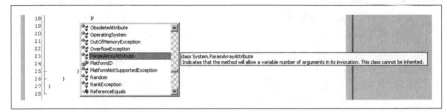

Figure 2-7. IntelliSense listbox, brought to you by the letter P

You can also press Ctrl-Space on a blank line and be shown a complete list of members in the current context. This is a great way to find a variable name that has slipped your mind. Figure 2-8 shows an example of this.

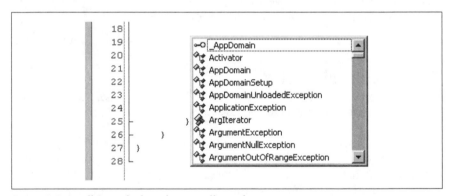

Figure 2-8. IntelliSense listbox showing all members

This shortcut can be even more useful if you name all of your private member variables with a common prefix; for instance, if all of your variables are prefixed with "_", by typing _ and then pressing Ctrl-Space, you would display a list of all of your variables to choose from.

Parameter Info

Another useful form of IntelliSense is the parameter information that is shown after you type the opening parenthesis of a method (it goes away when the parentheses are closed). When editing an already existing method, it would be nice to have this information again without having to delete and then reenter the opening parenthesis, wouldn't it? As long as the cursor is located inside of the method parameters parenthesis, pressing Ctrl-Shift-Space (Edit.ParameterInfo) will display the parameter information pop up. Figure 2-9 shows this pop up.

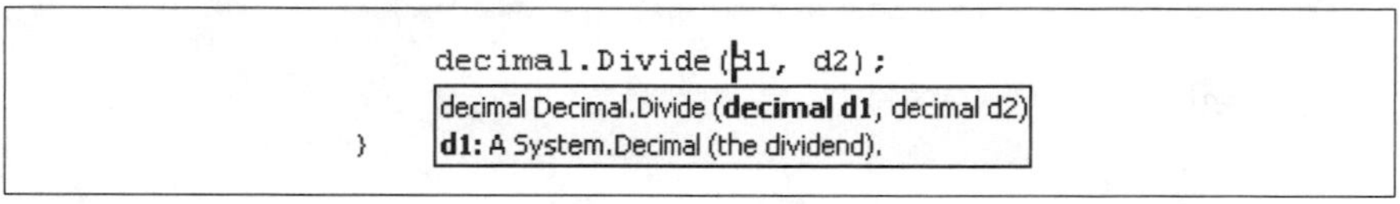

```
        decimal.Divide(d1, d2);
        decimal Decimal.Divide (decimal d1, decimal d2)
    }   d1: A System.Decimal (the dividend).
```

Figure 2-9. Parameter info IntelliSense pop up

Quick Info

When you move your mouse over a method or variable, you will see a small tool tip pop up that contains information about that method or variable. This is commonly called Quick Info. If you are navigating by keyboard, you can also get this small pop up by pressing Ctrl-K and then Ctrl-I (Edit. QuickInfo). Using this shortcut is also the only way to bring up this informational pop up during debug, since the default behavior is to show the value of the object you are hovering over when using the mouse.

Stub Completion

Another form of autocompletion called stub completion can be very useful when working with interfaces or event handlers or when overriding a method. This feature can be used to automatically *stub out* the methods required by the interface or the default code for an overridden method or event handler. This is a feature that was added to Visual Studio .NET 2003, but its presence is not always obvious when you are coding quickly.

Interface. When you first create a class and add the interface name after the colon (or the Implements in Visual Basic), a small yellow window will pop up for just a few seconds, offering you the ability to press the Tab key, as shown in Figure 2-10.

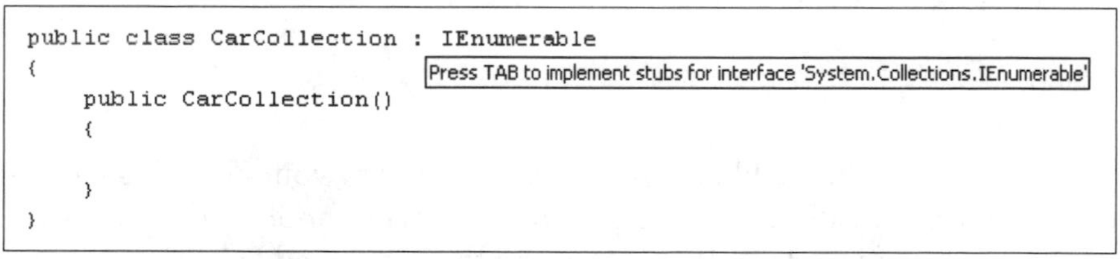

```
public class CarCollection : IEnumerable
{                              Press TAB to implement stubs for interface 'System.Collections.IEnumerable'
    public CarCollection()
    {

    }
}
```

Figure 2-10. Interface IntelliSense prompt

When you press the Tab key with this window still displayed, the methods required by the interface will be automatically added to your class, including TODO comments to remind you to complete the methods:

```
public class CarCollection : IEnumerable
{
    public CarCollection( )
    {

    }
    #region IEnumerable Members

    public IEnumerator GetEnumerator( )
    {
        // TODO:   Add CarCollection.GetEnumerator implementation
        return null;
    }

    #endregion
}
```

Overriding methods. When you type **override** into the document window, you will see a list of methods you can override in the base class. This can be seen in Figure 2-11.

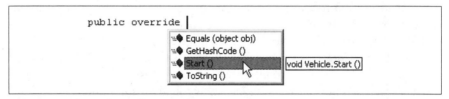

Figure 2-11. Override IntelliSense

When you select the method you want to override, Visual Studio will create the method and automatically add a call to the method you are overriding on your base class like this:

```
public override void Start( )
{
    base.Start ( );
}
```

Event handlers. When adding a new event handler to your class, Visual Studio will automatically create the stub of this event handler, much as when working with an interface. When you type the code to add an event handler to an event, you will see a prompt inviting you to press the Tab key, as shown in Figure 2-12.

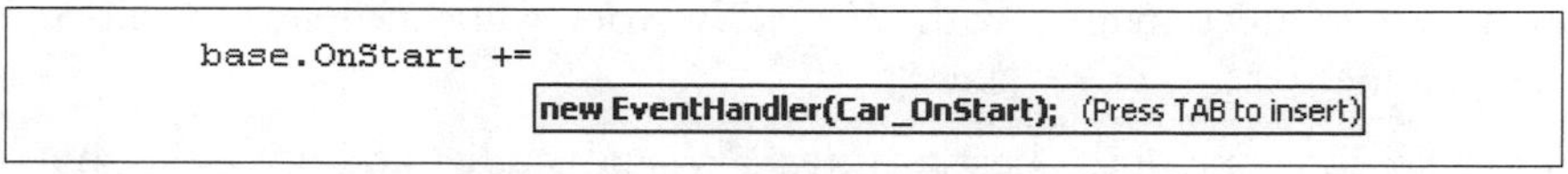

```
base.OnStart +=
        new EventHandler(Car_OnStart);   (Press TAB to insert)
```

Figure 2-12. EventHandler IntelliSense before pressing the Tab key

When you press the Tab key, you will then see the prompt shown in Figure 2-13.

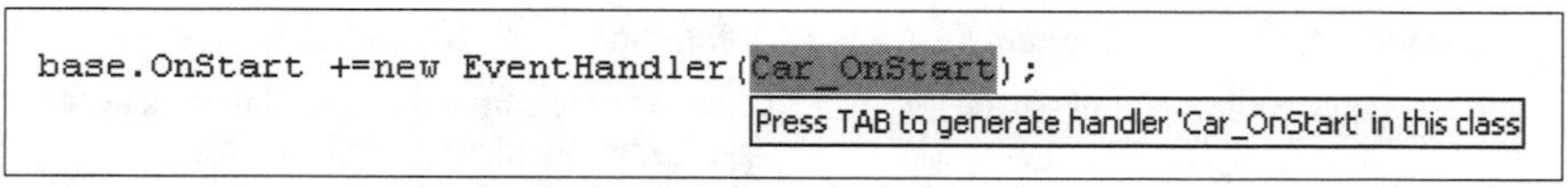

```
base.OnStart +=new EventHandler(Car_OnStart);
                                 Press TAB to generate handler 'Car_OnStart' in this class
```

Figure 2-13. EventHandler IntelliSense after pressing the Tab key

When you press the Tab key again, the following code will be inserted into your document:

```
private void Car_OnStart(object sender, EventArgs e)
{

}
```

IntelliSense Comments

When comments exist for a method or class, they are displayed in the IntelliSense pop up shown in Figure 2-14.

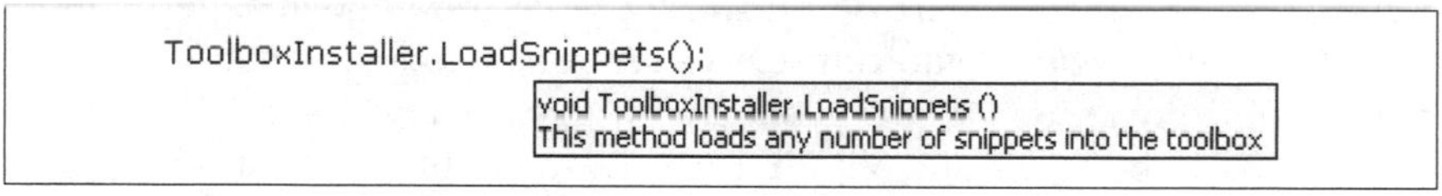

```
ToolboxInstaller.LoadSnippets();
                  void ToolboxInstaller.LoadSnippets ()
                  This method loads any number of snippets into the toolbox
```

Figure 2-14. IntelliSense comments

These comments can be created a number of different ways. If you are using C#, then these comments are pulled from the XML-based comments in your code, like the following example:

```
/// <summary>
/// This method loads any number of snippets into the toolbox
/// </summary>
public static void LoadSnippets()
```

If you are using C++, these comments are generated based on any comments at the end of the line for the member; if no comments exist at the end of the line, then any comments on the line directly above the member are used. Any comments on the declaration are used first; if there are no comments on the declaration, any comments on the definition are used. To get this same functionality with VB.NET, you will need to install the VBCommenter power toy [Hack #70].

IntelliSense is one of the best features of Visual Studio, and using the short-cut keys summarized in Table 2-1 will allow you to get the most out of this great feature.

Table 2-1. IntelliSense shortcut keys

Command	Shortcut keys	Description
Edit.CompleteWord	Ctrl-Space	Completes the current word or shows all available methods and properties for a class
Edit.ParameterInfo	Ctrl-Shift-Space	Shows the parameter information when the cursor is inside method parentheses
Edit.QuickInfo	Ctrl-K, Ctrl-I	Shows a quick description about whatever object the cursor is currently resting on

See Also

- "Enable IntelliSense for HTML and XML Documents" [Hack #32]

HACK #9 Master Regions

Tag, expand, and collapse regions. Visual Studio's regions let you make even the largest source files become instantly readable.

Regions are a valuable part of organizing your code and making it more readable. Using regions, you can select a section of code that you want to be able to logically group and also collapse. In this hack, you will learn how to use regions in both C# and VB.NET and learn about an add-in that makes working with regions even easier.

C# Regions

To use regions in C#, you simply need to surround the code you want to include in the region with #region and #endregion. Optionally, you can also include a string literal after #region that will be shown when the region is closed. Figure 2-15 shows an example of C# code surrounded by a region.

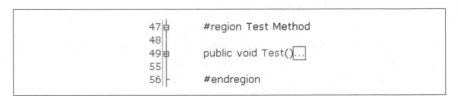

Figure 2-15. C# region expanded

Figure 2-16 shows this same region, except collapsed.

Figure 2-16. C# region collapsed

In C#, you can include regions anywhere in your source code file, even inside of methods or properties. (Whether this is a good idea is debatable.) Regions can also be nested inside of other regions.

VB.NET Regions

VB.NET regions are a little bit different than C# regions. In VB.NET, you surround the code that you want to include in the region with #Region and #End Region. You can also include a string after the #Region, but in VB.NET, the string will need to be enclosed in quotes. Figure 2-17 shows an example of VB.NET code surrounded by a region.

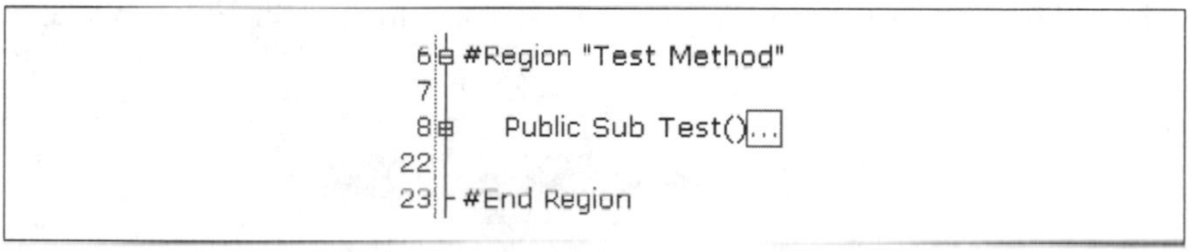

```
 6  #Region "Test Method"
 7
 8      Public Sub Test()...
22
23  #End Region
```

Figure 2-17. VB.NET region expanded

You might notice that in VB.NET, region tags are always moved to the complete left of the document. In VB.NET, you can include regions inside of other regions, but you can't include them inside of methods or properties.

Region Strategy

Regions are best used to group similar parts of your class. This makes finding a particular method or property easier and also makes the file more readable, since sections that you are not working with are hidden inside of a region. I am a big fan of the idea that all code, except for namespace declarations and using statements, should be in a region. Opening a file in which all of the private member variables are grouped inside of a region, the constructors in another region, the private methods in another region, and the public properties in yet another region make it extremely easy to find exactly what you are looking for. There are times when this organization might not make the most sense though. When implementing an interface, it is a good practice to group the method and properties that are used to implement the interface into a single region.

The best thing to do with regions is to define a standard for your project and then be sure that all of your developers follow that standard. A well-defined region strategy can make it easier to find and understand files, whereas a poorly defined strategy can lead to regions being more of a hindrance than benefit.

The Regions Add-in

To enclose a piece of existing code in a region, you need to find the top of the code, type in the #region statement, and then find the bottom of the code and type in the closing #endregion statement. While this is not all that difficult, wouldn't it be nice to be able to simply highlight a section of code and click a button that adds that code to a region? That is where the Regions Add-in comes into play. Using the Regions Add-in, you can select a piece of code using the mouse or keyboard and then right-click and select Add to New Region.

First, you will need to download and install the Region Add-in from *http://www.codeproject.com/dotnet/RegionsAddIn.asp.* After you have downloaded and installed the add-in, you will see two new items on your right-click menu. These are shown in Figure 2-18. (These items will be visible only when you have text selected.)

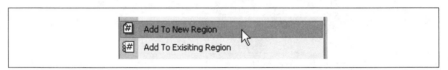

Figure 2-18. Regions Add-in menu items

If you select a block of code and then click the Add to New Region item, you will see the dialog shown in Figure 2-19.

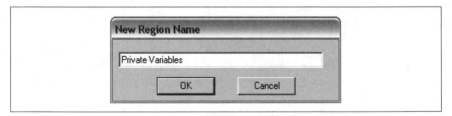

Figure 2-19. New Region Name dialog

After entering a name in the dialog box and clicking OK, the add-in will wrap the selected code in a region using the name you entered.

You can also use the add-in to add code into an existing region. Simply select a section of code and then right-click and choose the Add to Existing Region menu item. You will then see the Regions Dialog shown in Figure 2-20.

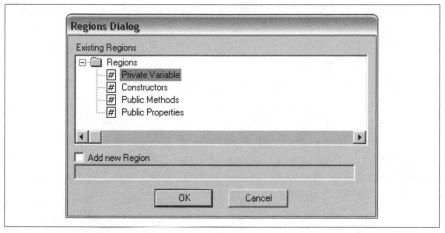

Figure 2-20. Regions Dialog

From the Regions Dialog, you can select the region you want to add the selected code to or you can decide to add it to a new region and click the Add New Region checkbox. This is particularly useful if you are adding a new property to the class; instead of opening the existing region and appending it to the end, you can write the property anywhere you want and then select it and move it to that region.

The Regions Add-in is a valuable tool that makes working with regions even easier than it already is.

Add Guidelines to the Text Editor

HACK
#10

If you've got to have everything line up just right, turn on guidelines and get everything pixel perfect.

One of the features missing from the text editor in Visual Studio is the ability to add vertical guidelines. Vertical guidelines are thin vertical lines that can be used as visual guides when aligning text. This feature is not actually missing though—using a simple registry hack, you can add up to 13 different guidelines to Visual Studio's text editor.

When editing the registry, you should always back up your registry or use the alternative registry method [Hack #30].

To add guidelines:

1. Close Visual Studio.
2. Open *regedit* (Start → Run → type **regedit**).

3. Navigate to *HKEY_CURRENT_USER\Software\Microsoft\VisualStudio\ <7.1>\Text Editor*.

4. Right-click on the Text Editor key and choose New → String Value and name it "Guides".

5. Set the value of the guides to RGB(128, 128, 128) 4, 16.

The first part of the value sets the color of the guidelines using common red, green, and blue values. 128, 128, and 128 sets the color of the guidelines to gray. The second numbers specify where the guidelines should appear. In this example, guidelines will be shown at the 4-space mark as well as the 16-space mark. You can add up to 13 different guidelines by simply adding more numeric values separated by commas.

After you have created your registry entry, you will see guidelines in the marks specified when you launch Visual Studio. Figure 2-21 shows an example of the results from the example settings.

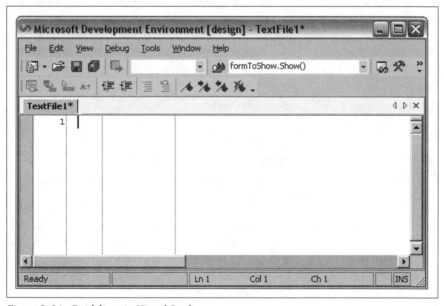

Figure 2-21. Guidelines in Visual Studio

Removing these guidelines is simply a matter of deleting the Guides registry key and restarting Visual Studio.

Guidelines are easy to add and can be very useful when trying to keep your code organized. Thanks to Sara Ford for posting about this hidden feature on her blog: *http://blogs.msdn.com/saraford*.

Select the Best Editor

Different editors can be used for different file types, including some hidden possibilities.

A large part of learning to work with any toolset is understanding what tool should be used and when it should be used. Visual Studio contains a number of different editors, including a Text Editor, XML Editor, CSS Editor, and many more. This hack is about determining what editor should be used in what situation and also explains how Visual Studio can be configured to use a third-party editor as opposed to the native editor.

So Many Editors

Visual Studio contains a host of different editors; you have probably encountered a number of them.

Text Editor. The editor you are probably most familiar with is the Text Editor, which is used to edit and work with most forms of text, including source code. The Text Editor contains a number of configuration settings that can be specified on a per-language basis; these settings can be accessed through the Tools → Options menu, which can be seen in Figure 2-22.

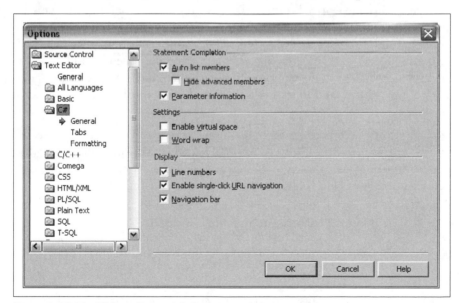

Figure 2-22. Text Editor Options dialog

Using the Options dialog, you can decide whether or not to enable word wrap, line numbers, and some other miscellaneous settings. Each language can be configured independently of the other languages; each is configured to different defaults initially.

> As of Visual Studio .NET 2003, the VB.NET editor is set to Hide Advanced Members automatically. This is something you will most likely want to turn off, as it stops certain methods and properties from showing up in IntelliSense. Some of the hidden methods, like `Page.RegisterClientScriptBlock`, are very valuable and encourage better development and so should not remain hidden. The idea behind this setting is to filter members that won't normally be used by your average developer, but as it turns out, some of the members it hides are indeed very useful. Methods marked with the attribute `[EditorBrowsable(EditorBrowsableState.Advanced)]` will be hidden when this option is enabled.

The Text Editor is used for programming languages, so it's the one you will probably work with the most.

HTML/XML Editor. The HTML/XML Editor is used to work with HTML, XML, and XML schemas. The HTML/XML Editor consists of a regular textual view of the HTML or XML as well as a number of different designers. Designers provide a visual representation of the HTML or XML that you are editing. A designer for HTML shows you how the HTML should look in the browser and provides WYSIWYG editing support. A designer for XML shows a "Data" view by creating rows and columns based on the structure of the loaded XML. A designer for XML schemas shows a visual representation of the schema and allows you to drag elements from a schema-specific toolbox.

For the most part, these editors are all self-explanatory and work perfectly, but if you are particular about your HTML then you probably don't like Visual Studio messing with it. Visual Studio has a nasty habit of not only reformatting your HTML, but sometimes even removing attributes or tags.

> Visual Studio is getting better and better at working with HTML. Visual Studio 2005 is light-years ahead of previous versions when it comes to leaving your HTML alone and generates even better HTML than previous editions.

HTML purists will always want complete control over their HTML, how it is formatted, and what is included. The best way to manage this in Visual Studio is to simply not use the designer, but since by default, all *.html* and *.xml* documents are opened with the designer, you will need to change some settings to get this behavior.

To switch the default behavior, you need to change the settings located under the HTML Designer folder in the Tools → Options dialog. These settings are shown in Figure 2-23.

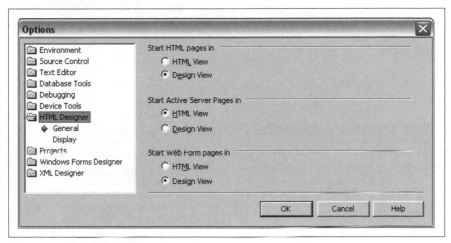

Figure 2-23. HTML Designer Options

On this Options screen, you can determine what view will be used for each type of file handled by the HTML designer. Changing the radio button to HTML View (in which you edit the raw HTML) for each of the file types will cause Visual Studio to also use the HTML view when opening these files. (You can later switch to design view if you like.)

Other editors. There are also editors for CSS files, resource files, and binary files. I am not going to cover these here since they are easy to use and don't have any hidden features that you need to worry about.

Choosing Your Editor

Visual Studio will also select what editor it feels is best, based on the extension of the file you select, but sometimes it is beneficial to use a different editor than the Visual Studio default. To select a different editor, you need to use the Open With command, which you can access in a couple of different ways. When selecting a file from the Solution Explorer, right-click the file and choose Open With from the context menu that appears. Or if browsing for a file with the File Open dialog, first select the file, then click the arrow on the Open button (see Figure 2-24), and choose Open With.

After selecting Open With, you will see the Open With dialog, which is shown in Figure 2-25.

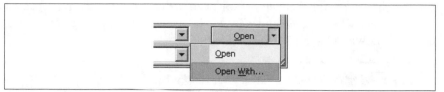

Figure 2-24. Open With option

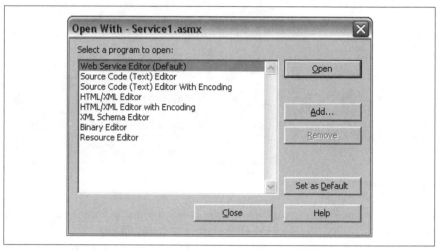

Figure 2-25. Open With dialog

You can see in Figure 2-25 that the Web Service Editor is the default editor for the *.asmx* extension. This is a great example of when you need to specify a different editor: by default you can view only a designer of the web service or the web service's *code behind* (the file that contains any C# or VB.NET for your web service) *.asmx* file. There is no way to actually view and edit the source code of the *.asmx* file—you must go through the designer. To overcome this restriction, select the HTML/XML Editor from this dialog, and you will be able to directly edit the *.asmx* file just as if it were a normal ASP.NET file.

This dialog also allows you to set the default editor for a file extension; this is particularly useful when working with a new extension that Visual Studio might not be set up to edit. Loads of different applications use different extensions for what boil down to be XML files. When you first open one of these files, just select the HTML/XML Editor and click the Set As Default button (shown in Figure 2-25). Whenever you open this file type in the future, Visual Studio will use that editor.

Use a Third-Party Editor

Although Visual Studio includes a number of nice editors, sometimes a third-party application does it better. I have a particular liking for a CSS editor application called TopStyle (*http://www.bradsoft.com*), and whenever I work with CSS files, I use it.

To configure TopStyle as an editor in Visual Studio, all I need to do is open a *.css* file, use the Open With option, and from the Open With dialog, click the Add button. I then see the Add Program dialog, which is shown in Figure 2-26.

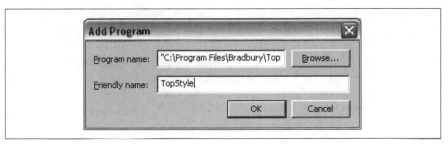

Figure 2-26. Add Program dialog

From the Add Program dialog, I can browse for the program executable and also give the application a friendly name, which will be shown in the editor list. After adding TopStyle as an editor, I can then click OK to return to the Open With dialog and there set TopStyle as the default editor for *.css* files by selecting it in the editor list and clicking the Set As Default button. Now whenever I double-click on a *.css* file, Visual Studio will launch an instance of TopStyle with the file open in it. If the file is under source control, you will need to manually check it out before opening it with the third-party editor.

HACK
#12

Customize Syntax Coloring
Specify the keywords you want Visual Studio to colorize, even in PHP!

When working with Visual Studio, you will notice that language keywords are highlighted in blue. This coloring makes code more readable. If you ever want to see the impact that this coloring has, open a code file in Notepad and notice how much less readable it is.

Unfortunately, most languages, including VB.NET and C#, won't let you change how keywords are colored in Visual Studio. One language that does provide a method for specifying your own keywords is C++. For example, you can add the word "DateTime" as a keyword to C++ with a few simple steps. First, you need to create a file named *usertype.dat*. This is a simple text file that contains all of the words that you want to be colored as keywords.

Start by creating a new text file in your favorite text editor, add the word DateTime to the top line of that file, then save that file with the name of *usertype* and the extension of *.dat*. Here is what your file should look like:

```
DateTime
```

Next, copy this file to the following directory: *<Visual Studio Directory>\ Common7\IDE* (for example, *C:\Program Files\Microsoft Visual Studio .NET 2003\Common7\IDE*).

Before Visual Studio will read this file, you need to restart the IDE; after the restart, you can open up a C++ source code file, and you should see DateTime colored as a keyword. You can then add additional keywords, each on its own line, and the IDE will pick these words up and treat them as keywords. Customizing the words that are colored is a great way to get confirmation that you typed the correct word and also increases the readability of your code.

Hacking the Hack

If you wanted all of your classes to be colored, it would take a quite a bit of time to add all of them to the *usertype.dat* file. Steve King has written a nice add-in that will look through your entire solution, add all of your classes to a temporary *usertype.dat* file, then load that file with Visual Studio. This way, you can have all of your classes colored without the labor of doing it yourself. The only downside to this add-in is that this file is not saved when you close the IDE, so you will need to run this command every time you open the IDE. (It was written this way to avoid overwriting any changes to the original *usertype.dat* file.)

This add-in actually does a number of other things that might be of interest to C++ developers, including adding regions, dependency and inheritance graphs, and the ability to search the Web.

The add-in can be downloaded from *http://www.codeproject.com/macro/ kingstools.asp*.

Add Coloring for Other Languages

Many people use Visual Studio to edit languages that it was never intended to edit. Out of the box, Visual Studio won't do syntax highlighting for these languages, but you can fix this with a small registry hack and a custom *usertype.dat* file. The first part of this hack is to hack the registry and tell Visual Studio to associate the language's filename extension with C++. It may seem a little strange to add the extension as a C++ extension, but this is the only way to get the IDE to use the custom *usertype.dat* file, since only C++ will use the *usertype.dat* file.

This example adds PHP as a supported language. First, you need to edit the registry and add the *.php* extension to the list of C++ file extensions.

Always back up your registry by exporting the key you are modifying before making modifications to it, or use the alternate registry method **[Hack #30]**.

To add the *.php* extension, create a new string value key under the File Extensions folder located here:

```
HKEY_LOCAL_MACHINE\SOFTWARE\Microsoft\VisualStudio\7.1\
Languages\File Extensions
```

Replace *7.1* with the version of Visual Studio that you are working with: 7.0 for Visual Studio .NET 2002, 7.1 for Visual Studio .NET 2003, and 8.0 for Visual Studio 2005.

The key needs to be named .php and the value of the key should be: {B2F072B0-ABC1-11D0-9D62-00C04FD9DFD9}. (Make this easy on yourself by copying this GUID from the .c key.) After this key is added, the *.php* extension will be treated as a C++ file, and any keywords entered in the *usertype. dat* file will be appropriately highlighted.

The next step is to add all of the PHP language keywords to the *usertype.dat* file. These keywords are shown in Table 2-2.

Table 2-2. PHP keywords list

abstract	array	as
boolean	break	case
class	default	define
do	echo	else
elseif	empty	eval
exit	extends	false
for	foreach	function
global	if	implements
in	include	include_once
instanceof	interface	new
null	php	php3
phpinfo	print	private
protected	public	require

Table 2-2. PHP keywords list (continued)

require_once	return	static
switch	true	unset
var	while	

You will need to add each of these keywords on its own line to *usertype.dat*, along with any other C++ keywords you may have defined. After you create this file and save it to the *<Visual Studio Directory>\Common7\IDE* directory, all the PHP language keywords will be highlighted whenever you open a *.php* file in Visual Studio.

Thanks to a blogger named David Cumps for discovering this method. You can also download a *.reg* file to create the registry key and a prefilled *usertype.dat* file from his blog, located at *http://weblogs.asp.NET/cumpsd/ archive/2004/02/22/77926.aspx*.

Edit the Most Recent File and Project Lists

#13   The list of recently used files is a good place to go back to the projects you've been working with a lot. You can tweak this list to your liking and make it even better.

Visual Studio maintains a list of the most recently opened file and project files. Whenever you open a file or project, it is added to the top of the most recently opened list. Visual Studio then uses the most recent file and project lists for a number of different purposes. The first is to populate two menu items that list the entire recent file and project lists; this is shown in Figure 2-27.

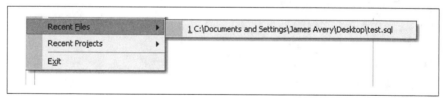

Figure 2-27. Recent Files list

The second use is to display recent projects on the default Visual Studio .NET 2003 start page, which is shown in Figure 2-28.

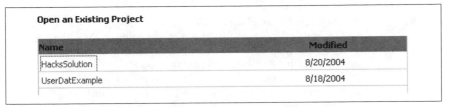

Figure 2-28. Visual Studio .NET 2003 start page

Modify Number of Items

By default, both of these lists display only four (or eight in Visual Studio 2005) of the most recent projects or files. By navigating to Tools → Options → General, you can set the number of items shown in these lists under the option called "Display *n* items in most recently used lists." This option can be seen in Figure 2-29.

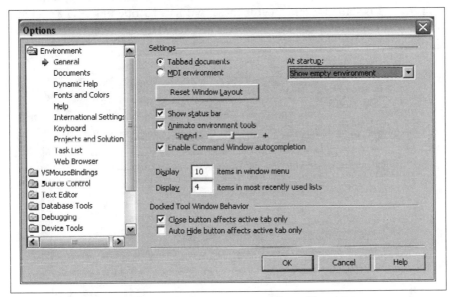

Figure 2-29. Number of items to display in most recently used lists

You can set the number of items to any number between 1 and 24. When you click OK, you will immediately see the new files and projects in Visual Studio.

Editing Most Recent Lists

There is no place in Visual Studio to edit either of these lists, but thankfully Microsoft has released a power toy called VSTweak to do so.

A *power toy* is a small utility released after the full release of an application. It is usually written by the some of the same people who worked on the original application and often includes features or functionality that they could not get done in time to build into the original application. You can find power toys for most Microsoft applications including, but not limited to, Visual Studio, Windows, OneNote, and more. Power toys are not supported by Microsoft.

The VSTweak power toy is one of the more useful power toys for Visual Studio and is the subject of a number of different hacks in this book. The VSTweak power toy can be downloaded from *http://workspaces.gotdotnet. com/vstweak*.

The *.zip* file that you download contains both an *.exe* and an *.msi* (Microsoft Installer): you can double-click on either of these to install VSTweak. After VSTweak is installed, you can edit these two lists by opening VSTweak and selecting the MRU (Most Recently Used) Lists Manager tab. This screen is shown in Figure 2-30.

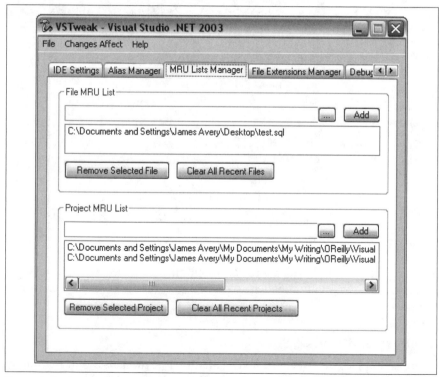

Figure 2-30. VSTweak—MRU Lists Manager

Using the Lists Manager, you can remove files and projects currently in the list or add new files or projects using the Add button. Normally you should not need to edit these lists, but from time to time I like to clear them out. And when doing a fresh install, I like to add my frequently used projects back to the list.

HACK #14 Refactor Your Code

Visual Studio 2005 puts this fundamental tenet of Extreme Programming into action. Use it to write better code.

Refactoring is a technique for improving a section of code by modifying its internal structure, but without affecting its external behavior. Refactoring is one of the key tenets of Extreme Programming; in a rapid development methodology, the idea is to create code quickly and then refactor it as you work with it. The goal of Extreme Programming is to create better quality code by concentrating on small deliverables and continuously testing and refactoring your code. Refactoring is not just limited to Extreme Programming—it is a valuable practice regardless of the methodology you happen to subscribe to. Visual Studio 2005 introduces a new Refactor menu. This menu is available whenever you right-click and provides a number of time-saving and code-improving functions.

> Refactoring is almost exclusively a C# feature. The only part of the Refactor menu that is available in VB.NET is the Rename function.

Figure 2-31 shows the menu and the various functions included there.

Extract Method

The first function available in the Refactor menu is Extract Method. This can be used to select a block of code and then extract that code into a separate method. This function has a number of applications, such as removing a section of code that deserves to be in its own method for code reuse purposes. Here is some existing code:

```
public class Car
{
    private bool _isStarted = false;
    private bool _hasFuel = true;

    public Car()
    {
```

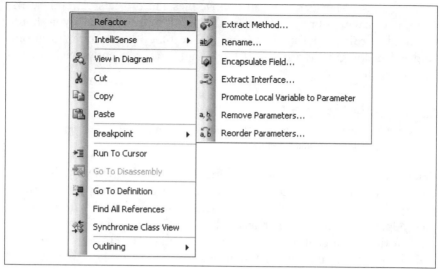

Figure 2-31. Refactor menu

```
//Start the Car
if (_hasFuel)
{
        _isStarted = true;
}
    }
}
```

That example has a little bit of code in the constructor that checks to see if the car has fuel and then "starts" the car by setting a Boolean value. If you decide that this class needs a second constructor, instead of duplicating this tiny piece of logic, you could extract this into a separate StartCar method and then call that method from both constructors. To accomplish this with the Refactor menu: highlight the code you want to extract and then right-click and select the Extract Method function from the Refactor menu. After you select Extract Method, you see a dialog box that asks for the name of the new method (see Figure 2-32).

Type in the new name of the method, in this case, **StartCar**, since it describes exactly what the method will accomplish. After you click OK, Visual Studio will modify the selected code by placing it in a new method named StartCar, then placing a call to the new method in the spot where the old code was. Here is the new code:

```
public Car()
{
    //Start the Car
    StartCar();
}
```

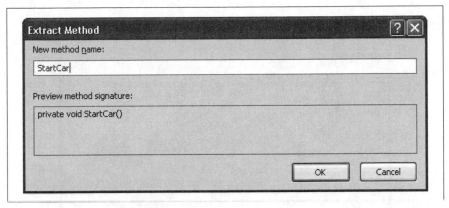

Figure 2-32. Extract Method dialog

```
private void StartCar( )
{
    if (_hasFuel)
    {
        _isStarted = true;
    }
}
```

Rename

The second function on the Refactor menu is the Rename function. This is one of the most time-saving functions on this menu. Suppose that you decide the name Car is a little shortsighted, since the system will need to work for Cars, Bikes, Trucks, and more. A more appropriate name would be Vehicle. Normally you would need to manually find all references to the name Car and change them; the Rename function does this for you automatically. First, right-click on the name Car and then select the Rename function from the Refactor menu; the Rename dialog will then be displayed (see Figure 2-33). The Rename dialog allows you to specify what to rename the class to; in this case, it's going from Car to Vehicle. A number of checkboxes are available; check all of them in this example. The first (Preview Reference Changes) lets you preview all of the changes to the files; the next two checkboxes (Search In Comments/Strings) tells Visual Studio to search for this name in comments as well as strings.

After clicking the OK button, you will see a confirmation dialog that shows all of the changes that will be made. As you can see in Figure 2-34, the Preview Changes dialog shows where Visual Studio is going to change the name Car to Vehicle. After you click Apply, Visual Studio will make all the changes to the project.

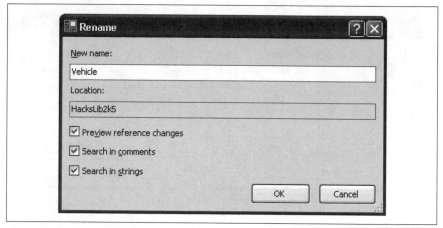

Figure 2-33. Rename dialog

One thing that Visual Studio does not change is the name of the StartCar method. Since Visual Studio does not look in method names when making these changes, you will have to change StartCar to StartVehicle yourself.

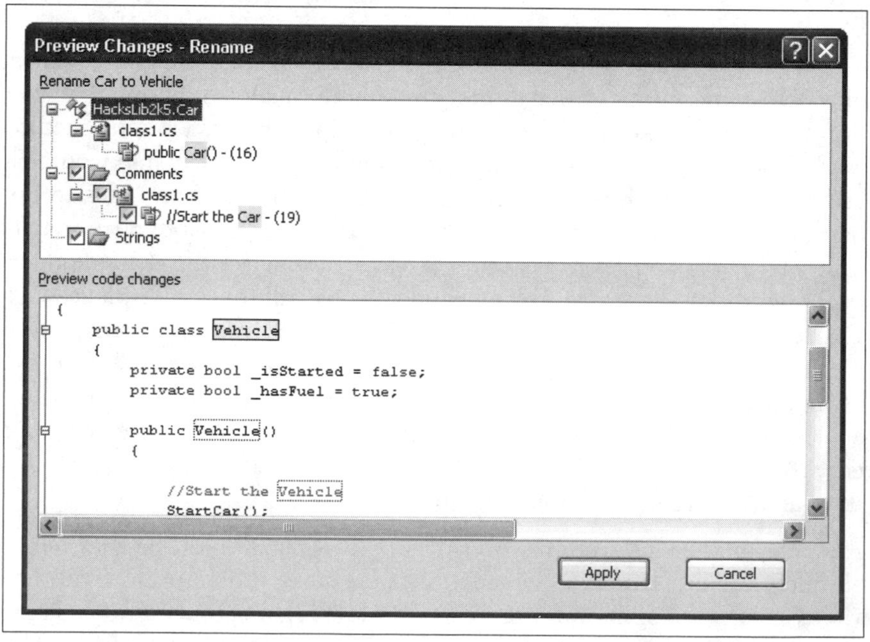

Figure 2-34. Preview Changes dialog

In addition to being a great time-saver, Rename removes any excuse you might make about why a class is not named appropriately.

Encapsulate Field

The Encapsulate Field function creates a public property that encapsulates your field. In the ongoing example, suppose that you need to create a public property for the _isStarted field. To do this, right-click on the field name and click the Encapsulate Field function on the Refactor menu. You are then shown the Encapsulate Field dialog, which is shown in Figure 2-35.

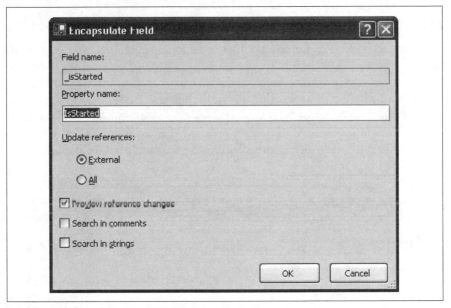

Figure 2-35. Encapsulate Field dialog

Visual Studio automatically sets the property name to be IsStarted and gives you the option to update references to the old field. Leave this setting as External so that code in your class is not changed to reference the public property and instead continues to use the private field. The other checkboxes are similar to the ones you saw in the Rename dialog and perform the same actions. After you click OK, you are shown a Preview Changes dialog—the same kind of dialog shown in Figure 2-34—which shows all of the changes that will result. After you accept the changes shown, the following code is added to the class:

```
public bool IsStarted
{
    get
    {
```

```
        return _isStarted;
    }

    set
    {
        _isStarted = value;
    }
}
```

This function comes in handy even when you are not refactoring. When creating a class for the first time, you can create the private fields and then use this function to create all of the necessary public properties.

Extract Interface

The Extract Interface function looks at your current class and creates an interface based on its public methods and properties. For example, suppose you want to create an interface for objects that can be "started"; this interface would include a Boolean property, in this case IsStarted, which, when set, has the side effect of "starting" the object (some kind of vehicle or item with an on/off switch). First, right-click on the class name and click the Extract Interface menu item; this displays the Extract Interface dialog, which is shown in Figure 2-36.

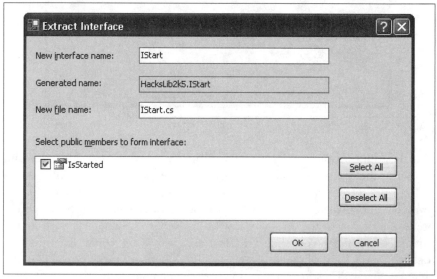

Figure 2-36. Extract Interface dialog

The default interface name is IVehicle; change it to IStart and then select the IsStarted property. After you click OK, Visual Studio creates a new file called *IStart.cs* with the following piece of code:

```
interface IStart
{
    bool IsStarted { get; set; }
}
```

Visual Studio will also modify the existing class to implement the new interface. The Extract Interface function is a great time-saver when you need to create an interface that is based on a current class.

Parameter Functions

The next three functions on the menu all focus on working with parameters. Since the sample class does not currently contain any methods with parameters, go ahead and add a new method with a number of different parameters. Here is a method called Collision that you can add to this class:

```
public void Collision(DateTime CrashDate, int Speed, int DamagePct)
{
    int costMultiplier = 1;

    // Do stuff
}
```

As you can see, this method has a local variable called costMultiplier and sets the value to 1. But suppose that costMultiplier varies from vehicle to vehicle. In this case, you'd want to pass in this multiplier as a parameter instead of creating it as a local variable. The first of the parameter refactoring functions will do just that. First, right-click on the costMultiplier variable and select the Promote Local Variable to Parameter function. This will take the local variable and add it as a parameter to the method. Here is a look at the modified code:

```
public void Collision(int costMultiplier, DateTime CrashDate,
    int Speed, int DamagePct)
{
    // Do stuff
}
```

You may be thinking that this is not a big deal; it is basically cut and paste. But Visual Studio also goes and looks for any calls to this method and modifies them as well. If you were calling this method before with the following line of code:

```
Collision(DateTime.Now, 60, 10);
```

this method call would be changed to the following:

```
Collision(1, DateTime.Now, 60, 10);
```

Notice that Visual Studio not only adds the new parameter, but also passes in the value that the local variable was set to as well, saving time and ensuring that existing code continues to work as it did before.

Suppose you decide that you don't need the CrashDate parameter. If you won't be using it in the method, you can remove this parameter using the second of these parameter refactoring functions, called Remove Parameters. First, right-click on the method name and click Remove Parameters in the Refactor menu. You'll be shown the Remove Parameters dialog, which is shown in Figure 2-37.

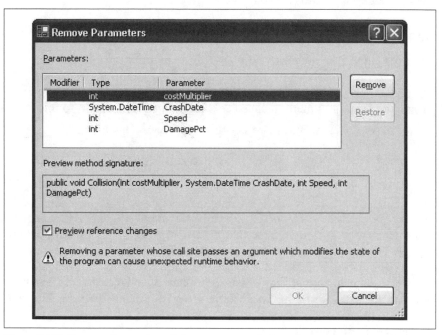

Figure 2-37. Remove Parameters dialog

In the Remove Parameters dialog, you can select the CrashDate parameter, click Remove, and then click OK. You are then shown a Preview Changes dialog showing the changes that will be made to any calls to this method. After clicking Apply on that screen, those changes will be made. Any calls to this method will have this parameter removed, and the parameter will be removed from the method signature.

Further, suppose you decide that you don't want costMultiplier to be the first parameter, but rather the last parameter. This is where the last of the parameter functions comes in. First, right-click on the method, then choose the Reorder Parameters menu item on the Refactor menu. This will display the Reorder Parameters dialog, which is shown in Figure 2-38.

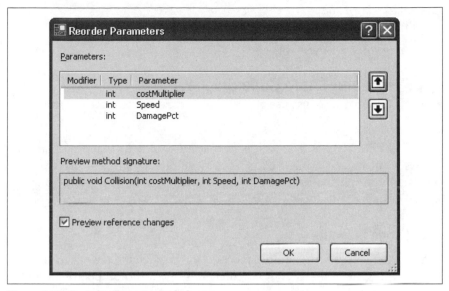

Figure 2-38. Reorder Parameters dialog

You can then select the `costMultiplier` parameter, move it down two spots, and click OK. You will again then be shown the Preview Changes dialog, where you can confirm the changes that will be made to any calls to this method. Click Apply, and the order of the parameters will be changed in the method signature and any calls to this method.

The Refactor menu is a great addition to Visual Studio and will make it much easier to refactor code. If you want to learn more about refactoring, the best resources are the book *Refactoring* (Addison-Wesley) and the companion web site, *http://www.refactoring.com*.

Want It Now?

Tired of waiting for Visual Studio 2005 or stuck using Visual Studio .NET 2003 for some reason? A number of commercial tools are available that add similar functionality into Visual Studio .NET 2003:

ReSharper
> From Jet Brains:
>> *http://www.jetbrains.com/resharper*

C# Refactory
> From XtremeSimplicity:
>> *http://www.xtreme-simplicity.NET/CSharpRefactory.htm*

C# Refactoring Tools
    From dotnetrefactoring.com:
       http://www.dotnetrefactoring.com

H A C K   Use and Share Code Snippets
#15
Tap into a whole universe of other people's code and share some of your own.

Visual Studio 2005 introduces a new feature called Code Snippets that allows you to insert a piece of example code directly into the class you are working with. At the time of this writing, this feature is available only for Visual Basic.

Insert Code Snippets

You can quickly insert example pieces of code by right-clicking in the area where you want to insert code, then clicking the Insert Snippet item on the context menu that appears. A list of code categories appears, as shown in Figure 2-39.

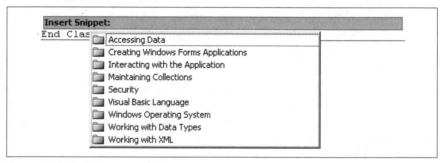

Figure 2-39. Code Snippet categories

After you select the category Accessing Data, you will see the list of examples that you can automatically insert, as shown in Figure 2-40.

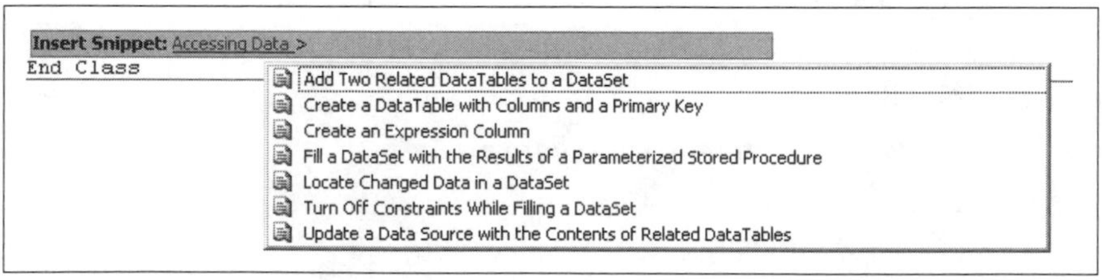

Figure 2-40. Accessing Data example list

You can then select the "Create a DataTable with columns and a primary key" snippet, and the following code will be inserted into the class:

```
Private Sub CreateTable( )
    Dim IDColumn As New DataColumn("ID")
    IDColumn.DataType = GetType(Integer)
    IDColumn.AutoIncrement = True

    Dim FNameColumn As New DataColumn("FirstName")
    FNameColumn.DataType = GetType(String)

    Dim LNameColumn As New DataColumn("LastName")
    LNameColumn.DataType = GetType(String)

    Dim EmployeeTable As New DataTable("Employees")
    EmployeeTable.Columns.Add(IDColumn)
    EmployeeTable.Columns.Add(FNameColumn)
    EmployeeTable.Columns.Add(LNameColumn)

    EmployeeTable.Constraints.Add("Key1", IDColumn, True)
End Sub
```

Of course, this code probably does not do *exactly* what you want it to do, but it gives you a great start to work from. Code Snippets are a great way to incorporate examples into your everyday coding, but wouldn't it be great if you could build your own library of code snippets?

Add Your Own Code Snippets

A large number of code snippets are already loaded into Visual Studio, but you can also add your own. This could be very useful if you want to create snippets for common pieces of code you use or code that is specific to your project or architecture. You will also be able to download and add code snippets from community sites as well; I have a feeling that it will become common for people to post snippet files on their sites and blogs. To add or modify code snippets, you need to first create a snippet file. For Visual Basic, this is a structured file with the extension of *.vbsnippet*.

The creation and editing for the *.vbsnippet* files is not complete in the Beta 1 release of Visual Studio 2005, so hopefully this will be easier in the future. For now, the best way to create new snippet files is to start with an existing snippet file. These can be found in the *Visual Studio Directory\Vb\Snippets\ 1033* directory. First, you need to make a copy of an existing snippet file, then open the copy in Visual Studio. At the time of this writing, Visual Studio will treat this file as a solution file and provide a number of property windows to set the name of the snippet as well as the author and other metadata. After entering your own snippet, you can save the modified file and then add it to Visual Studio using the Code Snippets Manager located under the Tools menu in Visual Studio 2005.

There won't be a complete editor included in the final version of Visual Studio 2005, but the team plans to release a separate application at or around the release of Visual Studio 2005 that will provide a rich code snippet editing experience.

Navigating Visual Studio

Hacks 16–23

Visual Studio is a rich development environment including windows, toolbars, commands, and editors. Knowing how to quickly and easily move around the development environment makes developing applications that much easier. Being able to quickly and easily find the information you are looking for is a key part of learning how to best work with Visual Studio, whether that information is a piece of source code or a property for a control. Any time spent fumbling around the IDE is time wasted.

The hacks in this chapter cover how to arrange and work with windows, find files quickly, search your files using incremental search and regular expressions, and navigate your source code using shortcuts and task list shortcuts. You'll also learn about a power toy that assigns commands to different mouse buttons and an add-in that enhances the tabs in the document window.

HACK #16 Take Control of Your Workspace

Dock, float, and size your windows, and save a layout for every mode and mood.

Visual Studio contains many ways to customize your workspace. Every window can be moved, docked, or hidden. Visual Studio includes different window layouts for different modes; modifying a window layout during debug mode will not affect your window layout while coding. There is even a full-screen mode. This hack delves into all the ways you can take control of your workspace.

Window Management

Visual Studio provides a plethora of windows that you can move around the IDE. Windows have a number of different states; they can be floating, docked, hidden, or in auto hide mode. Understanding these different states and how changes you make are saved is important to getting the most out of the Visual Studio IDE.

Window state is controlled by right-clicking on the window titlebar and selecting the state (see Figure 3-1) or by selecting a window option while the focus is on the window you want to change. Each of these states affects how the window behaves.

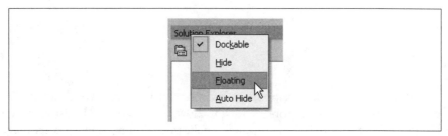

Figure 3-1. Choosing the window state

Dockable. This is the default state for most windows. When a window is set to be dockable, it can either float above other windows or be docked to the edges of the IDE window. To dock a window, you simply need to drag that window and, following the bold outline, choose where you want the window to be docked. When a window is docked, it will resize with and react to the other windows around it (including the IDE main window). Visual Studio 2005 includes a new method for docking that makes it easier to determine where that window will actually be docked. Figure 3-2 shows an example of the new docking interface.

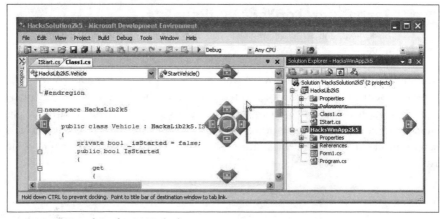

Figure 3-2. Visual Studio 2005 docking

The new interface makes it easier to determine where you are docking something. You can simply move your cursor over one of the blue icons and the window will dock there. Dropping it in the center circle will cause it to become a tabbed document along with the source code files.

Windows can be set to dockable but still be floating windows; *dockable* just means that you can dock them if you want to. Holding Ctrl while dragging the window will prevent it from docking so you can place it over a dock location without it docking to that location.

Floating. If a window is set to floating, it cannot be docked. It will float right above the IDE and will always be on top of any docked windows below it.

Hidden. Hiding a window simply means that it is not shown on your screen anywhere. It is the same as closing the window. If you hide a window, you can always show it again by going to View and then selecting the window in that list or under the Other Windows menu option.

Auto hide. Auto hide is a very cool feature that is best used through the little pin icon that appears on the menu at the top of each window. Click the pin when the window is docked to hide it; it will be replaced by a small vertical menu on the side of the screen. You can then click or hover over the icon on the vertical menu to make the window slide back into view; it will disappear a few seconds after you stop using it. Clicking on the pin again will pin it back on the IDE.

Tabbed document. Visual Studio 2005 introduces the ability to add a regular window as a tabbed document. To do this, right-click on the window and choose Tabbed Document from the context menu or drag the window to the blue round icon in the center, as shown in Figure 3-2. The window will now appear next to your code files in the document window.

Window Layouts

As you move around and customize your window layout, you may notice that sometimes your changes are undone or they change in certain situations. This is because Visual Studio uses different layouts that are active at different times (debug, full screen, etc.). Window layouts are stored for each user on a machine in a file called *devenv.xml*.

Sometimes the *devenv.xml* file can become corrupted. If you find that auto hide stops working, you can't open debug windows any more, or you are stuck with a black window that won't go away, quit Visual Studio and delete *devenv.xml* from your *\Documents and Settings\<username>\Application Data\Microsoft\Visual Studio\<7.1>* directory. When you restart Visual Studio, it will create a fresh version of the file for you, and your problem should be resolved.

By default, the *devenv.xml* file contains a number of different window layouts, including design layouts for each of the different languages as well as debug and full-screen layouts. Any changes you make to the window layouts are saved in this file and are remembered the next time you start Visual Studio. When you are in debug mode, any changes you make to the window layout will affect only the debug windows layout. Next time you enter debug mode, all of your windows will be in the same place. The other two main window layouts are design and full screen.

You can also create your own custom window layouts using the VSWindow-Manage power toy [Hack #26].

Document Window

The document window is the window you use to edit a file. Each time you open a new document, a new tab is created on the tab bar across the top of this window. The document window is one of the places where you will spend a lot of time when working with Visual Studio, and these shortcuts and features will make working with the window faster and easier.

You can easily move between open documents using the Window.NextDocumentWindow (Ctrl-Tab or Ctrl-F6) and Window.PreviousDocumentWindow (Ctrl-Shift-Tab or Ctrl-Shift-F6) commands. These two commands allow you to quickly switch between documents without the use of a mouse, and since they are similar to the Windows Alt-Tab command, they are easy to remember. You can also close the current document window with the Window.CloseDocumentWindow (Ctrl-F4) command, also similar to the Alt-F4 command used in Windows.

The Ctrl-Tab shortcut performs an additional action in Visual Studio 2005. It pops up a dialog (similar to the Windows Alt-Tab dialog) that shows all of the open documents. This new dialog can be seen in Figure 3-3.

Using this dialog, you can choose which file to open using the arrow keys or pressing Ctrl-Tab again. You can also use the arrow keys to select a tool window that you want to switch to.

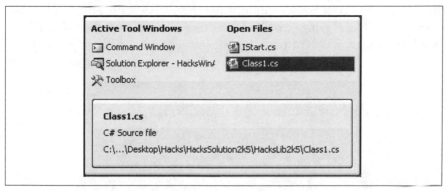

Figure 3-3. Ctrl-Tab dialog

Work with Tabs

Tabs are all over Visual Studio. One of the most common places you find tabs is when you dock multiple windows in the same spot. Visual Studio will create a tab list of all the different windows you have docked. Two shortcuts can be used to quickly toggle between tabs. The first is Window.NextTab (Ctrl-PageDown) and the second is Window.PreviousTab (Ctrl-PageUp). You can use these shortcuts any time the focus is set on a window that has tabs (for example, on the Solution Explorer window, you can use these shortcuts to toggle between the Solution Explorer, class view, etc.).

When in the document view, these commands do not change the tabs that are across the top of the document window, but rather the tabs that sometimes appear at the bottom of the document window. For example, when working with a file type that includes a designer, such as an ASP.NET file, there are two tabs at the bottom of the window (one for the design view and one for the HTML view). Use the keystrokes described in the previous section to move between the tabs across the top of the window—these are considered document windows.

Work with Panes

A *pane* is defined as any of the windows you can move and dock. The solution explorer, class view, and task list are all panes. Two commands can be used to quickly move between all the panes currently open in the IDE: Window.NextPane (Alt-F6) and Window.PreviousPane (Alt-Shift-F6). Both of these commands let you move around the IDE quickly and easily, without picking up your mouse.

Split-pane mode. You can split a document by grabbing the small bar at the top of the scrollbar with the mouse and then dragging down or by selecting the Window → Split menu option. This creates two different views for the same source file. Having two views into the same file is wonderful when you need to compare different parts of the same file; it is much preferred to having to scroll back and forth. Figure 3-4 shows an example of split-pane mode.

```
1  <%@ Page language="c#" Codebehind="WebForm1.aspx.cs" AutoEventWireup="false" Inherits="WebUI.WebForm1" %>
2  <!DOCTYPE HTML PUBLIC "-//W3C//DTD HTML 4.0 Transitional//EN" >
3
4  <html>
5    <head>
6      <title>WebForm1</title>
7      <meta name="GENERATOR" Content="Microsoft Visual Studio .NET 7.1">
8      <meta name="CODE_LANGUAGE" Content="C#">
9      <meta name=vs_defaultClientScript content="JavaScript">

1  <%@ Page language="c#" Codebehind="WebForm1.aspx.cs" AutoEventWireup="false" Inherits="WebUI.WebForm1" %>
2  <!DOCTYPE HTML PUBLIC "-//W3C//DTD HTML 4.0 Transitional//EN" >
3
4  <html>
5    <head>
6      <title>WebForm1</title>
7      <meta name="GENERATOR" Content="Microsoft Visual Studio .NET 7.1">
8      <meta name="CODE_LANGUAGE" Content="C#">
9      <meta name=vs_defaultClientScript content="JavaScript">
10     <meta name=vs_targetSchema content="http://schemas.microsoft.com/intellisense/ie5">

Design   HTML
```

Figure 3-4. Split-pane mode

Two shortcut commands also allow you to move between split panes: Window.NextSplitPane (F6) and Window.PreviousSplitPane (Shift-F6). When you are done working in split-pane mode, you simply need to drag the window separator all the way up to the top of the window or select the Window → Remove Split Menu option.

Full-Screen Mode

Visual Studio includes a full-screen mode that can be toggled using the View.FullScreen command, by either using the Shift-Alt-Enter keystroke or clicking View → Full Screen. Figure 3-5 shows an example of full-screen mode.

As you can see, full-screen mode hides all the other windows and provides an incredible amount of space for just coding. I frequently find myself using full-screen mode whenever I am focusing on writing code, and I really enjoy the added real estate in the editor window. The same keystroke (Shift-Alt-Enter) switches you back out of full-screen mode.

Find Files Quickly
#17   Visual Studio's Solution Explorer gives you a quick view of your files, but you'll be able to search through thousands of files quickly with a free add-in.

The Solution Explorer shows you all of the files in your solution in an easy-to-use tree. Each project is a node, and under that node is any number of

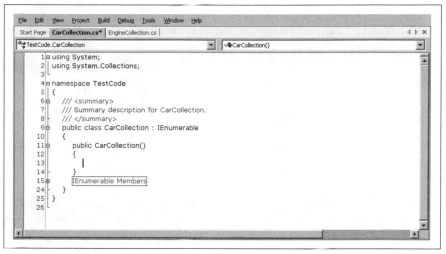

Figure 3-5. Full-screen mode

files and folders. The Solution Explorer usually works perfectly; however, it starts to fall short when you have a lot of projects and files. If your solution has six projects and 500 files, finding one of those files starts to become quite a task.

Find Files

A free add-in that provides a new interface for finding files anywhere in your solution is available. It is called the VS File Finder and can be downloaded from the following link:

http://www.zero-one-zero.com/vs

The first step is to download the add-in and run the installation file. The installation does not include any choices and can be completed by simply launching the *.msi* file. Once the add-in is installed, it will show up as a new window the next time you start Visual Studio. If it does not automatically appear or if you'd like to show the window again after you close it, you need to click View → VS File Finder, and the window will be displayed. Figure 3-6 shows the VS File Finder interface, which includes a list of all the files in all the projects in my solution.

The text box at the top of the window lets you enter any number of characters—the list below will be filtered based on what is entered in the window. Unlike the IntelliSense provided by the command window, this window will search for the entered string in any part of the filename. Figure 3-7 shows the string "Collection" entered in the text box and the filtering that the tool provides.

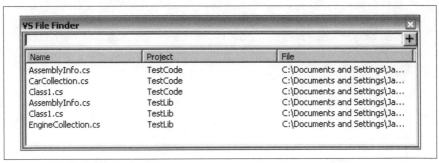

Figure 3-6. VS File Finder window

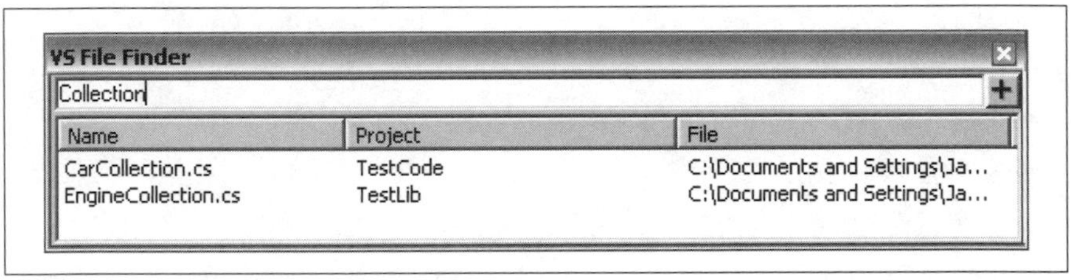

Figure 3-7. VS File Finder with results

After the string "Collection" is entered, the tool shows only the files whose name contains the word "Collection." This type of searching is very useful if you maintain common naming conventions in your project. You can also click on the headings for the list and sort it based on the name, project, or file.

Exclude Files

The VS File Finder also includes the ability to exclude certain files from the search list. If you wanted to exclude all *.css* files from the search list, you first need to click on the blue plus sign to the right of the text box. This brings up the Options screen for VS File Finder, which is shown in Figure 3-8.

Next, you need to click the Add button to see the Add Exclude Filter dialog, which is shown in Figure 3-9.

Next, you need to enter a description for your exclusion; in this example, "CSS Files" will work perfectly. Then you enter your filter (in this example, *.css*, which will exclude all CSS files) and click OK. The filter works a little differently than the search in that it needs to be an actual extension; it can't be any part of the filename. After you enter your exclusion filter, all *.css* files will be excluded from the search. This is particularly useful if you

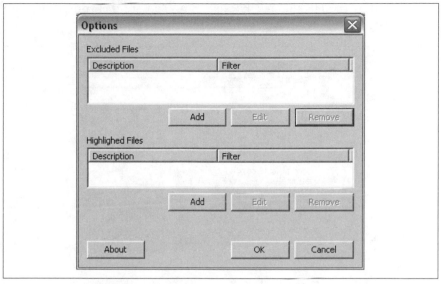

Figure 3-8. VS File Finder Options

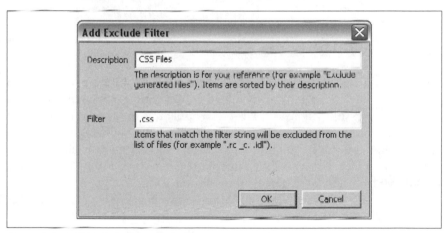

Figure 3-9. Add Exclude Filter dialog

include files in your project that you are not actively working on. For example, you might have a number of *.css* files that are part of a company standard that you would not want to edit and thus can be excluded from your search list.

Highlight Files

The VS File Finder add-in provides a method to highlight certain files in the search list. This is configured in the Options screen that was shown back in Figure 3-8. To highlight a certain type of file, you simply need to click the

Add button in the Highlighted Files section. You are then prompted with the Add Highlight Filter dialog, which is shown in Figure 3-10.

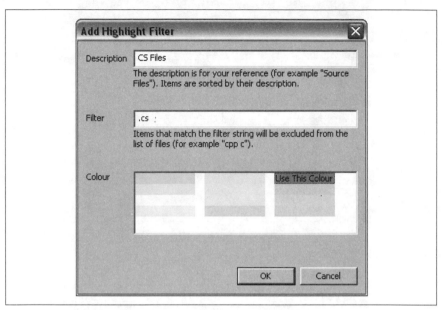

Figure 3-10. Add Highlight Filter dialog

First you need to specify a description of the file type. In this example, I am going to specify that all *.cs* files be highlighted with a particular color and that my description will be "CS Files." To apply this to files ending in the *.cs* extension, you need to specify *.cs* in the Filter box. And last, you need to choose what color to highlight the files with; this is done by clicking on the color in the box filled with different colors. After you add this filter, all *.cs* records will be highlighted with the selected color. This is a useful technique for spotting certain types of files in the search list.

Shortcut

During installation, VS File Finder also adds a command to Visual Studio. You can use this command to assign a shortcut key to VS File Finder. Since this add-in is about speed, it makes sense to be able to quickly launch the add-in with a shortcut key, as opposed to using the mouse.

To create a shortcut for VS File Finder, you simply need to wire a shortcut key to the VSFileFinder.Connect.ShowVSFileFinder command. For more information on creating shortcuts, see "Create Your Own Shortcuts" **[Hack #24]**.

VS File Finder is a very valuable tool that has the capacity to greatly speed up the search for files in your solutions. VS File Finder was written by Jonathan Payne and is available at *http://www.zero-one-zero.com/vs*. The source code for this add-in is also available from that web site.

HACK #18 Search Files Quickly

Visual Studio's default Find function is pretty run-of-the-mill. Perk it up with incremental search.

Most users of Visual Studio are already familiar with the normal Find functionality, which lets you enter a search term, and then Visual Studio will look for that term in your current file. There is another type of search, an *incremental search*, that lets you enter your search term character by character while Visual Studio actively finds the first instance of that string in your current document. You can then quickly jump to each instance that is found in your document. All of this can be done with just a couple of quick keystrokes.

The first keystroke you need to remember is Ctrl-I (Edit.Incremental-Search). First, you will need to open a document, then press this keystroke. This will turn incremental search on, which turns your cursor into what can only be described as a pair of binoculars with a down arrow. The next thing you need to do is simply start typing your search term character by character. Visual Studio will jump to the first match for that character combination and continue to search when you enter more characters. There is no text box area to type in; just start typing and you will see Visual Studio react. Figure 3-11 shows incremental search in action. After having typed in the string "Car", you can see that it is now selected.

Visual Studio has highlighted the first instance of this search term, but you may be looking for a different instance of this term. You can simply press Ctrl-I again and Visual Studio will jump to the next matching instance in this document. You can also step backward by pressing Ctrl-Shift-I (Edit. ReverseIncrementalSearch). This keystroke will jump back to the previous matching instance in the document.

You can cancel your search at any time by pressing Esc or clicking anywhere with the mouse.

Incremental search is simple but can save a lot of time, especially when you are trying to jump quickly between different sections of a file or looking for every instance of a certain term.

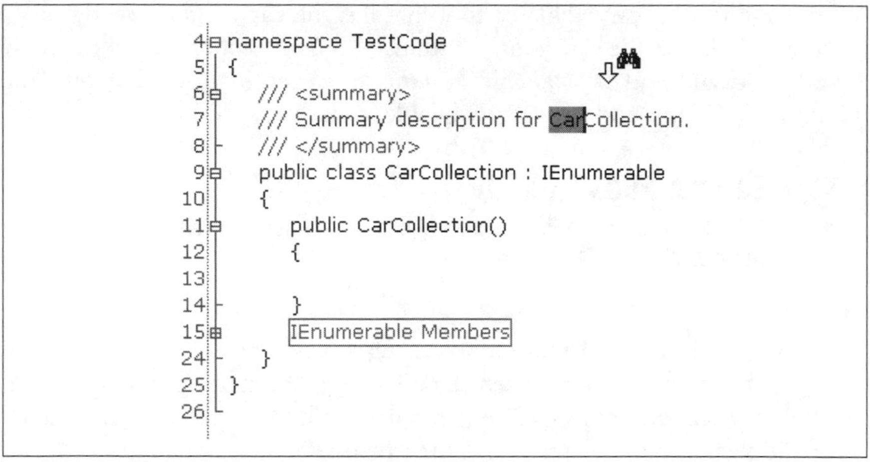

```
 4⊟ namespace TestCode
 5│  {                                    ⇩🔍
 6⊟     /// <summary>
 7│     /// Summary description for [Car]Collection.
 8├     /// </summary>
 9⊟     public class CarCollection : IEnumerable
10│     {
11⊟        public CarCollection()
12│        {
13│
14├        }
15⊟        IEnumerable Members
24├     }
25│  }
26└
```

Figure 3-11. Incremental search

Search for Patterns in Your Files

HACK
#19

Unleash the power of regular expressions to make everyday searches and Find and Replace operations more powerful.

Regular expressions are an extremely versatile text-matching language that gives you incredible power when searching your documents and when used with replace operations, can greatly assist with repetitive changes to blocks of code.

Searching

The basic regular expression search is easily done. You simply open the Find dialog through the Edit → Find and Replace → Find menu or with Ctrl-F (Edit.Find). Enable regular expression searching by ensuring the Use checkbox is selected and the drop-down list has Regular Expressions selected, as shown in Figure 3-12.

In Visual Studio 2005, the Find dialog has changed. To enable regular expressions searching, you will need to expand the Find Options section of the dialog. Figure 3-13 shows the new Find dialog with the Options section expanded.

Enter your regular expression into the Find What text box and click on Find Next. The next match of your expression will be found in the document. As with normal matches, clicking Find Next again will find the next match. The next step is to learn the regular expression (also known as *regex* or *regexp*) syntax. Searching will never be the same.

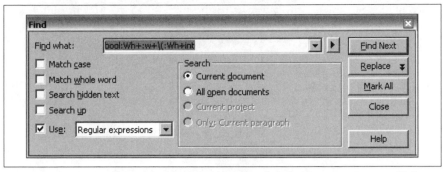

Figure 3-12. Visual Studio .NET 2003 Find dialog with Regular Expressions enabled

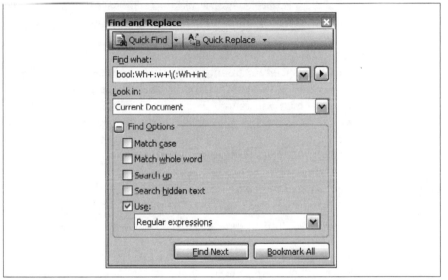

Figure 3-13. Visual Studio 2005 Find and Replace dialog with Regular Expressions enabled

Basic Expressions

Regular expressions can be very complex, but basic expressions can be easy to master. Unlike normal searches, regular expressions designate a pattern of characters to match instead of a constant string. For example, square brackets in a regular expression define a set of characters (a *character class*). When you execute the search, it will match any one character out of the set of characters inside the brackets, so the expression [abcd] would match *a*, *b*, *c*, and *d*—but not *z*. You can also specify character ranges inside the brackets, so [a-d] is equivalent to the expression [abcd]. If you need to specify more than one range, simply add it to the first, so [a-z0-9] will match any letter or number. Regular expression characters in Visual Studio are not case sensitive unless you select the Match Case option in the Find dialog. This is a departure from most other regular expression syntax.

Normal alphabetic characters outside of special expressions match characters literally, similar to a normal Find, but can be combined with regular expressions to make them more flexible. This means that combining the set match with a literal match gives us a pattern such as var[12], which will match var1 and var2 but not var3.

> If you want to match the string var[12], you'd need to escape the special characters, as in var\[12\].

Matching quantities. Matching a single character isn't particularly useful, so you want to be able to specify a quantity. You can either specify an exact number of times with the pattern ^n, where *n* is the number of matches you are seeking, or use *, which will match 0 or more repetitions of the pattern. Thus, [abcd]* would match *ababcd*, *a*, or an empty string, but not *abzd*. If you want to be sure that there is at least one match, you can use the + character, which matches one or more repetitions of the pattern.

Preventing matches. Sometimes preventing a match is the desired behavior. The pattern bool~(ean) uses the ~ operator to match only *bool* where it is not followed by *ean* (the parentheses group the ean so that the ~ acts on it as a group). It is also possible to specify a set of characters you do not want matched. In this case, you simply specify the character set with a ^ before it. Thus, the expression [^abc] will match any single character except for those specified.

Basic Replacements

After you have a search pattern, replacing it with a constant string is the same as doing a normal Find/Replace, but the real power of regular expressions comes in the ability to use the string that was matched in the replacement. In order to do this, you need to select the portion of the match expression you wish to reuse by tagging it inside of curly braces. For example, if you create a Find expression such as var{[12]}, this will put the 1 or 2 into the first tagged buffer.

In the Replace expression, you can access these buffers with a backslash. Thus, if you create a Replace expression of indicator\1, you will change any text reading "var1" to "indicator1". If you had a list of variables like this:

```
var1
var2
var3
```

they would be converted into:

```
indicator1
indicator2
indicator3
```

You may, of course, create as many tagged expressions as you wish. You can also access the entire string that the regular expression matched with \0.

Advanced Patterns

Basic expressions can take you a long way, but there are a number of more advanced operators that you can use with regular expressions to perform even more finely targeted searches.

Shortcuts. Several shortcuts for various character sets are built into the regular expression framework so that you do not have to constantly specify sets for commonly used groups. For example, :c matches one alphabetic character—it is the same as specifying [a-zA-Z]. Table 3-1 shows a few of the more useful character sets.

Table 3-1. Commonly used expression shortcuts

Shortcut	Definition
:c	Alphabetic character. Equivalent to [a-zA-Z].
:d	Decimal character. Equivalent to [0-9].
:i	Identifier. This shortcut will match an identifier (such as a variable, class, or method name). This is one of the most useful shortcuts. It is equivalent to ([a-zA-Z_$][a-zA-Z0-9_$]*)
:q	Quoted string. Matches a string bounded by either double quotes or single quotes.
:Wh	Whitespace. Matches any whitespace character.
\n	Newline. This can be useful to build multiline strings.

Positional characters. Several characters in regular expressions indicate that a portion of the regular expression needs to occur at a specific place in the text being matched. For example, ^ indicates the beginning of a line. So in the expression ^a, the *a* must occur as the first character in a line for the expression to match, including whitespace characters such as tabs or spaces; so ^a wouldn't match a line that starts with spaces or tabs. The positional character $ matches the end of line, so the pattern ^a$ will match only if *a* is the only character on a line.

Escaping characters. We have now discussed several different types of special characters that are used to designate parts of a regular expression. If you want to match those characters literally, you need to tell the regular expression engine to not interpret them as special portions of an expression. For example, if you wish to match the character [, you need to escape it with a backslash and use \[in the expression.

Example expressions. Table 3-2 and Table 3-3 display a few example expressions to show some of the flexibility of the syntax.

Table 3-2. Example Find expressions

Find what	Effect
bool:Wh+:w+\(:Wh+int	Matches method definitions that take an integer for the first parameter and return a Boolean
///.*$	Matches a C# documentation comment
/*([^*]|\n)**\/	Matches a C# multiline comment
'.*$	Matches a VB.NET comment

Table 3-3. Example Find/Replace syntax

Find what	Replace with	Effect
private:Wh+{:i}: Wh+_{:i}:Wh*;	\0\npublic \1 \2\n{\ nget{return _\2;}\nset{ _\2 = value ; }\n}	Takes a private variable definition in the form private int _prop and creates a public property accessor
(System\.)*String	string	Changes variables and parameters defined as System.String to use the C# native string

Regular Expressions in Your Code

The .NET Framework includes classes in the System.Text.Regular-Expressions namespace that allow you to include functionality using regular expressions in your code. Unfortunately, the regular expression syntax Microsoft uses inside of the Visual Studio IDE differs from the syntax used by the .NET regular expression interpreter. Much of the syntax is identical; however, many of the character sets and characters indicating the type of expression or tagged expressions for replacement are different. It is also important to note that by default the .NET regular expression classes are case sensitive in their matching.

For in-depth coverage of regular expressions, see *Mastering Regular Expressions* (O'Reilly).

See Also

- "Test Regular Expressions in Visual Studio" [Hack #100]

—Ben Von Handorf

Navigate Your Source Code

Visual Studio lets you go way beyond moving around with the arrow, Page Up, and Page Down keys. Learn some keyboard tricks that let you move around in different ways.

Visual Studio provides a number of ways to navigate through your source code. This hack will cover how to use a number of helpful shortcuts as well as how to use bookmarks to quickly move around in your code.

Navigation Shortcuts

The normal method of moving around in your source code with the mouse is perfectly acceptable, but it is also slow. When you are busy typing, it takes time to reach for the mouse, orient the cursor, and then move to another section of code by clicking on a line. Visual Studio contains a number of navigational shortcuts that can keep your hands on the keyboard and help you write code faster.

Navigation history. The first two commands that you can use to navigate are the View.NavigateBackward (Ctrl and -) and View.NavigateForward (Ctrl-Shift and -) commands. These keystrokes can best be described as undo and redo commands, but instead of undoing or redoing actions, these keystrokes undo and redo navigation. For instance, if you are working in one method, then use the mouse to move over to another method, you can jump back to the previous method using the NavigateBackward keystroke. After changing something in that method, you could then jump forward again using the NavigationForward keystroke. These shortcuts also work fine across files and projects. If you are working in one file and switch to another, you can quickly jump back using the NavigateBackward shortcut keystroke.

Mouseless scrolling. Usually when you want to scroll, you end up reaching for the mouse. The nice thing about scrolling is that it does not move the cursor, whereas using the regular up and down arrows does move the cursor. Thankfully, Visual Studio includes commands to scroll the file without moving the cursor. The Edit.ScrollLineUp and Edit.ScrollLineDown commands can be accessed by simply pressing Ctrl while also pressing either the up or down arrow.

Go-to brace. Visual Studio includes a number of commands that will jump to the next occurrence of a code element. Possibly the most useful is Edit. GoToBrace (Ctrl-]), which will jump to the corresponding brace, parenthesis, or bracket in the document. If the cursor is on a closing brace, it will jump back to the opening brace; if the cursor is on the opening brace, it will jump to the closing brace. This keystroke will work only when the cursor is on a line that includes a brace and only with languages that use braces (C#, C++, etc.).

End and Home. Visual Studio also supports the End and Home keys through the commands Edit.LineEnd and Edit.LineStart. Pressing the End or Home key will move you to the end of the current line or the start of the current line, respectively. Visual Studio also includes two commands called Edit. DocumentEnd and Edit.DocumentStart (Ctrl-End and Ctrl-Home), which will move you to the end or beginning of the current document.

Bookmarks

Bookmarks are one of the few computing analogies that make perfect sense. Bookmarks allow you to mark a place in your code that you want to come back to, just like a regular bookmark you would use in a paper book. Creating and using bookmarks is incredibly easy and when used properly can save time that would otherwise be wasted scrolling and searching with the mouse.

You can set a bookmark on a specific line in a file using the command Edit. ToggleBookmark (the keystroke chord **[Hack #24]** Ctrl-K, Ctrl-K). After setting a bookmark, you will see a small blue indicator next to that line where a breakpoint would normally appear. You can remove the bookmark by simply using the Edit.ToggleBookmark command again. You can also quickly move between bookmarks using two other commands, Edit.NextBookmark (Ctrl-K, Ctrl-N) and Edit.PreviousBookmark (Ctrl-K, Ctrl-P). Using these two commands, you can quickly jump through all of your bookmarks much faster than manually searching for that last line you were on using the mouse.

Bookmarks are removed when you close a file, but if you leave files open and close the solution, they are saved in your user options file **[Hack #4]** and will still be there next time you open the solution. You can also manually clear all bookmarks by calling the Edit.ClearBookmarks (Ctrl-K, Ctrl-L) command.

Bookmarks can also be used with the mouse through the Edit → Bookmarks menu.

Never Forget a TODO Again

Place reminders for yourself or for other developers that are nearly impossible to miss.

The task list (Ctrl-Alt-K/View.TaskList) is a handy tool that is most often used to view errors or warnings from the compilation of your code. In Visual Studio .NET 2003, when you compile your project, any errors or warnings are displayed in the task list. You can read the message and double-click on the item to jump to the offending line in your code. (Visual Studio 2005 includes a separate error list.)

The task list also has another use; it can be used to leave reminders for yourself or other members of your team in comment form.

Comments

By default, the task list includes three different comments; these are `//TODO`, `//UNDONE`, and `//HACK`.

> Visual Studio 2005 includes only the `//TODO` comment by default; the other comments can still be added through the process outlined later in this hack.

You can use these comments anywhere throughout your code, and they will show up in the task list when the file with the comment is open. Visual Studio .NET 2003 uses this functionality by default when you create a new class; it adds the following code to the constructor of every new class:

```
//
// TODO: Add constructor logic here
//
```

First make sure that the task list is configured to show comments, and then you will see in the task list that this comment has been added as an item, as shown in Figure 3-14.

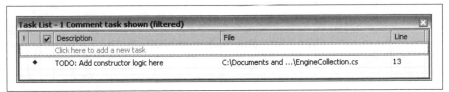

Figure 3-14. Task list comments

The task list does not always show every comment. It needs to be configured according to what you are currently working on. If you are trying to find and fix compilation errors, chances are that you don't want to also see a bunch of comments. What the task list displays is configurable in Visual Studio .NET 2003 through the Show Tasks list under the View menu in the toolbar. There are options to show just build errors, tasks in the current file, all, or comments.

In Visual Studio 2005, the options list has moved to the task list itself. You will now see a drop-down list at the top of the task list that lets you choose what should be displayed in the task list. You will also notice that errors are no longer displayed in the task list in Visual Studio 2005; instead, there is a separate error list just for build errors and warnings.

For the purpose of this hack, options will need to be set to All or Comments.

You can then click on this comment and be taken to the place where you need to add code. The other two comments work much the same way. You simply need to use //HACK: and a task list item will be created for that comment. You can use shortcuts to step back and forth between tasks as well. The View.NextTask (Ctrl-Shift-F12) and View.PreviousTask (no default shortcut) commands can be used to step through the tasks listed in the task list.

You can also click in the area at the top of the task list with the text "Click here to add a new task," or in Visual Studio 2005, you can click the Create User Task button. This creates a user task for you and acts much like the tasks portion of Outlook. You can also tag any line in your project as a task by using the Edit.ToggleTaskListShortcut (Ctrl-K, Ctrl-H) command. Whenever you call this command, it will add a shortcut to the task list pointing to this line of code. You can then add text that says what should be done to the line of code. It is a quick and easy way to add something to the task list to tackle later on. These tasks will appear only on your system and not on the systems of your team members.

Task list comments are a great way to remind you or others of something that still needs to be done or something that may need to be revisited for enhancement.

Custom Comments

You can also define and use custom comments with the task list. Custom comments can be very useful if you want to create a more specific comment. You can set a priority level higher than the other comments so you can differentiate the comments easier. I'll walk through creating a custom comment called REFACTOR. You could use this comment to mark places that you feel need to be refactored. I will also create a second custom comment called BROKEN that will have a higher priority (since you don't want broken code in your project for long).

To add a new comment, you first need to go to Tools → Options and then select Task List under the Environment folder. Then simply type the name of the new comment in the Name textbox, and the Add button will become active. These comments are case sensitive, so using all caps will help to ensure that the names do not get mistyped—this is also consistent with the default Visual Studio tokens. Figure 3-15 shows an example of adding a REFACTOR comment.

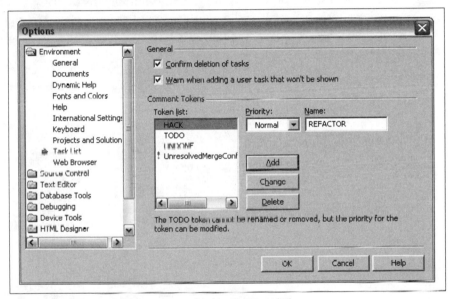

Figure 3-15 New task list comment added in Options dialog

You can select a priority of Normal for this comment. After you click Add, this comment will be added to the list. Next, you need to do the same thing for the BROKEN comment by simply repeating the same process, except this time set the priority to High.

After you have added both of the custom comments, you will be able to use them in your code. Figure 3-16 shows your task list after adding both REFACTOR and BROKEN comments to your document.

Custom comments can be a valuable tool when trying to relay information to other members on your team or just as a way to remind yourself of something that needs to be done.

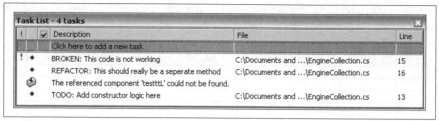

Figure 3-16. Task list with custom comments

 ### Hack the Mouse

#22   Assign commands to every button on your mouse.

Many people now use a mouse with five different buttons. Most likely you use only two of those in Visual Studio (and the rest of them in Halo). Using a freely available power toy, you can assign each of your mouse buttons to a Visual Studio command. First, you will need to download and install the VSMouseBindings power toy from *http://www.gotdotnet.com/team/ide*. Once you have installed the power toy, it will add a new folder to your Tools → Options window, which is shown in Figure 3-17.

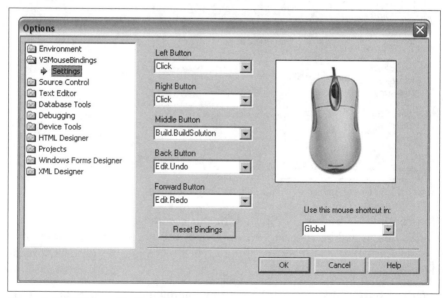

Figure 3-17. VSMouseBindings Options

These options are fairly straightforward. You will notice that you can set a command for each of the different buttons on your mouse. Whenever you click a button on your mouse, the command you assign to that button will be executed. Figure 3-17 shows some of my favorite settings, making undo and redo easily accessible on the Back and Forward buttons, and also putting BuildSolution on the middle button. You can configure the mouse to execute whatever commands make sense for you.

> These are the same commands that you use in the Command window [Hack #46] and when creating keyboard shortcuts [Hack #24]. Any command that you can use from the command window or assign to a keyboard shortcut can be assigned to one of your mouse buttons.

Just as when working with shortcut keys, you can set the scope of your command assignments. Using the drop-down labeled "Use this mouse shortcut in:", you can set the scope of your command. The available scope settings are Global, HTML Source Editor, HTML Designer, and Source Editor. When determining scope, the more specific settings will override the global settings. You might have the middle button configured to be BuildSolution at the global level, but set to be OpenFile in the source editor. This means that the setting for the source editor will override the global settings; if you click the middle button on your mouse in source code view, the OpenFile command will be called.

The VSMouseBindings power toy is easy to download, easy to use, and can definitely make it easier to move around in Visual Studio.

 ## HACK #23 Enhance the Tabs in Visual Studio

Visual Studio's tabs can get crowded. Use a free add-in that can cut the number of tabs in half.

One of the more frustrating things about Visual Studio is that, when you have a dozen or so files open, you've got double that for files having multiple tabs for code-behind or design, and you end up with a huge list of tabs that you have to navigate through. This is time consuming and somewhat annoying. There is a freely available add-in that works to alleviate some of this pain, though. The add-in, called VSTabs and written by Jonathon Payne, can be downloaded from *http://www.zero-one-zero.com/vs*.

> This tool is referred to as a Technical Preview by its author. For the most part, this add-in works perfectly, but you may encounter a bug or two. Luckily, the code for the add-in is available, so if you want to fix the bug yourself, you can do so.

Once you have downloaded and installed the add-in, you will see a new tab along the top of the document window. The new tab can be seen in Figure 3-18.

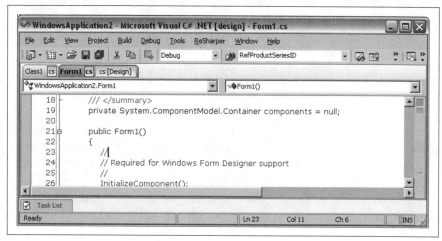

Figure 3-18. VSTabs

Notice how the new tab groups the design view and the *.cs* view for Form1 under a single tab. You can switch between the two by simply clicking on that section of the tab, and that document will be loaded. The tab control will group documents under the same tab whenever there are two views for the same file—this includes ASP.NET pages, Windows Forms, and web services.

This add-in also adds another piece of functionality. It allows you to close a tab by clicking on it with the middle mouse button. If you are a user of the Firefox browser, you are probably already familiar with this type of functionality—you can middle-click on a tab in that browser, and it will close the tab. This is another great timesaving feature, since you no longer need to select the tab and then move your mouse over to the Close button, but can instead simply middle-click on the tab.

This is a quick and easy add-in to install and start using right away.

Customizing Visual Studio

Hacks 24–35

Customizing Visual Studio is a great way to get the most out of this application. Through the course of using an application, you sometimes realize that it would be a lot easier if there were a shortcut key for this command or perhaps a toolbar item for that command. One of the nice things about Visual Studio is that, for the most part, you can customize just about any part of the IDE.

The hacks in this chapter cover how to create your own shortcut keys, customize menus and toolbars, create custom windows layouts, customize the toolbox, and much more.

> Visual Studio saves many of its settings only when you exit Visual Studio. This is important to remember if you are running more than one instance of Visual Studio. If you close the version of Visual Studio you have customized before you close the other instance, the latter instance overwrites your changes.

H A C K   Create Your Own Shortcuts

#24

Visual Studio lets you do a lot with the keyboard configuration. You can customize the keyboard mapping and even copy these mappings from one machine to another.

Keyboard shortcut keys are a big part of working with Visual Studio. Throughout this book, we have identified a number of different shortcuts that are in Visual Studio by default, but in this hack you will learn how to create new shortcuts as well as edit the existing shortcut keys. Visual Studio provides an excellent interface to edit and add new shortcuts. Everything in

Visual Studio works off the idea of commands. Although this is a fairly common pattern, with Visual Studio you see it much more, since you can create shortcuts for various commands and can also see commands when using the command window **[Hack #46]**.

Visual Studio includes hundreds of different commands. A small portion of these commands already have shortcut keys, but through the Options screen (Tools → Options), you can add a shortcut for any of these commands. You can also remove shortcuts that you never use, freeing up more key combinations for shortcuts you might use more often.

Adding a Custom Keystroke

In this example, you will create a shortcut for the Build.RebuildSolution command, which does not normally have a shortcut assigned to it. The first thing you need to do is go to Tools → Options and select the Keyboard item under the Environment folder. This brings up the interface (Figure 4-1) you will use to edit and create shortcuts.

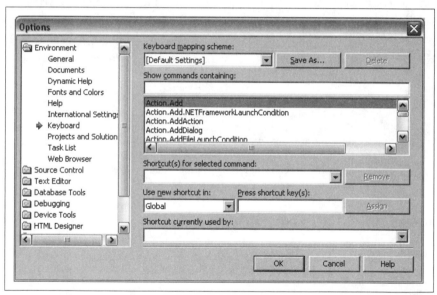

Figure 4-1. Keyboard mapping options

Visual Studio does not allow you to make changes to the default keyboard mappings. You need to first create a copy of the default keyboard mappings for yourself. Start with whatever keyboard mapping you are currently using, then click the Save As button. This will prompt you to name your new scheme. After you create a name, Visual Studio will save the scheme and set it as your selected scheme. Now you are ready to modify shortcuts.

The next step is to find the command that you want to create a shortcut for. This is done in the long listbox of commands. Thankfully, you can enter part of the command and the list will find it for you as you type. In this example, you are going to select the Build.ReBuildSolution command from the list. To add the shortcut:

1. Click in the Show Commands Containing box and type **Build.Re**. The list will narrow to just a few commands. Click once on Build.ReBuild-Solution to select it.

2. Next, you need to decide at what scope you want your shortcut to operate. This is configured using the drop-down list under the "Use new shortcut in:" heading. Leave the scope set to Global so the shortcut will work everywhere, but for more specific shortcuts, you would limit the scope to a particular designer or editor. (For instance, you might have a shortcut that is specific to ASP.NET so you would want it to be valid only while using the HTML Editor Design View.)

3. Your last step is to decide what shortcut key you want to assign to the command. This is more difficult than it sounds. Because of the number of commands and current shortcuts, it can be a task to find an empty shortcut. You can test shortcut keys by typing them into the Press Shortcut Key(s) box. The box below will then be populated with any current mappings for this shortcut key combination. My initial instinct for this rebuild command was Ctrl-Shift-R, since Ctrl-Shift-B is used to build a solution, but Ctrl-Shift-R is already used to record a macro. You could eliminate one of the current mappings by simply overwriting it, but instead I am going to use the unused Ctrl-K, Ctrl-R.

 Visual Studio supports *keystroke chords*. Similar to musical chords, keystroke chords are the combination of two or more key combinations in quick succession. The Ctrl-K, Ctrl-R shortcut is performed by pressing Ctrl-K and then Ctrl-R immediately after it. This is a testament to the number of shortcuts already existing in Visual Studio that they came up with this solution. Ctrl-K is the default first key for chords, but you can create chords using any keys that you want. The only thing to remember is that after a key is used as the first part of a chord, it can no longer be an individual shortcut key because Visual Studio will be listening for the second part of the chord.

In this book, chords will be shown separated by a comma, as in Ctrl-K, Ctrl-R.

Figure 4-2 shows your Options screen right before you click Assign to add your new shortcut key.

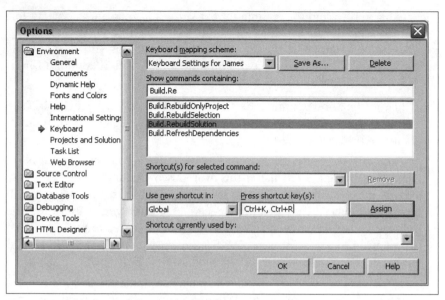

Figure 4-2. Adding a new shortcut key for Build.RebuildSolution

Once you click the Assign button, your new shortcut will be added to your keyboard mapping and you can start using it right away. Creating shortcut keys is something that you should do over time as you notice yourself accessing something over and over again through the menu structure. Everything is faster with the keyboard, especially when writing code. Developing your own set of keyboard shortcuts over time is a great way to improve the speed of your development.

Hacking the Hack

So now that you have spent time to create your own set of shortcut keys, tailored to your own style of development, what happens when you switch machines? While there is a way to save and move keyboard settings manually, it is much easier and less troublesome to use the excellent power toy VSTweak to move the settings for you. VSTweak provides an interface to export and then import keyboard mapping schemes quickly and easily.

The VSTweak power toy is one of the more useful power toys for Visual Studio and is the subject of a number of different hacks in this book. The VSTweak power toy can be downloaded from *http://workspaces.gotdotnet. com/vstweak*.

After you have downloaded and installed the VSTweak power toy, look for the section dealing with keyboard mapping schemes—it's on the first tab, as shown in Figure 4-3.

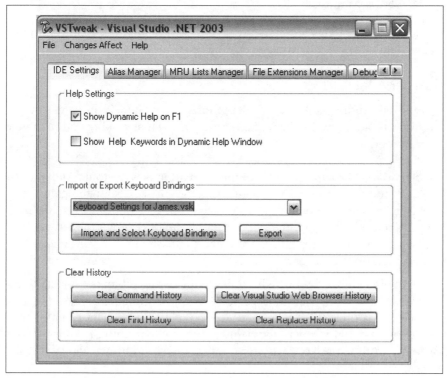

Figure 4-3. VSTweak keyboard mapping schemes

VSTweak provides an easy-to-use interface with which you can export your keyboard bindings by selecting them in the drop-down list and then clicking the Export button. VSTweak will save a *.vsk* file to the location of your choosing. You then need to copy this file to your other system, fire up VSTweak, then use the "Import and select keyboard bindings" button to find and import that file.

VSTweak makes this process relatively easy and painless, but if you wanted to do it manually, you could. The *.vsk* file is stored in your own profile located in the following directory: *\Documents and Settings\<username>\ Application Data\Microsoft\VisualStudio\<7.1>*. You can take this *.vsk* file and copy it to another machine. When you restart Visual Studio, you will see the new scheme in the Keyboard Options window and you can select it.

Customize Menus and Toolbars

HACK #25

You can make Visual Studio work just the way you want. After you create your own menu and toolbar items, you can even move these settings between machines.

Visual Studio includes an impressive number of menus and toolbars. In this hack, you will learn how you can customize them.

Customize Toolbars

The Visual Studio toolbar can be customized in a number of ways, including ways to add new toolbars and buttons, as well as modify and rearrange current toolbars.

Modify existing toolbars. Before looking at creating new custom toolbars, let's look at modifying the existing toolbars. One of the easiest things to do is move buttons around on an existing toolbar or move buttons from one toolbar to another. This can be done by simply holding down the Alt key and dragging and dropping a button from one toolbar to another or into a different position on the current toolbar.

You can also add and remove buttons from existing toolbars using the Customize screen, which can be accessed a couple of different ways. The first way to access this screen is to go to Tools → Customize. You can also click on the small down arrow to the right of every toolbar, select Add or Remove Buttons, and then select Customize. Either approach brings you to the dialog shown in Figure 4-4.

Once you are in this dialog, it puts the entire IDE in a special customization mode. You can use the tabs here to customize any of the existing toolbars. Clicking on a checkbox in the Toolbars list will cause that toolbar to be displayed on the screen, which is the first step if the toolbar you want to modify is not already shown. In this example, let's add a Rebuild Solution button to the Build Toolbar:

1. Click the checkbox to the left of the Build toolbar; this will show the toolbar on the screen.
2. Click on the Commands tab in the Customize dialog. This tab is shown in Figure 4-5.
3. On the Commands tab, select Build from the Categories list and then drag the Rebuild Solution command from the Commands list to your toolbar.

After performing these steps, you will have a toolbar that looks like the one in Figure 4-6.

Figure 4-4. Toolbars tab in Customize dialog

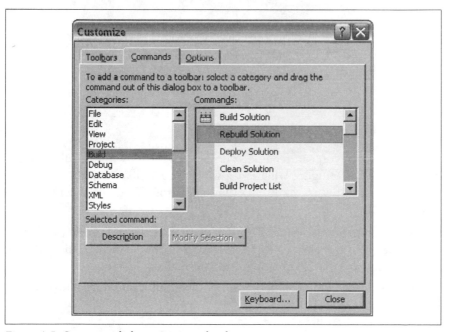

Figure 4-5. Customize dialog—Commands tab

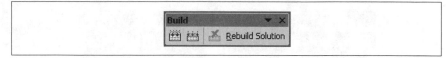

Figure 4-6. Build toolbar

Now that you have the Rebuild Solution command on the toolbar, it would be nice to replace the text with a nice, easy-to-use icon. To do this, right-click on the item (make sure the Customize dialog is still open), and you will see the menu shown in Figure 4-7.

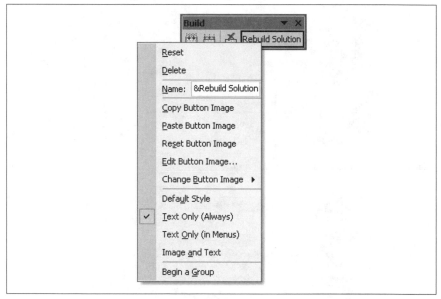

Figure 4-7. Right-click menu for toolbar item

From this menu, you can rename your item and work with the image of the item, as well as configure what is shown on the toolbar. Suppose you want to base your button on the Build Solution button. To derive a button from that one:

1. Right-click on the Build Solution icon (the second from the left in Figure 4-6), and click Copy Button Image from the menu. This will copy the image for that command to the clipboard.

2. Right-click on your Rebuild Solution item and click Paste Button Image from the menu. This will add the icon from the normal Build Solution item to the new item.

3. Next, you need to change your image a little bit so you can differentiate between the two. This can be done using the Edit Button Image command in the menu. Click on the Edit Button Image command, and you will see a small image editor that you can use to modify the image. In this example, simply replace the blue arrows of the image with red arrows. This is a minor change, but should be enough to remind you that this button is for rebuilding whereas the other button is for building.

4. After changing the icon, you can change the display style to Default Style; this will cause just the image to be shown on the menu.

The end result is shown in Figure 4-8.

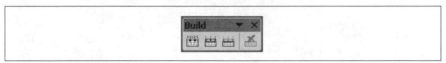

Figure 4-8. Finished Build toolbar

Adding new toolbars. Adding a new toolbar is similar in many ways to modifying an existing toolbar. Instead of starting with an existing toolbar, you need to create your own. This is done from the Customize screen found by going to Tools → Customize. On this screen, you need to click the New button. You will then be prompted to name your new toolbar. After you name the toolbar, it will be saved and will show up in the list of toolbars, and you can edit it just as if it were a preexisting system toolbar.

Customize Menus

Customizing menus is very similar to customizing toolbars. Open the Customize screen through Tools → Customize. Once open, instead of working on the Toolbars tab, you simply switch right to the Commands tab and customize the menus from there. Once the Customize dialog is open, you can customize menus much as if they were toolbars. You simply need to click on the menu to open it, and then you can drag a new command to the menu, rearrange items, or right-click on an item to modify its image or text. Figure 4-9 shows an example of adding the Select Project Template command to the File → New menu.

Reset Changes

Sometimes things get botched up. Toolbars may disappear and won't reappear. Buttons from a toolbar may not show up any more. Thankfully, Visual

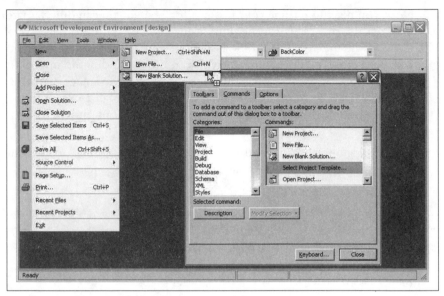

Figure 4-9. Adding a command to a menu

Studio provides a method to reset all the toolbars and menus. This can be done using the following procedure:

1. Close all running instances of Visual Studio.

2. Open the Visual Studio Command Prompt **[Hack #77]**.

3. Type **devenv /setup**.

4. This will reset all the toolbar and menu customizations and hopefully fix whatever problems you are running into.

Hacking the Hack

Now that you have made all these different customizations to the menus and toolbars on the IDE, how can you save these settings and move them to another computer? Unfortunately, there is no power toy available to do this automatically, but thankfully, it is not too hard. All of the changes are located in one file in your user profile. All you need to do is copy this file to the same directory on your new system. The file is called *CmdUI.PRF* and is located in the following directory:

*\Documents and Settings\<username>\Application Data\Microsoft\
VisualStudio\<7.1>\1033*

All you need to do is copy this file to your new system, and all of your changes should be moved.

Create Custom Window Layouts

HACK #26

Visual Studio's windows are a dashboard view of your project. You can create different window layouts and even switch between them on the fly.

In "Take Control of Your Workspace" [Hack #16], I discussed how to modify your window environment in the Visual Studio IDE. You can rearrange your windows in a number of different ways, including the ability to dock, float, hide, and auto hide windows. Back in that hack, I also mentioned that there are a number of default windows layouts. For instance, there is a layout for design mode and a layout for debug mode. Modifications to those window layouts are done independently from each other. Changes to the window layout while in debug mode don't affect the window layout of design mode.

By default, Visual Studio includes a number of different window layouts but does not include a way to create your own custom layouts or switch between layouts. Thankfully, the Visual Studio team has released a power toy called VSWindowManager which will allow you to do this.

You can download the VSWindowManager power toy from *http:// workspaces.gotdotnet.com/vswindowmanager*. Be sure to close all instances of Visual Studio before installing the power toy. After you have installed the power toy, it will add two new items to the Window menu in Visual Studio, as shown in Figures 4-10 and 4-11.

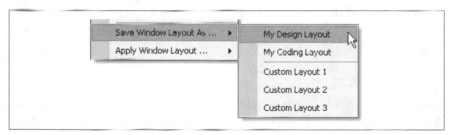

Figure 4-10. VSWindowManager Save Window Layout As... menu

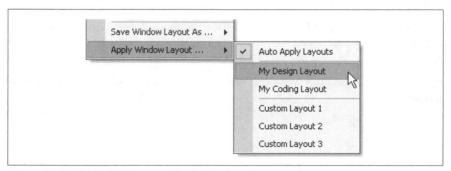

Figure 4-11. VSWindowManager Apply Window Layout menu

These new menu items allow you to create your own custom window layouts and switch between these layouts at any time. To try out this new feature, first customize your window layout for when you design forms, whether Windows Forms or ASP.NET—for example, you might customize it so as to keep the toolbox or the Solution Explorer open, and so on. Once you have configured the window layout the way you like it for design, click on the Save Window Layout As... menu item and select My Design Layout. This will save the current window layout as your design layout.

Next, configure the window layout for when you are writing code. The toolbox is probably hidden; perhaps the task list is now visible. Once you have the windows laid out the way you want, click on Save Window Layout As... again, and this time choose My Coding Layout.

Now that you have two different layouts saved, you can quickly switch between the two layouts using the Apply Windows Layout menu item. You simply need to click that menu item, then select the window layout that you want to switch to. Visual Studio will then relatively quickly switch to the other window layout.

The VSWindowManager power toy is a great tool that allows you to save custom window layouts and then quickly switch between those window layouts. Creating and using different window layouts is a great way to get the most out of the IDE and save time when moving between different coding modes. It is nice to always have Visual Studio configured the way that you like it without the hassle of hiding and showing windows each time you switch tasks.

Hacking the Hack

After creating these custom window layouts, it is nice to be able to move them to another machine. This can be done by copying a single file from your profile to your new system. The file is called *devenv.xml* and is located in the following directory:

> *\Documents and Settings\<username>\Application Data\Microsoft\VisualStudio\<7.1>*

This file can be copied from this directory to the same directory on your new system, and all of your window layouts should be available on your new system.

Customize the Toolbox

Everything you need can be at your fingertips in Visual Studio's toolbox. In this hack, learn how to enhance the toolbox with custom controls and code snippets.

The toolbox is used to store controls and code snippets. The controls and code snippets can be dragged from the toolbox to either the editor or the code window. The toolbox is designed to save time during development. Instead of writing control code manually, you can drag and drop controls or code snippets.

Controls and the Toolbox

The most common use of the toolbox is for Windows controls and web controls (including HTML controls). When you work with either the Windows Forms designer or the Web Forms Designer, you will constantly interact with the toolbox to drag and drop controls onto the designer. By default, the toolbox contains controls from within the .NET Framework, but you can also add custom controls to the toolbox. Adding new controls to the toolbox is a relatively simple procedure.

First, right-click on the tab of the toolbox you want to add the control to and select Add/Remove Items; this will display the dialog shown in Figure 4-12.

From this dialog, you simply need to select your control from the list of .NET Framework Components or COM Components or use the Browse button to manually browse for the control. When browsing for controls, you need to select the assembly that the control is in, either the assembly that you created for your custom controls or the assembly provided by the control author.

One of the Windows Forms controls not added to the toolbox by default is the PropertyGrid control. Follow these steps to add this control to your toolbox:

1. Right-click on the Toolbox tab to which you want to add the control and select Add/Remove Items.

2. Scroll through the .NET Framework Components list and find the control labeled PropertyGrid.

3. Check the box next to the control.

4. Click the OK button.

You will then see the PropertyGrid control added to your tab. You can see the PropertyGrid control added to the toolbox in Figure 4-13.

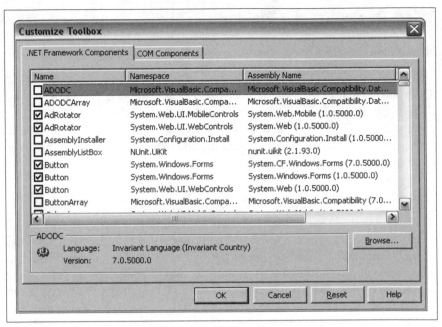

Figure 4-12. Customize Toolbox dialog

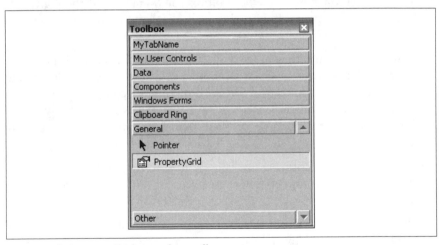

Figure 4-13. PropertyGrid control in toolbox

When a control does not include a custom icon, you will see a small gear next to the control in the toolbox, as seen in Figure 4-14. This is the default icon used when the control author does not provide a custom icon.

If you are building your own control, it's easy to add a custom toolbox icon: create a 16 × 16 bitmap and add it to your project. You will need to ensure that the name of the bitmap is the same as the name of the control and the bitmap is set to be an embedded resource.

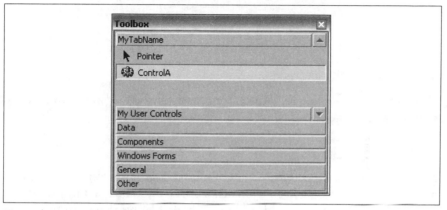

Figure 4-14. New control in toolbox

Code Snippets and the Toolbox

The normal use of the toolbox includes adding and removing tabs and controls, but you can also use the toolbox to store code snippets. Whether you want to store a method call to get a connection string, a commonly used piece of JavaScript, or an architecture specific piece of code, the toolbox is a great place to save those pieces of code that you constantly find yourself typing.

Before adding any code snippets to the toolbox, it is a good idea to add a separate tab to the toolbox for your code snippets: right-click on the toolbox and select Add Tab, then enter a name for the tab (such as **Code Snippets**) in the text box that appears at the bottom of the toolbox.

Storing a piece of code in the toolbox is simple: select the code from the document window and drag it over to the toolbox. After dropping the code on the toolbox, you will see a snippet like the one shown in Figure 4-15.

This code snippet can now be dragged and dropped from the toolbox to the document window, and the included code will be pasted into the document. You can also rename the snippet by right-clicking on the item, selecting Rename Item, and then specifying the new name. Changing the name of the item will not affect the text that is copied to the document window.

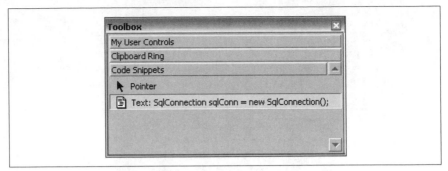

Figure 4-15. Toolbox code snippet

Using the toolbox as a method to store code snippets is an effective way to reduce coding time and increase your own consistency.

Hacking the Hack

Now that you have customized the toolbox, it is important to be able to move those settings between systems. To move toolbox settings from one machine to another, you need to copy a single file from your profile on the current machine to your profile on the target machine. The file is called *toolbox.tbd* and is located in the following directory:

> *\Documents and Settings\<username>\Local Settings\Application Data\ Microsoft\VisualStudio\<7.1>*

This file can be copied to the target system, and all of your toolbox settings will be moved to the new system when you restart Visual Studio. Keep in mind that for custom controls, any assemblies that the toolbox references would need to be copied as well.

Package Your Toolbox Settings

#28
If you want to be able to deploy the same toolbox settings on a bunch of different machines, you can write a program to add custom controls or code snippets to the toolbox.

One of the big challenges of team development is creating consistent code across all developers. One way to encourage consistent code is to provide each developer with the same set of controls and code snippets. This way, each individual developer has all the same tools as the other developers (whether they use them is another matter).

In "Customize the Toolbox" [Hack #27], we covered a method for moving toolbox settings, but using this as a method of distribution is not a good idea.

The method outlined involved copying a user-specific file to another system. This is a great solution for moving your own personal settings, but trying to use this method as a means of distribution would result in the overwriting of any custom controls or code snippets each developer may have created.

A better method for adding custom controls and code snippets to each developer's system is to create a small program that adds these controls and snippets through the Visual Studio Common Environment Object Model. In this hack, you are going to learn how to create just such a program.

For simplicity's sake, we are going to create a Windows Forms application that, upon the press of a button, will add a number of custom controls to the Visual Studio toolbox. In practice, you may find it easier to create an installation package or command-line tool, but the code will be the same. The first thing you need to do is create a Windows Forms Project in Visual Studio using your favorite .NET language. (I am using C# for these examples, but a version of VB.NET is available for download from the book's web site, which is described in the Preface.) Next, you will need to create a reference to the *envdte.dll* assembly—this assembly contains the objects we will work with to modify the Visual Studio environment. This is called the Common Environment Object Model and can be used to modify just about every aspect of the Visual Studio IDE **[Hack #86]**.

After you create the obligatory using or Imports statement for the EnvDTF namespace, you can start to work with the Visual Studio environment.

> When working with EnvDTE, you may run across frequent "Call was rejected by the Callee" errors. These are due to timeouts and occur more frequently on slow machines, but they can pop up on fast machines as well. To prevent these errors refer to **[Hack #87]**.

The next thing you need to do is to get an instance of the current DTE (see "Access Visual Studio from Standalone Applications" **[Hack #87]**). This is not as easy as it sounds. Because the DTE objects for Visual Studio .NET 2002 and Visual Studio .NET 2003 are exactly the same, we have to get the class using the progid, as shown here:

```
Type latestDTE = Type.GetTypeFromProgID("VisualStudio.DTE.7.1");
EnvDTE.DTE env = Activator.CreateInstance(latestDTE) as EnvDTE.DTE;
```

> You can get a reference to the currently executing instance of Visual Studio using this line of code:
>
> ```
> EnvDTE.DTE dte =
>     (DTE)Marshal.GetActiveObject("VisualStudio.DTE.
>         7.1");
> ```
>
> This will return a reference to the currently executing instance of Visual Studio as opposed to a reference to a new instance of Visual Studio.

The DTE object can be used to modify many different parts of Visual Studio. To get the toolbar window, you need to access the Windows collection of the DTE object using the vsWindowKindToolBox constant, then you need to cast the object to the ToolBox type as shown in this code:

```
Window win = env.Windows.Item(Constants.vsWindowKindToolbox);

ToolBox toolBox = (ToolBox) win.Object;
```

The next thing you need to do is check to see if the tab you want to add is already there. If it is not already there, you will want to add it:

```
ToolBoxTab tab = null;

// Loop through the tab collection and see if the tab already exists
foreach (ToolBoxTab tb in toolBox.ToolBoxTabs)
{
    if (tb.Name == "Our Controls")
    {
        tab = tb;
    }
}

// The tab does not exist so add it
if(tab == null)
{
    tab = toolBox.ToolBoxTabs.Add("Our Controls");
}
```

Now there is a little dirty work. The following things need to be done because working with the DTE object can often be an adventure in bugs. Rather than simply adding the control to the Toolbox tab, first you need to show the property window, activate the tab, and then select the first item. All of this is necessary to get the process to run correctly, though admittedly does not make a lot of sense:

```
// Show the PropertiesWindow for bugs sake
env.ExecuteCommand("View.PropertiesWindow","");

// Activate the tab
```

```
//(Because the Add method will only add to the active tab)
tab.Activate( );

// Select the first item
//(Because this is the only way to make it work)
tab.ToolBoxItems.Item(1).Select( );
```

Then you need to add the toolbox item to the tab by calling the Add method and passing in the path to the *.dll* that contains your controls and the type of item you are adding. When adding a code snippet, the first string is the name of the snippet and the second is the value of the snippet. When adding controls, the first string is not used; the name of the control is used instead. Visual Studio uses the assembly specified in the second string and looks inside it to determine the name of the control.

In this example, I am using *System.Web.dll*, which will add all of the controls in that assembly to the toolbox. In practice, you will want to point to the assembly that contains your custom controls.

```
// Add new toolbox items for our custom controls
ToolBoxItem tbi1 = tab.ToolBoxItems.Add("not used", _
    @"C:\windows\Microsoft.NET\Framework\v1.1.4322\System.Web.dll",
    vsToolBoxItemFormat.vsToolBoxItemFormatDotNETComponent);
```

The last thing you need to do is close the environment:

```
// Close the environment
env.Quit( );
```

After running this code, whether in an installation procedure or a simple Windows Form, you can open Visual Studio and you will see all of the controls in *System.Web.dll* added to your new Toolbox tab. (You may need to right-click on the toolbox and select Show All Tabs to see the new tab.)

> At the time of this writing, attempting to add code snippets to the toolbox in this manner works for only Visual Studio .NET 2002—all attempts to get this working in Visual Studio .NET 2003 and VIsual Studio .NET 2005 have ended with only the tab being added and no code snippets being saved. Hopefully this will be fixed before the final release of Visual Studio 2005.

If you are shipping your own custom controls, or even using a set of custom controls internally, this code presents a great way to install these controls in the toolbox for all of your users. The complete application can be downloaded in both C# and VB.NET from this book's web site (see *http://www.oreilly.com/catalog/visualstudiohks*).

HACK #29   Add Support for Nonstandard File Extensions

Use the VSTweak power toy to tell Visual Studio how to handle file types that aren't supported by default.

Creating custom file extensions allows you to specify your own file extensions that will be treated like another already existing file type in Visual Studio. This is very useful if you have created a custom file type for your application but want Visual Studio to treat it like a regular file.

To create and manage custom file extensions, you can use a power toy called VSTweak. The VSTweak power toy is one of the more useful power toys for Visual Studio and is the subject of a number of different hacks in this book. The VSTweak power toy can be downloaded at *http://workspaces.gotdotnet. com/vstweak*.

Once you have installed and launched VSTweak, click on the File Extensions Manager tab, shown in Figure 4-16.

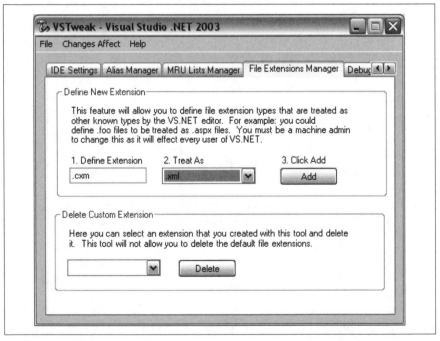

Figure 4-16. File Extensions Manager

To add a new custom extension, you simply need to enter the custom extension in the Define Extension text box, select what kind of file this extension should be treated as in the Treat As drop-down, and then click the Add button shown in Figure 4-16. The extension *.cxm* will be added to Visual Studio and treated like an *.xml* file.

You can also remove custom extensions by selecting the extension from the drop-down and clicking the Delete button. Changes made to custom extensions are made for *all* users of your machine, not just you.

> To edit custom file extensions, you must be logged in as administrator on your machine, or you must launch the VSTweak application by right-clicking on it and choosing Run As, then log in using an administrator account.

Managing custom file extensions is very useful, especially when creating custom file types or when hacking Visual Studio to do something it was never intended to do (such as adding the ability to edit *.php* files [Hack #12]).

Hack the Registry
#30 Visual Studio has some settings that you can get to only through the registry. You'll need to be careful, but you can do some incredible things in there.

The Visual Studio registry contains a host of settings. Some of these settings can be accessed from the normal Tool → Options dialog; others can be edited with Visual Studio power toys; some can be edited only directly in the registry. In this hack, you are going to learn how to make these changes, how to use an alternative registry, and how to move these settings from machine to machine.

Registry Settings

Visual Studio stores most settings in two different places in the registry. The first section is located under *HKEY_CURRENT_USER/Software/Microsoft/VisualStudio/<7.1>* and stores all of the user-specific settings. This section includes settings for the various editors, external tools, source control, and just about everything located in Tools → Options.

The other place that Visual Studio stores settings is under *HKEY_LOCAL_MACHINE/Software/Microsoft/VisualStudio/<7.1>*. The systemwide settings are stored in this location. Any changes here will affect all users of the system as opposed to just your own settings.

Between these two locations, you can modify just about any setting in Visual Studio. Most of the registry keys and values are human readable. Figure 4-17 shows an example of some of the settings that can be modified in the registry.

I am not going to cover individual registry settings in this hack, since we cover those in other hacks. Many of the settings that once had to be edited

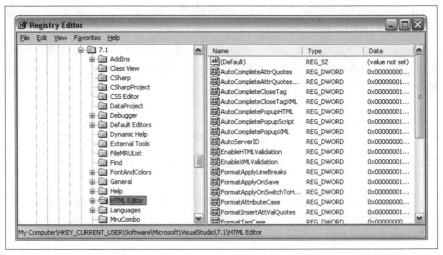

Figure 4-17. Registry Editor

directly through the registry, like the recent file and projects list **[Hack #13]** and custom file extensions **[Hack #29]**, can now be edited using a power toy like VSTweak.

Some settings can still be edited only through the registry, and if there is something you can't find in any of the power toys or on the Tools → Options screen, then the next place to look is the registry.

Moving Registry Settings

Moving registry settings is a fairly simple procedure, but one that can often be fraught with danger. A good rule of thumb to follow is to move only settings that you understand. Your instinct might be to copy the entire settings tree, and while this might work, it can also cause some issues (especially with recent file and project lists, since those file and projects might not be in the same place and could cause huge delays when opening Visual Studio).

To move registry settings from one machine to another, all you need to do is open *regedit* (Start → Run → type **regedit**) on your machine, find the group of settings you want to copy, then right-click on the parent key and choose Export. This is shown in Figure 4-18.

After clicking Export, you will be prompted for a place to save a *.reg* file. After saving this file, you can move it to another machine—when you double-click on the file on the new machine, you will be prompted to confirm that you want to add this information to your registry. After clicking Yes,

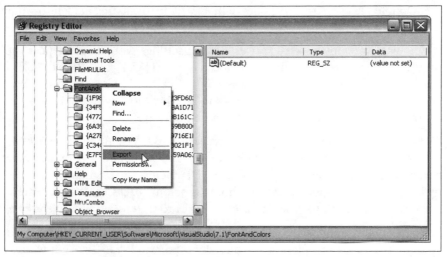

Figure 4-18. Registry Editor dialog—Export tab

you will see another prompt confirming that the information has been entered into your registry. Moving registry settings between computers using this method is relatively easy and is the only way to move settings like Font and Colors or editor settings between systems (unless you are using Visual Studio 2005 **[Hack #31]**).

Use an Alternate Registry Tree

We authors always encourage our readers to back up their registry before playing with it—if the wrong things are changed in the registry, Visual Studio won't start or won't work properly. Sometimes a reinstallation of Visual Studio is necessary, which we all know uses hours of your time that you won't ever get back.

Visual Studio includes an alternative to backing up your registry. You can actually switch the registry that Visual Studio uses! This way you can make a copy of the current registry, tell Visual Studio to use that registry, hack the registry settings to your heart's content, and then if you have any issues, just switch back to the old registry location.

The process for switching to an alternate registry is as follows:

1. Make a copy of the current registry. Using *regedit*, go to *HKEY_LOCAL_MACHINE\SOFTWARE\Microsoft\VisualStudio\<7.1>*, right-click on the folder, and export the entire key to a *.reg* file.

2. Open the *.reg* file in a text editor and replace all instances of "\7.1" with "\7.1Hacks". (7.1 being the version of Visual Studio that you are using.)

3. Double-click on the *.reg* file, which will load all the keys into your registry.

If you also want to move your user-specific settings, you should repeat the preceding process for the key located at *HKEY_CURRENT_USER\ SOFTWARE\Microsoft\VisualStudio\<7.1>*. You don't have to copy over your user settings though; when you start Visual Studio with the new registry tree, it will create a new set for you automatically.

After creating the new registry, you next need to tell Visual Studio to use the new registry by using the /rootsuffix switch. Go to Start → Run and type **devenv.exe /rootstuffix Hacks**—this will launch Visual Studio using the new registry tree. Notice that you should type only **Hacks** and not **7.1Hacks**, since Hacks is the suffix that you are adding onto the end of the current key.

When Visual Studio opens, it will be running using the new registry, and you can play around as much as you want and switch back by simply closing Visual Studio and opening it without using the switch. If you wanted to switch to a different registry for an extended amount of time, you could always create a shortcut that includes the switch.

HACK #31   Save and Move Your IDE Settings

Move all your customizations from one computer to another with Visual Studio 2005.

Throughout this chapter, we have looked at numerous ways that you can customize Visual Studio to your needs, and in each section, we have looked at ways to move those customizations between machines, usually involving a power toy or manually copying a file to another system.

Visual Studio 2005 adds another way to move settings between machines by using a new import and export settings dialog. This dialog can be accessed by going to Tools → Import/Export Settings. You will then see the screen shown in Figure 4-19.

From this dialog, you can select the settings that you want to export from the tree view. The tree view list includes just about all of the settings that we have talked about in this chapter, including all of the settings in the Tool → Options window. After you click Export Settings, Visual Studio will save a *.vssettings* file to the location of your choice.

The *.vssettings* file is a mixture of XML and binary data (the structure of the file is XML, but the value of some nodes is binary). Take a look at the file using any text editor, and you will notice that settings like key bindings are

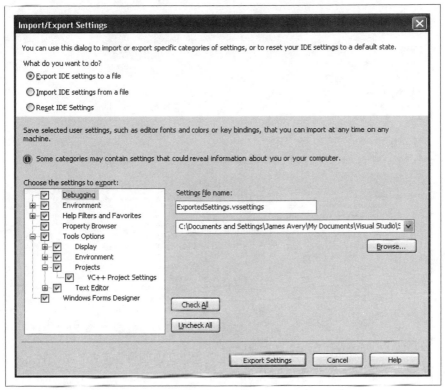

Figure 4-19. Import/Export Settings dialog with Export selected

stored in binary and are not easily editable. Some of the other settings are stored as plain text and could be changed manually if you wanted to do so.

The *.vssettings* file can be copied to another system and then imported using this same window. You simply need to select the second radio button labeled "Import IDE settings from a file," and you will see the dialog shown in Figure 4-20.

After selecting the file that you exported, you will see it listed on the left side; on the right side, you will be able to select what settings you would like to import from the file. After selecting the file to import from, as well as the settings to import, click the Import Settings button, and Visual Studio will then import all of these settings into the new installation of Visual Studio.

You can also restore Visual Studio to one of the default configurations. To do so, you first need to select the Reset IDE Settings option in the options

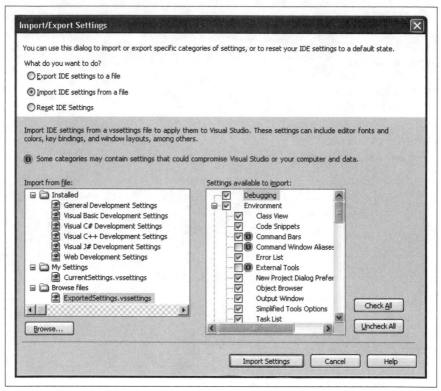

Figure 4-20. Import/Export Settings dialog with Import selected

group at the top of the window. You will then see the screen shown in Figure 4-21.

This screen displays the default Visual Studio configurations. You can select one of the configurations from the list and then click Reset Settings to restore all the Visual Studio settings to one of the default configurations.

This method of moving configuration settings is much preferred to the myriad of things you had to do manually with previous versions of Visual Studio, including copying files, using power toys, and backing up the registry.

> A cool byproduct of this feature is the ability developers now have to easily share their Visual Studio configurations. If you want to show someone how you set up Visual Studio, you can simply send them your *.vssettings* file or even post it out on your blog for the entire world to check out (and ridicule you for using granny fonts or green type on a black background).

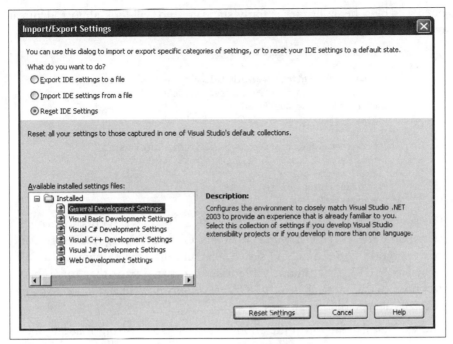

Figure 4-21. Import/Export Settings dialog with Reset selected

HACK #32 Enable IntelliSense for HTML and XML Documents

Eliminate errors in XML and HTML editing by adding IntelliSense support for your configuration sections and controls.

Visual Studio provides developers with IntelliSense in code by interrogating compiled objects or assemblies, but it is unable to provide the same assistance when editing XML, HTML, or ASPX files. In this hack, you will learn how to enable IntelliSense in these documents using an XML schema.

IntelliSense in HTML and XML documents relies on XML schema. ASP. NET has schemas defined for the built-in types (DataGrid, TextBox, etc.), but if you find yourself editing custom sections in application configuration files or want to add IntelliSense to your custom controls, you can create your own schema and reference it from your files. Visual Studio will then add the elements you define in your schema to the default ones and provide you with the same level of support you expect from the built-in controls.

Basic Structure of an IntelliSense Schema

The schema you need to create is composed of three basic sections: the header, the names, and the types.

Header. The schema header is fairly standard and will look almost identical for each schema you create:

```
<?xml version="1.0" encoding="utf-8" ?>
<xsd:schema
    targetNamespace="http://www.orbitalspacelaser.com/schemas"
    xmlns="http://www.orbitalspacelaser.com/schemas"
    elementFormDefault="qualified"
    xmlns:xsd="http://www.w3.org/2001/XMLSchema"
    xmlns:vs=
    "http://schemas.microsoft.com/Visual-Studio-Intellisense"
    vs:friendlyname="Custom Intellisense Forms Controls"
    vs:ishtmlschema="false"
    vs:iscasesensitive="false"
    vs:requireattributequotes="true">
```

The sections that you will need to change are the `targetNamespace`, the `xmlns`, and the `vs:friendlyname` attribute. Generally, `targetNamespace` and `xmlns` should be the same and set to some unique schema namespace. The format is a URL that uniquely identifies the namespace that this schema describes. A format such as *http://OrganizationName/schema/ProjectName* is generally acceptable.

The `vs:friendlyname` attribute should be set to some string that succinctly describes the set of items you are providing for IntelliSense with this schema.

Note that the schema must have a matching close tag (`</xsd:schema>`) at the end of the document for it to be validated and used.

Names. Following the header section are the names of the items that are valid in the schema. This section is basically a simple list of items that are valid in the document you will be editing, be it a list of custom control names that are valid in an ASPX or elements that are valid in a XML configuration file:

```
<xsd:element name="AlphaControl" type="AlphaControlDef" />
```

The `name` attribute will determine what Visual Studio matches in the file. Thus, the preceding element will match `<AlphaControl>` in the XML file you are editing (remember that ASPX files are XML files). The type of the element will be defined in the next section. For most situations, using the name and adding "Def" to the end should be sufficient.

Types. The types defined in the schema are actually what Visual Studio will use to create the IntelliSense prompts when you are editing a file. Types can be very complex and can also be nested, so if you have a hierarchy (with custom controls, for example) you can mirror that in the schema:

```
<xsd:complexType name="AlphaControlDef">
    <xsd:attribute name="Alpha" type="xsd:boolean" />
    <xsd:attribute name="Delta" type="xsd:double" />
    <xsd:attribute name="Gamma">
        <xsd:simpleType>
            <xsd:restriction base="xsd:string">
                <xsd:enumeration value="ValueOne" />
                <xsd:enumeration value="ValueTwo" />
                <xsd:enumeration value="ValueThree" />
            </xsd:restriction>
        </xsd:simpleType>
    </xsd:attribute>
    <xsd:attributeGroup ref="BaseClassAttributes" />
</xsd:complexType>
```

This type represents a few simple attributes that demonstrate much of the flexibility of the schema. Our element contains three attributes and also a group of attributes defined elsewhere. Both Alpha and Delta have simple xsd types set, and Visual Studio will simply prompt you to enter a value of the appropriate type, providing a list of choices where applicable (such as True/False with Boolean attributes).

The attribute definition for Gamma defines a custom simpleType, which allows us to enhance the built-in xsd types. We start with a string, but we add a restriction to it. When we edit this type in Visual Studio, this restriction tells Visual Studio that the value for Gamma can only be one of the options listed in the enumeration, so it will prompt the developer to pick one of them, as shown in Figure 4-22.

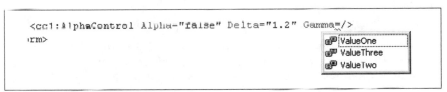

Figure 4-22. IntelliSense for attributes with enumerations defined

XML schemas provide a great many options on how to build these attributes, but these simple options should cover most controls and configuration sections you will need to create.

Considerations for Application Configuration Files

Application configuration files are straight XML and will generally be custom to an application, so creating the schema is a fairly straightforward process. In general, your use of attribute groups and other more complex constructs will be limited in these situations.

Considerations for Custom Controls

Creating schema for a custom control often involves extending the existing schema of one of ASP.NET's built-in controls. In this situation, we can eliminate a lot of typing and create a more useful schema by copying the appropriate portions of the default ASP.NET schema. After creating your schema file, locate and open the file *<VS Install Directory>\Common7\Packages\ schemas\xml\asp.xsd*. This file contains the schema for all the built-in controls. Find and copy into your new schema the appropriate `attributeGroup` elements that apply to your control.

 Editing the *asp.xsd* is a bad idea. Not only are you potentially breaking IntelliSense for the built-in controls, but the next time you upgrade or patch Visual Studio, your changes will probably be lost.

In most cases, you will be able to use the `ControlAttributes` group even if no other groups apply. After pasting these definitions into your schema, you can simply reference them with an attribute group tag inside the appropriate type:

```
<xsd:attributeGroup ref="ControlAttributes" />
```

After that, your type will automatically provide all the attributes defined in the referenced attribute group.

Installing the Schema

After you have created the schema, you need to place it where Visual Studio expects to find it. The normal directory will be *<VS Install Directory>\ Common7\Packages\schemas\xml*. After you copy your new schema to this directory, Visual Studio will be able to reference it in files in which the appropriate XML namespace is imported. Be sure to restart your Visual Studio environment to ensure the new schema is recognized.

Referencing the Schema

Referencing a schema after it has been installed is a matter of adding an attribute to the document you are editing to make Visual Studio use the XML namespace you created. To do this, simply add an `xmlns` attribute to the root element in the file with a value equal to the `targetNamespace` you defined in your schema.

Application configuration files. It's easy to set configuration files to use a schema. Simply add the `xmlns` to the node below which your schema should apply. For example, if your schema defines the elements your application would expect in the appSettings node of the file, the types and attributes you had defined in your schema would apply beneath that point, such as with this schema, which provides assistance adding a ConnectionString attribute to your appSettings (Figure 4-23 shows it in action):

```xml
<?xml version="1.0" encoding="utf-8" ?>
<xsd:schema
    targetNamespace=
     "http://www.orbitalspacelaser.com/schemas/config"
    xmlns="http://www.orbitalspacelaser.com/schemas/config"
    elementFormDefault="qualified"
    xmlns:xsd="http://www.w3.org/2001/XMLSchema"
    xmlns:vs=
     "http://schemas.microsoft.com/Visual-Studio-Intellisense"
    vs:friendlyname="Custom Intellisense Forms Controls"
    vs:ishtmlschema="false"
    vs:iscasesensitive="false"
    vs:requireattributequotes="true">

    <xsd:element name="ConnectionString" type="ConnectionStringDef"/>

    <xsd:complexType name="ConnectionStringDef">
        <xsd:attribute name="Server" type="xsd:string"/>
        <xsd:attribute name="Database" type="xsd:string"/>
        <xsd:attribute name="User" type="xsd:string"/>
        <xsd:attribute name="Password" type="xsd:string"/>
    </xsd:complexType>

</xsd:schema>
```

Figure 4-23. An appSettings node with IntelliSense schema applied

Unfortunately, if you apply a schema to one of the default configuration sections (*system.web* in a *web.config* for example), .NET will be unable to parse the configuration file. If IntelliSense is required on a default node, you can add the *xmlns* attribute, but you *must* remove it before running the application or the parsing of the configuration file will fail.

ASPX files. For an ASPX file, this means changing the body tag to include the namespace and giving it an alias:

```
<body xmlns:cc1="http://www.orbitalspacelaser.com/schemas/controls">
```

The `cc1` will then be the alias for this namespace. If you are referencing a custom control library, it should match the TagPrefix defined in the Register directive at the top of the page:

```
<%@ Register TagPrefix="cc1"
Namespace="CustomControlIntellisense"
Assembly="CustomControlIntellisense" %>
```

Now when you wish to reference the control, simply open a tag with the alias defined, as shown in Figure 4-24.

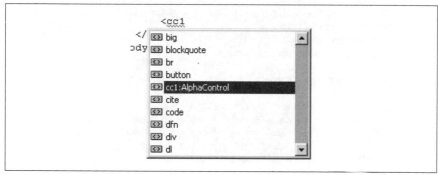

Figure 4-24. Adding a tag with the defined alias

Visual Studio will now display your types in the list of available tags and will provide IntelliSense for the defined attributes.

—Ben Von Handorf

Add an External Tool
#33
Enhance Visual Studio by plugging in all kinds of external tools such as ILDASM.

Visual Studio provides the functionality to include external tools in the Tools menu. If you go to the Tools menu, you will see a listing of tools including those like Error Lookup and Create GUID. These are all external tools that have been configured to be listed in this menu. You can modify the existing external tools and add your own external tools to this list quite easily.

To modify the existing tools or to add new tools of your own, you simply need to go to Tools → External Tools. You will then see the dialog shown in Figure 4-25.

Figure 4-25. External Tools dialog

This dialog lists all of the tools currently configured in Visual Studio. You can use the Move Up and Move Down buttons to rearrange the order of these tools in the menu. You can also click on each of the tools and modify any of its properties or use the Delete button to remove a tool from the menu.

You can add a new external tool by clicking the Add button. This will clear out all of the fields and allow you to enter new values and save a new external tool. In this example, I am going to add a link to the tool ILDASM. ILDASM is a tool that can be used to examine the IL of an assembly [Hack #63].

Following are the steps to add ILDASM as an external tool:

1. Click the Add Button.
2. Specify a Title of **ILDASM**.
3. Specify a command location of **C:\Program Files\Microsoft Visual Studio .NET 2003\SDK\v1.1\Bin\ILDASM.exe** (this path may vary depending on the version of Visual Studio you are running).
4. Click on the arrow to the right of the Arguments box and choose Target Path. This will send the complete path of your assembly to ILDASM.
5. Click the OK button.

ILDASM will now be added as an external tool to the Tools menu. You can click on the ILDASM link and the tool will open with your assembly already loaded in the tool. Adding external tools for utilities that you commonly use is a great way to save time and avoid the hassle of pointing the tool to your assembly or file.

External Tool Arguments

In the ILDASM example, I used the Target Path argument to pass the name and location of the project's assembly to the external tool. The 15 different argument variables that you can use when configuring an external tool are listed in Table 4-1.

Table 4-1. External tool argument variables

Name	Argument	Description
Item Path	$(ItemPath)	The path to the active document.
Item Directory	$(ItemDir)	The directory where the active document is located.
Item File Name	$(ItemFileName)	The name of the active document.
Item Extension	$(ItemExt)	The file extension of the active document.
Current Line	$(CurLine)	The line position where the cursor is currently resting.
Current Column	$(CurCol)	The column position where the cursor is currently resting.
Current Text	$(CurText)	Either the word where the cursor is located or a single line of selected text.
Target Path	$(TargetPath)	The path (including filename) to the current target. (The target is what your project is compiling into, e.g., the assembly.)
Target Directory	$(TargetDir)	The directory where the target is.
Target Name	$(TargetName)	The filename of the target.
Target Extension	$(TargetExt)	The file extension of the target.
Project Directory	$(ProjDir)	The drive and directory where the current project is located.
Project File Name	$(ProjFileName)	The complete path to the current project.
Solution Directory	$(SolutionDir)	The drive and directory where the current solution is located.
Solution File Name	$(SolutionFileName)	The complete path to the current solution.

Using these variables, you can pass all kinds of information directly to your external tool, saving you the time of supplying this information by hand.

You can also set the initial directory where this tool should be run. This is set using the Initial Directory option. The initial directory can be set to Item Directory, Target Directory, Target Name, Project Directory, or Solution Directory. (These arguments are the same as the arguments defined in Table 4-1.)

External Tool Options

A number of options can also be set when configuring external tools:

Use Output Window
> When this option is enabled, any response from the command line will be shown in the output window. If you were calling a command-line utility that reported statistics on your assembly, instead of having to view the results in the open command prompt, you could have those results shown in the output window. "Follow the Rules with FxCop" [Hack #65] includes an example of doing this with the FxCop command-line utility.

Prompt for Arguments
> When this option is enabled, you will be prompted every time the tool is run and allowed to modify or change the arguments being passed to the external tool. A good example of when this might be useful is when you have a tool to which you want to pass the project, solution, or item path, depending on the circumstances. By prompting you each time, it allows you to choose which argument you want to pass into the tool.

Close on Exit
> This option determines whether the command prompt will be closed after your command has been executed. Normally this will be set to true, but if the tool you are calling returns results in the command window, you would not want it to close. This option is also very handy when debugging an external tool that is not working, since you can see the error it returns.

Adding and configuring external tools is a great way to customize the IDE and can save a lot of time that would otherwise be wasted looking for programs and pointing them at your assemblies or files.

HACK
#34

Customize Your Project Build Process

Find out how to automate tasks that occur prior to, during, or after a build.

While the Visual Studio build process is familiar for all .NET developers, not everyone realizes the build customization capabilities that can be accomplished with just a little work. You can easily put together tasks that occur before, after, and even during a build.

> With the release of Visual Studio 2005 (Whidbey), a new build tool—called MSBuild—will be used within the Visual Studio environment. This tool will provide many build process workflows and will be similar to NAnt in capability.

Pre- and Post-Build Event Commands

In nonweb projects, you can create pre- and post-build event commands. As their names suggest, these are commands that you can customize to run just prior to or after a build. You can even control whether the post-build event executes at all depending on the outcome of the build. You can find these settings on the project properties under the Build Events tab (see Figure 4-26).

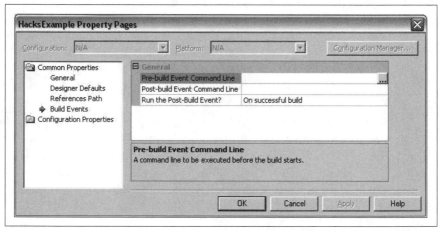

Figure 4-26. Project build events

Just type in the command you want to occur for each event type. When you select the text box to enter the command, you can click on the button on the righthand side of the text box to expand the command window and gain access to the list of macros or variables available. These variables help provide some shortcuts to including pathnames, project output locations, and other information into your event commands. Note that the variables are sensitive to the type of build you are compiling, so if you switch to a release build, the variables referencing the output directory will be correctly pointed at the *\bin\release* directory (or wherever you have set up the output directory to be). Table 4-2 provides a few examples of the macros available.

Table 4-2. Macro examples

Name	Description
$(TargetPath)	The full directory path to the output directory, including the project output filename. Example: *c:\CSharpWinFormApp\bin\debug\CSharpWinFormApp. exe.*
$(TargetDir)	The full directory path to the output directory. Example: *c:\ CSharpWinFormApp\bin\debug\.*
$(ProjectDir)	The full directory path to where the project file exists. Example: *c:\ CSharpWinFormApp\.*

The build event command lines are simply command-line operations that will be executed at the specified time. In fact, the command line you enter in the properties tab actually gets copied out into a batch file (stored in the output directory for the project). These batch files will be named *PreBuildEvent. bat* or *PostBuildEvent.bat* and are handy to help troubleshoot your build events if necessary.

Note that a failing build event will be shown in the build output and listed in the Build Error task list along with any other build errors. A failing pre-build event will cause the build to stop, while a failing post-build event will still mark the build as a failure even if the build of the code succeeded without errors. You can choose to have the post-build event occur every build, only if the build succeeded, or when the project output (the resulting *.dll* or *.exe*) actually changes.

A great example of using a custom post-build event is when you have multiple configuration files. When you add an *app.config* file to your project, it will automatically be copied to the output directory of the project and renamed to match up with the project output file (e.g., *CSharpWinFormApp. exe.config*), but the IDE will not do the same with other custom configuration files. What if your project had multiple *.config* files to break up the settings? For example, you have *app.config* to store application configuration but then you also have an *EndUser.config* file to store user-specific settings that you didn't want to mix with the application settings. By default, this configuration file would not be copied to your output directory, and the application would receive an exception if it went looking for the file during execution. To get around this, a custom post-build event can copy the *EndUser.config* file to the output directory every time a build succeeds.

In the Build Events tab, choose to run a Post-Build event when a successful build occurs and add a Post-Build event command line of:

```
copy "$(ProjectDir)EndUser.config" "$(TargetDir)"
```

Note the use of quotes around the variables and commands—the quotes are there because there may be spaces in the file and pathnames. Also, the variables that generate pathnames will append an ending slash automatically. After a successful build of this project the current version of the *EndUser.config* file in the project directory will be copied to the output directory.

Copying files after a build is just one example of how these build events can be useful. More complex operations can be performed as well. For example, a Windows script or executable could be run when a build completes to kick off a set of test scripts against the newly built output. The build event could just as easily automatically create and register an output type library for use with COM or even register a newly built component with the GAC.

Pre- and post-build commands are available only to nonweb C# applications in Visual Studio .NET 2003, but they are also available to nonweb Visual Basic .NET applications in Visual Studio 2005.

Handling Build Events

Some of the limitations of the custom pre- and post-build command events are that they are available for only nonweb projects and are only project specific. They don't give you the flexibility to deal with building a multiproject solution or provide a way of handling more complex build outcomes other than a successful build, a failed build, or a changed project output. For more advanced handling of build events, we turn to the Visual Studio Macro Environment.

To hook into the IDE build events, all we need to do is create some simple macros. Open up your Macro IDE (from Tools → Macros → Macro IDE) [Hack #51]. If you haven't used the Macro IDE before, the first thing you'll notice is that it resembles the regular VS.NET IDE, except the Macro IDE is used solely for the creation, editing, and compiling of macros that can be used within your Visual Studio IDE.

Open up the MyMacros project and see if it already contains an EnvironmentEvents module. If it doesn't, go ahead and copy the one from the Samples directory into your MyMacros project. The code looks like this:

```
Option Strict Off
Option Explicit Off
Imports EnvDTE
```

```
Imports System.Diagnostics

Public Module EnvironmentEvents

#Region "Automatically generated code, do not modify"
'Automatically generated code, do not modify
'Event Sources Begin
<System.ContextStaticAttribute()>
    Public WithEvents DTEEvents As EnvDTE.DTEEvents
<System.ContextStaticAttribute()>
    Public WithEvents DocumentEvents As EnvDTE.DocumentEvents
<System.ContextStaticAttribute()>
    Public WithEvents WindowEvents As EnvDTE.WindowEvents
<System.ContextStaticAttribute()>
    Public WithEvents TaskListEvents As EnvDTE.TaskListEvents
<System.ContextStaticAttribute()>
    Public WithEvents FindEvents As EnvDTE.FindEvents
<System.ContextStaticAttribute()>
    Public WithEvents OutputWindowEvents As EnvDTE.OutputWindowEvents
<System.ContextStaticAttribute()>
    Public WithEvents SelectionEvents As EnvDTE.SelectionEvents
<System.ContextStaticAttribute()>
    Public WithEvents SolutionItemsEvents _
        As EnvDTE.ProjectItemsEvents
<System.ContextStaticAttribute()>
    Public WithEvents MiscFilesEvents As EnvDTE.ProjectItemsEvents
<System.ContextStaticAttribute()>
    Public WithEvents DebuggerEvents As EnvDTE.DebuggerEvents
'Event Sources End
'End of automatically generated code
#End Region

End Module
```

This sets up the types of IDE events you can hook into. Now if you open the
EnvironmentEvents module in your MyMacros folder, you can select the
BuildEvents from the Class Name drop-down (the left drop-down box above
the code). Then from the right Method Name drop-down, you can select
one of four build events to hook into:

OnBuildBegin
> Will fire when any build operation is fired from the IDE. It fires only
> once for a full solution or multiproject build operation.

OnBuildDone
> Will fire when a build operation completes. This event fires only once
> for a full solution or multiproject build operation.

OnBuildProjConfigBegin
> Will fire when a project build begins. This event is used to catch each
> project build event within a solution or multiproject build operation.

OnBuildProjConfigDone

Will fire when a project build completes. This event is used to catch the completion of each project build within a solution or multiproject build operation.

 These events fire even if build errors or warnings occur, and the default behavior of Visual Studio is to build all projects in a solution even if projects earlier in the build have failed.

For an example, you can add the capability to stop the build process when a project fails and display a message box in the IDE to note when the build process is complete (in case someone isn't paying attention to the Build output).

Canceling a failed build. The normal behavior of Visual Studio is to build every project in a solution, even if one or more of those projects fails. If you have a half-dozen projects in your solution, then this can sometimes take a little while. It is much faster if the build quits when any of the projects fails. By handling a build event, you can ensure that.

Start by selecting the OnBuildProjConfigDone event from the Method Name drop-down above the code. The Macro IDE will automatically generate the method signature to hook the event:

```
Private Sub BuildEvents_OnBuildProjConfigDone( _
        ByVal Project As String, _
        ByVal ProjectConfig As String, _
        ByVal Platform As String, ByVal SolutionConfig As String, _
        ByVal Success As Boolean) _
            Handles BuildEvents.OnBuildProjConfigDone
    End Sub
```

Since this event will fire whenever a project completes a build, you can easily stop the rest of the build from occurring by using the `ExecuteCommand` method of the DTE object to send a `Build.Cancel` command to the IDE. The DTE object **[Hack #86]** is a reference to the Visual Studio IDE, and using `DTE.ExecuteCommand` method to cancel the build is the same as hitting Ctrl-Break during a build or typing `Build.Cancel` into the IDE command window. Using the Success parameter of the event signature, you can determine whether you want to stop the build. The code looks like this:

```
Private Sub BuildEvents_OnBuildProjConfigDone( _
        ByVal Project As String, ByVal ProjectConfig As String, _
        ByVal Platform As String, ByVal SolutionConfig As String, _
        ByVal Success As Boolean) _
```

```
            Handles BuildEvents.OnBuildProjConfigDone
    If Success = False Then
        'The build failed...cancel any further builds.
        DTE.ExecuteCommand("Build.Cancel")
    End If
End Sub
```

Alert the user on a successful build. Now, the idea was to capture the end of the build process to alert the user that the build was complete. For that you hook into the OnBuildDone event the same way you did for the project build complete. This time, you'll use a standard Windows message box to display an informative alert:

```
Private Sub BuildEvents_OnBuildDone( _
    ByVal Scope As EnvDTE.vsBuildScope, _
    ByVal Action As EnvDTE.vsBuildAction) _
        Handles BuildEvents.OnBuildDone
    'Alert that we finished building!
    System.Windows.Forms.MessageBox.Show("Build is complete!")
End Sub
```

These are some pretty simple examples, but you have the power of the .NET Framework in your hands for any of these events so you are limited only by what you can come up with to handle. You can share these with other developers by just sending them the code to include in their own macro project or take it a step further and create a Visual Studio add-in that hooks these events and distribute it that way. If you take a look at the other IDE events you can tap into, you will understand why the Visual Studio IDE is so extensible.

Something to consider when you are implementing custom build events is that they are handled within the IDE only. Build events implemented using the extensibility of the IDE (macros or add-ins) will not fire if the build is run from the command line [Hack #78]. However, pre and post build event commands will execute even if the build is being run via the command line with devenv.exe /build. This could be important if you want to automate your build process on a build machine.

—Michael Wood

Modify the Build Output and Navigate the Results

Find out how to add your own information into the build output, as well as get more out of the standard results by jumping directly to source of the problem.

The build output window is very important to developers. It tells us when we have errors and warnings in our builds, provides a means of tracking those issues down, and gives us a view into the progress of the build process.

Modifying the Build Output Results

You have the capability of modifying the output of the build results to provide some extra information. All you need to do is tap into the build events [Hack #34] and add your own output. For example, a failed build of a project looks like the screen shown in Figure 4-27.

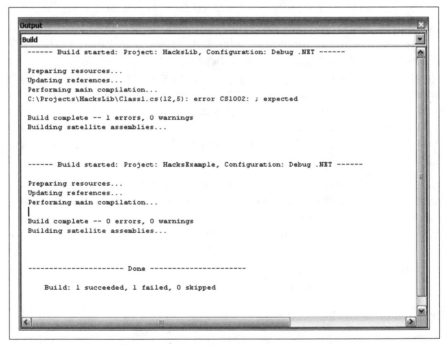

```
Output                                                                    ×
Build                                                                     ▼
------ Build started: Project: HacksLib, Configuration: Debug .NET ------

Preparing resources...
Updating references...
Performing main compilation...
C:\Projects\HacksLib\Class1.cs(12,5): error CS1002: ; expected

Build complete -- 1 errors, 0 warnings
Building satellite assemblies...


------ Build started: Project: HacksExample, Configuration: Debug .NET ------

Preparing resources...
Updating references...
Performing main compilation...
|
Build complete -- 0 errors, 0 warnings
Building satellite assemblies...


-------------------- Done --------------------

    Build: 1 succeeded, 1 failed, 0 skipped
```

Figure 4-27. Failed build output

If you use the hack to stop a build process when one of the project builds fail [Hack #34], then on a large solution build, you'll want to know exactly which project is causing the build to die. Starting with the code from *"Customize Your Project Build Process"* [Hack #34], the code in the Macro Explorer looks like this:

```
Private Sub BuildEvents_OnBuildProjConfigDone( _
        ByVal Project As String, _
        ByVal ProjectConfig As String, _
        ByVal Platform As String, _
        ByVal SolutionConfig As String, _
        ByVal Success As Boolean) _
        Handles BuildEvents.OnBuildProjConfigDone
    If Success = False Then
        'The build failed...cancel any further builds.
        DTE.ExecuteCommand("Build.Cancel")
    End If
End Sub
```

You want to add some code to add a little more information into the output window. To do this, you simply need to add the following lines of code:

```
Dim win As Window = _
    DTE.Windows.Item(EnvDTE.Constants.vsWindowKindOutput)
Dim OW As OutputWindow = CType(win.Object, OutputWindow)
OW.OutputWindowPanes.Item("Build").OutputString( _
    String.Format( _
    "Build Stopped with a failure on the {0} project. {1}", _
    Project, _
    System.Environment.NewLine))
```

This code gets a reference to the output windows, then the Build output windows specifically. It then uses the OutputString method to write out a formatted string indicating that the build failed and on what project.

 The default Visual Studio settings will open the Task List window when a build fails. This action usually hides the output window completely, so you will need to first close the Task List window to see the output or configure Visual Studio to not automatically open the task list through Tools → Options → Project and Solutions → "Show Task List window if build finishes with errors".

The final code looks like this:

```
Private Sub BuildEvents_OnBuildProjConfigDone( _
    ByVal Project As String, _
    ByVal ProjectConfig As String, _
    ByVal Platform As String, _
    ByVal SolutionConfig As String, _
    ByVal Success As Boolean) _
        Handles BuildEvents.OnBuildProjConfigDone
    If Success = False Then
        Dim win As Window = _
      DTE.Windows.Item(EnvDTE.Constants.vsWindowKindOutput)
      Dim OW As OutputWindow = CType(win.Object, OutputWindow)
      OW.OutputWindowPanes.Item("Build").OutputString( _
        String.Format( _
```

```
"Build Stopped with a failure on the {0} project. {1}", _
        Project, System.Environment.NewLine))
        'The build failed...cancel any further builds.
      DTE.ExecuteCommand("Build.Cancel")
      DTE.ExecuteCommand("View.Output")
    End If
End Sub
```

The output on a failed build now looks like the screen shown in Figure 4-28.

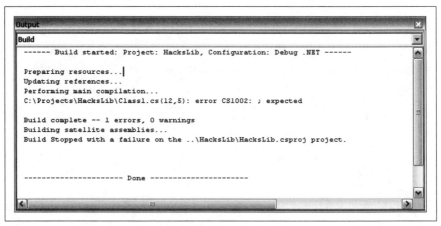

Figure 4-28. Failed build output with custom information

Of course, on a single project build this hack doesn't help much, but if you have a large number of build errors this little hack will quickly show you at the bottom of your results which project is the culprit.

You can use this technique to write information to any of the IDE windows you wish. Just modify which window you assign to the variable win by altering the constant value for the window, or change the item you are looking for in the OutputWindowPanes collection (to write to the Database output window, for example). By altering the output to the Build output window, you can provide yourself with more information about the build, including the progress of any processes you have added.

Navigate Build Results with the Output Window

By default, Visual Studio will list all of the build warnings and errors as tasks within the Task List window after a build. This task list can then be used to navigate to the specific lines of code that are causing those warning and errors; however, there is also another way to navigate the build results—by using the build results in the Build output window.

To navigate the errors listed in the Build output window if the build results have scrolled in the window, you can use the F8 key (Edit. GoToNextLocation) to move the next error or warning and Shift-F8 (Edit. GoToPreviousLocation) to move to the previous one. This will also bring up the source file and position the cursor on the error.

You can also double-click on an error or warning listed in the Build output window and the IDE will bring up that source code file and place the cursor on the line indicated by the build results. The same effect can be accomplished by right-clicking the Build output window line and choosing Go To Error or Go To Tag for the same result.

—Michael Wood

CHAPTER FIVE

Debugging
Hacks 36–43

The ability to debug an application is arguably what turns an excellent text editor into an interactive development environment. Without debugging, Visual Studio is really just a feature-rich text editor that allows you to compile applications. With debugging, Visual Studio turns into an invaluable development tool. If I were to argue the merits of using an IDE versus using just a normal text editor to develop applications, debugging would be one of the pillars of my argument.

Visual Studio provides a rich debugging experience. You can set breakpoints in your code, step through application execution line by line, and read and set the value of variables while the application is executing.

The hacks in this chapter show you how to get the most out of debugging with Visual Studio. You will learn how to set breakpoints, troubleshoot breakpoints, and halt the execution of your application when exceptions are thrown. You will also learn how to debug scripting languages like Java-Script and VBScript, as well as how to debug T-SQL that's running on an instance of SQL Server.

This chapter will help you learn how to better debug your applications, leading to more productive development and more efficient bug resolution.

 All of the code discussed in this chapter can be downloaded from the book's web site (see the Preface for more details).

Set Breakpoints

HACK
#36

Visual Studio's breakpoints appear pretty trivial at first, but you can create some that have quite a bit of intelligence.

Visual Studio offers a powerful debugger to aid with testing and trouble-shooting your applications. One of the most common uses of a debugger is to set *breakpoints*, which are positions in the code that, when reached, cause the program execution to pause, allowing the developer to inspect the code and state of the program. When a breakpoint is reached and the application suspended, the application is in *break mode*. In break mode, you, the developer, can examine and change the values of the program variables. With Visual Studio 2005, you can even change the program's code during this time.

In its simplest form, a breakpoint interrupts program execution whenever it is reached. However, Visual Studio allows for more intelligent breakpoints, ones that suspend the program only if a certain condition has been met or if the breakpoint has already been passed over a certain number of times.

Enter Break Mode Whenever a Particular Line of Code Is Reached

Developers often want to suspend their program's execution and enter break mode when a specific line of code is reached, such as the first line of code for a particular method or a line of code inside a conditional statement. The simplest way to add a breakpoint to a particular line of code is to click in the margin for that line of code. As Figure 5-1 shows, this will add a red circle in the margin, indicating that a breakpoint has been set

Figure 5-1. Breakpoint set for a specific line of code

Clicking in the margin toggles the breakpoint for that line of code, so to remove a breakpoint, click the red circle. The F9 key (Debug.ToggleBreakpoint) will also toggle the breakpoint for the line of code on which the cursor is located.

Breakpoints can also be added through the New Breakpoint dialog. To launch the New Breakpoint dialog, go to the Debug menu and choose the New Breakpoint menu option or press Ctrl-B (Debug.NewBreakpoint). This will display the New Breakpoint dialog shown in Figure 5-2.

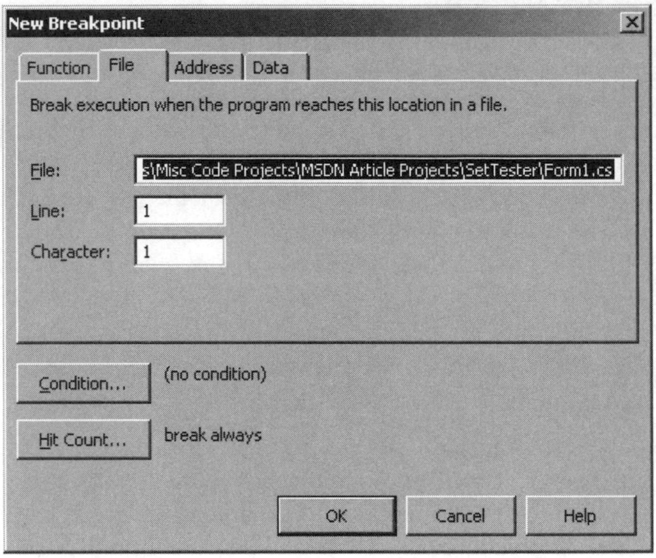

Figure 5-2. New Breakpoint dialog—File tab

The New Breakpoint dialog has four tabs:

Function
Used to add a breakpoint to a specific line of a specific function.

File
The tab shown in Figure 5-2; adds a breakpoint to a specific line in a specific file in the solution.

Address
Adds a breakpoint to a specific memory address. Commonly used when debugging unmanaged code.

Data
Used to add a breakpoint on a variable. When the variable changes, the breakpoint will be hit. Data breakpoints can be used only when debugging unmanaged code.

To add a breakpoint to a specific line of code, use the File tab. As Figure 5-2 shows, the File tab prompts you for the file and the line number for the breakpoint.

Enter Break Mode When a Function Is Called

In addition to being able to break on a particular line of code, Visual Studio makes it easy to break when a particular function is invoked. From the

Function tab of the New Breakpoint dialog—shown in Figure 5-3—you can enter the name of the function where the breakpoint should be added.

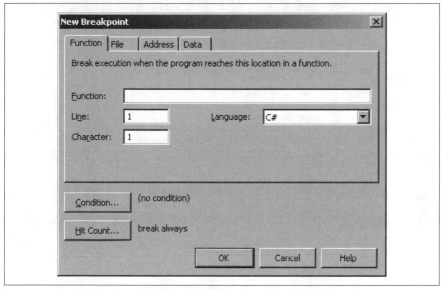

Figure 5-3. New Breakpoint dialog—Function tab

In order to set the breakpoint, the function name needs to be fully qualified. That is, you need to specify the function name as: namespace.class. methodName. For example, suppose you have a C# Solution named skmDataStructures, which contains, among others, a class named BST with a method named Add. To place a breakpoint at this method, simply type in the function name as **skmDataStructures.BST.Add**. However, if you type in just the method name or the class name and method name, Visual Studio is smart enough to determine the fully qualified name. In fact, if there are any conflicts, you will be prompted to select to what method(s) to add break points, as shown in Figure 5-4.

You can also configure the debugger to break on a particular function call by using the Call Stack window. When in debug mode, display the Call Stack window by going to the Debug menu's Window submenu and choosing the Call Stack menu option. The Call Stack, as its name implies, lists the functions on the call stack, along with the parameter types and values. To add a breakpoint through the Call Stack window, right-click on the function name and choose the Insert Breakpoint option from the context menu, as shown in Figure 5-5.

Adding breakpoints through the Call Stack window is a handy technique when debugging recursive functions.

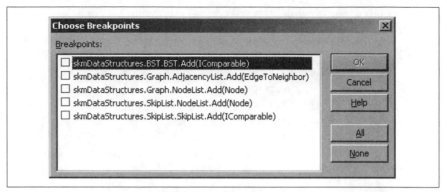

Figure 5-4. Choose to add a breakpoint to any of the matching function names

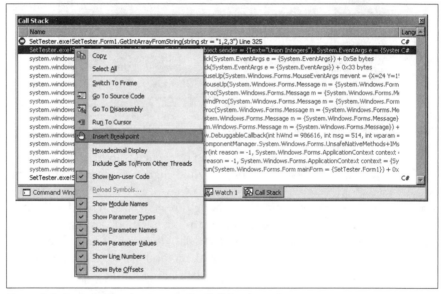

Figure 5-5. Inserting breakpoints via the Call Stack window

Review Breakpoints in the Breakpoints Window

The Breakpoints window provides a list of the current breakpoints and allows you to enable or disable breakpoints, delete breakpoints, add new breakpoints, and edit the properties of existing breakpoints. To display the Breakpoints window, go to the Debug menu's Windows submenu and select the Breakpoints option. You can also display this window by pressing Ctrl-Alt-B (Debug.Breakpoints). Figure 5-6 shows the Breakpoints window.

To add a new breakpoint, click the New icon in the upper-left corner, which will display the New Breakpoint dialog. To delete a breakpoint, select the

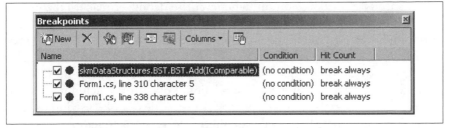

Figure 5-6. Manage breakpoints through the Breakpoints window

breakpoint and click the Delete icon or delete all breakpoints in one go by clicking the Clear All Breakpoints icon or pressing Ctrl-Shift-F9 (Debug. ClearAllBeakpoints). From the Breakpoints window, you can disable breakpoints without deleting them, either by unchecking a particular breakpoint or by clicking the Disable All Breakpoints icon. To edit a breakpoint, select the breakpoint and click the Properties icon, or right-click on the breakpoint from this window and choose the Properties option. This will display the Breakpoint Properties dialog, which is analogous to the New Breakpoint dialog, but with the selected breakpoint's values shown.

Break Only on Certain Conditions

Breakpoints in Visual Studio can be configured to cause the program to enter break mode only when a particular condition holds. To add a condition to a breakpoint, view the breakpoint's properties by selecting the breakpoint from the Breakpoints window and clicking on the Properties icon. From any of the tabs, you will find a button titled Condition. Clicking on this will display the Breakpoint Condition dialog, where you can specify the condition to be watched. Figure 5-7 shows the Breakpoint Condition dialog.

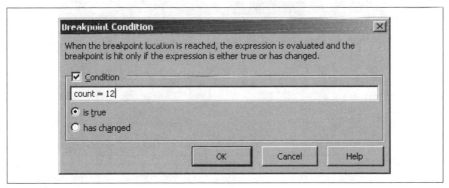

Figure 5-7. Add a condition to a breakpoint in Breakpoint Condition dialog

If you specify a break condition, whenever the debugger reaches the breakpoint, it evaluates the condition, and if the condition is met, the program enters break mode. If, however, the condition is not met, then the program continues execution. The break condition specified can be any valid debugger expression, which may include the relational operators <, >, ==, !=, and so on, along with many nonrelational operators, including +, -, &&, ||, and so on. Variables as well as object properties can be used in expressions. For a complete list of valid debugger expressions, refer to:

http://msdn.microsoft.com/library/default.asp?url=/library/en-us/vsdebug/html/vchowusingexpressionsindebugger.asp

Finally, the breakpoint condition can be configured so that the program enters break mode when the condition is true or when the condition has changed.

Control How Often to Break on a Breakpoint

Breakpoints, by default, cause the program to enter break mode whenever they are hit and their condition, if any, is met. However, you can configure a breakpoint to enter break mode based on the breakpoint's *hit count*. The hit count of a breakpoint is the number of times the breakpoint has been reached and the condition, if specified, has been met. Through the Breakpoint Properties dialog box, you can indicate when a breakpoint should cause the program to enter break mode based on its hit count value.

To configure this information, open up the properties for a breakpoint and click the Hit Count button Clicking on this button will display the Breakpoint Hit Count dialog, shown in Figure 5-8.

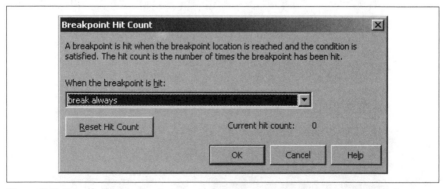

Figure 5-8. Specify the breakpoint's break behavior in Breakpoint Hit Count dialog

From the Breakpoint Hit Count dialog, you can specify how often a breakpoint should cause the program to break. As you can see in Figure 5-8, the default is to break always. You can, however, specify it to break when the hit count equals, is a multiple of, or is greater than or equal to a specified value, as shown in Figure 5-9.

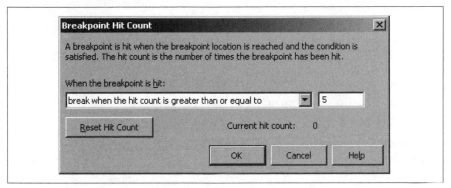

Figure 5-9. Breakpoint Hit Count set to greater than or equal to 5

With this setting, the breakpoint won't cause the program to enter break mode until it has been reached five times. The hit count technique is especially useful when you want to place a breakpoint within a loop, but are interested in breaking only in specific cycles of the loop. For example, if you wanted to break only after the loop had iterated a dozen times, you could set the breakpoint to break only when its hit count was greater than or equal to 12. You could also configure the debugger to stop on each tenth iteration of the loop by configuring the breakpoint to break only when its hit count is a multiple of 10.

A large part of the life cycle of a computer program is testing and debugging. Visual Studio's powerful debugger enables developers to rapidly debug applications. One of the most common tools used in debugging are breakpoints. Breakpoints in Visual Studio can be added to specific lines of code or particular functions and can be given conditions on when to break and how often, based on a hit count.

—Scott Mitchell

Troubleshoot Breakpoints

Use an online web application to figure out why your breakpoints aren't working.

In "Set Breakpoints" [Hack #36], we discussed the various ways to set and use breakpoints, but sometimes your breakpoints just don't work. Andy Pennell, the development lead at Microsoft responsible for the Visual Studio debugger, has created a small web application that will help you troubleshoot problems with your breakpoints. To use this tool, you simply answer the questions and then follow any steps or recommendations that the tool makes. Let's take a look at the tool in action.

The breakpoint helper can be found at *http://www.controlav.com/bphelper* and is shown in Figure 5-10.

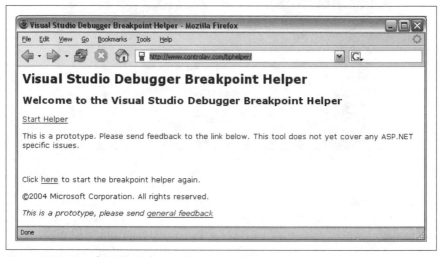

Figure 5-10. Visual Studio Debugger Breakpoint Helper

To start using the helper, simply click Start Helper. The next screen asks you what version of Visual Studio you are using and is shown in Figure 5-11.

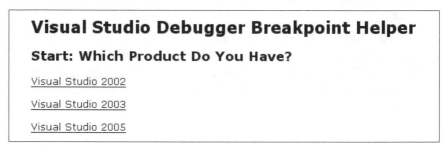

Figure 5-11. Which Product Do You Have?

Select the version of Visual Studio that you are currently using. For this example, I am going to select Visual Studio 2003. The next screen asks you what kind of breakpoint you are currently using and is shown in Figure 5-12.

For this example, I am going to select File/Line, the most common type of breakpoint. The next screen asks what kind of code this breakpoint is set on and is shown in Figure 5-13.

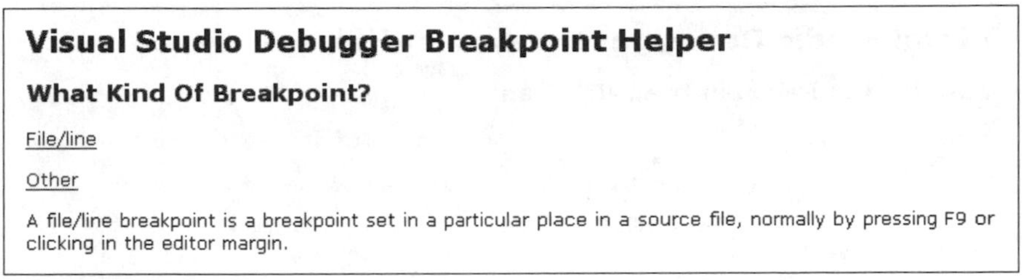

Visual Studio Debugger Breakpoint Helper

What Kind Of Breakpoint?

File/line

Other

A file/line breakpoint is a breakpoint set in a particular place in a source file, normally by pressing F9 or clicking in the editor margin.

Figure 5-12. What Kind of Breakpoint?

Visual Studio Debugger Breakpoint Helper

What kind of code is your breakpoint set in?

Native code

Managed code

Other (e.g. Script, T-SQL)

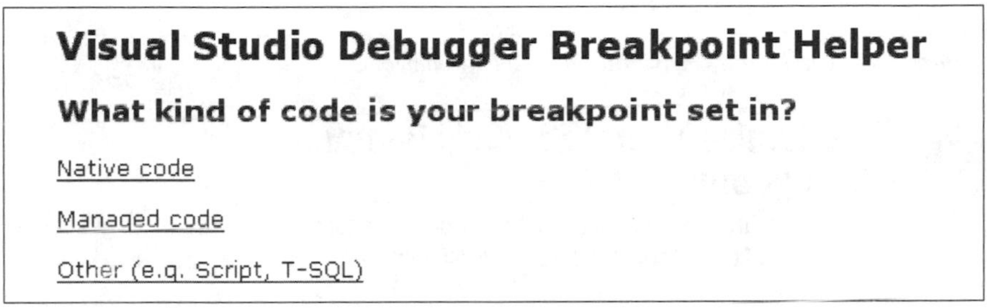

Figure 5-13. What kind of code is your breakpoint set in?

From here, I am going to choose Managed Code. The next screen asks whether any breakpoints are working and is shown in Figure 5-14.

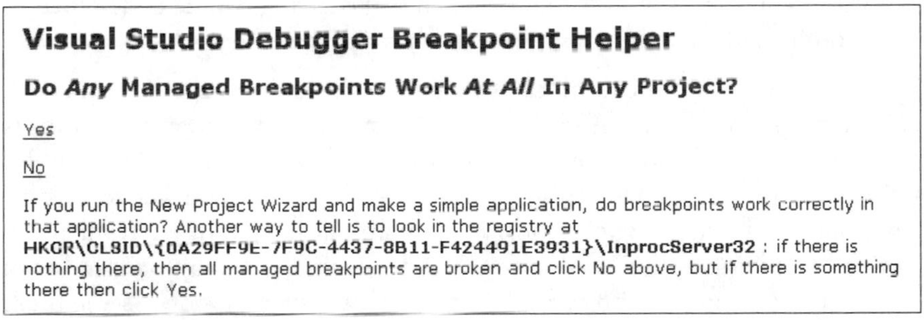

Visual Studio Debugger Breakpoint Helper

Do *Any* Managed Breakpoints Work *At All* In Any Project?

Yes

No

If you run the New Project Wizard and make a simple application, do breakpoints work correctly in that application? Another way to tell is to look in the registry at **HKCR\CLSID\{0A29FF9E-7F9C-4437-8B11-F424491E3931}\InprocServer32** : if there is nothing there, then all managed breakpoints are broken and click No above, but if there is something there then click Yes.

Figure 5-14. Do Any Managed Breakpoints Work At All In Any Project?

This step tells you to try creating a new blank project and see if the breakpoints work in that project. Let's suppose that they don't work in the new project either, so I click No and then see the screen in Figure 5-15.

The breakpoint helper has determined that I would need to reinstall the .NET framework to fix this issue. The breakpoint helper is a very valuable tool and should be the first place you turn whenever you have problems with your breakpoints not working correctly.

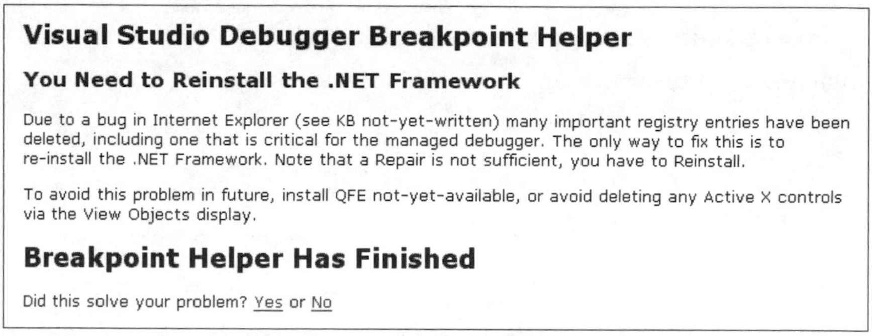

Visual Studio Debugger Breakpoint Helper

You Need to Reinstall the .NET Framework

Due to a bug in Internet Explorer (see KB not-yet-written) many important registry entries have been deleted, including one that is critical for the managed debugger. The only way to fix this is to re-install the .NET Framework. Note that a Repair is not sufficient, you have to Reinstall.

To avoid this problem in future, install QFE not-yet-available, or avoid deleting any Active X controls via the View Objects display.

Breakpoint Helper Has Finished

Did this solve your problem? Yes or No

Figure 5-15. You Need to Reinstall the .NET Framework

HACK #38 Customize Visual Studio's Reaction to Exceptions

Exceptions are a sometimes-frustrating part of debugging and developing. You can configure Visual Studio to deal differently with certain exceptions.

When debugging a program in Visual Studio, a number of situations may cause the debugger to enter break mode. When the debugger enters break mode, program execution is suspended, allowing you—the developer—the opportunity to examine and change the program variables. With Visual Studio 2005, you can even alter the program's underlying source code when in break mode and have the program continue with the edited source.

A common way that break mode is entered is through breakpoints [Hack #36]. Another way that break mode is regularly entered is when an exception is raised that is not handled by your application. Any exception that bubbles up out of your user code will cause the Visual Studio debugger to display information about the exception. While you will likely always want to be notified of an unhandled exception when debugging, you may want to break when an exception is thrown, regardless of whether or not it's handled. Visual Studio can be easily customized to break immediately when a particular type of exception is thrown.

Use the Exceptions Dialog Box

To customize Visual Studio's behavior when encountering exceptions, go to Debug → Exceptions or press Ctrl-Alt-E (Debug.Exceptions). This will display the Exceptions dialog, shown in Figure 5-16.

The Exceptions dialog allows you to specify Visual Studio's behavior when encountering an exception of a specific type. As discussed earlier, the default

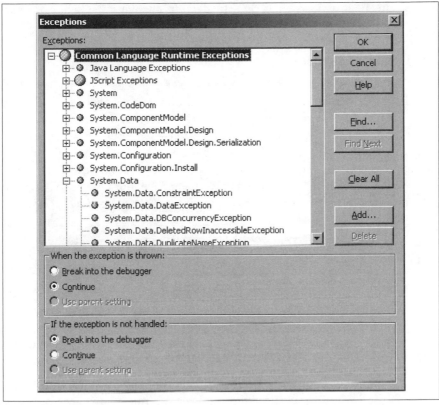

Figure 5-16. Exceptions dialog

behavior is to continue when the exception is thrown and to break into the debugger if the exception is not handled. To modify these settings for a particular exception type, simply choose the exception type from the tree of exceptions and customize the radio buttons, indicating the debugger's behavior.

> The Express versions of Visual Studio 2005 do not offer the complete debugging experience provided by the full version of Visual Studio 2005. At the time of this writing, the Express versions allow specifying the exception behavior only for *all* exceptions, not for specific ones as shown in the Exceptions dialog in Figure 5-16.

Understand that changing the setting for a particular exception modifies the behavior for any of those derived exception types whose Use Parent Setting option is selected. By default, all derived exceptions have this Use Parent

Setting checked, which means that, by default, changing the behavior of an exception will propagate those changes to its derived exceptions.

Add Custom Exceptions

The Exceptions dialog allows you to change the debugger's behavior when working with system-defined exceptions, but you may want to tailor the behavior of custom exception types you have created. To accomplish this, select the topmost item in the tree of exceptions—Common Language Runtime Exceptions—and click the Add button. This will display a dialog prompting you to enter the name of your custom exception (see Figure 5-17). The exception name is case insensitive, but be sure to enter the fully qualified name of your exception, including the namespace.

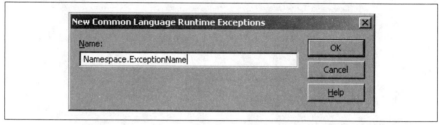

Figure 5-17. Enter the name of your custom exception

Once a custom exception has been added to the list, you can remove it by selecting the exception and clicking the Delete button; you can remove all custom exceptions by clicking the Clear All button.

Quickly Finding Exception Names

While the Exceptions dialog lists the Common Runtime Language exceptions in an easy-to-navigate tree, there may be times when you don't know where in the tree the exception resides, or you may know the name of the exception and don't want to have to scroll through the tree interface. Fortunately, the Exceptions dialog offers a Find button that, when clicked, will prompt you for the name, or part of the name, of the exception.

Once you have entered the exception name and click OK, the Exceptions dialog will highlight those exceptions in the tree that match your search. You can click the Find Next button to enumerate through the matches.

—Scott Mitchell

Debug Scripting Code

Visual Studio isn't just a great IDE, it's a great debugger for all sorts of Windows programming tasks. You can even use it to debug VBScript or JavaScript as it runs inside your web browser.

I spent a lot of time writing web applications without the benefit of Visual Studio. Before ASP.NET, I would usually use a web tool like HomeSite to write web applications. When ASP.NET came out and I started using Visual Studio, I got very spoiled using the debugging capability of Visual Studio for my ASP.NET code, but I always wished I could do the same for JavaScript or VBScript. Thankfully, Visual Studio provides this exact functionality. This hack details how you can set up Visual Studio to debug VBScript and JavaScript while it runs in your browser.

The first thing you have to do to enable debug scripting is to enable script debugging in Internet Explorer 6:

1. Open Internet Explorer.
2. Navigate to Tools → Internet Options.
3. Select the Advanced tab, which is shown in Figure 5-18.
4. Uncheck the box titled "Disable script debugging (Internet Explorer)".

After this checkbox is unchecked, script debugging will be enabled in Internet Explorer.

> It is important to understand that when debugging script code, you are debugging the actual code run by the browser, not your ASP.NET server-side code. When debugging script code, you will be looking at the code the same as you would if you used View → Source in the browser.

Once script debugging has been enabled, you can start debugging a script in a number of different ways. The first option is two menu items that are available in Internet Explorer under the View → Script Debugger menu. From this menu, you can choose Open and you will then be able to jump into the debugger and place breakpoints in your document. The second option is Break at Next Statement, which will cause Internet Explorer to break into the debugger whenever the next piece of script is run.

You can also debug from inside Visual Studio. Open your Web Project in Visual Studio and start the debugger. (You can start the debugger using the Play button, which will launch a new browser, or you can attach to an already existing Internet Explorer instance [Hack #41].) Once the debugger is started, you need to access the Running Documents window. This can be

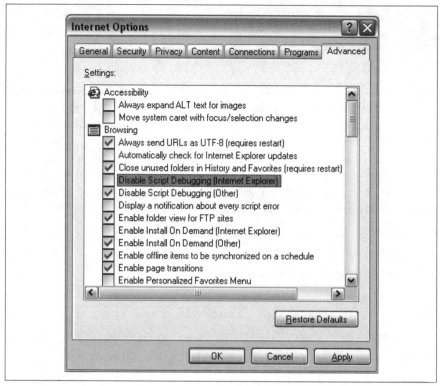

Figure 5-18. Internet Options dialog—Advanced tab

done through the Debug → Windows → Running Documents or by using the shortcut key Ctrl-Alt-N (Debug.RunningDocuments).

The Running Documents window shows a list of all the currently running web documents—usually this contains only a single document. (In the case of frames or iframes, more than one document can show up here.) The Running Documents window is shown in Figure 5-19.

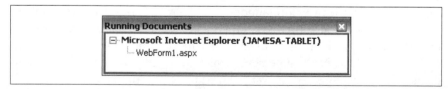

Figure 5-19. Running Documents window

In this window, you need to select the document you want to debug—the rendered HTML output of that document will be shown as a normal HTML file. You will then be able to set breakpoints and step through client-side script just as if it were any other code file, as shown in Figure 5-20.

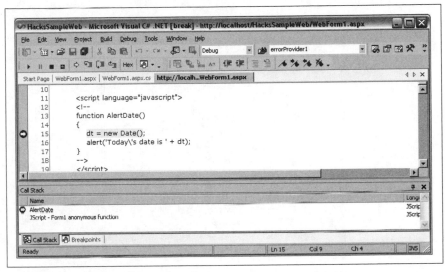

Figure 5-20. Debugging client-side script

Web applications are constantly trying to behave more like their Windows client brethren, and this means more and more client-side scripting. The ability to debug client-side script can save tremendous amounts of time when trying to find bugs in it or when simply trying to understand the flow of the application.

HACK #40 Debug SQL Server

Learn how to use Visual Studio to debug Transact SQL stored procedures or functions.

SQL statements can be difficult to diagnose and debug. SQL Server does not include any default way to debug and step through a stored procedure, but Visual Studio does. Using the Server Explorer, you can step through the execution of a stored procedure or function right inside of Visual Studio. The first step is to open the Server Explorer and create a data connection to your database [Hack #74].

You will then see the stored procedures and functions of your database listed in the Server Explorer; these objects for the Northwind database are shown in Figure 5-21.

From the Server Explorer, you can right-click on a stored procedure or function and you will see a menu item named Step Into Stored Procedure, as shown in Figure 5-22.

When you select Step Into Stored Procedure, you will see the Run Stored Procedure dialog that is shown in Figure 5-23.

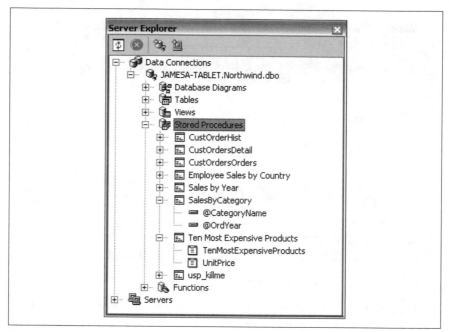

Figure 5-21. Server Explorer—Northwind database

After specifying the values for any parameters the stored procedure has, click the OK button. Visual Studio will now execute the stored procedure and open it in the document window, stopping in the first line of execution. This is shown in Figure 5-24.

You can now step through the stored procedure as it executes. You can set breakpoints just as you would in normal code—the only limitation is that you can specify only location and hit count breakpoints. The applicable debug windows also work. Figure Figure 5-25 shows an example of the Locals window displaying the values of the various parameters.

Because T-SQL is inherently different than .NET languages, the debugging experience is a little bit different. Here are some of the limitations with SQL debugging:

- You can use only location and hit count breakpoints in T-SQL stored procedures and functions.

- You cannot use Step Into to step from .NET managed code to T-SQL. You can set breakpoints in the stored procedure though, and the debugger will break when it comes across them.

- You cannot use Break while a SQL statement is already running.

- You can't use the Set Next Statement function as you might in managed code.

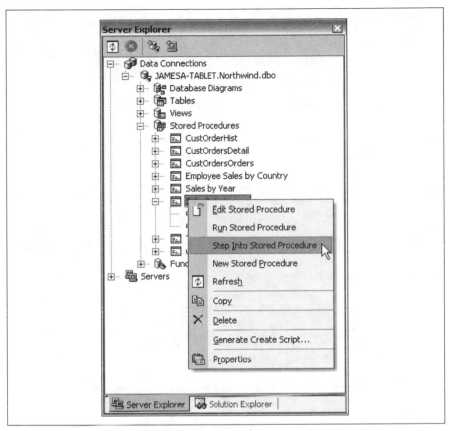

Figure 5-22. Step Into Stored Procedure command

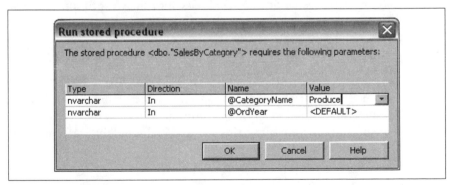

Figure 5-23. Run Stored Procedure dialog

Some other differences are the facts that you can't use the memory or registers windows, as they just don't apply to SQL. Unfortunately, SQL Print statements are not shown in the output window either.

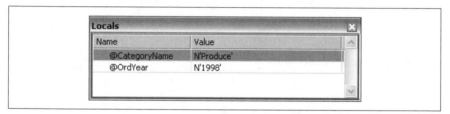

Figure 5-24. Debugging a stored procedure

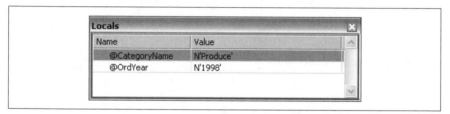

Figure 5-25. Locals window

You cannot run triggers directly, but you can set breakpoints in triggers, and if they are triggered, Visual Studio will break into their execution on those breakpoints.

Running Remote

You can configure Visual Studio and SQL Server to debug stored procedures and functions that are located on a remote server. Enabling this has security implications, and I would not recommend it on a production SQL Server. The process for enabling this feature includes quite a few steps, which are detailed at *http://msdn.microsoft.com/library/default.asp?url=/library/en-us/vsdebug/html/vxlrfSettingUpSQLDebugging.asp*.

Being able to debug T-SQL stored procedures, functions, and triggers can be extremely helpful when trying to find errors or follow the execution of your application.

HACK #41 Debug a Running Process

Avoid having to re-create bugs by attaching directly to a process that you started outside of the IDE's control.

Have you ever found yourself 20 minutes into a test session when you find that you have *finally* reproduced that bug that people have been complaining about for months? But you're not running in the debugger, so you'll never figure out how you got the application in this state. By attaching to the process directly without running your project, you can examine memory, look at the call stack, and work out the bug—all without losing the state of your application.

Attaching to a Process

In order to attach to a running process, you first need to load the project you want to debug. For a Windows Forms application or a service, simply select the Debug → Process menu item (for ASP.NET applications, see the next section). Then select the process you wish to debug from the Processes dialog shown in Figure 5-26. After selecting the process, click Attach.

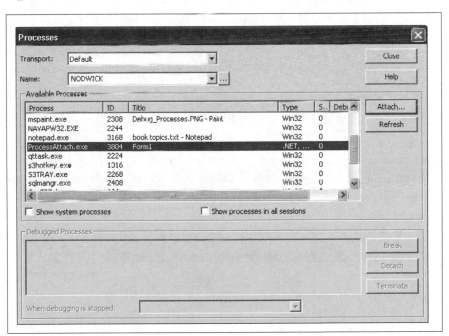

Figure 5-26. Process dialog

You are then prompted to determine which types of code you wish to debug in the Attach to Process dialog, which is shown in Figure 5-27.

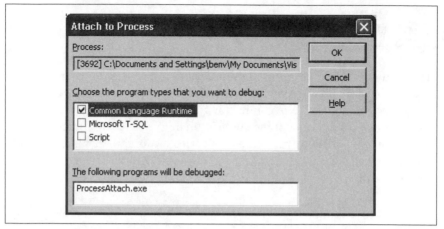

Figure 5-27. Attach to process dialog

You will almost always want to select Common Language Runtime in the list of process types to debug. If you are debugging client-side script and attaching to Internet Explorer, select Script as well. Next, select OK and close the Processes dialog. Your IDE is now connected to the process you selected. You can set breakpoints, watch variables, and participate in any normal debugging task. If the code is in a loop, the Debug → Break All option will stop the application wherever the current execution point is. You can then examine the call stack and variables and determine what may be broken.

Debug ASP.NET Applications Quickly

For those writing ASP.NET applications, the world is even simpler. You will always be attaching to the same process, the ASP.NET worker process. Simply open the Debug → Processes dialog and find the *aspnet_wp.exe* (or *w3wp.exe* on Windows Server 2003) process as shown in Figure 5-28.

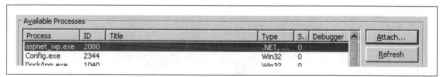

Figure 5-28. Select aspnet_wp.exe for debugging

It's always the same for all ASP.NET applications, since all ASP.NET applications run inside the ASP.NET worker process as opposed to individual processes.

In Windows Server 2003, you can have multiple application
pools; each of these application pools has its own worker
process or worker processes. All of these processes will be
named *w3wp.exe*. This makes attaching to the right process
somewhat difficult. Once you have identified the correct process based on trial and error, you can recognize it based on
its ID.

Connecting to ASP.NET in this way gives you several advantages. You can
start debugging without reinitializing the application and thus losing any in-
process session or cache information. It's also faster—by attaching to the
process, you don't have to wait for the browser to start or navigate back to
where you were in the application. When a bug is discovered, you can simply attach to the process, place your breakpoints, and refresh the browser
window to start the debugging session.

Special Considerations for Services

If you find yourself writing Windows services the only way to debug your
service is by attaching. Simply ensure that the Show System Processes checkbox is checked, and attach to your service.

However, you will find it to be practically impossible to debug the Start
event of the service. The only way to really debug this event is to put a call
to System.Threading.Thread.Sleep(1000) in the beginning of the Start event
to give you time to attach the debugger. This should be done inside of a
#debug block or removed before you move the service to production. You
could also add a call to System.Diagnostics.Debugger.Launch( ), which
would launch an instance of the debugger. Use whichever of these solutions
works best in your situation.

Detaching from a Process

Another option the Debug → Processes dialog gives you is a choice of what
to do when you are done debugging your process—this is shown in
Figure 5-29. Normally, ending debugging will kill a Windows Forms application (assuming you started it from the debugger rather than attaching to it
as before), but that may not always be desirable.

Simply select the process that you are working with and click either the
Detach (peacefully release it) or Terminate (stop debugging and kill the
application) button to disconnect the debugger in the desired fashion.

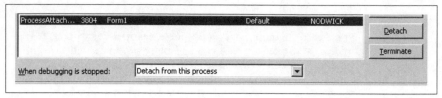

Figure 5-29. Options for detaching from a process

Hacking the Hack

Remember how attaching to an ASP.NET application is so easy because it's always the same process? In fact, it's so easy that even a machine can do it—and you can write a macro to do it for you. Go to Tools → Macros and select Macros IDE. This will open the Macro IDE which is a Visual Studio look-alike specifically for editing Macros. Right-click on My Macros and add a new Module. Name the module "Debugging" or something similar. Then add the following code into the new module:

```
Public Sub AttachToIIS( )
    AttachToProcess("aspnet_wp.exe")
End Sub

Private Sub AttachToProcess(ByVal ProcessName As String)
    Dim Processes As EnvDTE.Processes = DTE.Debugger.LocalProcesses
    Dim Process As EnvDTE.Process

    For Each Process In Processes
        If Process.Name.Substring(Process.Name.LastIndexOf("\") + 1) _
                        = ProcessName Then
            Process.Attach( )
            Exit Sub
        End If
    Next
End Sub
```

Modify the name of the process to *w3wp.exe* if you are using Windows Server 2003. Next, save the module and close the Macro IDE.

Now, in your Visual Studio IDE, go to Tools → Macros → Macro Explorer. Browse into your new module and find the AttachToIIS macro. Double-click to run it, and your project should attach to IIS and go into debugging mode. You could then create a toolbar button and a keyboard shortcut for your macro [Hack #51]. For those of you who are writing a Windows Forms application or a Service and who spend a long time working on the same application, you can clone the AttachToIIS macro to create an AttachToMyApplication macro. (You'll also need to change the application name to match the one you want to debug.)

—*Ben Von Handorf*

HACK #42 Debug a Failing Application

Launch the debugger when an application starts to crash.

Just-in-time debugging, or JIT debugging for short, is the ability to attach to a running program that has failed by throwing an unhandled exception. For instance, you might be testing an application, but not running the application in the debugger, and the application throws an exception. Without JIT debugging, you would have to try and reproduce the error after restarting the application in the debugger. With JIT debugging, you can immediately attach to the program and investigate the exception.

> JIT debugging does not have anything to do with Just-in-time compilation; the abbreviation may mean the same thing but represents vastly different things. Just-in-time compilation is the part of the Common Language Runtime that compiles intermediate language into machine code "just in time" for the machine to process it. (Literally when you call a method, the JIT compiler checks to make sure the code for that method exists; if it does not, then it is compiled from the IL **[Hack #63]**.)

Using JIT Debugging

Using JIT debugging is pretty simple. When you are running an application that throws an unhandled exception, you will see the dialog shown in Figure 5-30.

The Just-in-Time Debugging dialog offers you a number of different debuggers that you can attach to your application based on the debuggers that are currently installed on your machine. The first debugger listed is the instance of Visual Studio that is currently open on my machine. The two versions of the Microsoft CLR Debugger (*DBGCLR.EXE*) are the free debuggers that ship with each version of the .NET framework (1.0 and 1.1). The next two debuggers are the two versions of Visual Studio installed on my machine (2002 and 2003). From this dialog, you can attach the application to any one of these debuggers. If you select a version of Visual Studio and click Yes, the next dialog you will see is shown in Figure 5-31.

The dialog shown in Figure 5-31 is the standard Attach to Process dialog. After clicking the OK button, you will be given the standard exception dialog where you can choose to continue on in the execution of the program or break in the current location.

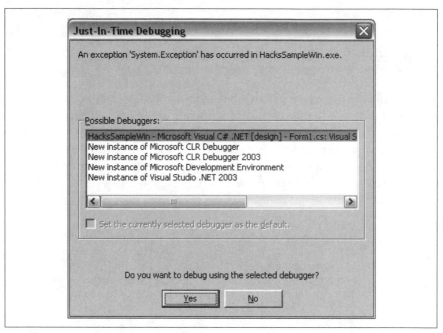

Figure 5-30. Just-in-Time Debugging dialog

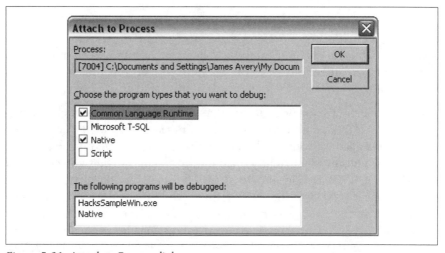

Figure 5-31. Attach to Process dialog

JIT debugging is a valuable feature that can save time when trying to debug hard to find bugs. Knowing how to use and configure this feature will help save you from the frustrating task of re-creating hard to find bugs.

Windows Forms JIT Debugging

When you first try JIT debugging with a Windows Forms application, it probably won't work. By default, Windows Forms will display a dialog that gives you the ability to see the details of the exception, continue, or quit, but not the ability to attach a debugger to the process. To enable JIT debugging with Windows Forms, you will need to add a configuration setting either to the *app.config* of your application or, if you want to enable JIT debugging for all Windows Forms applications, to the *machine.config*. To enable JIT debugging, you need to add the following element inside the <configuration> element:

```
<system.windows.forms jitDebugging="true" />
```

This will enable JIT debugging either for the application (if you added it to the *app.config*) or for all Windows Forms applications on your machine (if you added it to the *machine.config*).

> If your application does not already have an *app.config*, you will need to create one by right-clicking on the project, selecting Add New Item, and then selecting the application configuration file from the list of files.

If you want to modify the *machine.config* file to enable JIT debugging for all Windows Forms applications, the file can be found in the following directory:

```
%SystemRoot%\Microsoft.NET\Framework\v1.1.4322\machine.config
```

The *machine.config* file actually already has this element—it simply needs to be uncommented.

JIT Settings

A number of settings, in both Visual Studio and the registry, allow you to control how JIT debugging works. The first way that you can configure JIT debugging is through the Tool → Options window. Under the Debugging folder is an item for JIT debugging, which is shown in Figure 5-32.

On this screen, you can disable JIT debugging for any of the various program types. Disabling JIT debugging here overrides any settings in your configuration files. When an exception is thrown, you will see a dialog stating that JIT debugging is disabled.

A number of registry settings can also be used to configure JIT debugging and the .NET framework. Both keys are located at:

```
HKEY_LOCAL_MACHINE\SOFTWARE\Microsoft\.NETFramework
```

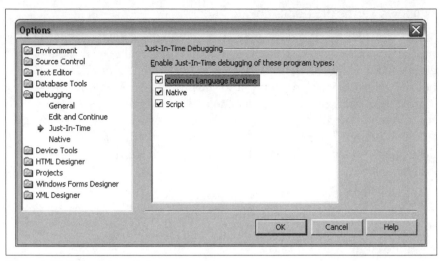

Figure 5-32. Just-in-Time Debugging settings

The first key is called `DbgManagedDebugger` and specifies what application should be launched when an exception is detected. The default value for this is *vs7jit.exe*, which launches the standard Visual Studio .NET JIT debugger dialog that was shown in Figure 5-30. The second key is `DbgJITDebugLaunchSetting`, which specifies what should be done when an unhandled exception is caught. Table 5-1 shows the possible values for this key.

Table 5-1. DbgJITDebugLaunchSetting key values

Value	Behavior
0	Will prompt you with a dialog giving you two options: *OK* Terminates the application *Cancel* Calls the application specified in `DbgManagedDebugger`
1	Disables JIT debugging and passes control back to the application and the default error handler.
2	Control is immediately passed to the application specified in `DbgManagedDebugger`. **This is the default behavior.**

Using the settings available in Visual Studio and the registry, you will be able to configure JIT debugging to your specific needs.

**HACK
#43**

Write a Custom Visualizer

View complex data types with custom visualizers in Visual Studio 2005.

Have you ever been debugging an application and decided that you need to view the contents of a DataSet that is being shown in your Locals or Watch window? Well, if you tried this before Visual Studio 2005, you would have had quite a hard time actually getting to the rows and values of the data-grid—it is no small task. You would need to go from DataSet → Tables → List → [0] (first table in the array) → Rows → List → [0] (row array) → Item Array. You would then see the window shown in Figure 5-33.

Locals	
Name	Value
Item	<cannot view indexed property>
ItemArray	{Length=3}
[0]	"James Avery"
[1]	"Infozerk Inc."
[2]	"555.555.1212"
newRecord	3
oldRecord	-1
RowError	""
rowID	3

Figure 5-33. DataSet in Locals

This view is hard to get to, hard to use, and doesn't even include column names.

Visualizers make this process much easier and more enjoyable. Visualizers provide customized views of data while debugging. Instead of the normal limitations of the debug windows, visualizers are custom Windows Forms that can display the data in any way imaginable. If you had a type that represented an image, you could display the actual image using the visualizer, instead of the text you would normally see in the debugger window.

When you are debugging an application, a small magnifying glass will appear next to the variable in the debugging window if a visualizer exists for that type. You can click on the magnifying glass to launch into the custom visualizer for this type. This can be seen in Figure 5-34.

By clicking on the magnifying glass, you can select a visualizer to use for this data type (there is a drop-down because multiple visualizers can be associated with a single type). This drop-down menu allows you to choose which visualizer you want to use.

After choosing the DataSet Visualizer, you will see your DataSet displayed in an easy-to-view form, as shown in Figure 5-35.

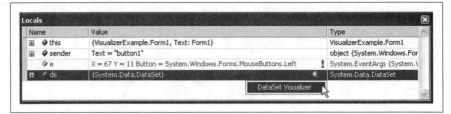

Figure 5-34. Visualizer icon

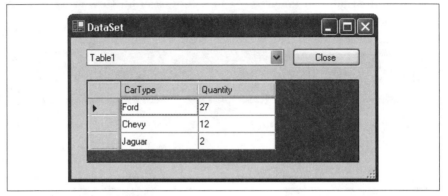

Figure 5-35. DataSet Visualizer

As you can see, the visualizer provides an easy-to-understand view of the data contained in the DataSet.

Write Your Own

By this point, you may be thinking, "Hey, I have complex types that I use all the time and I wish I could write a visualizer for them." Well, you can. In this section, I am going to cover how to do exactly that by writing a visualizer for a simple class called Car that includes four properties with the following names: CarID, CarMake, CarModel, and EngineType. Because I need to reference the same class from both the visualizer and the application, I am going to put this class in its own project called CarLib.

The first step is to create a new Class Library project in the language of your choice. I am going to call the project CarVisualizer. After creating the project, the next thing you need to do is create a reference to the *Microsoft. VisualStudio.DebuggerVisualizers.dll*, which can be found on the .NET tab of the Add Reference dialog. This assembly contains all of the interfaces and classes that you will need to create a custom visualizer.

Create the visualizer form. The next step is to create a new class, which I will call CarForm. This class will be the form that displays data about the class. Since this is a class library project, you will need to add references to the *System.Windows.Forms* and *System.Drawing* assemblies (Located under the .NET tab in the Add Reference dialog) and then also add a using statement for both namespaces to the top of the class file. Next, you will need to set this class to inherit from Form. Once this is done, you will be able to edit the file just as if it were a form in a Windows Forms Project. When creating your visualizer form, you should create a constructor that takes an instance of your class. This way, when creating the form, you simply need to pass the object from Visual Studio to your form in the constructor.

Create the Visual Studio Interface. After designing the visualizer form, you need to create the class that will interface with Visual Studio. The job of this class is to receive the call from Visual Studio and then create a new instance of your form, passing in the value of the object. To do this, you need to add another class to your project, which I will call DebuggerInterface. The first thing you will need to do is add a using statement for the *System.Diagnostics* namespace; this will give you access to the interface you need to implement. Next, you need to tell your class to implement the IDebugVisualizer interface. Using the smart tag, you can autoimplement this interface explicitly [Hack #8], and Visual Studio will add the following code for you:

```
void IDebugVisualizer.Show(IServiceProvider windowService,
IVisualizerObjectProvider objectProvider, VisualizerUIType uiType)
{
    throw new NotImplementedException();
}
```

Now you need to replace the line throwing a NotImplementedException with actual code: first get your object, and then call your form, passing in the object:

```
Car carClass = (Car) objectProvider.GetObject();
new CarForm(carClass).ShowDialog();
```

When Visual Studio calls your Show method, you will first get the Car class from the object provider using the GetObject() method, and then you will create and show an instance of your custom form class, passing in the object.

Telling Visual Studio about the visualizer. Next, you need to add an attribute to your namespace, but using the assembly: target:

```
[assembly:DebuggerVisualizer(
typeof(VisualizerObjectSource),
typeof(CarVisualizer.DebuggerInterface),
```

```
VisualizerUIType.Modal,
Target = typeof(CarLib.Car),
Description = "Car Visualizer")]
Namspace
```

This attributes parameters specify the following things:

- The first parameter tells Visual Studio what object source to use; in this case the default VisualizerObjectSource should work just fine.
- The second parameter tells Visual Studio the type that should be called.
- The third parameter tells Visual Studio that your visualizer is of type Modal.
- The Target parameter tells Visual Studio the type that your visualizer is written for.
- The Description parameter specifies the text that will be shown in the menu during debugging.

Deploy the visualizer. For Visual Studio to detect and use the visualizer, you will need to copy it to *\Documents and Settings\<username>\Visual Studio\ Visualizers*, which would make the visualizer available only to you; alternatively, you could copy it to *<Visual Studio Install Directory>\Common7\ Packages\Debugger\Visualizers*, which would make it available to all users of your system.

> For now you will also need to add any assemblies that your visualizer uses to the Global Assembly Cache; hopefully this will be fixed before the final release.

Visualizer in action. Now you need to throw together a quick little application that uses your Car class and that you can use to test out the visualizer. The test application will need to reference the CarLib assembly that contains the Car class. The test application simply needs to create a car class and populate its fields.

You can now start the sample application and launch the debugger. When you hover over the Car class, you will see the visualizer in the list, as shown in Figure 5-36.

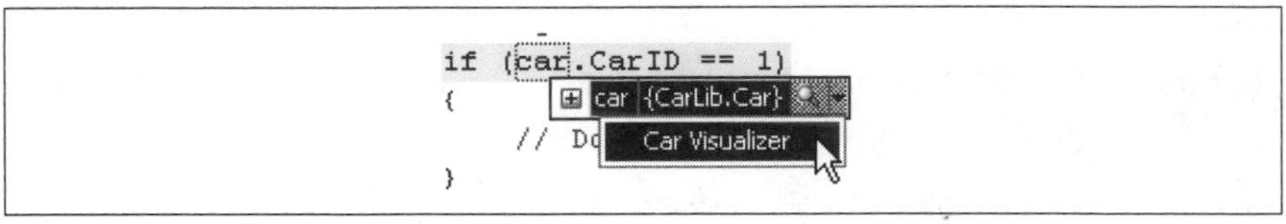

```
if (car.CarID == 1)
{                ⊞ car {CarLib.Car}
    // Do        Car Visualizer
}
```

Figure 5-36. Car Visualizer in the debugger

After you select the visualizer, you will see the custom form with the object's data, as shown in Figure 5-37.

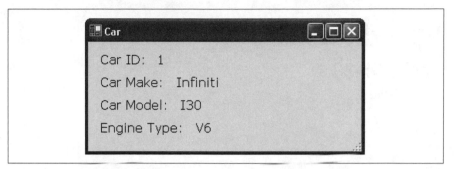

Figure 5-37. Custom visualizer form

Custom visualizers are a great improvement over the limited amount of data you could see in previous versions of Visual Studio. If you have a complex object, it will be well worth the time to write a custom visualizer to make debugging that much easier.

Speed Hacks
Hacks 44–58

Developers are constantly looking for ways to more efficiently write code. We don't want to toil for three hours to write code when we can spend an hour writing something that will create this code for us. Being able to write code faster is not about moving your fingers faster; rather it is about finding more efficient ways to get the same code.

The hacks in this chapter describe a number of different ways to help you more quickly write code and work with Visual Studio. You will learn how to create and run macros that can save you time during the development process. These hacks include macros that will create connection strings, automatically sign assemblies, and update project references. You will also learn how to create and run custom tools that can generate code based on an input file.

Learning how to develop applications faster is also about optimizing your tools. You'll learn how to optimize Visual Studio to start up faster as well, how to load files into the current instance of Visual Studio instead of waiting for a new instance to start up, and how to use the command window.

HACK #44 Speed Up Visual Studio

Visual Studio does a lot—perhaps too much—at startup. Cut out a lot of the less important bits to get into your code that much faster.

No one has ever accused Visual Studio of being the fastest application in the world. One particular sore spot is the time it takes to launch a new instance of Visual Studio. If you are a frequent user of Visual Studio, this is not news to you. There are a couple of things you can do to speed up how Visual Studio starts—although it won't be the fastest app in the world, it will be much more bearable.

Disable the Start Page

The start page is the web page that is displayed by default when Visual Studio first starts up. By default, this page shows a list of recent projects and includes tabs that list online resources and allow you to edit your Visual Studio profile. The start page does not really add any functionality that you can't access somewhere else. The reason the start page is both a security threat and a slowdown factor is that it launches Internet Explorer. Visual Studio .NET 2003 fixes this issue slightly by loading Internet Explorer only if you are using a customized start page, so needless to say, using a customized start page is discouraged.

 Visual Studio 2005 adds a completely new start page that should not affect the startup time of Visual Studio and should not create any security issues.

If you don't get a lot of use out of the start page, it is easily disabled in the Options menu. While the performance gain won't be the same between Visual Studio editions, it will be enough to be worth the effort. To disable the start page, simply go to Tools → Options, then choose General under the Environment folder (General should be selected by default). On the right of that screen, you will see a drop-down where you can specify what Visual Studio should do on startup. I recommend choosing Show Empty Environment; this means Visual Studio will not do anything special on startup.

Turn Off Dynamic Help

Another issue that Visual Studio .NET 2003 helped to resolve was Dynamic Help starting during startup. Dynamic Help is another part of Visual Studio that tends to slow everything down. It is a good idea to make sure the Dynamic Help window is not open when you start up Visual Studio—this is done by simply making sure the window is closed when you close Visual Studio.

If you never really use Dynamic Help, you can disable it completely. To do this, you need to delve into the registry and change the value of the key located here:

*HKEY_CURRENT_USER\Software\Microsoft\Visual Studio\<7.1>\
Dynamic Help*

The name of the key is Never Show DH on F1, and you will need to change the value of this key to YES. Doing this will disable Dynamic Help.

Start from the Run Dialog

As with starting any application, part of the time it takes to start Visual Studio is spent hunting for it in your Start menu. Many developers find it much easier to simply open the Run dialog and enter the name of the application executable. To do this with Visual Studio, all you need to do is open the Run dialog (Windows Key-R or Start → Programs → Run), then type **devenv** and press Enter. This is by far the fastest way to get the application up and running. There is also a switch for devenv called /nosplash, which will suppress the splash page for Visual Studio. So, you can type **devenv /nosplash** into the Run dialog (or the command prompt) to have Visual Studio start up without the splash page.

Keep MRU Lists Under Control

One sure way to slow down the startup of Visual Studio is to have a lot of files and projects in the recent file and recent project lists. This is especially apparent if you have any projects in the MRU list that are located on a network share. Visual Studio checks various file attributes, and if there is a problem with the network connection (or if you're simply not connected to it when you start up), Visual Studio will hang while trying to access these files.

The best thing to do is simply keep these lists under control using the method outlined in "Edit the Most Recent File and Project Lists" **[Hack #13]**. If you notice any slowdowns in startup, a quick trip to VSTweak to clear out these lists is a good idea.

HACK #45   Load Files from the Command Prompt

If you're a command-line junkie, the command prompt can cut down on your mousing. Here's a way to open your files without taking your hands off the keyboard.

VSEdit is a freely available Visual Studio power toy that adds the ability to load files from the command prompt directly into a current instance of Visual Studio. This is definitely a hack for people who still love the command prompt. If you would rather use the mouse and menus, this is not for you.

First, you will need to download and install the VSEdit power toy from:

> *http://workspaces.gotdotnet.com/vsedit*

The installation for this power toy will add a help file and command prompt shortcut to your Start menu, but you really don't need either of these to start using this tool right away.

You can use VSEdit via the shortcut installed in the Start menu or simply open a normal command prompt (Start → Run → type **cmd**), or just use the Start → Run command to open the Run dialog. You can then type **vsedit** followed by the name of an existing file (e.g., **vsedit Form1.cs**). Figure 6-1 shows an example of loading a file using VSEdit.

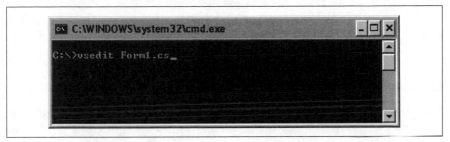

Figure 6-1. Using VSEdit

After you execute this command, VSEdit will then look and see if an instance of Visual Studio is open. If an instance is open, it will load this file into that existing instance of Visual Studio. If not, it will open a new instance and then load this file.

If the file you specify cannot be found, VSEdit will still open an instance of Visual Studio and then report in the command prompt that the file cannot be found. Normal command prompt rules apply—you either need to be in the same directory as the file you want to open or must specify a relative or absolute path to the file.

VSEdit allows you to open multiple files by simply adding them one after another separated by a space. You could type **Vsedit Form1.cs Form2.cs Form3.cs**, and all of these files would be opened in Visual Studio.

VSEdit also has a couple of different switches that can be useful. The first switch is /?, which will provide a brief description on the usage of VSEdit. The second is /c, which can be used to specify the command line that will be used to open Visual Studio. For instance, you could type **vsedit /c "devenv.exe /nosplash" Form1.cs**, and the /nosplash switch would be used when launching Visual Studio. Even when specifying the command, VSEdit will open a new instance only if there is not an already open instance of Visual Studio.

The VSEdit power toy is simple to use—if you are the kind of developer who lives inside the command prompt, then it is right up your alley.

Master the Command Window

Although Visual Studio is, er...well, rather visual, command-line junkies don't need to fear it.

Visual Studio has hundreds of menus, windows, and dialog boxes. This you are probably aware of; what you may not be aware of is that you can avoid using all of these and use the command line inside the command window instead. This hack looks at some of the different commands available to you, how to use existing aliases, and how to create and manage your own aliases.

Command Window Basics

So why would you want to use a command window when you could just use some part of the IDE? Using the command window is sometimes faster than using the IDE, and when you are writing code with both of your hands on the keyboard, it is often easier and faster to type a command than to reach for the mouse. Many people who are used to the good old days of the command prompt find themselves right at home with the command window, but whether or not you are one of these people, I encourage you to explore its functionality.

The main keystroke to remember is Ctrl-Alt-A (View.CommandWindow); this is the shortcut to open the command window.

The open command is the first command I am going to cover. Using the open command, you can open any file in either the filesystem or the current solution. (I think the real added value here is opening a file in the current solution, since the command window provides IntelliSense.) Figure 6-2 shows the command window and the IntelliSense available for the open command.

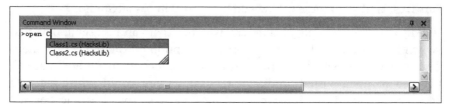

Figure 6-2. Command Window open command

This might not seem like much, but if you have a dozen projects with hundreds of files, this becomes much faster than digging through the Solution Explorer with your mouse.

You can use any Visual Studio command directly through the command window (through this book, whenever we mention a keyboard shortcut, we've also been mentioning the command). Any command can be used through the command window.

Twenty of the most useful commands are shown in Table 6-1. You can either type the full command or use the alias.

Table 6-1. Useful Visual Studio commands and aliases

Command	Alias	Description
File.OpenFile	open	Opens the file specified as a parameter
File.NewFile	nf	Creates and opens a new file
File.NewProject	np	Creates and opens a new project
File.AddNewProject	addProj	Creates and adds a new project to the current solution
File.SaveAll	SaveAll	Saves all the currently open files
File.Close	close	Closes the selected file
View.FullScreen	FullScreen	Switches to full-screen mode in the IDE
View.Toolbox	toolbox	Shows the toolbox window
View.PropertiesWindow	props	Shows the properties window
Edit.GotoBrace	GotoBrace	Skips to the corresponding brace (e.g., the closing brace of an if statement)
Edit.SelectAll		Selects all the text in the current document
Edit.Undo	undo	Equivalent to Edit → Undo
Edit.Redo	redo	Equivalent to Edit → Redo
Edit.NextBookmark	NextBook	Jumps to the next bookmark
Edit.PreviousBookmark	PrevBook	Jumps back to the previous bookmark
Edit.CollapsetoDefinitions	StopOutlining	Collapses all collapsible section of code (classes, regions, etc.)
Build.BuildSolution	build	Builds the current solution
Debug.Print	?	Shows the value of the variable passed in as a parameter
Debug.QuickWatch	??	Displays the quick watch dialog for the variables passed in as a parameter
Tools.Alias	alias	Lists all currently defined aliases or defines a new one

When in doubt, you can sometimes fall back on old MS-DOS command prompt habits: for instance, the command cls will clear the command window. You can find a complete list of commands in the Tools → Options → Keyboard screen [Hack #24].

Debugging with the Command Window

Perhaps the most useful function of the command window is the ability to use it to view the values of variables during the debugging process. You can use a number of different commands during the debugging process to read and set the values of variables. You can simply type a question mark, a space, and then the name of a variable, and when you press Enter, the value of that variable will be printed to the screen. Here is an example of this command:

```
>? i
0
```

In this example, the value of the variable i is zero. You can also set the value of a variable through the command window by using the question mark, a space, the name of the variable, and then an equals sign and the value that you want to set the variable to. Here is an example of setting the value of a variable through the command window:

```
>? i =2
2
```

As an alternative to using the question mark, you can also set the command window to *immediate mode*; this turns the command window into an immediate window and you no longer need to use a question mark. You can set the command window to immediate mode by typing in the command immed. Following is a transcript of using the command window in immediate mode:

```
>immed
i
0
```

To switch the command window back into command mode, you simply need to type in any command prefixed with >. For instance, you could type >cmd and the window would switch back to command mode.

Another benefit to viewing the value of a variable in the command window is that it is easy to copy the value of that variable *out of* the command window. If you are working with a large string of XML, it might be valuable to get the value of that XML document and then copy it to your favorite XML application to view the data in a friendlier format.

Create Window Aliases

Aliases are a way of creating a custom command that is short for a longer command. The Open command shown earlier is actually an alias that Visual Studio defines for the more verbose command File.OpenFile. To create new aliases you simply need to type **alias**, the name of the alias, then the command that you want to execute for this alias. Here is an example of creating an alias for the Edit.SelectAll command:

```
>alias selectall Edit.SelectAll
```

You can now select all the text on the screen by calling the alias selectall. You can also create aliases that include a parameter for a command. You can create a command called openClass1 that calls the File.OpenFile command and also specifies which file to open. Here is an example of this command:

```
>alias openClass1 File.OpenFile Class1.cs
>openClass1
```

This way you can call the openClass1 command at any time to open the *Class1.cs* file. You can also remove aliases that you have already created by simply adding the /delete switch at the end of the alias command. Here is an example of how to remove the openClass1 alias:

```
>alias openClass1 /delete
```

View and Edit Command Window Aliases

While you can create and edit aliases directly in the command window, the VSTweak power toy provides an easy-to-use graphic interface for these command window aliases. Using this interface, you can add, edit, or delete command window aliases.

The VSTweak power toy is one of the more useful power toys for Visual Studio and is the subject of a number of different hacks in this book. The VSTweak power toy **[Hack #13]** can be downloaded from *http://workspaces. gotdotnet.com/vstweak*. Figure 6-3 shows an example of this interface.

Using the Alias Manager, you can create, edit, and delete aliases using a nice graphical interface. The Available Commands button will show all of the available commands that you can create aliases for. The View File button shows the *aliases.ini* file, which stores all of the command window aliases.

The command window offers a lot of features that can be used to increase your productivity while working with Visual Studio, particularly when debugging.

HACK #47 Build a Custom Tool

You can write code, or you can write tools that write code. How much is your time worth?

Custom tools can be used to generate code based on an input file. The most familiar custom tool is probably *xsd.exe*, which will create a strongly typed DataSet based on an XML file **[Hack #49]**. In this hack, I am going to cover how to create your own custom tool that takes an XML file and then generates a piece of code based on that XML. The example I cover here will be somewhat simplistic, but it will demonstrate the basic principles of building a custom tool and will provide you with the information you need to create your own custom tool.

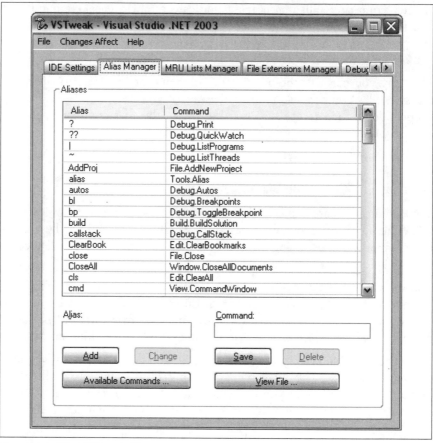

Figure 6-3. The VSTweak Alias Manager

Write the Code

To create a custom tool, you first need to create a new project in the language of your choice and then create a new class in that project. The next thing you need to do is set your class to inherit from a class called BaseCodeGeneratorWithSite.

In Visual Studio .NET 2002, this class was available in the *Microsoft.VSDesigner.dll* assembly. However, starting with Visual Studio .NET 2003, this class was made private and you could no longer inherit from it. Thankfully, someone at Microsoft has made this class available for download from GotDotNet, so before you can inherit from this class, you must first download it from *http://www.gotdotnet.com/Community/UserSamples/Details.aspx?SampleGuid=4AA14341-24D5-45AB-AB18-B72351D0371C.*

The zip file downloaded from this link contains all the code for the class, but all you really need is the *BaseCodeGeneratorWithSite.dll*. Reference this *.dll* from your project, add the using or Imports statement for the CustomToolGenerator namespace, and then you can inherit from the BaseCodeGeneratorWithSite class in your code.

After inheriting from BaseCodeGeneratorWithSite, you will need to implement the abstract method GenerateCode. This is the method where your generator will receive the XML file and where you will need to return the generated code for Visual Studio to include in the project.

Here is what your code should look like so far (this example is in C#, but a Visual Basic example is available in the sample code download—go to *http://www.oreilly.com/catalog/visualstudiohks* to obtain the sample code for this book):

```
using System;
using CustomToolGenerator;

namespace CustomToolProject
{
    public class CustomGenerator : BaseCodeGeneratorWithSite
    {
        protected override byte[] GenerateCode(
            string file, string contents)
        {
            return null;
        }
    }
}
```

Next you will need to implement your GenerateCode method. For this example, I am going to simply return some arbitrary code shown here:

```
protected override byte[] GenerateCode(string file,
                        string contents)
{
    string code = @"using System;
namespace Vehicles
{
public class Car { }
}
";
    return System.Text.Encoding.ASCII.GetBytes(code);
}
```

For Visual Studio to use your generator, you have to register your custom tool as a COM class, which means you need to decorate it with the Guid attribute and include a unique GUID. To get a new GUID, you can use the Tools → Create GUID tool. This generates a new GUID using the registry format and then place it in the Guid attribute on your class. Here is what your code should now look like:

```
using System;
using System.Runtime.InteropServices;
using CustomToolGenerator;

namespace CustomToolProject
{
    [Guid("8696CA73-4FD7-4e5f-B267-48C9F3CB8F07")]
    public class CustomGenerator : BaseCodeGeneratorWithSite
    {
        protected override byte[ ] GenerateCode(string file,
                                    string contents)
        {
            //Code from the preceding example goes here
        }
    }
}
```

Add the Tool to Visual Studio

After you have written the code to generate the code for your custom tool, the next step is to register your custom tool with Visual Studio. The first thing to do is register your class as a COM component using the *regasm* tool. Here are the steps to register your class:

1. Run the Visual Studio Command Prompt (Start → Visual Studio 2003 → Visual Studio .NET Tools → Visual Studio .NET 2003 Command Prompt).

2. Navigate to the directory where your *.dll* file is located (most likely *Your Project/bin/debug*).

3. Type the following command: **regasm /codebase *your_assembly.dll***.

4. Next, you will get a warning if your tool is not signed with a strong name. You can ignore this for now (although signing your tool before distributing it is recommended).

Now that your tool is registered, you need to tell Visual Studio where and what the tool is. This is done through the registry. You will need to add a new key under the following key:

HKEY_LOCAL_MACHINE\SOFTWARE\Microsoft\VisualStudio\<7.1>\ Generators

Under this key, you will find a list of GUIDs. Each of these GUIDs represents a language, and the first step is to find the language that you would like to add your custom tool to. Table 6-2 shows a list of the GUIDs and the languages they correspond to.

Table 6-2. Language GUIDs

GUID	Language
{164B10B9-B200-11D0-8C61-00A0C91E29D5}	VB.NET
{E6FDF8B0-F3D1-11D4-8576-0002A516ECE8}	J#
{FAE04EC1-301F-11d3-BF4B-00C04F79EFBC}	C#

After choosing what language type to add your custom tool to, the next step is to create a new key under that value. This key should be named the same as your custom tool and will need to include three values; these values are shown in Table 6-3.

Table 6-3. Custom tool key values

Name	Type	Description
(Default)	REG_SZ (String)	A description of your custom tool
CLSID	REG_SZ (String)	The GUID for your custom tool (as defined in the Guid attribute)
GeneratesDesignTimeSource	REG_DWORD (DWORD)	Specifies whether your custom tool creates a new file: 1 = True, 0 = False

Figure 6-4 shows the registry keys and values for this example custom tool.

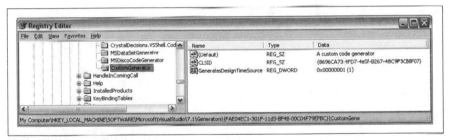

Figure 6-4. Custom tool registry settings

Running the Tool

Now your custom tool should be ready to use. Inside Visual Studio, you can create a file and specify that it should be handled by your custom tool in the Properties window, as shown in Figure 6-5.

Whenever this file is saved, the custom tool will be run and your code will be generated. You can view this generated code by clicking the Show All Files button in the Solution Explorer. You will then see a plus sign next to your file, and when you click that plus sign, you will see the generated file as shown in Figure 6-6.

Figure 6-5. Specifying the custom tool

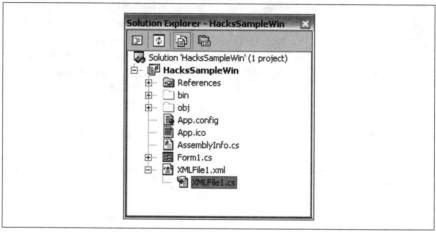

Figure 6-6. Viewing the generated file

You can then double-click on the *.cs* file and view the code that was generated by your custom tool; in my example, you would see the following code:

```
using System;
namespace Vehicles
{
    public class Car { }
}
```

This was a very simple example. Custom tools are limited only by what you can think of to generate; they are very powerful tools and have great potential to save time through code generation.

Extend the Application Configuration File

#48 Use an open source custom tool to add your own configuration sections to your *app.config* file.

Custom configuration sections are a valuable tool for storing application-specific settings. With .NET, you can extend the normal configuration files and include your own custom configuration sections. Normally, creating your own custom configuration section involves writing classes and a configuration section handler to access your custom settings. There is an easier and much quicker way to handle the creation of a custom configuration section and all the code that you need to work with it.

The open source custom tool, ConfigBuilder, can be used to automatically generate configuration section handlers, as well as custom objects that can be used as data containers for the settings.

To use the ConfigBuilder custom tool, you will need to download and run the installation file from *http://workspaces.gotdotnet.com/configbuilder*.

Building the Configuration Template

To start using ConfigBuilder, you first need to add a new XML file to your project. This XML file is called the *configuration template file* and will be used to specify the format of your configuration section. This file will then used to generate the code to access this configuration section. The configuration template can be named whatever you like and should be in the location where you want the code to be stored. (The code will appear underneath this XML file in the Solution Explorer, exactly like other custom tool-generated code.)

The first step to building your configuration template file is to add a root element named configuration, the same as a normal configuration file. Next you will need to declare your custom sections by creating an element for the section and then any number of attributes. The name of the section and the name of the attributes should be the same as the names that will be used in the configuration section, but instead of specifying values, you will need to specify the type that this attribute expects. To specify the type, you will need to use C# type keywords such as string, int, short, and so forth.

Here is an example of declaring a custom section called DatabaseSettings:

```
<configuration>
    <DatabaseSettings server="string"
        username="string" timeout="int" />
</configuration>
```

Extend the Application Configuration File

In this file, I am creating a single element called DatabaseSettings that has three different attributes; the first two are strings and the last is an integer.

You can also define default values for attributes in the template file. In this example, suppose that I want to set a default value for the timeout attribute parameter. I can do this by simply adding a colon after the type and then specifying my default value. My template file would now look like this:

```
<configuration>
    <DatabaseSettings server="string"
        username="string" timeout="int: 60" />
</configuration>
```

By declaring a default value, the attribute is no longer required. If the timeout attribute is omitted in the configuration section for this application config file, the code will simply assume the value is 60. (When declaring default values for strings, you must use [Empty] to signify an empty string.)

You can also specify the number of times a section can appear, create section groups, and specify comments to be included in the generated code. Explanations of these features can all be found in ConfigBuilder's documentation.

Running the ConfigBuilder

To execute the template file and generate the code, you need to specify ConfigBuilder as the custom tool for this file. This is done by simply entering **ConfigBuilder** into the Custom Tool field in the .XML file's property window as shown in Figure 6-7.

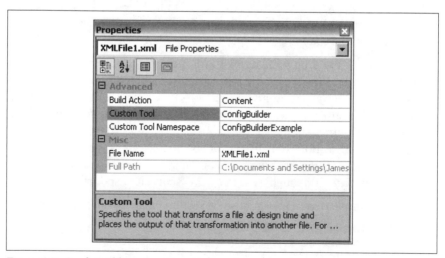

Figure 6-7. ConfigBuilder set as the custom tool

Once ConfigBuilder is specified as the custom tool for this file, it will be run every time the file is saved, regenerating the code based on any changes to the template file.

After you specify ConfigBuilder as the custom tool, a plus sign will appear next to the .XML file. The plus sign can be expanded to show the code that has been generated based on the template. Here is a look at the code generated based on the template from the preceding example (I have removed comments for the sake of brevity):

```
namespace ConfigBuilderExample
{
using System;
using System.Configuration;
using System.Xml;

public sealed class DatabaseSettingsSectionHandler
                 : object, IConfigurationSectionHandler
{

    public const string SectionName = "DatabaseSettings";

    public static DatabaseSettingsConfig Config
    {
      get
      {
        object oConfig = ConfigurationSettings.GetConfig(
              DatabaseSettingsSectionHandler.SectionName);
        if ((oConfig == null))
        {
          throw new ConfigurationException(
          "The application configuration file must have the
          \'DatabaseSettings\' configuration" +
          " section defined.");
        }
        return ((DatabaseSettingsConfig)(oConfig));
      }
    }

    object IConfigurationSectionHandler.Create(object parentConfig,
                    object webContext, XmlNode sectionNode)
    {
      XmlElement sectionElement = ((XmlElement)(sectionNode));
      return DatabaseSettingsConfig.Create(sectionElement);
    }

    internal static object GetValue(XmlElement element,
                          string attributeName,
                          Type attributeType,
                          string defaultVal)
    {
      try
```

```
        {
            string attrVal = element.GetAttribute(attributeName);
            if ((attrVal.Length == 0))
            {
                if ((defaultVal == null))
                {
                    throw new ConfigurationException(String.Format(
                     "Missing value for required attribute \'{0}\' of
                     element \'{1}\'.", attributeName, element.Name));
                }
                attrVal = defaultVal;
            }
            if (attributeType.IsEnum)
            {
                return Enum.Parse(attributeType, attrVal);
            }
            return Convert.ChangeType(attrVal, attributeType,
            System.Threading.Thread.CurrentThread.CurrentCulture);
        }
        catch (ConfigurationException )
        {
            throw;
        }
        catch (Exception ex)
        {
            throw new ConfigurationException(String.Format(
            "Failed to extract value for attribute \'{0}\'
            from element \'{1}\'.", attributeName,
            element.Name), ex);
        }
    }
}

public class DatabaseSettingsConfig
{
    private String _server;
    private String _username;
    private int   _timeout;

    public DatabaseSettingsConfig(String server,
                                  String username,
                                  int   timeout)
    {
        this._server = server;
        this._username = username;
        this._timeout = timeout;
    }

    public String Server
    {
```

```
        get{return this._server;}
    }

    public String Username
    {
        get{return this._username;}
    }

    public int  Timeout
    {
        get{return this._timeout;}
    }

    internal static DatabaseSettingsConfig Create(
                    XmlElement configElement)
    {
        String server = ((String)(
            DatabaseSettingsSectionHandler.GetValue(
            configElement, "server", typeof(String), null)));
        String username = ((String)(
            DatabaseSettingsSectionHandler.GetValue(
            configElement, "username",
            typeof(String), null)));
        int  timeout = ((int )(
            DatabaseSettingsSectionHandler.GetValue(
            configElement, "timeout", typeof(int ), " 60")));
        return new DatabaseSettingsConfig(
                server, username, timeout);
    }
  }
}
```

Using the Code

To use this configuration section in your configuration file, you need to
declare your custom section in the configSections section of the configuration file for your application:

```
<configSections>
    <section name="DatabaseSettings"
        type="ConfigBuilderExample.DatabaseSettingsSectionHandler" />
</configSections>
```

ConfigBuilderExample is the name of my namespace in this example. Next,
you need to actually add your configuration section to the application configuration file:

```
<configuration>
    <DatabaseSettings server="localhost"
        username="notsa" timeout="55" />
</configuration>
```

Then you can read these values from the configuration file using the following code anywhere in your application:

```
DatabaseSettingsConfig config = (DatabaseSettingsConfig)
System.Configuration.ConfigurationSettings.GetConfig(
                        "DatabaseSettings");

MessageBox.Show(config.Server);
```

The first line of this code gets an instance of the DatabaseSettingsConfig class from the configuration file. You can then access any of the configuration settings by simply accessing the properties of this class. In this example, the value of the server element is shown to the user through a message box.

This custom tool is a great time-saver and makes it extremely easy to create and use custom configuration sections.

HACK #49   Generate Strongly Typed DataSets

Make DataSets a little smarter by using Visual Studio and the XSD tool to generate typed DataSets.

ADO .NET's DataSet objects provide powerful functionality when working with data. They allow you to easily scroll, filter, search, and sort data, as well as work with hierarchical data and its relationships. However, your typical DataSet object is untyped, meaning it doesn't really know and understand what it is storing. It's just a smart container for your data. You can make a DataSet object even smarter by turning it into a strongly typed DataSet object.

When working with an untyped DataSet, accessing the value of a row looks something like this:

```
String artistName =
    ds.Tables["Artists"].Rows[0]["Artist"].ToString();
```

When working with a typed DataSet, you will have IntelliSense for the list of tables as well as the column names, and best of all, each property is stored in its correct type. This means you don't need to call ToString() or cast the type when pulling it out of the DataSet. Performing the same operation with a typed DataSet would look like this:

```
string artistName = ds.Artists[0].Artist;
```

Creating a strongly typed DataSet object is done one of three ways: by writing the code yourself, by letting Visual Studio help you, or by using the *xsd. exe* tool. Hand-writing the code to make strongly typed DataSet objects can be long and tedious, so it's best to use one of the other two methods to do the heavy lifting for you.

Let Visual Studio Help

Visual Studio provides a nice shortcut to creating your own strongly typed DataSet objects. Follow these simple steps:

1. Open your Visual Studio Project (or create a new one).
2. Select the project in the Solution Explorer and click the Show All Files button.
3. Right-click on the project in the Solution Explorer, click Add, and select Add New Item.
4. In the Add New Item dialog box, select the DataSet template. In the Name field, type the name of your DataSet (e.g., *Customers.xsd*) and click Open.

You will see that the XSD file was added to your project. There are two things to note here. First, right-click on the XSD file and select Properties. This is where you can specify a custom tool to generate your strongly typed DataSet objects. By default, the custom tool is named MSDataSetGenerator, which is provided out of the box by Visual Studio (see Figure 6-8).

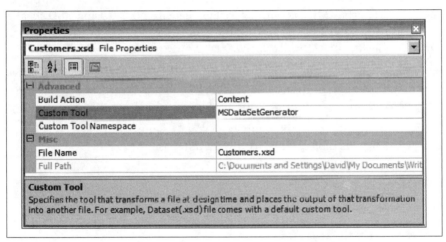

Figure 6-8. Properties of DataSet XSD file

The other thing to know is that the class file for the strongly typed DataSet object was autogenerated for you. You can see it by turning on Show All Files and expanding the XSD file. Figure 6-9 shows that the *Customers.cs* class file was autogenerated to create a DataSet object of type Customers.

Using the xsd.exe Tool

The .NET Framework SDK includes a tool named *xsd.exe* that can be used for a few different reasons; one of the handiest is for creating strongly typed

Figure 6-9. Autogenerated DataSet class file

DataSet objects. The best and easiest way to accomplish this is by first creating your own XML schema definition file (**.xsd*). Because a DataSet object natively supports XML (as with everything else in .NET), using XSD files as the basis for your data and its structure makes the creation of strongly typed DataSet objects rather simple.

Assuming your XSD file is already created, using the *xsd.exe* tool will save you a significant amount of time because it generates your classes automatically based on the information contained in your XML schema definition.

To get started, let's first take a quick look at a sample XSD, which is based on the Customers table in the Northwind database:

```xml
<?xml version="1.0" standalone="yes"?>
<xs:schema id="Customers"
targetNamespace="http://www.tempuri.org/Customers.xsd"
xmlns:mstns="http://www.tempuri.org/Customers.xsd"
xmlns="http://www.tempuri.org/Customers.xsd"
xmlns:xs="http://www.w3.org/2001/XMLSchema"
xmlns:msdata="urn:schemas-microsoft-com:xml-msdata"
attributeFormDefault="qualified" elementFormDefault="qualified">
<xs:element name="Customers" msdata:IsDataSet="true">
<xs:complexType>
<xs:choice maxOccurs="unbounded">
<xs:element name="Customer">
<xs:complexType>
<xs:sequence>
    <xs:element name="CustomerID" type="xs:string" />
    <xs:element name="CompanyName" type="xs:string" />
    <xs:element name="ContactName" type="xs:string" minOccurs="0" />
    <xs:element name="ContactTitle" type="xs:string" minOccurs="0" />
    <xs:element name="Address" type="xs:string" minOccurs="0" />
```

```
    <xs:element name="City" type="xs:string" minOccurs="0" />
    <xs:element name="Region" type="xs:string" minOccurs="0" />
    <xs:element name="PostalCode" type="xs:string" minOccurs="0" />
    <xs:element name="Country" type="xs:string" minOccurs="0" />
    <xs:element name="Phone" type="xs:string" minOccurs="0" />
    <xs:element name="Fax" type="xs:string" minOccurs="0" />
  </xs:sequence>
  </xs:complexType>
  </xs:element>
  </xs:choice>
  </xs:complexType>
  <xs:unique name="Constraint1" msdata:PrimaryKey="true">
    <xs:selector xpath=".//mstns:Customers" />
    <xs:field xpath="mstns:CustomerID" />
  </xs:unique>
  </xs:element>
  </xs:schema>
```

Notice that the XSD is rather simple, but does contain some database schema information. For instance, by studying the *Customers.xsd*, you can see that the CustomerID and CompanyName fields are required but all other fields can be null and that the CustomerID field is the primary key.

To create a strongly typed DataSet object of type Customers, feed the *Customers.xsd* file into the *xsd.exe* tool and have it generate the Customers class for you. To do this, perform the following:

1. Open the Visual Studio .NET command prompt and browse to the directory where your XSD file exists.

2. Type the following at the prompt: **xsd.exe SchemaName.xsd /DataSet /language:CS**, where *SchemaName.xsd* is the name of your XSD file. In this example, the command line looks like this: xsd.exe Customers.xsd /DataSet /language:CS. For Visual Basic .NET, use **/language:VB**.

3. Look for your generated class file. In this sample, a file named *Customers.cs* will be created.

There are several options and flags for the *xsd.exe* tool, but the important flag for creating your strongly typed DataSet object is the /DataSet flag. This tells the tool to parse through the XSD file and autogenerate a strongly typed DataSet object for you. A view of the command line looks like this:

```
C:\>xsd.exe Customers.xsd /DataSet /language:CS
Microsoft (R) Xml Schemas/DataTypes support utility
[Microsoft (R) .NET Framework, Version 1.1.4322.573]
Copyright (C) Microsoft Corporation 1998-2002.
All rights reserved.

Writing file 'C:\Customers.cs'.

C:\>
```

Again, you can see the class file that was generated in this example was named *Customers.cs*. Taking a look at this class, you can see that the *xsd.exe* tool created a class named Customers that inherits from the DataSet class, thus creating a strongly typed DataSet object:

```
[Serializable( )]
[System.ComponentModel.DesignerCategoryAttribute("code")]
[System.Diagnostics.DebuggerStepThrough( )]
[System.ComponentModel.ToolboxItem(true)]
public class Customers : DataSet {
```

Including all of the code here would be excessive—the generated class is more than 600 lines long, but it is important to note that the Customers class is not the only class contained in this file. The following classes were also generated:

CustomerDataTable
CustomerRow
CustomerRowChangeEvent
CustomerRowChangeEventHandler

I would encourage you to examine the generated classes further to better understand how strongly typed DataSets work.

—*Dave Donaldson*

HACK #50   Define Templates for Generating Code

Whenever possible, take a shortcut. You can use the CodeSmith custom tool to generate code from templates that you create.

CodeSmith is a popular .NET code generation tool. The normal CodeSmith application is a Windows Forms application that allows you to create templates in an ASP.NET-like syntax, and then generate code using those templates. The templates can be based on simple variables specified at the time of the template execution, or they can be based on database tables or other objects.

CodeSmith is an excellent time-saver because you can generate any part of your application using the completely customizable templates. And while the normal CodeSmith application is valuable, another part of CodeSmith is built directly into Visual Studio.

The normal CodeSmith application performs what is called *passive code generation*. Passive code generation is when you generate code and then add it to your application as separate steps. The code in your application could even be edited after generation, meaning that you could not generate the code again without losing your changes to the code. The CodeSmith custom tool performs what is called *active code generation*. Active code generation is when code is generated on the fly, usually during the build process of your solution. Using active code generation, you almost never modify the code generated, since it would simply be overwritten the next time you build your solution. The CodeSmith custom tool is a little bit different in that it generates the code when you save the file, as opposed to during the build process, but the result is the same. (You could also create a custom build step to execute the templates [Hack #34].)

The first step in using CodeSmith is downloading and installing it. Code-Smith can be downloaded from *http://www.ericjsmith.NET/codesmith*. During the installation process, you will be asked if you want to add support for Visual Studio—be sure to answer yes.

Creating a Template

To make use of this tool, you first need to add a new CodeSmith template to your Visual Studio Project by right-clicking on your project and choosing Add New Item. From the Add New Item dialog, choose Text File and save the file with a *.cst* extension. (You could also create a new template from the CodeSmith Explorer window.)

Here is a simple CodeSmith template to generate a dictionary-based collection—you can put this in your *.cst* file to try it out:

```
<%@ CodeTemplate Language="C#" TargetLanguage="Text"
         Description="Sample Template" %>
<%@ Property Name="className" Type="System.String"
         Description="This name of the class" %>

public class <%=className%>Dictionary :
         System.Collections.DictionaryBase
{
    public <%=className%> this[int <%=className.ToLower()%>ID]
    {
    get { return ((<%=className%>)(
        Dictionary[<%=className.ToLower()%>ID])); }
    set { Dictionary[<%=className.ToLower()%>ID] = value; }
    }

    public ICollection Keys
    {
      get  {return( Dictionary.Keys );}
    }

    public ICollection Values
    {
      get  {return( Dictionary.Values );}
```

```
      }

      public bool Contains(int <%=className.ToLower( )%>ID)
      {
        return Dictionary.Contains(<%=className.ToLower( )%>ID);
      }

      public void Add(int <%=className.ToLower( )%>ID,
              <%=className%> <%=className.ToLower( )%>)
      {
        Dictionary.Add(<%=className.ToLower( )%>ID,
                    <%=className.ToLower( )%>);
      }

      public void Remove(int <%=className.ToLower( )%>ID)
      {
        Dictionary.Remove(<%=className.ToLower( )%>ID);
      }
  }
```

This template will generate a strongly typed dictionary class based on a single property. At the top of the template, you can see that it expects the name of the type, its sole parameter. Using this property, CodeSmith will fill in this template and create the output. If you look at the syntax of the template, it is very similar to ASP.NET and you can see where the value of the property will be inserted between the <% and %> symbols.

This template could be executed as-is from the normal CodeSmith application, but to use the custom tool, you need to do a little more work.

Creating the XML

The next step is to create an XML file that will be used by the custom tool. First, add a new XML file (right-click on your project and click Add → Add New Item, then select XML File from the list) to your project and then enter the following XML:

```xml
<?xml version="1.0" encoding="utf-8" ?>
<codeSmith>
    <!-- template that will be used to generate code -->
    <template path="SimpleClass.cst" />

    <!-- namespace for the generated code -->
    <namespace>Vehicles</namespace>

    <!-- namespaces that should be imported -->
    <imports>
        <import namespace="System" />
        <import namespace="System.Collections" />
    </imports>

    <!-- list of property sets which each get
```

```
loaded into the template and executed -->
<propertySets>
    <propertySet>
        <property name="className">Car</property>
    </propertySet>
    <propertySet>
        <property name="className">Truck</property>
    </propertySet>
</propertySets>
</codeSmith>
```

The template element specifies the name of the template you want to execute. The namespace element specifies what namespace your generated class should be included in. The imports element lists all of the namespaces that should be included in your generated class. With this template, you will need to include System and System.Collections as the Dictionary class is in the System.Collections namespace. Finally, the propertySets element contains any number of property sets that will be passed to the template. In this sample XML file, I have specified two *property sets*, one with the class name of Car and the other with the class name of Truck. Property sets are the automated method of specifying parameters when running the template. The property set contains exactly what you would specify if you were running the template through the normal GUI.

Execute in Visual Studio

The next step is to set up and execute the CodeSmith custom tool. Just as with other custom tools, you need to specify the name of the custom tool in the properties page of the XML file. The name of the CodeSmith custom tool is CodeSmithGenerator. A configured XML Properties page is shown in Figure 6-10.

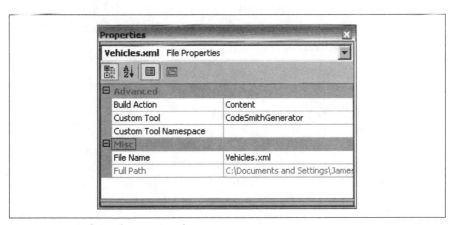

Figure 6-10. CodeSmith custom tool

Once you have specified the custom tool, you will see the generated code in the *Vehicles.cs* file. (Remember, to see files created by a custom tool **[Hack #47]**, you will need to click the Show all Files button on the Solution Explorer.)

Here is the code that CodeSmith generated:

```
//--------------------------------------------------
// <autogenerated>
//      This code was generated by CodeSmith.
//      Version: 2.6.0.117
//
//      Changes to this file may cause incorrect behavior
//      and will be lost if the code is regenerated.
// </autogenerated>
//--------------------------------------------------
using System;
using System.Collections;

namespace Vehicles
{
public class CarDictionary : System.Collections.DictionaryBase
{
    public Car this[int carID]
    {
    get { return ((Car)(Dictionary[carID])); }
    set { Dictionary[carID] = value; }
    }

    public ICollection Keys
    {
        get {return( Dictionary.Keys );}
    }

    public ICollection Values
    {
        get {return( Dictionary.Values );}
    }

      public bool Contains(int carID)
      {
          return Dictionary.Contains(carID);
      }

    public void Add(int carID, Car car)
      {
         Dictionary.Add(carID, car);
      }

      public void Remove(int carID)
      {
```

```
            Dictionary.Remove(carID);
        }
    }

    }
```

I am showing only the first class generated for brevity's sake. As you might imagine, the second class is exactly the same except for a different class name. You can modify the XML file and add additional property sets, or you can modify the template and the custom tool will always keep your code up-to-date.

CodeSmith is an extremely valuable tool, and I encourage you to explore it further. More information can be found at the home page for CodeSmith, which is at *http://www.ericjsmith.NET/codesmith*.

HACK #51 Create a Macro

Learn how to create and run macros that automate mundane development activities.

Creating a macro to help you with your daily tasks is an excellent way to automate and improve repetitive operations. There are several ways to create a macro: either recording your actions in the IDE or creating a macro from scratch. After you have your macro built and tested, you can also create a toolbar button that launches your macro or create a keyboard shortcut.

Recording Macros

The quickest way to automate simple macros is by recording your interactions with the IDE. To activate the macro recorder, go to Tools → Macros → Record TemporaryMacro. This will start the macro recorder. From this point until you stop the recording, your interactions with the IDE will create code in the new macro. You can pause recording to interact with the IDE without recording those actions in your macro. The recorder toolbar is shown in Figure 6-11.

Figure 6-11. Macro recording toolbar

After you have performed the actions you want to record, select Stop Recording from the macro recording toolbar or from the Tools → Macros menu. Visual Studio will then create the macro corresponding to your actions.

If you select Macro Explorer from the Tools → Macros menu and open the Recording Module, you will see a new macro called TemporaryMacro. This is where the code for your actions during recording is created. Because the Macro Recorder will always create the same macro routine, you must now either copy the code to another macro module or at least rename the macro created by the recording process, or your macro will be lost the next time you record a macro. To change the name of the macro, right-click on the macro in the Macro Explorer and select Rename.

Macro recording is a powerful way to quickly create fairly simple macros, but it also has some major limitations. First, any selections in the Solution Explorer or Class View will be specific to the file or class selected, so it will be linked to the filename or class name. This can be overcome by editing the recorded macro and using variables in place of the filenames.

Second, some actions, such as attaching to a process to debug, will not be recorded. Most of these actions can be coded into macros, but you will have to code these by hand.

Creating Macros from Scratch

If the limitations of the macro recorder make it impractical for your situation or if you are creating a complex macro, then you can create a macro from scratch. To create macros from scratch or to edit existing macros, you will use the Macro IDE (Tools → Macros → Macros IDE).

Before looking at the Macro IDE, it is a good idea to first create a new Macro Project to store your macros in. A Macro Project is just like a regular Visual Studio Project in that you can use it to store a number modules and classes that include macros. To create a new macro project, click on Tools → Macros → New Macro Project. You will then be prompted to name your project and choose where it will be saved.

After creating a new project, you are ready to start writing new macros using the Macro IDE. The Macro IDE is a miniature version of Visual Studio used exclusively for creating and editing macros. The Macro IDE is shown in Figure 6-12.

As you can see, the Macro IDE is similar to the Visual Studio IDE, including familiar windows like the document window and the project explorer.

Macros are written using Visual Basic .NET and a special set of objects to access the capabilities of the IDE, allowing you to create files, examine projects, and edit documents. Because these are COM objects instead of part of the native .NET Framework, you will find that IntelliSense support is often somewhat inconsistent.

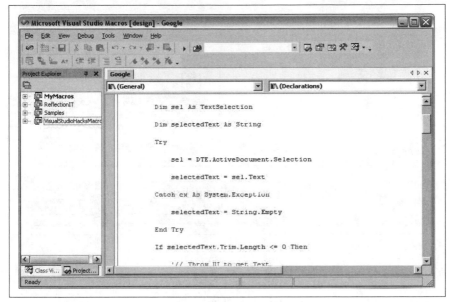

Figure 6-12. The Macro IDE

The base object for almost all macro commands is DTE, which stands for Development Tools Extensibility [Hack #86]. It represents your Visual Studio IDE session and has a large number of object collections and properties. For macros in which you want to edit the text of the current file, the ActiveDocument property will be the one you are primarily concerned with. For operations such as Find and Replace, there is a Find property in the DTE. The documentation for the DTE object is fairly complete, but often using the macro recorder will allow you to figure out which methods or properties are involved in a given operation.

Macros are organized into modules for convenience, so before you start creating a macro's functions and subs, it is best to create a new module to put them in. To add a new module, right-click on your project in the Project Explorer and choose Add New Item. The Add New Item dialog is shown in Figure 6-13.

From this dialog, you can name your module, and when you click Open, the module will be added to your project and opened in the document window. From this point, you can start writing your macro.

For a short sample macro, this code will add the specified text to the beginning of the active document:

```
Public Module NewModule
    Public Sub SampleMacro()
        DTE.ActiveDocument.Selection.StartOfDocument()
```

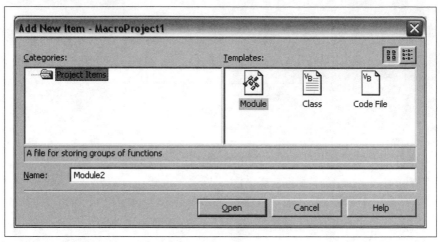

Figure 6-13. Adding a new item

```
            DTE.ActiveDocument.Selection.NewLine()
            DTE.ActiveDocument.Selection.Text = "This is a test"
            DTE.ActiveDocument.Selection.NewLine()
        End Sub
    End Module
```

The first line of the Sub called `StartOfDocument()` will move the cursor to the top of the document. The second line will create a new line. The third line of this macro will insert the string "This is a test", and the last line will create another new line.

After you have written your macro in the Macro IDE, you can save the file and then close the IDE. Your macro will now appear in the Macro Explorer and can be run from the IDE.

Adding a Toolbar Button

Many macros will be useful in your daily life, so having to locate them through the Macro Explorer each time can be inconvenient. Thankfully, macros can be added to a toolbar.

To avoid cluttering existing toolbars, it is a good idea to create a new toolbar. First, select Customize from the View → Toolbars menu. Click the New button and specify the name for your new toolbar, as shown in Figure 6-14.

After creating the toolbar, a ghost of it will appear, as shown in the bottom right of Figure 6-15. You can now select the Commands tab where you can add your macro to the new toolbar.

In order to select the macro, you must first select the Macros category in the Categories listbox. After scrolling past the sample macros (if they are

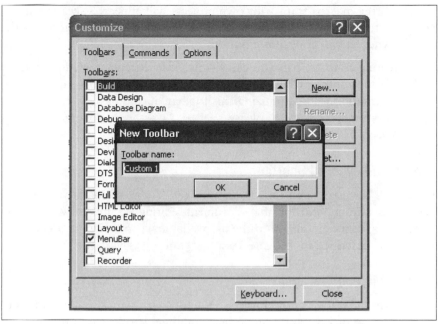

Figure 6-14. Enter the name for the new toolbar

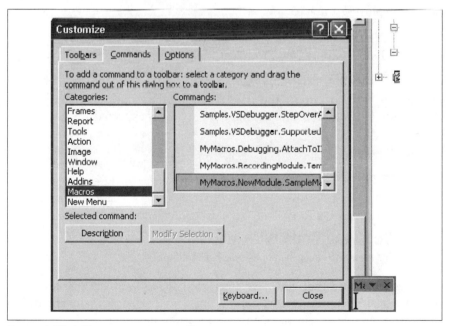

Figure 6-15. Adding a macro to a toolbar

installed), the macros from your own projects will appear. Select the macro you want to create a button for and drag it into the desired position on the toolbar where it will appear as a button.

After creating your toolbar, you can simply close the customization window and dock the toolbar wherever it is convenient for you in your IDE. For more information on customizing this toolbar, including how to create an image for your toolbar item, please refer to "Customize Menus and Toolbars" [Hack #25].

Creating a Keyboard Shortcut

Creating a keyboard shortcut is an even easier way to make your macro accessible during your normal document editing. A macro will simply appear as another command in the list available when assigning a keyboard shortcut as described in "Create Your Own Shortcuts" [Hack #24].

Sharing Macros

Unlike normal Visual Studio Projects, Macro Projects are contained in a single file instead of a separate file for each module. If you have a module you wish to share among multiple users, you must first export it. Here is the process for exporting a macro:

1. Open the module you wish to export.
2. Click File → Export NewModule (Ctrl-E).
3. Choose where to save the file to.

When you wish to import the module on another machine, simply select Add Existing Item and locate the file you previously exported.

See Also

- "Generate Code with Macros" [Hack #52].

—Ben Von Handorf

HACK #52 Generate Code with Macros

Use macros to help generate repetitive sections of code.

Often you will find that you have blocks of code in a project that are virtually identical. Generating this code using a macro has the advantages of ensuring the code is the same in each location and saving valuable developer time.

Creating a Simple Generation Macro

Suppose you want to create a function for each value in an enumeration. Code generation is useful for creating an initial set of functions and can be done using a more typical generation tool such as CodeSmith **[Hack #50]**. However, often you will find that after hand-editing some of the generated functions, the prospect of regenerating the entire set is undesirable when all you wish to do is add a single function. At the same time, for more complex examples, copy-pasting an existing example may result in a lot of editing. Using a macro to generate a single example gives you another option for cases in which you know there will be edits later.

Recording a code template. The simplest way to create a macro to generate repetitive blocks of code is to use the macro recorder to record the creation of one of the blocks, and then edit the macro to parameterize it. Open the file you wish to create the function in and start the macro recorder **[Hack #51]**. Create the function as you normally would, then stop the macro recorder.

> For VB.NET users, it is important to turn off the "Automatic insertion of end constructs" option before both recording and playing back your macro. This option can be configured through Tools → Options → Text Editor ▸ Basic ▸ VB Specific. Otherwise, your macro will insert multiple end constructs (such as End If).

Here is a sample of a recorded macro:

```
Sub TemporaryMacro( )
    DTE.ActiveDocument.Selection.NewLine( )
    DTE.ActiveDocument.Selection.Text = _
        "private void RecordFoo( Enum.Foo value )"
    DTE.ActiveDocument.Selection.NewLine( )
    DTE.ActiveDocument.Selection.Text = "{"
    DTE.ActiveDocument.Selection.NewLine( )
    DTE.ActiveDocument.Selection.Text = _
        "BusinessLogicCall.RecordEnum( value, OurEnum.Foo ) ;"
    DTE.ActiveDocument.Selection.NewLine( )
    DTE.ActiveDocument.Selection.Text = "}"
End Sub
```

Generalizing the macro. After recording the macro, open the macro editor. You can now parameterize your macro by changing the variable portions of your function with variables and reading the desired settings either from the environment or with InputBox functions that allow the user to enter simple data. I have changed the function name from TemporaryMacro to Macro1 so it will not be lost if I record another macro.

```
Sub Macro1( )
    Dim var As String = InputBox("Enter enum name")
    DTE.ActiveDocument.Selection.NewLine( )
    DTE.ActiveDocument.Selection.Text = _
      "private void Record" + var + "( int value )"
    DTE.ActiveDocument.Selection.NewLine( )
    DTE.ActiveDocument.Selection.Text = "{"
    DTE.ActiveDocument.Selection.NewLine( )
    DTE.ActiveDocument.Selection.Text = _
      "BusinessLogicCall.RecordEnum( value, OurEnum." + var + " ) ;"
    DTE.ActiveDocument.Selection.NewLine( )
    DTE.ActiveDocument.Selection.Text = "}"
End Sub
```

Resulting code. In this example, you now have a macro that is useful for generating new versions of the Record function when new items are added to the OurEnum enumeration. This can be useful when providing a Business Layer interface in which you wish to provide a distinct function for each value of the enumeration.

If you type **NewValue** into the InputBox prompt, the macro will create the following function:

```
private void RecordNewValue( int value )
{
    BusinessLogicCall.RecordEnum( value, Enum.NewValue ) ;
}
```

—*Ben Von Handorf*

HACK #53 Create Connection Strings Quickly

Database connection strings can be tricky and confusing. Use a macro to automatically generate your connection strings.

Connection strings are one of those things that you usually create only when you are starting a new project or if you have to change databases, so it is easy to forget how to write a connection string. Instead of hunting around for an example or documentation, there is a quick macro you can use to automatically generate your connection string using the Data Link object.

To create the macro:

1. Open the Macro IDE.

2. Create a new module and name it ConnectionStringMacro.

3. Copy the following code into the module:

```
Public Sub InsertConnectionString( )
        Dim links As Object = CreateObject("DataLinks")
        Dim cn As Object = CreateObject("ADODB.Connection")

        links.PromptEdit(cn)
```

```
        If cn.connectionstring = "" Then Exit Sub
        Dim sel As TextSelection = ActiveDocument( ).Selection
        sel.Text = cn.connectionstring
    End Sub
```

4. Close the Macro IDE.

You can then run this macro from the Macro Explorer in your project. First, select the place in your document where you want to insert the connection string, then double-click on the macro; you will see the Data Link Properties page. You will then need to select the provider for your connection by clicking on it in the Provider tab shown in Figure 6-16.

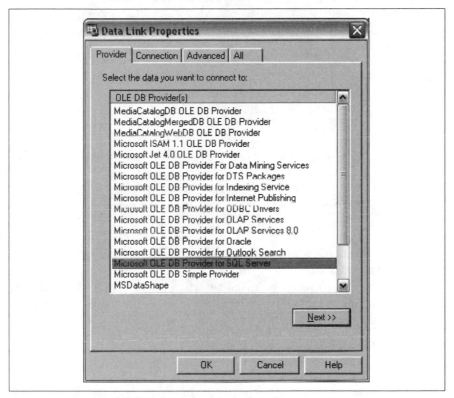

Figure 6-16. Data Link Properties dialog—Provider tab

From this tab, select the type of data that you want to connect to—the OLEDB provider for SQL Server is selected in Figure 6-16. Next, you will need to specify the details of the connection on the Connection tab, which is shown in Figure 6-17.

From this tab, you will need to choose the server name, specify the username and password, and then select the database that you want to connect

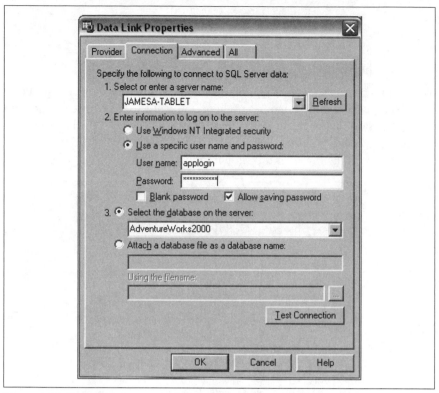

Figure 6-17. Data Link Properties dialog—Connection tab

to. You will also need to check the Allow Saving Password checkbox; otherwise, the password will not be included in the connection string. Don't worry, your password won't be saved anywhere other than in the generated connection string. When you click OK, the following string will be inserted into your document:

```
Provider=SQLOLEDB.1;Password=apppassword;
Persist Security Info=True;User ID=applogin;
Initial Catalog=AdventureWorks2000;Data Source=JAMESA-TABLET
```

Using this macro, you can quickly create connection strings without needing to research the correct syntax. Thanks to Roy Osherove who published this macro on his blog, which can be found at *http://weblogs.asp.net/rosherove.*

Quickly Sign Assemblies

Use a macro to sign an assembly with a strong name.

Strongly signing assemblies is one of the more tedious processes that you have to perform when developing with the .NET Framework. The normal process to strongly sign an assembly is as follows:

1. Create a *.snk* file using the *sn.exe* command prompt utility.

2. Move the *.snk* file into your project.

3. Point to the *.snk* file using the `AssemblyKeyFile` attribute.

This is the process that you will reproduce using a macro. Follow these steps to create a macro that will automatically sign assemblies for you:

1. Open the Macro IDE.

2. Create a new module.

3. Copy the following code into the module:

```
Imports EnvDTE
Imports System.Diagnostics
Imports Microsoft.VisualBasic
Imports Microsoft.VisualBasic.ControlChars
Imports System.Windows
Imports System.Windows.Forms
Imports System

Public Module Module1

Public Class WinWrapper
    Implements System.Windows.Forms.IWin32Window

Overridable ReadOnly Property Handle() As System.IntPtr Implements _
        System.Windows.Forms.IWin32Window.Handle
    Get
        Dim iptr As New System.IntPtr(DTE.MainWindow.HWnd)
        Return iptr
    End Get
  End Property
End Class

Sub AddStrongNameToProject()

    Dim init_dir, outfile_name, outdirectory As String
    Dim stemp, Macroprojname As String
    Dim prjSolution As EnvDTE.Project
    Dim prjVSProject As VSLangProj.VSProject
    Dim openfile As Forms.FileDialog
    Dim result As Forms.DialogResult
    Dim snPath As Microsoft.Win32.RegistryKey
    Dim winptr As WinWrapper
```

```
Dim myProj As EnvDTE.Project

Try
  winptr = New WinWrapper( )
  openfile = New Forms.OpenFileDialog( )

  ' set the initial directory to SystemDrive
  init_dir = System.Environment.SystemDirectory( )
  init_dir = Left(init_dir, InStr(init_dir, "\", _
    CompareMethod.Text))
  openfile.InitialDirectory = init_dir

  If openfile.ShowDialog(winptr) = result.OK Then

    ' create the output filename
    outfile_name = Right(openfile.FileName, _
          Len(openfile.FileName) - _
          Len(System.Environment.CurrentDirectory) - 1)
    outfile_name = Left(outfile_name, InStr(outfile_name, ".", _
          CompareMethod.Text) - 1)
    outfile_name = outfile_name & ".dll"

    ' set the output directory to the VsMacros dir
    outdirectory = Left(DTE.FullName, InStr(DTE.FullName, _
          "devenv.exe", CompareMethod.Text) - 1)
    outdirectory = outdirectory & "PublicAssemblies\"

    snPath = _
      Microsoft.Win32.Registry.LocalMachine.OpenSubKey( _
        "software\microsoft\.NETFramework")

    If Not snPath Is Nothing Then
      stemp = snPath.GetValue("sdkinstallroot", "") & "bin"
    End If

    If stemp = "bin" Then
      MsgBox("Unable to get sn.exe location from registry")
      Exit Sub
    End If

    Dim strsnkFileName As String
    strsnkFileName = openfile.FileName.Replace(".dll", ".snk")

    Microsoft.VisualBasic.ChDir(stemp)

    ' Shell out to the CMD sn.exe file
    Microsoft.VisualBasic.Shell("cmd /c sn.exe -k """ & _
    strsnkFileName & """", AppWinStyle.NormalFocus, True)

    ' Add the snk file to the project
    DTE.ItemOperations.AddExistingItem(strsnkFileName)

    ' Navigate to the AssemblyInfo file
```

```
        Dim projItem As ProjectItem
        projItem = DTE.Solution.FindProjectItem("AssemblyInfo.cs")
        projItem.Open(EnvDTE.Constants.vsViewKindTextView).Activate()

        'Update the Assembly file with the location here
        Dim ts As TextSelection = DTE.ActiveWindow.Selection
        ts.SelectAll()
        Dim strNewStrongNameLoc As String
        strNewStrongNameLoc = "[assembly: AssemblyKeyFile(@" & _
            Chr(34) & strsnkFileName & Chr(34) & ")]"
        ts.ReplacePattern("[assembly: AssemblyKeyFile("""")]", _
            strNewStrongNameLoc)

      End If

    Catch err As System.Exception
       MsgBox(err.Message)
    End Try
  End Sub

  End Module
```

4. Save and close the macro

Before running the macro, be sure to compile the project whose assembly
you want to sign and make sure the project is selected in the Solution
Explorer. When you run the macro, it will first prompt you for the location
of your assembly. Then the macro will execute *sn.exe* for you, copy the *.snk*
file to your project, and then populate the AssemblyKeyFile attribute for your
assembly.

Once you have used this macro, you won't ever want to go back to manually signing assemblies again.

Thanks to Doug Doedens for writing this macro and posting at the C#
Corner, which is located at *http://www.c-sharpcorner.com/Code/2002/July/
AddStrongNamesMacro.asp*.

Update Project References Quickly

Use a macro to quickly update multiple references without updating each one
individually.

When working with a large solution that contains a number of projects, you
will often have multiple project references pointing to the same assemblies.
You might have an assembly that contains the exception management portion of your application. This assembly would naturally be referenced by
every one of your other projects. But what if you had to move to that assembly's location? You would then need to update each and every reference to
that assembly individually. This macro will automate that process for you.

You will be able to run this macro and select the new location of your reference, and then the macro will look for any other references to the same assembly and update those references as well.

To create this macro:

1. Open the Macro IDE.

2. Create a new module.

3. Copy the following code into the module:

```
Imports EnvDTE
Imports System.Diagnostics
Imports Microsoft.VisualBasic
Imports Microsoft.VisualBasic.ControlChars
Imports System.Windows
Imports System.Windows.Forms
Imports System

Public Module UpdateReferences

Public Class WinWrapper
        Implements System.Windows.Forms.IWin32Window

Overridable ReadOnly Property Handle( ) As System.IntPtr _
Implements System.Windows.Forms.IWin32Window.Handle
        Get
                Dim iptr As New System.IntPtr(DTE.MainWindow.HWnd)
                Return iptr
        End Get
    End Property
End Class
Public Sub UpdateReference( )

Dim startDir
Dim newAssembLocation
Dim outdirectory As String
Dim stemp, Macroprojname As String
Dim prjSolution As EnvDTE.Project

Dim openfile As Forms.FileDialog
Dim result As Forms.DialogResult
Dim tlbimppath As Microsoft.Win32.RegistryKey
Dim winptr As WinWrapper

winptr = New WinWrapper
openfile = New Forms.OpenFileDialog

'set the initial directory to SystemDrive
startDir = System.Environment.SystemDirectory( )
startDir = Left(startDir, InStr(startDir, "\", _
                        CompareMethod.Text))
openfile.InitialDirectory = startDir
```

```
If openfile.ShowDialog(winptr) = result.OK Then

newAssembLocation = Right(openfile.FileName, _
    Len(openfile.FileName) - _
    Len(System.Environment.CurrentDirectory) - 1)

End If

Dim myProj As Integer
Dim prjVSProject As VSLangProj.VSProject

Try
    For myProj = 1 To DTE.Solution.Projects.Count

    prjVSProject = DTE.Solution.Projects.Item(myProj).Object

    If prjVSProject Is Nothing Then
       MsgBox("Unable to get reference to solution file")
       Exit Sub
    End If

    Dim myRef As VSLangProj.Reference

    ' Strip off the .dll ext so we can use the find command
    newAssembLocation = newAssembLocation.Replace(".dll", "")

    myRef = prjVSProject.References.Find(newAssembLocation)

    If Not myRef Is Nothing Then

        ' remove the old reference
        myRef.Remove()
        ' add the new one
        prjVSProject.References.Add(openfile.FileName)

    Else

        ' We did not find a reference to this assembly here
    End If
    Next
Catch err As System.Exception
End Try
End Sub
End Module
```

4. Save and close the macro.

First make sure that the solution whose references you want to update is
open, and then activate your newly created macro. When you run the
macro, you will see the Open File dialog; using this dialog, select the new
location of your assembly. Once you have selected the new location, Visual

Studio will search through the solution for any other references to the same assembly. Any references found will be updated to the new location.

This macro is a great time-saver when you are reorganizing projects or solutions and is a great alternative to updating all your references manually.

Thanks to Doug Doedens for writing this macro and posting at the C# Corner (see *http://www.c-sharpcorner.com/Code/2002/July/SolutionMacros.asp*).

HACK #56 Automatically Add using and Imports Statements

Use a macro to scan your code and determine which namespaces need to be imported.

The .NET Framework is built around namespaces. Every class in the .NET Framework belongs to a namespace; you need to tell the compiler that you want to use the classes in that namespace. This is done through the use of a using statement in C# or an Imports statement in VB.NET. One of the annoyances that this creates is then realizing that you have not added a using or Imports statement for a class that you added. This means you have to find out what namespace you need to add for this class and then go to the top of your document and add the name of the namespace. Alternatively, you could fully qualify the class you are using, meaning that you prefix the name of the class with the full name of the namespace (e.g., System.Data. SqlClient.SqlConnection).

A set of macros that will do either of these for you automatically is available. The first macro is called AddDirective and will look for your class and then add the Imports or using statement for you. To use this macro, you simply need to highlight the name of your class and then run the Add-Directive macro. If you highlight SqlConnection and run the macro, it will add using System.Data.SqlClient; or Imports System.Data.SqlClient to the top of your document.

The other macro is called AddNamespace and will, instead of adding a using or Imports statement, fully qualify the name of your class. If you highlight SqlConnection and run the macro, it will add System.Data.SqlClient to the front of your class.

The macro works by cycling through all the assemblies referenced by your project. If it finds a class in multiple namespaces, the first namespace found is used.

This macro was written by a developer named Jan Tielens, and its code is shown here (this one is pretty long; you may want to download it from the book site):

```
'TypeFinder Macro, version 2.11
'For Visual Studio.NET
'By Jan Tielens, http://weblogs.asp.NET/jan
'With the help of:
'- Yves Hanoulle, http://www.hanoulle.be/
'- Thomas Freudenberg
'- Guillaume Roberge


Imports EnvDTE
Imports System
Imports System.Collections
Imports System.Diagnostics
Imports System.Reflection
Imports System.IO

Public Module TypeFinder
    Private Class TypeCache
        Public Shared Cache As Hashtable = New Hashtable
    End Class

    Private Function SearchTypeInAssembly( _
        ByVal typename As String, _
        ByVal assm As Reflection.Assembly) As Type
        DTE.StatusBar.Text = "Searching for '" & _
        typename & "' " & assm.GetName.Name & "..."

        If (Not TypeCache.Cache.ContainsKey(typename)) Then
            Dim t As Type
            For Each t In assm.GetTypes
                If t.Name.ToLower = typename Then
                    TypeCache.Cache.Add(typename, t)
                    Return t
                End If
            Next
        Else
            Return TypeCache.Cache.Item(typename)
        End If
    End Function

    Private Function SearchType(ByVal typename As String) As Type
        typename = _
        typename.ToLower.Trim.Replace(";", "").Replace(".", "")
        Dim assm As [Assembly]
        Dim currentAssm As String
        Dim currentPath As String
        Dim t As Type
        Dim p As [Property]
```

```
'search in principal assembly
assm = Reflection.Assembly.LoadWithPartialName("mscorlib")
t = SearchTypeInAssembly(typename, assm)
If Not t Is Nothing Then Return t

'search in assemblies in solutions
Dim proj As Project
For Each proj In DTE.ActiveSolutionProjects
    'search in references of current project
    Dim ref As VSLangProj.Reference
    For Each ref In proj.Object.References
        assm = Reflection.Assembly.LoadFrom(ref.Path)
        t = SearchTypeInAssembly(typename, assm)
        If Not t Is Nothing Then Return t
    Next

    currentAssm = ""
    currentPath = ""

    'obtain properties to get assembly
    'associated with project
    For Each p In proj.Properties
        If (p.Name = "OutputFileName") Then
            currentAssm = p.Value
        ElseIf (p.Name = "LocalPath") Then
            currentPath = p.Value
        End If
        If currentAssm.Length > 0 _
            And currentPath.Length > 0 Then Exit For
    Next

    'search in the assembly associated with the project
    currentAssm = currentPath + "bin\" + _
    DTE.Solution.SolutionBuild.ActiveConfiguration.Name _
    + "\" + currentAssm
    Dim tempAss As String = currentAssm + "2"

    Try
        Try
            If (File.Exists(tempAss)) Then
                File.Delete(tempAss)
            End If
        Catch
        End Try

        'we copy the assembly to be sure that when the
        'compilation will be launch the file
        'could be written
        File.Copy(currentAssm, tempAss)
        assm = Reflection.Assembly.LoadFrom(tempAss)
        t = SearchTypeInAssembly(typename, assm)
        Try
            File.Delete(tempAss)
```

```
                Catch
                End Try
                If Not t Is Nothing Then Return t
        Catch ex As Exception
        End Try
    Next

    DTE.StatusBar.Text = "Could not find type '" _
    & typename & "'"

    DTE.StatusBar.Highlight(True)
    Return Nothing
End Function

Public Sub AddNamespace()
    Dim text As TextSelection = DTE.ActiveDocument.Selection
    If (text.Text.Length = 0) Then text.WordLeft(True)
    Dim t As Type = SearchType(text.Text)
    If Not t Is Nothing Then
        text.Text = t.FullName
        text.EndOfLine()
        DTE.StatusBar.Text = "Ready"
    End If
End Sub

Public Sub AddDirective()
    Dim text As TextSelection = DTE.ActiveDocument.Selection
    If (text.Text.Length = 0) Then text.WordLeft(True)
    Dim t As Type = SearchType(text.Text)
    If Not t Is Nothing Then
        Dim keyword, suffix As String
        Dim line As Integer = text.AnchorPoint.Line
        text.Text = t.Name

        Select Case DTE.ActiveDocument.Language
            Case "CSharp"
                keyword = "using"
                suffix = ";"
            Case "Basic"
                keyword = "Imports"
                suffix = String.Empty
            Case Else
                Throw New System.Exception("Invalid Language: " _
                & DTE.ActiveDocument.Language)
        End Select

        Dim alreadyUsed As Boolean = False
        text.StartOfDocument()

        'Skip the headers
        text.WordRight(True, 2)
        While text.Text.StartsWith("/*") _
        Or text.Text.StartsWith(" *") _
```

```
        Or text.Text.StartsWith("//") _
        Or text.Text.StartsWith("'")
            text.LineDown( )
            text.StartOfLine( )
            text.WordRight(True, 2)
    End While
    text.StartOfLine( )
    text.WordRight(True)

Dim lineTarget As Integer = text.AnchorPoint.Line
Dim correctPlace As Boolean = False
While text.Text.StartsWith(keyword) And _
Not alreadyUsed And Not correctPlace
Dim startpt As EditPoint = text.BottomPoint.CreateEditPoint( )
Dim endpt As EditPoint = text.BottomPoint.CreateEditPoint( )
endpt.EndOfLine( )

If DTE.ActiveDocument.Language = "CSharp" Then
'Skip ';'
endpt.CharLeft( )
End If

Dim currentText As String = endpt.GetText(startpt)
        If currentText = t.Namespace Then
            alreadyUsed = True
        ElseIf (currentText < t.Namespace) Then
            text.LineDown( )
            text.StartOfLine( )
            text.WordRight(True)
        Else
            correctPlace = True
            lineTarget = text.AnchorPoint.Line
        End If
    End While
    text.StartOfLine( )

    If alreadyUsed Then
        DTE.StatusBar.Text = "Namespace " & t.Namespace _
        & " is already imported."
        DTE.StatusBar.Highlight(True)
        text.MoveToLineAndOffset(line, 1)
    Else
        If (correctPlace) Then text.GotoLine(lineTarget)
        DTE.UndoContext.Open("Add Namespace Directive")
        text.Insert(keyword & " " & t.Namespace _
                & suffix & vbCrLf)
        DTE.UndoContext.Close( )
        DTE.StatusBar.Text = "'" & keyword & " " _
        & t.Namespace _
        & suffix & "' added to the document."
        DTE.StatusBar.Highlight(True)
        text.MoveToLineAndOffset(line + 1, 1)
    End If
```

```
            text.EndOfLine( )
        End If
    End Sub
End Module
```

All you need to do is download or transcribe this code into the Macro IDE [Hack #51]. You will then see the two macros in the Macro Explorer and can start using them right away.

Insert Commonly Used Code Automatically
Discover an add-in that will provide code templates and code completion to enable you to write code faster.

Throughout this book, we have talked about different ways to handle code snippets, including storing them in the toolbox or using other add-ins to handle your code snippets. The Code<Template>.NET add-in allows you to create and manage code templates, which are code snippets that contain variables. Instead of just having a piece of text you can drag to your document, you will be able to specify variables that you will be prompted for. What differentiates this add-in from other code snippet management add-ins is the ability to define variables as well as the ability to automatically insert your code template using a predefined keyword and shortcut key.

Contrary to the misleading angle brackets, this add-in does not have anything to do with C++ templates or .NET 2.0 generics.

First you will need to download and install the Code<Template>.NET add-in from *http://www.codeproject.com/useritems/CodeTemplateNET.asp*. The installation is relatively painless, and the next time you start Visual Studio you will see the CodeTemplate toolbar, which is shown in Figure 6-18.

It is from this menu that you will work with the add-in. First, let's add a new code template to the tool. Click Open <codetmpl.cs> on the CodeTemplate menu. The *codetmpl.cs* file contains all of the code templates that this tool manages. It is to this file that you will need to add your own code templates. As you can see, the format of this file is a little confusing—here is a look at one of the standard code templates:

```
#{Subsection Header|subh

//////////////////////////////////////////////////////
// <%?Subsection name%>
}#
```

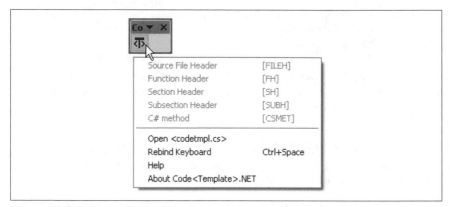

Figure 6-18. CodeTemplate toolbar

Each snippet starts with #{ and then the name of the snippet, in this case Subsection Header. After the name of the template is a | character followed by a keyword, which will be used to autoinsert the code into your document. What follows next is the actual code that will be inserted into the document. This can also include variables. In this case you see <%?Subsection name%> in the text. When the template is inserted, the add-in will prompt you with a dialog like the one shown in Figure 6-19.

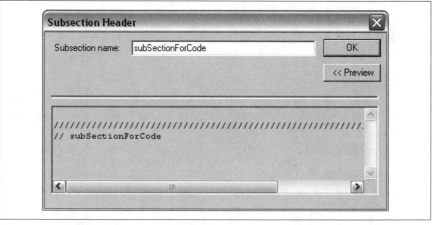

Figure 6-19. CodeTemplate variable dialog

This dialog allows you to specify the variable at the time of insertion. The last part of the code template is the ending }#. So let's add a new code snippet to this file:

1. First you need to open the template and create a name and shortcut key for it:

   ```
   #{SQLConnection|sqlc
   ```

2. Next you need to specify the actual text that will be inserted, including any variables:

   ```
   SqlConnection sqlConn = new SqlConnection(
       ConfigurationSettings.AppSettings["<%?ConfigKey%>"]);

   using(sqlConn)
   {

   }
   ```

3. Then you need to close the template:

   ```
   }#
   ```

4. Next you simply need to save the file, and the menu will be updated.

Now that the code template is added to the file, it can be invoked in two different ways. The first is to select the code template from the menu; the second is to type **sqlc** into the document and then press Ctrl-Space (You may want to reassign this shortcut key, as it tends to interfere with the normal Ctrl-Space shortcut.) After performing either of these functions, you will be presented with the variable dialog shown in Figure 6-20.

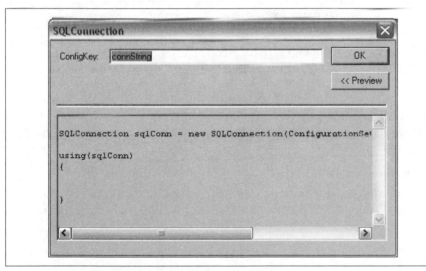

Figure 6-20. SQLConnection variable dialog

First, you need to specify the variable for this snippet. After you press the OK button, the code shown here will be inserted into the document.

```
SQLConnection sqlConn = new SQLConnection(
    ConfigurationSettings.AppSetting["connString"]);

using(sqlConn)
{


}
```

As you can see, this add-in can help quickly insert code snippets, including code snippets that include variables.

This add-in also includes a number of default keywords that can be used in your templates; these are used by enclosing the keyword between <% and %> characters. (Notice that, unlike ConfigKey in the preceding example, there is no question mark; those are used only for variables that will be specified by the user.) You can insert any of the keywords shown in Table 6-4 in the template, and the keyword will be replaced with the value specified in the table.

Table 6-4. Template keywords

Keyword	Value
SOLUTION	The name of the current solution
PROJECT	The name of the current project
FILE	The name of the current file
NOW	The current date and time
TODAY	The current date
GUID	A new GUID
TEMPLATE	Includes the text generated by another template

The TEMPLATE keyword is particularly interesting since it allows you to nest templates within each other. Here is an example of how to use this keyword:

```
<%template:sqlc%>
```

This would insert the output from the template defined earlier into another template. You will still be prompted for any variables when the parent template is executed.

The Code<Template>.NET add-in is a great way to decrease the amount of time you spend typing the same code over and over again.

Move Quickly Between Source Control
#58 Providers

*Using multiple version control systems is normally a tedious operation. Here's
a free utility that makes it a snap.*

Visual Studio provides a model for source control vendors to write source
control providers that plug into Visual Studio. A third-party source control,
or even Microsoft's GotDotNet Workspaces source control, can work just
like using SourceSafe from Visual Studio. This is a great thing when you
switch between various source control providers, since the functionality and
UI are consistent across all tools when used through Visual Studio.

One problem though: it is not the easiest thing to switch between source
control providers. There is no quick switch in the IDE to choose what
source control provider you want to use, but thankfully Harry Pierson (better known as DevHawk) has written an easy-to-use utility called SccSwitch
that will allow you to do just that.

To use this utility, you first need to download the tool from *http://devhawk.
NET/art_sccswitch.aspx*. The source and executable are both included in the
zip file. After extracting the executable and running it, you will see a screen
like the one shown in Figure 6-21.

Figure 6-21. SccSwitch

To switch source control providers, simply check the box of the provider
you want to use and then click the Update button. This will switch what
provider you use, and the next time you start Visual Studio you should
notice the change.

If you would rather not download a utility, you can also make these changes
right in the registry. The key you will need to modify is HKEY_LOCAL_MACHINE\
SOFTWARE\SourceCodeControlProvider. The value of this key is a string that
identifies what source control provider is the active provider. The possible
values for this key are stored in a subkey called InstalledSCCProviders. Any

of the data values from this key can be substituted for the current provider in the `SourceCodeControlProvider` key. Making these changes in the registry is easy, but using the utility is even easier.

As a consultant, I find this tool especially valuable, since going from project to project you never know what source control you will be using. (Plenty of times I use multiple source code providers on the same day.) This tool is especially helpful if you get involved with projects on GotDotNet.

CHAPTER SEVEN

Help and Research
Hacks 59–67

To be an efficient developer you have to know how to best get help and perform research. It is not a coincidence that most developers discovered Google before normal users did and probably use Google more than most users. Looking for documentation and researching problems and bugs is a large part of any programmer's job. Knowing the best ways to get help and do your own research goes a long way to making you a more efficient developer.

The hacks in this chapter cover how to use the help built into Visual Studio as well as a number of different ways to search Google and other search engines directly from Visual Studio.

You'll also see how to delve into the internals of the .NET Framework using both ILDASM and Reflector, how to use FxCop to enhance the quality of your code, and how to use the Allocation Profiler that examines the garbage collection heap.

Get Help
Visual Studio's help is of the F1 variety, but it also goes way beyond that. Learn how to get the most from Visual Studio's built-in help.

Visual Studio includes a rich help experience, one that improves even more with the release of Visual Studio 2005. Knowing how to best use help can help make you a more efficient and faster developer.

Press F1 for Help

Like most applications, the main key to remember with the Visual Studio help system is F1. Visual Studio's F1 is a little smarter than most applications though. Instead of just opening a generic help window, F1 pays attention to the context in which you are asking for help. For instance, if you select the Solution Explorer window and press F1, Visual Studio will display a help document about how to use the Solution Explorer.

While you are developing, you can select a piece of code and press F1. This will call up the documentation for whatever you happened to highlight. When you do this, Visual Studio is performing an index search for the item that you highlighted. If you have no code highlighted, it will provide help for the best match based on context. For example, if your cursor is on the .Clone method of a String variable, F1 will take you to the help page for the String. Clone method. If there is more than one result for the item you highlighted, you will see the index search dialog shown in Figure 7-1.

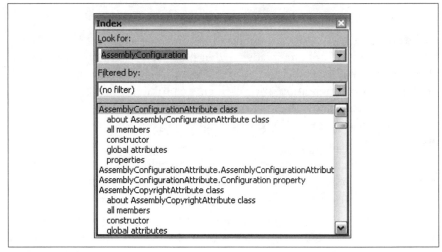

Figure 7-1. Index search dialog

In this example, I highlighted AssemblyConfiguration in my code and pressed F1. If I highlighted the term int and pressed F1, it would take me right to the documentation about integers instead of showing me the index screen. You can also access the Index search screen directly by going to Help → Index.

Dynamic Help

Dynamic Help can be both a curse and a blessing. Elsewhere in the book, we have recommended that you disable this feature to improve the performance of the IDE [Hack #44]. Dynamic Help can be a very useful tool; you just need to weigh the performance versus the helpfulness of this tool for you. If you find Dynamic Help to be useful, then its small performance hit will well be worth the benefit.

What Dynamic Help does is display a window with help topics that might be helpful based on the action you are currently performing. Figure 7-2 shows the Dynamic Help window.

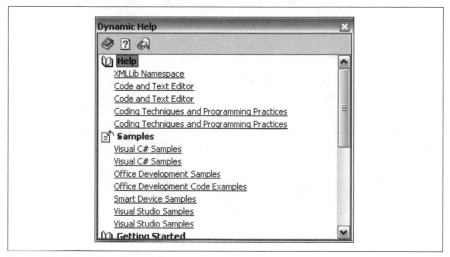

Figure 7-2. Dynamic Help window

In this example, I happen to have a code file from the XMLLib Namespace open so it shows the documentation for that namespace under Help. You can also use Dynamic Help much like F1. If you simply select the word int in your code file without pressing any keys, you will then see the window shown in Figure 7-3.

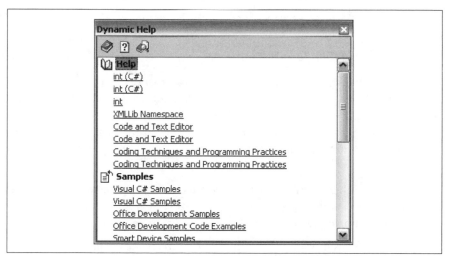

Figure 7-3. Dynamic Help picking up on what you've highlighted

Notice how Dynamic Help picked up on the fact that you highlighted the word int and now displays multiple help documents pertaining to the int type. Dynamic Help can be a great tool for a learning developer—targeted help topics will always be at your fingertips whatever you happen to be working on.

Contents and Search

If normal F1 and Dynamic Help are not providing the information you need, it is time to turn to either the Contents window or the Search window. Both of these portions of help require more work on your part to find what you need. The Contents window is a simple table of contents for all the .NET help installed on your machine and is shown in Figure 7-4.

Figure 7-4. Help Contents window

Using the Contents window, you can browse through all the help collections installed on your machine. A help collection is a group of help documents pertaining to a particular topic. In Figure 7-4, each of the top-level nodes is a separate help collection—you can tell from this that I have certain tools like ReSharper and Visual Studio .NET Help Integration Kit installed.

If you would rather not browse through this tree structure, you can use the Search window, which will perform a full-text search on help using keywords that you provide. The Search window can be seen in Figure 7-5.

After clicking Search, you will see the results screen shown in Figure 7-6.

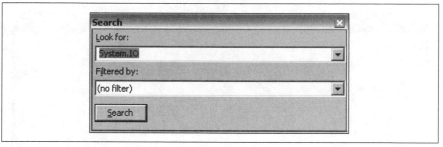

Figure 7-5. Help Search window

Title	Location	Rank
Framework Services Namespaces in Visual Studio	Visual Basic and Visual C# Concepts	1
Framework Services Namespaces in Visual Studio	Visual Basic and Visual C# Concepts	2
System.IO Namespace	.NET Framework Class Library	3
System.IO Namespace	.NET Framework Class Library	4
File Access with Visual Basic .NET	Visual Basic Language Concepts	5
Microsoft Win32 to Microsoft .NET Framework API Map	.NET Development (General) Technical Articles	6
Object Hierarchy	.NET Framework Class Library	7
Object Hierarchy	.NET Framework Class Library	8
Enum Hierarchy	.NET Framework Class Library	9

Search Results for System.IO - 500 topics found

Figure 7-6. Search Results window

While Visual Studio's search is somewhat good, you may find turning to your favorite online search engine more helpful. However, read on for some improvements in Visual Studio 2005 that extend the help system and even include online sources.

Visual Studio 2005 Help System

Visual Studio 2005 includes all the help features you have become accustomed to in prior version of Visual Studio, but also includes a number of new helpful features.

How do I? The first new feature in Visual Studio 2005 help is the How Do I tab in the new help window. In Figure 7-7, you can see this tab inside the new help window.

The How Do I tab includes links to a number of tutorials on various tasks you might want to perform while in Visual Studio. From Figure 7-7, you can also see the new help window, which gives you a central window from which to work with all the different parts of help. This window also includes new features like Help Favorites, which allow you to bookmark help topics or search results and access them from a single window.

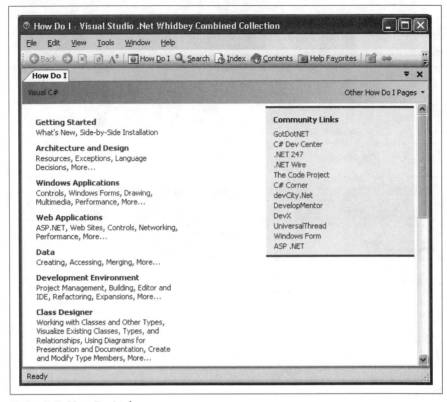

Figure 7-7. How Do I tab

Online Search

One of the best new features in Visual Studio 2005 is the ability to search online resources directly from Visual Studio. Using this new online search feature, you can search not only MSDN online but also any of the sites that are part of the CodeWise community of sites. The first time you use help in Visual Studio 2005, you'll be asked to choose how you want to use online help. The default is to use local help as the primary source, but to also consult online help when you are connected to the Internet. You will need to agree to the online help privacy policy if you choose to use it.

> The CodeWise community is a collection of Microsoft endorsed technical sites. Chances are you have run across some of these sites as they include favorites like CodeProject, DotNetJunkies, and the ASPAlliance. For more information, please refer to *http://www.gotdotnet.com/content/codewise*.

By default, online search will be enabled and is integrated into the same help that appears when you press F1. If you select "bool" in your document and press F1, you will see the screen shown in Figure 7-8.

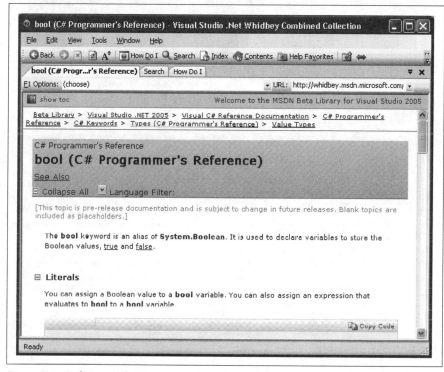

Figure 7-8. Online search

This is just the beginning of what you can do though. If you click on the Search button at the top, you can enter any term you want and search MSDN and all the CodeWise sites and MSDN Online as well. This search is shown in Figure 7-9.

In the results pane you will see three different sections of results: MSDN Online results, Local Help results, and Code Wise Community results. You can click on any of these results, and they will be loaded into the list on the left (replacing MSDN Online results), where you can then scroll through the results and find what you are looking for.

The new help features in Visual Studio 2005 make it even easier to find the information you are looking for.

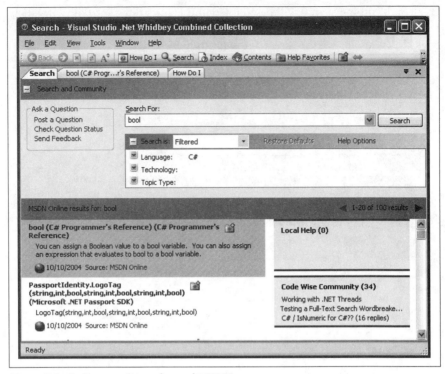

Figure 7-9. Online search goes beyond MSDN

Use Safari from Help

Visual Studio 2005 includes the ability to extend the help system and add additional search locations to the help system. O'Reilly has done a wonderful thing and added the ability to search through the entire Safari online library when you search help.

Safari is a huge electronic reference library that includes not only O'Reilly books but also books from more than a dozen other publishers. You can search through the text of books and then view the contents of the books, all online.

To install this new search location, you simply need to go to *https://secure. safaribooksonline.com/?mode=promo&promocode=vshi2005&portal=msdn.*

From here, you will need to either sign up for a trial account or log in if you already have a Safari account. Once logged in, you will see a link for the VS2005 Help Tool along the top menu. When you click this link, you will be able to download a simple *.reg* file. When you run the *.reg* file, it will add registry settings that add a search function for the Safari online library. The next time you search help, Safari will appear just like MSDN Online or the CodeWise Community sites. Search results from the Safari library can be seen in Figure 7-10.

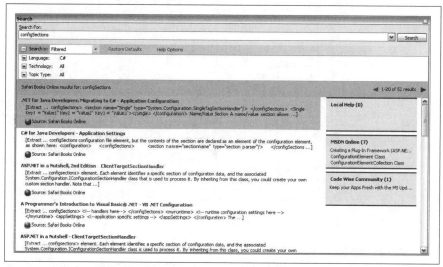

Figure 7-10. Safari search

You can look forward to a number of these search enhancements being added as we get closer to the final version of Visual Studio 2005.

Search the Internet from Visual Studio

Visual Studio's help searches can extend well beyond the boundaries of the IDE and your hard drive. Learn how to make it consult online sources of wisdom.

The Internet has become an indispensable tool when researching programming tasks. If you have ever tried programming on a disconnected machine, you will quickly realize how frustrating it can be when valuable tools like MSDN Online and Google are not available. The Visual Studio team has released a power toy called VSOnlineSearch that allows you to search the Internet from directly inside the text editor, passing whatever text you have selected to the search engine of your choice.

The first step to using this power toy is to download the tool from *http://www.gotdotnet.com/team/ide* and then install the tool using either the *.msi* or *.exe* file included in the *.zip* file. Once you have installed the add-in, you will find a new menu available when you right-click in the editor, which is shown in Figure 7-11.

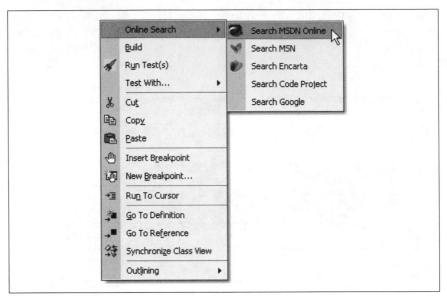

Figure 7-11. VSOnlineSearch right-click menu

To use this power toy, you should first select a piece of text in the text editor and then right-click and select the search engine you would like to search. The power toy will then pass the selected text to the search engine you chose and open the page in the built-in browser, as shown in Figure 7-12.

Because the source is also available online (follow the same link as before), you could add your own searches to the menu if you were so inclined. (I would love to see a Google groups search item.) The VSOnlineSearch power toy is simple to install, easy to use, and makes it very easy to search for something without leaving the IDE.

HACK Redirect Help to Google
#61

Supercharge Visual Studio's help by hooking up a macro to Google and other search engines.

In "Search the Internet from Visual Studio" [Hack #60], you saw a way to highlight text and then query a search engine using that selected text. This hack is similar in that it allows you to select text and then search Google with that text. The difference between these hacks is that this hack uses a macro. This makes it easier to wire up to a shortcut key and to change the search engine to use.

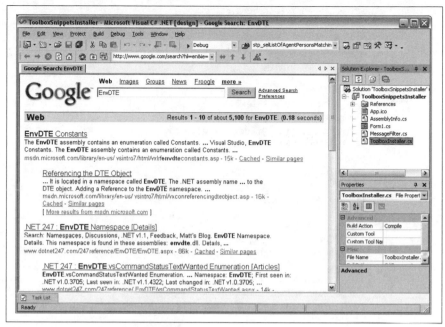

Figure 7-12. VSOnlineSearch results

The first step to using this macro is creating a managed class to interact with from the macro. Here is the process to do this:

1. Open the Visual Studio .NET 2003 command prompt under Start → Programs → Visual Studio .NET 2003 → Visual Studio .NET Tools.

2. Enter the following command into the command prompt:

   ```
   tlbimp %SystemRoot%\system32\shdocvw.dll /out:"%VSINSTALLDIR%\
   PublicAssemblies\Interop.hdocvw.dll"
   ```

Next, you will need to create the actual macro—for detailed instructions on how to create macros, please refer to "Create a Macro" [Hack #51]:

1. Add a reference to your macro project to the Interop.SHDocVW assembly, which will be listed under the .NET tab.

2. Add a reference to the System.Web assembly.

3. Add the following line of code to the top of your module:

   ```
   Imports Interop
   ```

4. Add the following code to the body of your module:

   ```
   Sub DoGoogleSearch( )

       Dim sel As TextSelection
       Dim selectedText As String
       Try
   ```

```
            sel = DTE.ActiveDocument.Selection
            selectedText = sel.Text
        Catch ex As System.Exception
            selectedText = String.Empty
        End Try

        If selectedText.Trim( ).Length < 1 Then
            '// Throw UI to get Text
            Dim criteria As String = InputBox("Enter Search Criteria")
            If (criteria.Trim( ).Length = 0) Then
                Exit Sub
            Else
                selectedText = criteria
            End If
        End If

        Dim url As String = _
    String.Format("http://www.google.com/search?hl=en&ie=UTF-8&q={0}", _
    System.Web.HttpUtility.UrlEncode(selectedText))

        '// Get the WebBrowser/Help Window
        Dim win As Window
        win = DTE.Windows.Item(EnvDTE.Constants.vsWindowKindWebBrowser)
        win.Visible = True

        '// Get the interface
        Dim br As SHDOCVW.WebBrowser
        br = CType(win.Object, SHDOCVW.WebBrowser)

        '// Do The Navigation
        br.Navigate(url, Nothing, Nothing, Nothing, Nothing)
    End Sub
```

The next step is to add a shortcut key or toolbar item for your macro. For information on performing either of these actions, please refer to "Create a Macro" [Hack #51].

Once your macro is created and accessible, you will be able to select a bit of text and then press your shortcut key (I like to assign Alt-F1 for this macro), and you will be shown a search results screen for that bit of code, as shown in Figure 7-13.

The nice thing about this being a macro is that it is so easy to change which search engine this macro uses. If you wanted to create a macro to search Google groups instead of Google web, you would simply need to copy this macro and change the following line from:

```
    Dim url As String = _
    String.Format("http://www.google.com/search?hl=en&ie=UTF-8&q={0}", _
       System.Web.HttpUtility.UrlEncode(selectedText))
```

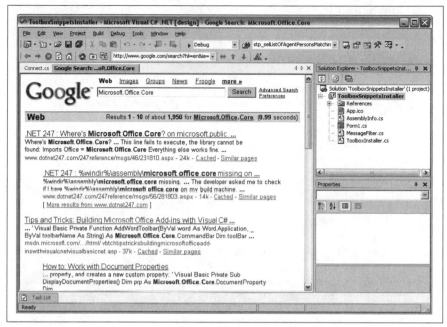

Figure 7-13. Google help

to the following:

```
Dim url As String = _
    String.Format("http://groups.google.com/groups?q={0}", _
    System.Web.HttpUtility.UrlEncode(selectedText))
```

As you can see from this example, it would be very simple to change this to any online resource that has a predictable query string format.

Thanks to Marty Garins for writing this macro and posting it on his web log, which can be found *http://www.little-garins.com/Blogs/marty.*

Use P/Invoke with Ease

P/Invoke can be extremely tricky. With the help of a wiki and an add-in, you can make it as easy as a cut and paste.

The .NET Framework includes a large amount of functionality, but it does not include everything. For a lot of different functions, you will find yourself using something called *P/Invoke*, which is short for platform invoke. P/Invoke allows you to call Win32 or other unmanaged APIs from your managed code, but it is not the easiest thing to do. To make a P/Invoke call, you need to create the correct signature, invoke the method, and hope that all goes well. Because you are working with an unmanaged API, this process is much more susceptible to error. This is where PInvoke.NET comes into play.

Using PInvoke.NET

PInvoke.NET is a wiki that acts as a reference for P/Invoke signatures and unmanaged APIs.

> A wiki is a web site that can easily be edited by anyone using the web site—and I mean anyone. This allows a large number of people to pool their knowledge and research in a single location. For more information about wikis, please refer to the original wiki at: *http://c2.com/cgi/wiki?WikiWikiWeb*.

Using PInvoke.NET, you can look for, and usually find, the P/Invoke signature call that you are looking for. The PInvoke.NET main screen is shown in Figure 7-14.

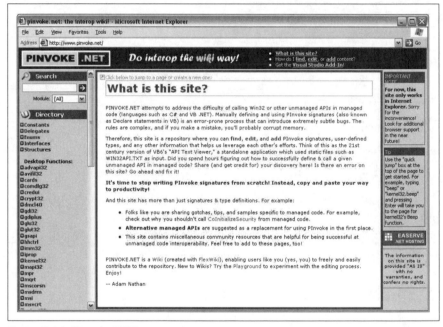

Figure 7-14. PInvoke.NET

As an example, let's look for the signature for the FindWindow API.

If you knew that FindWindow was located in *user32.dll*, you could browse using the tree on the left of the screen. Or you could simply enter the term FindWindow in the Search box and the first result would be the page shown in Figure 7-15.

This page contains a number of details about the FindWindow API. The first item on the page is the C# signature needed to call this API from C#. The

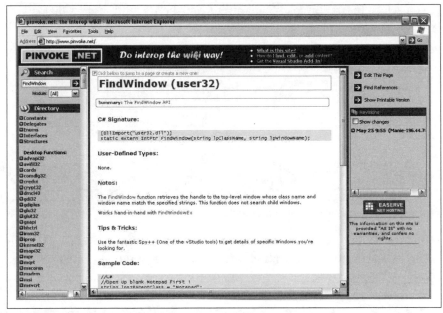

Figure 7-15. PInvoke.NET signature page

page also includes notes on the API as well as a tip on how to find the name for the specific window you might be using. The page also includes sample code that you could cut and paste directly into Visual Studio.

Using the Add-in

The PInvoke.NET wiki becomes even more valuable when you take advantage of the Visual Studio add-in. The first step is to download and install the add-in, which can done by clicking on the "Get the Visual Studio add-in" link at the top of the PInvoke.NET page or by going to the following link:

> *http://www.gotdotnet.com/Community/UserSamples/Details.*
> *aspx?SampleGuid=75122f62-5459-4364-b9ba-7b5e6a4754fe*

Once you have installed the add-in, you can use it by simply right-clicking on your document and selecting Insert PInvoke Signatures from the right-click menu, which is shown in Figure 7-16.

Figure 7-16. PInvoke add-in menu

If you select Insert PInvoke Signatures from the menu, the next dialog you will see is shown in Figure 7-17.

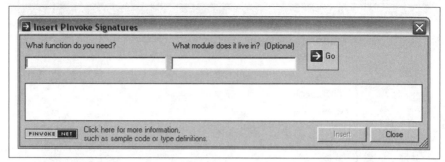

Figure 7-17. Insert PInvoke Signatures dialog

Using this dialog, you can search for any function. In this example, I am going to search for the FindWindow function. The results of that search are shown in Figure 7-18.

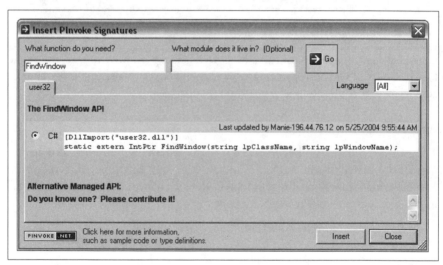

Figure 7-18. Function search results

As you can see in Figure 7-18, the add-in found a matching signature and has selected it for you. You simply need to click the Insert button, and the following code will be inserted into your document:

```
[DllImport("user32.dll")]
static extern IntPtr FindWindow(
    string lpClassName,
    string lpWindowName);
```

You can also use the add-in to contribute new signatures to the wiki. This can be done by selecting the "Contribute PInvoke signatures and types" item in the right-click menu. You will then see the dialog shown in Figure 7-19.

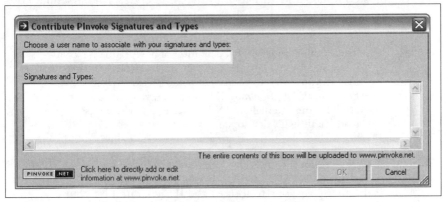

Figure 7-19. "Contribute PInvoke signatures and types" dialog

Using this dialog, you can enter signatures and types, and they will be uploaded to PInvoke.NET. To add notes or code samples, you will need to visit the site in your browser.

PInvoke.NET and its companion add-in were developed by Adam Nathan whose blog can be found at *http://blogs.msdn.com/adam_nathan*. Both the wiki and add-in are extremely useful tools for working with one of the most error-prone and frustrating parts of .NET development.

HACK #63 Examine the IL Generated by Your Code

Use ILDASM to unearth insight into what your code is doing under the hood.

Microsoft's .NET platform is in large part built upon the common intermediate language (CIL, MSIL, or IL for short).

> Hold on. Three abbreviations? What's the deal with that? CIL stands for Common Intermediate Language and is the standard created by Microsoft and certified by numerous parties. MSIL stands for Microsoft Intermediate Language and is Microsoft's implementation of the CIL standard. IL stands for Intermediate Language and is used by many as a catchall term for whatever form of Intermediate Language you happen to be discussing at the moment.

All of the various languages that you can use with .NET, Visual Basic.NET, C#, J#, Cobol.NET, and so forth are compiled into IL. When you compile a

C# Project, your code is not compiled into machine code (as a nonmanaged C++ application would be), but instead is compiled into IL. When your application is run, the IL of your application is then compiled by the JIT (just-in-time) compiler and turned into machine code. This machine code can then be executed and your application can be run.

> This is an extremely quick definition of how IL, the JIT compiler, and the CLR work together. If you have not already read it, you owe it to yourself to read *Applied Microsoft .NET Framework Programming* (Microsoft Press). This book covers how the internals of .NET function and is an essential read for all .NET developers.

Most of the time, you don't have to even think about the IL that your code is compiled into, but sometimes being able to examine this IL can be very useful. Among the many reasons to look at the IL generated by your code, you may want to:

- Better understand what your code is doing
- Compare the performance of different coding approaches
- Compare the differences between various .NET languages
- Diagnose difficult bugs

In this hack, you will learn how to examine IL to compare two different ways of performing the same action. The .NET Framework includes a large number of different ways to do the same things. You can add strings together using the normal addition sign or the StringBuilder object, you can set a string to empty using empty double quotes ("") or the string.Empty property, and so on. IL presents an interesting way to view how each of these is treated when compiled into IL.

Microsoft Intermediate Language Disassembler (ILDASM)

MSIL Disassembler (ILDASM) is an application that is included with the Microsoft .NET Framework SDK. You don't even need Visual Studio to use ILDASM. (But if you don't have Visual Studio, I really don't know why you bought this book.)

Using ILDASM you can examine the IL contained in your assemblies or executables. The easiest way to launch ILDASM is to open the Visual Studio command prompt and type in **ildasm**. You can also find the file in the following locations:

Visual Studio .NET 2002
> *%ProgramFiles%\Microsoft Visual Studio .NET\FrameworkSDK\Bin*

Visual Studio .NET 2003
> *%ProgramFiles%\Microsoft Visual Studio .NET 2003\SDK\v1.1\Bin*

If you have only the framework SDK installed, it will be in the *<SDK Directory>\Bin* directory.

You can see the ILDASM application in Figure 7-20.

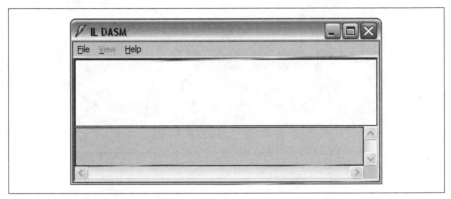

Figure 7-20. ILDASM main window

This is a pretty plain window and doesn't hint at the true potential of this application. First, I am going to set up a small example of two different ways to create an empty string, and then using ILDASM, I'll determine which method is more efficient. Here is the first method using simple empty quotations:

```
public class ILDASMTest {

public string GetBlankString1( )
{
    string s = "";
    return s;
}
```

The second method uses the string.Empty field:

```
public string GetBlankString2( )
{
    string s = string.Empty;
    return s;
}
}
```

Now I will need to compile both of these methods into an assembly and load that assembly into ILDASM. You can compile it at the command line with csc /t:library /out:ILDASMTest.dll ProgramName.cs or create a project and compile it. To open the assembly in ILDASM, click on File → Open and then select the assembly in the file dialog. After selecting the assembly, you will see the screen shown in Figure 7-21.

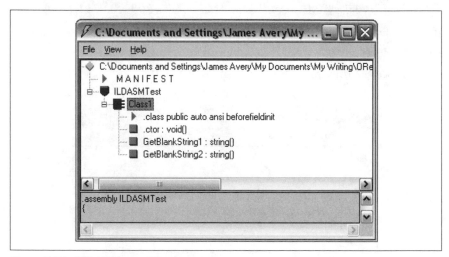

Figure 7-21. ILDASM assembly view

From this screen, you can see the two methods in the assembly. Double-clicking on each of these methods will show the IL that makes up this method. Here is the IL for the first string method:

```
.method public hidebysig instance string
        GetBlankString1( ) cil managed
{
  // Code size       12 (0xc)
  .maxstack  1
  .locals init ([0] string s,
           [1] string CS$00000003$00000000)
  IL_0000:  ldstr        ""
  IL_0005:  stloc.0
  IL_0006:  ldloc.0
  IL_0007:  stloc.1
  IL_0008:  br.s         IL_000a
  IL_000a:  ldloc.1
  IL_000b:  ret
} // end of method Class1::GetBlankString1
```

And here is the IL from the second string method:

```
.method public hidebysig instance string
        GetBlankString2( ) cil managed
{
  // Code size       12 (0xc)
  .maxstack  1
```

```
.locals init ([0] string s,
          [1] string CS$00000003$00000000)
IL_0000:  ldsfld     string [mscorlib]System.String::Empty
IL_0005:  stloc.0
IL_0006:  ldloc.0
IL_0007:  stloc.1
IL_0008:  br.s       IL_000a
IL_000a:  ldloc.1
IL_000b:  ret
} // end of method Class1::GetBlankString2
```

At first glance, IL is a little confusing, and I don't plan on trying to teach you everything about IL in this hack. But looking at these two simple examples, you will see one major difference. In the first method, you will see that the IL_0000: line contains this line of code:

```
IL_0000:  ldstr      ""
```

And on the same line in the second method is this line of code:

```
IL_0000:  ldsfld     string [mscorlib]System.String::Empty
```

To understand these two lines, you first need to understand what the commands ldstr and ldsfld actually do. The IL command ldstr creates a new string (or most likely pulls it from the string pool). The IL command ldsfld loads a static field from a class. Using the first string method creates a new string object, whereas the second method simply loads the value of a static field. To be sure, this is a tiny difference in these two procedures. You would probably never notice the performance difference between these two methods, even if you ran the process hundreds of times. But understanding the difference and how the .NET Framework works is what's important. The second method of creating an empty string (using string.Empty) is technically more efficient than the first method. (Of course, after I learned this. I have always used string.Empty because there is no reason not to.)

This is a simplistic example of using ILDASM, but it does an excellent job of demonstrating how ILDASM can be used to better understand the .NET Framework.

Advanced ILDASM

ILDASM also includes an advanced mode. This advanced mode can be activated by calling the *ildasm.exe* executable using the /ADV switch. This enables a number of different extra views that are not available when running ILDASM in normal mode. One of the more interesting views is the statistics view that is shown in Figure 7-22.

```
Statistics                                                    _ □ X
File size            : 16384
PE header size       : 4096 (496 used)    (25.00%)
PE additional info   : 987                ( 6.02%)
Num.of PE sections   : 3
CLR header size      : 72                 ( 0.44%)
CLR meta-data size   : 1108               ( 6.76%)
CLR additional info  : 0                  ( 0.00%)
CLR method headers   : 36                 ( 0.22%)
Managed code         : 31                 ( 0.19%)
Data                 : 876                ( 5.35%)
Unaccounted          : 9178               (56.02%)

Num.of PE sections   : 3
  .text    - 4096
  .rsrc    - 4096
  .reloc   - 4096

CLR meta-data size   : 1108
  Module       -   1 (10 bytes)
  TypeDef      -   2 (28 bytes)     0 interfaces, 0 explicit layout
  TypeRef      -  15 (90 bytes)
  MethodDef    -   3 (42 bytes)     0 abstract, 0 native, 3 bodies
  MemberRef    -  15 (90 bytes)
```

Figure 7-22. ILDASM Statistics

This view reports on all kinds of interesting information including the size of the file and what percentages different parts of the file contribute to the whole.

For more information on the advanced mode of ILDASM, please refer to the *ILDasmAdvancedOptions.doc* file that is in the same directory as the ILDASM executable.

HACK #64 Examine the Innards of Assemblies

ILDASM is great for digging into assemblies, but Reflector is a powerful, free tool that gives you even more.

When you compile your source code in Visual Studio, the compiler translates the high-level source code, not into machine-specific instructions, but into an intermediate language known as Microsoft Intermediate Language (MSIL). This Intermediate Language (IL), along with additional security, versioning, sharing, and other related metadata, is packaged into one or more DLLs or executable files. The complete package is referred to as an assembly. As you saw in "Examine the IL Generated by Your Code" **[Hack #63]**, there are free tools that can examine the IL of an assembly.

While examining the IL of an assembly can be useful at times, it requires familiarity with MSIL. More often than not, the average developer is much more comfortable with a high-level programming language like C# or Visual Basic rather than IL. Fortunately, a free tool called Reflector can translate the intermediate language of a .NET assembly into either C# or Visual Basic code. In addition to converting IL to C# or Visual Basic code, Reflector provides an outline of the assembly's classes and its members, the ability to view the IL for an assembly, and support for third-party add-ins.

Download and Run Reflector

Reflector is a free program created by Lutz Roeder, a Microsoft employee. It is one of those essentials that every serious .NET developer should have in her toolbox. Reflector is updated frequently; the latest version is available at *http://www.aisto.com/roeder/dotnet*. At the time of this writing, when you download Reflector, you download a zip file containing just two files: *Reflector.exe* and *ReadMe.htm*. After unzipping these two files to some directory, you can run Reflector by simply double-clicking the *Reflector.exe* file.

By default, Reflector opens a handful of common assemblies: *mscorlib*, *System*, *System.Data*, *System.Drawing*, and so on. Each opened assembly is listed in Reflector's main window (see Figure 7-23). Clicking on the + icon next to an assembly will expand the tree, showing the assembly's namespaces. Each namespace has a corresponding + icon next to it as well that, when clicked, will show the namespace's classes. Additionally, each class can be expanded to show the class's members—its events, fields, methods, and properties.

To view the details of other assemblies, such as assemblies you've created, go to the File menu and choose Open. Next, browse to the assembly you want to view. Once you have selected a valid .NET assembly, the assembly will be displayed in Reflector's main window along with the default assemblies. To remove an assembly from Reflector's main window, right-click on the assembly and choose Close.

Disassemble Assemblies with Reflector

While being able to browse through assemblies, namespaces, and classes is handy, Reflector's true usefulness shines through in its disassembling capabilities. Once you have drilled down to a class-level member, you can disassemble the class-level member by going to the Tools menu and choosing Disassembler. This will open up a second pane, showing the disassembled content in either C#, Visual Basic, Delphi, or IL. (You can specify what language the disassembled output should be shown in through the View → Options dialog or via the drop-down list in the toolbar.) Figure 7-24 shows the disassembled contents of the DataSet class's GetXml( ) method in C#.

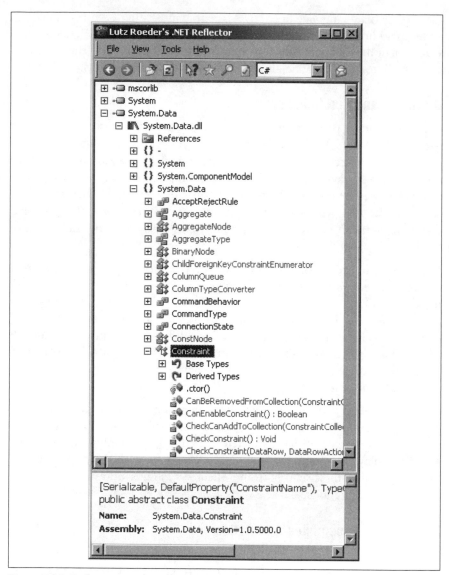

Figure 7-23. Reflector main window

With its disassembling capabilities, Reflector makes it easy to investigate the guts of the .NET Framework Base Class Library. You can also examine the source code of assemblies that you have created or are using but don't have the original source code for.

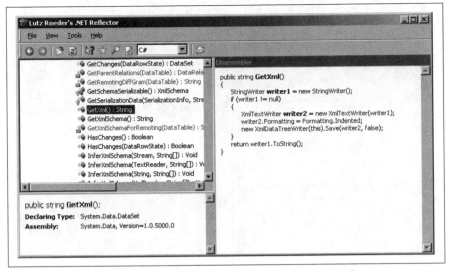

Figure 7-24. Disassemble methods in your language of choice with Reflector

 Seeing that Reflector can provide source code view of an assembly might give you pause if your company generates its revenue from selling a .NET application. The last thing you'd likely be interested in is having your customers—or worse, your competitors—examining the source code of the application. There's no way to prevent anyone from viewing the IL of a .NET assembly (and thereby disassembling it to C# or Visual Basic), but you can *obfuscate* the IL. Obfuscation is the process of changing the IL so that it still behaves as intended, but is illegible and unreadable for a human. A number of .NET obfuscation products —such as: PreEmptive Solution's Dotfuscator **[Hack #80]**, WiseOwl's Demeanor, and Remotesoft's .NET Obfuscator—are available.

Additional Reflector Features

In addition to serving as an object browser and disassembler, Reflector can display call and callee graphs for class and class members, offer one-click access to search Google or MSDN, and provide a framework that allows third-party developers to create add-ins for Reflector.

To view the call or callee graphs, simply select a member in the tree view, go to the Tools menu, and select the Call Graph or Callee Graph option. The Call Graph lists the members called by the selected item, whereas the Callee Graph lists those members that call the selected item. For example, as Figure 7-25 shows, the ArrayList class's Clone() method calls the System.Array.Copy() method and the ArrayList's constructor (as it created a new ArrayList instance), and works with the ArrayList's _items, _size, and _version private member variables.

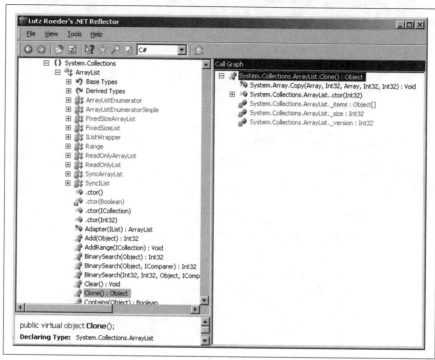

Figure 7-25. Call Graph shows members called by selected item

The callee graph is the inverse of the call graph. It shows those members that call the selected item. For example, the ArrayList's Clone( ) method's callee graph shows that the System.NET.SocketPermission class's Copy( ) method and the System.Xml.XPath.XsltFunction class's Clone( ) members, among others, call the ArrayList's Clone( ) method.

Reflector's functionality can be further extended through the use of add-ins. There are add-ins for displaying assembly dependency graphs, for automatically loading the currently running assembly, for outputting the disassembled contents of an entire assembly, and for hosting Reflector within Visual Studio. These add-ins, and more, are listed at *http://www.freewebs.com/csharp/Reflector/AddIns* and are all worth checking out.

Using Reflector Within Visual Studio

Of particular interest is the Reflector.VisualStudio Add-In. This add-in, created by Jaime Cansdale, allows for Reflector to be hosted within Visual Studio. With this add-in, you can have Reflector integrated within the Visual

Studio environment. To get started, you will need to have the latest version of Reflector on your machine. Once you have downloaded Reflector, download the latest version of the Reflector.VisualStudio Add-In from *http://www.testdriven.NET/reflector*. The download contains a number of files that need to be placed in the same directory as *Reflector.exe*. To install the add-in, drop to the command line and run:

```
Reflector.VisualStudio.exe /install
```

After the add-in has been installed, you can start using Reflector from Visual Studio. You'll notice a new menu item, Addins, which has a menu option titled Reflector. This option, when selected, displays the Reflector window, which can be docked in the IDE (see Figure 7-26). Additionally, the add-in provides context menu support. When you right-click in an open code file in Visual Studio, you'll see a Reflector menu item that expands into a submenu with options to disassemble the code into C# or Visual Basic, display the call graph or callee graph, and other related choices. The context menu also includes a Synchronize with Reflector menu item that, when clicked, syncs the object browser tree in the Reflector window with the current code file.

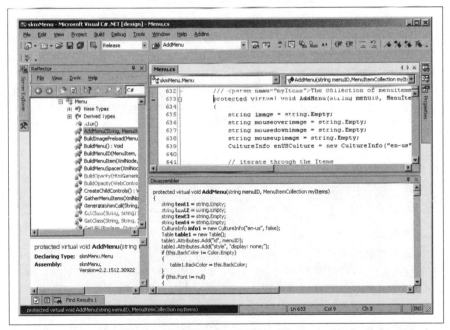

Figure 7-26. With the Reflector.VisualStudio Add-In, Reflector can be hosted in Visual Studio

Reflector is an object browser, disassembler, and so much more, all wrapped up into one program that can be hosted through Visual Studio. Reflector is useful for inspecting the source code of the .NET Framework's Base Class Library, as well as a helpful tool for inspecting your own assemblies. With its bevy of features and add-ins, Reflector is an indispensable tool that every .NET developer should know of and use.

—Scott Mitchell

HACK Follow the Rules with FxCop
#65
Determine whether your code and assemblies play by the rules and guidelines.

A common problem in the realm of software development is how to properly enforce coding standards and design guidelines (this is especially true in large corporations where a project team typically consists of several developers, each with his own coding style). In the majority of projects, these issues are addressed in a manual effort, occurring in the form of code reviews and design reviews. While absolutely necessary, these types of reviews often occur too late in the process; thus, problem areas identified in those reviews might not always get the proper attention they deserve.

To help alleviate these issues, Microsoft developed a free code analysis tool named FxCop (*http://www.gotdotnet.com/team/fxcop*). FxCop checks .NET assemblies for conformance to the Microsoft .NET Framework Design Guidelines (*http://msdn.microsoft.com/library/default.asp?url=/library/en-us/ cpgenref/html/cpconnetframeworkdesignguidelines.asp*). It uses reflection, MSIL parsing, and call graph analysis to inspect assemblies for defects in the following areas:

- Library design
- Localization
- Naming conventions
- Performance
- Security

Although primarily targeted at class library developers, FxCop can be used on any managed code assembly, and it's recommended that developers use it. FxCop includes both GUI and command-line versions of the tool, as well as an SDK to create custom rules.

An interesting aspect of using FxCop is that it can be used as a learning tool, especially to design guidelines and best practices. So even if you don't use FxCop to strictly enforce certain guidelines, you can use it to at least gain insight as to why the guidelines are in place and what they mean.

Create an FxCop Project

To use FxCop (assuming you've already downloaded and installed it), you'll first need to create a project in Visual Studio and compile that project; in this case, I've created a class library project named MathLibrary. You can create an FxCop Project by following these steps:

1. Start an instance of FxCop.
2. Click File → Project → Add Targets (Ctrl-Shift-A).
3. Browse to your .NET assembly, select it, and click Open. You'll now see your assembly listed under the Targets tab.
4. Click File → Save Project (Ctrl-S).
5. In the Save As dialog box, type a name for your FxCop Project, select a location, and click Save. Note that all FxCop Project files are saved with an *.fxcop* extension; however, these are just XML files that contain all the information needed for your project.

Analyze Your Assemblies

Now that you've created and saved an FxCop Project, you can use it to analyze your .NET assemblies for code and design conformance. To do this, click Project → Analyze (or press the F5 key).

Once FxCop has completed its analysis, you'll more than likely see several messages appear in the righthand pane of the tool, as shown in Figure 7-27.

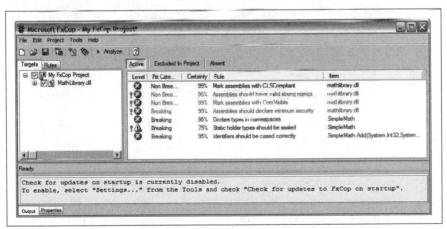

Figure 7-27. An analyzed assembly with FxCop

There are a couple things to take note of in Figure 7-27. First, you can see that FxCop assigns a certainty to each message. For instance, FxCop is 95% certain that the class SimpleMath does not belong to a namespace, therefore violating the rule "Declare types in namespaces". Also note that FxCop tells you exactly what item is in violation of a particular rule and gives each item a Fix Category, such as Breaking or Non Breaking.

You can view a summary of the analysis by clicking Project → Analysis Summary. This will show you how long the analysis took to execute, the number of checks performed, and how many issues were found. The summary for the MathLibrary assembly is shown in Figure 7-28.

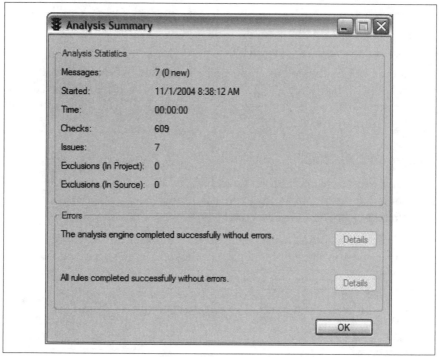

Figure 7-28. Analysis Summary

You can view even more details of a particular message by selecting it from the list. For this example, let's investigate further the message with the rule violation "Identifiers should be cased correctly", shown in Figure 7-29.

The Properties tab displays information that is much more useful to you. Here you can see that the Add method in the SimpleMath class contains a parameter named Expression1, which is PascalCased, and the guidelines say parameters should be camelCased. You also see the suggested resolution as well as the source of the rule violation. The source of the rule violation is shown in the Location line, which shows the file and line of code in violation (*C:/MathLibrary/SimpleMath.cs*, line 12 in this example).

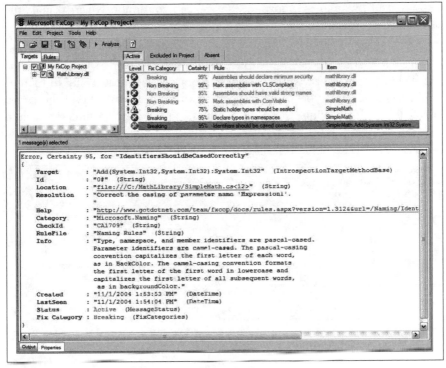

Figure 7-29. Properties tab for a given issue in FxCap

The Properties tab also shows you where to find help for the violation and the rule file used in the analysis. When I mentioned earlier that FxCop is a good learning tool, it was because of the information provided in this tab. As you can see, the tool provides insight as to why the message was generated.

Fix a Message—and Watch It Disappear

Great, you've written a class library that you think is rock solid, but then you run FxCop on it, which generates more issues than you care to admit. Chances are you'll choose to ignore some messages (for various reasons), but you'll want to take care of others. The good news is that FxCop identifies exactly where the issues are, so most of the work of tracking down the violations has already been done for you. All you have to do is fix the problem and recompile your assembly.

Previous versions of FxCop would keep a lock on the .NET assembly you were trying to analyze; thus, when you went to modify your code and recompile the assembly with FxCop still open, you would get an Access Denied error. To get around this, you had to shut down FxCop, recompile your code, then open FxCop again. Luckily, Version 1.30 and above of

FxCop fixed this major annoyance, so you can continuously run Visual Studio and FxCop side by side.

To see your number of FxCop messages decrease, make the necessary code changes in Visual Studio, recompile, then flip back over to FxCop and hit the F5 key to reanalyze your assembly. In our example, I'm going to fix two messages: "Declare types in namespaces" and "Identifiers should be cased correctly". After fixing these two issues, my FxCop results look like Figure 7-30.

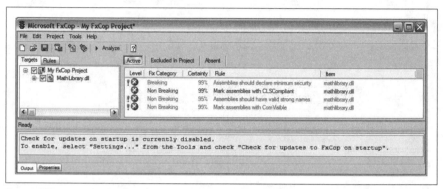

Figure 7-30. FxCop results after code fixes

A Look at the Rules

Now that you've seen how to use FxCop and what it's good for, you must be wondering where all those rules are and whether you really need to analyze all your assemblies against every single rule FxCop has. The answer is no. Although that is strongly suggested, the FxCop team understands that not everyone can abide by all the rules set forth in the .NET Framework Design Guidelines all the time. Therefore, they've made it very easy to pick and choose which rules will be used in the analysis of your .NET assemblies. By default, all rules are used during the analysis, but that can be easily changed.

To see the rules, click the Rules tab in the left pane of FxCop. You will see Figure 7-31.

Notice that all rules are expandable and can be checked or unchecked as needed. For instance, if you choose to ignore all interoperability rules, you would simply uncheck the Interoperability Rules box. If you did so, your rules selection would now look like Figure 7-32.

It's clearly visible in Figure 7-32 that each set of rules contains several individual rules that can also be selected or unselected as required for your

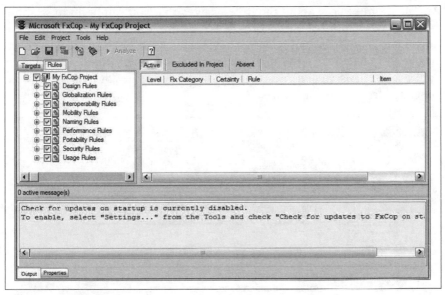

Figure 7-31. FxCop rules

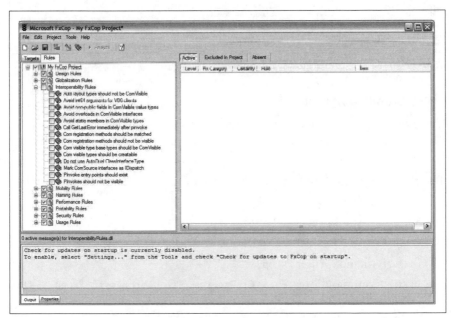

Figure 7-32. FxCop rules with Interoperability Rules ignored

project. I'll leave the exploration of the other sets of rules up to you, but it's easy to see that FxCop allows you to customize your code and design analysis as you see fit.

Another item of note about the Rules view is that you can begin to see how your rules violations are categorized. For example, if you wanted to know how many of your overall number of messages were based on design issues, you would switch to the Rules view and select Design Rules, as shown in Figure 7-33. This view shows that five messages of my overall issues were generated from the design rules.

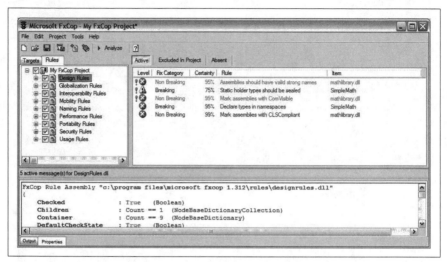

Figure 7-33. Messages specific for design rules

Visual Studio Integration

Up to this point, I've demonstrated the preferred way of using FxCop. However, FxCop provides a command-line interface that can be used from within Visual Studio.

The first thing that you must do is to set up FxCop as an external tool in Visual Studio [Hack #33]. To do this:

1. Start an instance of Visual Studio.
2. Click File → Tools → External Tools → Add.
3. In the Title box, enter **FxCop**.
4. In the Command box, enter **C:\Program Files\Microsoft FxCop 1.312\ FxCopCmd.exe**. (The actual path will vary based on the version of FxCop and where you installed it.)
5. In the Arguments box, enter:

    /c /f:$(TargetPath) /r:"C:\Program Files\Microsoft FxCop 1.312\Rules"
6. You can leave the Initial Directory box empty.

7. Check the Use Output Window box. Then click OK.

8. Click File → Tools, and verify that you now see FxCop as an option.

Figure 7-34 shows a completed External Tools dialog.

Figure 7-34. Completed dialog for adding FxCop as an external tool

Now that FxCop is set up as an external tool in Visual Studio, you can run FxCop on your .NET assemblies very easily:

1. Open a Visual Studio Project.

2. Click Tools → FxCop.

3. The Output window will appear and show the results of the analysis (see Figure 7-35).

More FxCop Resources

The goal of this hack is to expose you to when, why, and how you would use FxCop. However, there is much more to FxCop that cannot be covered in detail here, such as the ability to create your own rules. Here are additional FxCop resources:

FxCop integrated help
> You can find out much more about the tool and how to best use it by reading its built-in help functionality.

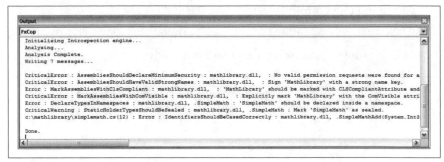

Figure 7-35. Output window showing FxCop analysis

FxCop web site (http://www.gotdotnet.com/team/fxcop)

In addition to more documentation, here you can find the latest downloads, readme files, and samples. You can also find custom rules that other developers have created for use in your own FxCop Projects.

FxCop blog (http://blogs.msdn.com/fxcop)

Although not updated very often, this site does provide some good information.

MSDN Magazine (http://msdn.microsoft.com/msdnmag)

John Robbins wrote two excellent articles about FxCop for the June and September 2004 issues of *MSDN Magazine*. These are highly recommended reads.

—*Dave Donaldson*

HACK #66 Generate Statistics on Your C# Code

You'll write a lot of code in Visual Studio. Now, learn about a free tool that lets you view assorted statistics and information about your C# Visual Studio Projects.

Have you ever wondered how many files, classes, or lines of code exist in one or more of your Visual Studio Projects? While you can certainly count these metrics manually, there is a free Visual Studio add-in that will provide these statistics (and more!) in a flash. Once installed, this add-in, called devMetrics, adds an Analyze menu option to the Visual Studio Tools menu. When selected, the projects in the currently loaded Visual Studio Solution are examined, and their statistics are presented in an easy-to-read report. (Unfortunately, devMetrics generates reports for only C# Projects.)

The devMetrics reports provide useful information at the click of a mouse. The report's statistics include information that can be used to measure the progress of a code project, show what classes are undercommented, and point out what classes and methods are exceedingly complex and in need of refactoring.

Download and Install devMetrics

Before you can generate statistical reports on your code, you'll first need to download and install the devMetrics add-in, which is a free product from Anticipating Minds (*http://www.anticipatingminds.com*) and is available at *http://www.anticipatingminds.com/Content/Products/devMetrics/devMetrics. aspx.* Download the devMetrics installer to your computer, and then double-click the file to begin the installation process.

Once installed, devMetrics can be run in two ways:

From Visual Studio
> To view the statistics for a C# Project through Visual Studio, open Visual Studio and load the solution or project to analyze. Then, from the Tools menu, choose the devMetrics submenu, and select the Analyze menu option, as shown in Figure 7-36. Once the project(s) have been analyzed, the statistical report will be automatically displayed in Visual Studio.

From the command line
> To run the devMetrics analyzer from the command line, navigate to the *Program Files\Anticipating Minds\devMetrics* directory and run the *devMetrics.exe* executable, specifying the directory that contains the C# Projects that you want to analyze, such as: devMetrics "C:\My Projects\ Some Visual Studio Project Folder". (devMetrics will recursively iterate through the directory's subdirectories and include reports on all C# Projects found.) After completing, devMetrics will automatically launch Internet Explorer, displaying the report.

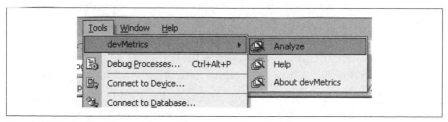

Figure 7-36. devMetrics Analyze menu option

Study the Report

After analyzing either a Visual Studio Project or Solution, devMetrics displays the resulting project report (see Figure 7-37). This report lists each C# Project analyzed, along with the following metrics:

Files
> The number of C# files in the project.

Types
> The number of classes, interfaces, and structures in the project.

Members
> The number of fields, properties, events, methods, and constructors.

Lines
> The total number of lines of code in the project, including blank lines and comments.

Statements
> The total number of statements in the project.

Average and maximum code complexity
> devMetrics uses the cyclomatic code complexity algorithm as defined by the Software Engineering Institute (see *http://www.sei.cmu.edu/str/ descriptions/cyclomatic_body.html*). The complexity is a measure of linearly independent paths through a program module and is calculated for each member that contains statements. The code complexity measurement results in a numerical evaluation, with lower values meaning less complex code. The maximum code complexity is the highest complexity value for all members in the project; the average code complexity is the average complexity of all members.

In addition to showing these metrics for each project, the project report also displays a summary row.

As Figure 7-37 shows, the name of each project in the report is displayed as a hyperlink. Clicking on the link will expand the project node and show you a list of the types in that particular project. For each type in the project, the number of statements and members are shown along with the cyclomatic complexity. Figure 7-38 shows the report with the project node expanded.

From the Type Declaration list, you can expand the node of each type and view a list of the type members, including the number of statements and complexity of each member.

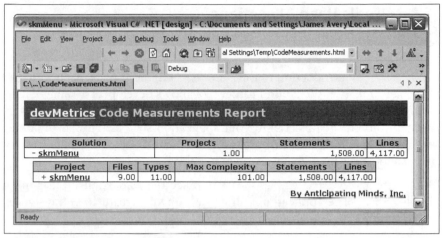

Figure 7-37. devMetrics project report

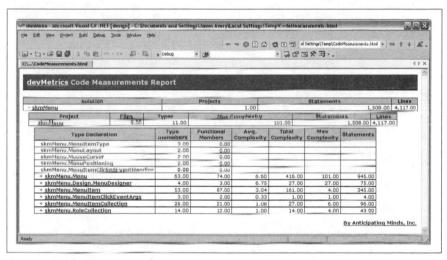

Figure 7-38. devMetrics member report

The devMetrics add-in can provide quick summary data about your C# code on a project-by-project level as well as a member-by-member level. The cyclomatic code complexity, statements/member, and members/class metrics can assess what portions of your code are unduly verbose and what portions would benefit from being refactored.

—Scott Mitchell

Profile Heap Allocations

HACK #67

Use the Allocation Profiler to research how your objects are being handled on the heap.

This hack is an introduction to the Allocation Profiler tool available at *www. gotdotnet.com*. The Allocation Profiler tool allows developers to analyze allocations on the garbage collection heap. The Allocation Profiler answers questions about the object(s) in your application such as: How many times was my object created in memory? At what point in execution time was my object allocated? How long was my object alive?

Let's write a very basic C# application to see the Allocation Profiler in its simplest form. The application will run a loop and create 10,000 instances of our simple class.

Here is the code for *AP_example1.exe*:

```
// main.cs
using System;

namespace AP_example1
{
    /// <summary>
    /// Summary description for main.
    /// </summary>

    // basic class that creates a string object
    public class AP_example_class
    {
        string s = String.Empty;
    }

    public class AP_example1
    {
        public static void Main( )
        {
            // create 10,000 instance of our class
            for(int x=0;x<10000;x++)
            {
                AP_example_class aec = new AP_example_class( );
            }

        }
    }
}
```

After compiling *AP_example1*, open *AllocationProfiler.exe*, which is shown in Figure 7-39.

Figure 7-39. AllocationProfiler

The Profiling Active box should be checked and Allocations should be chosen from the Profile radio button list on the right.

Choose Profile Application from the File menu and browse to *AP_example1.exe*.

The Allocation Profiler will execute your application and log everything that goes through the garbage collector. When the application has finished executing, it will automatically launch the Allocation Graph, which is shown in Figure 7-40.

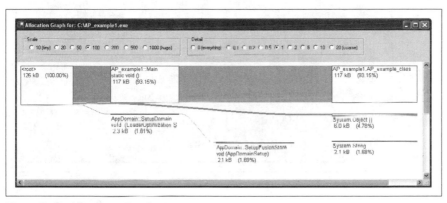

Figure 7-40. Allocation Graph

The Scale option allows you to choose the number of pixels to display proportional to allocated memory.

The Detail option shows more objects the lower you go in the scale. If you choose 0 (everything), you will see every object allocated. By choosing 20 (coarse), you will get a higher-level view of the core objects in your application.

Figure 7-40 shows you a hierarchical drill-down of the managed memory allocated in your application. In this example, the application has allocated 126 KB of managed memory. Of the initial 126 KB (100%), 117 KB (93.15%) has been initialized from the AP_example1::Main method. Since the only thing in the main method was a loop creating the AP_example_class object, AP_example1.AP_example_class is also 117 KB (93.15%) of the managed memory in the application.

The lowest levels of objects in the graph represent the percentage of the entire application, not the percentage of their parent.

From the main menu, choose View → Histogram Allocated Types. The result is shown in Figure 7-41.

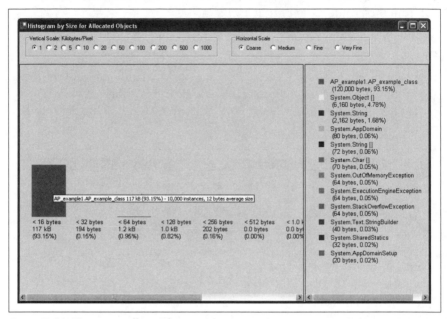

Figure 7-41. Histogram allocated types

Figure 7-41 shows you kilobytes allocated by object. By hovering over each item in the histogram, it will show you the number of instances created and their average size. You can right-click on the bar to show where the instance(s) were allocated and export the data.

From the main menu, choose View → Objects by Address to open the window shown in Figure 7-42.

In Figure 7-42, each vertical bar shows you an address range for each GC heap. There are two heaps for the system build, the normal heap and the large object heap. In this example, if you hover over the first bar in the graph, it will show you the object address for each instance you allocated. In addition, it will show you the size (in bytes) and how long the object was allocated in memory.

From the main menu, choose View → Histogram by Age, which is shown in Figure 7-43.

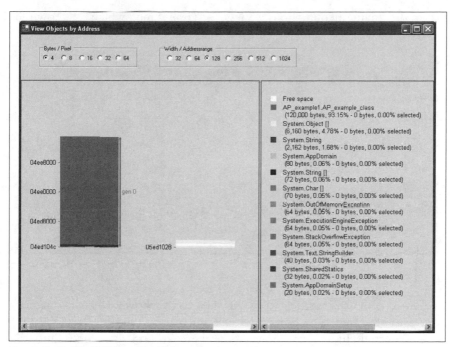

Figure 7-42. View Objects by Address window

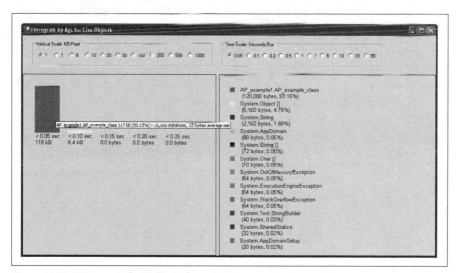

Figure 7-43. Histogram by Age window

In Figure 7-43, each vertical bar in this graph shows you a histogram of created objects by time. The time the object was in memory determines which bucket the object's instance will be included in.

From the main menu, choose View → Time Line, which is shown in Figure 7-44.

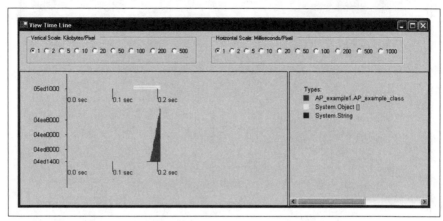

Figure 7-44. View Time Line window

In Figure 7-44, the vertical axis of this chart shows you the memory addresses allocated. The horizontal axis shows you the time in which they were allocated. In this example, somewhere around .2 seconds into the application, almost 100% of the objects were allocated. You can right-click at any point in the timeline to view objects by address at that time or by any of the recent features I covered in this hack.

The preceding example was intended to show you the analysis the Allocation Profiler provides. In a real-life application, you would use the Allocation Profiler to verify that the allocated objects are the ones you expected, view potential memory leaks, view how long objects are on the GC heap, and view what percentage each object allocates in your overall application memory usage. For more information, download the Allocation Profiler from www.gotdotnet.com and refer to the included documentation.

—Jayme Davis

Comments and Documentation
Hacks 68–72

A big part of developing a high-quality application is properly documenting that application. Documentation starts during the design process with your design documents (UML diagrams, use cases, stories, etc.) and then continues during the process of creating that application. A large part of documenting an application you are developing is correctly commenting it. Good comments are even more important with the .NET Framework because you can generate documentation based on your comments.

Two types of comments can be used with the .NET Framework. The most common type is line comments (whenever you use // with C# or ' with VB. NET to mark a line as a comment). This type of comment is usually used to explain what the current or next line of code is doing. While these types of comments are very valuable (and I would hate to try and understand an application with none of these), the focus of this chapter will be on another type of comment, XML comments. These comments document a class or method using a piece of XML. The comments can then be used for a number of different things, not least of which is generating API documentation for your application. Here is an example of XML comments applied to a C# method:

```
/// <summary>
/// This method accepts a string and then
/// displays that string using a message box
/// </summary>
/// <param name="textToDisplay">The string to display</param>
private void HelloWorld(string textToDisplay)
{
    MessageBox.Show(textToDisplay);
}
```

To use XML comments with VB.NET, you have to do a little more work [Hack #70].

The hacks in this chapter will cover how to get the most out of XML comments, how to create comments faster using an add-in, how to create documentation from your comments, how to use XML comments with VB.NET, and how to integrate your own documentation into Visual Studio.

HACK #68   Master C# XML Comments

Comment your code with a sprinkling of XML, and give IntelliSense and documentation tools plenty of grist for their mills.

XML comments are a compelling addition to any project. Using XML comments, you can document all of your public classes, methods, and enumerations while you program. The basics of XML comments are very simple—precede your comments with ///, and Visual Studio will add a basic summary and an element for each of the parameters on your method. You can then enter the summary and parameter descriptions. But there is much more to XML comments; there are 20 different tags that can be used in XML comments. In this hack, you are going to learn how to use all of these tags to create better documentation.

To insert XML comments, simply type /// on a line preceding a class, interface, method, field, or property declaration. As soon as you type these characters, IntelliSense will give you a skeletal XML comment with an empty `<summary>` element:

```
/// <summary>
///
/// </summary>
public void Foo( )
```

Technically you can put anything you want in your XML comments. You can make up an XML element and use it without having to do any sort of configuration or work. The only problem is that most tools won't recognize your custom element. By default, documentation generation tools like NDoc [Hack #71] recognize only the standard XML comments. Visual Studio also uses the standard tags to populate IntelliSense comments for your types.

Primary Tags

The first group of comment tags are the primary tags. The primary tags are the tags that you can use independently of other tags. Another set, called the secondary tags, can be used inside of the primary tags to mark up text. The primary tags are used by documentation generation tools to create documentation. When a tool sees a `<summary>` tag, it knows that the text inside that tag is used to summarize whatever the XML comments are describing.

<remarks>. The <remarks> tag is used to describe a type. You might not know this because when you insert XML comments in Visual Studio, it inserts a <summary> tag rather than a <remarks> tag. The difference is not huge, but the C# documentation recommends using <remarks>, so it is a good idea to do so. Here is an example of the <remarks> tag describing a class:

```
/// <remarks>
/// Vechicle is used as a base class for other specific classes.
/// It includes virtual methods like Start and TurnOff
/// </remarks>
public class Vehicle
```

The <remarks> tag should explain the purpose of your type.

<summary>. Since it appears by default, the <summary> tag is probably the most familiar of these tags. It should be used to document the general purpose of all public methods, properties, and fields of a type. Here is an example of the <summary> tag being used to describe the purpose of a method:

```
/// <summary>
/// Classes that inherit from Vehicle should override
/// this method and implement a function that starts
/// the vehicle.
/// </summary>
public virtual void Start( )
```

<value>. Similar to the <summary> and <remarks> tags, the <value> tag describes the value of a property. The usage is similar to the other tags:

```
/// <value>
/// This property contains the number of doors that this vehicle has.
/// </value>
public int NumOfDoors
```

Each of your properties should include a <value> tag describing what exactly the property represents.

<param>. The <param> tag is used to document each of a method's parameters. This is one of the most useful comments because it is sometimes hard to discern the purpose of a parameter just from its name. You might have a parameter called startDate, but what is this the start date of? The <param> tag can be used to answer those questions. Here is an example of using the <param> tag to document the parameters of a method:

```
/// <summary>
/// This method sets the owner of this vehicle
/// in the database table VehicleOwner
/// </summary>
```

```
/// <param name="ownerID">The userID of the owner</param>
/// <param name="startDate">
/// The date that this user took ownership of this vehicle
/// </param>
public void SetOwner(int ownerID, DateTime startDate)
```

Notice that the <param> tag includes an attribute called name that is used to specify which parameter this comment is describing. You should be sure and specify the exact name of the parameter, as it is case sensitive. The <param> tag is especially valuable because it is used in the IntelliSense pop up for parameters. Below the normal IntelliSense information, you will see your comment displayed.

<returns>. The <returns> tag is used to define the return type of a method. From the signature of the method, you know what type it returns, so simply stating "integer" is pointless. Instead, you should explain what the integer represents. Here is an example of using the <returns> tag to document the return value of a method:

```
/// <summary>
/// This method retrieves the owner of this vehicle
/// </summary>
/// <returns>The userID of the vehicle's owner</returns>
public int GetOwnerID()
{
    return new int();
}
```

<exception>. The <exception> tag is used to specify the exceptions a type can throw. This tag uses an attribute called cref. The cref attribute is used to reference another type and is covered in more detail in the "Secondary Tags" section of this hack. Using the <exception> tag, you should document any specific exceptions that your method might throw with the cref attribute and then explain when the exception could be thrown. Here is an example of using the <exception> tag:

```
/// <summary>
/// This method retrieves the owner of this vehicle
/// </summary>
/// <returns>The userID of the vehicle's owner</returns>
/// <exception cref="IDNotFoundException">
/// If an owner is not found for this vehicle
/// this exception will be thrown
/// </exception>
public int GetOwnerID()
```

Knowing what exceptions a method might throw is very important to developing high-quality applications. Since .NET does not allow you to specify the exceptions a method might throw in the method signature, this is the next best option.

<example>. The <example> tag can be used to provide an example of how to use your method, property, or field. Examples are a key part of high-quality documentation, and nothing can better show developers how to work with your types. Using the <example> tag in conjunction with the <code> tag (one of the secondary tags), you can provide code examples directly in your code. Here is an example of using an <example> tag:

```
/// <summary>
/// This method sets the owner of this vehicle
/// in the database table VehicleOwner
/// </summary>
/// <param name="ownerID">The userID of the owner</param>
/// <param name="startDate">
/// The date that this user took ownership of this vehicle
/// </param>
/// <example>
/// <code>
///     // Get the user
///     User user = User.Get(userID);
///     // Call the setOwner method using his ID and the current date
///     SetOwner(user.ID, DateTime.Now);
/// </code>
/// </example>
public void SetOwner(int ownerID, DateTime startDate)
```

This example shows the user how to get the userID and then call the SetOwner method. The <example> tag should be used whenever the use of your type is not straightforward. To reinforce the importance of using this tag, imagine trying to use the MSDN documentation without examples.

<permission>. The <permission> tag allows you to specify who is allowed to access your type. The <permission> tag can also include the cref attribute and almost always points to System.Security.PermissionSet. Here is an example of using the <permission> tag to describe the permission setting for a method:

```
/// <summary>
/// Classes that inherit from Vehicle should override
/// this method and implement a function that starts
/// the vehicle.
/// </summary>
/// <permission cref="System.Security.PermissionSet">
/// Public Access
/// </permission>
public virtual void Start()
```

In this example, I simply state that the Start( ) method is available for public use.

<seealso>. The <seealso> tag can be used to reference other classes or documents that might be of interest to the person reading the documentation. You can include any number of <seealso> tags that point to other types or type members. Here is an example of the <seealso> tag:

```
/// <summary>
/// This method retrieves the owner of this vehicle
/// </summary>
/// <returns>The userID of the vehicle's owner</returns>
/// <seealso cref="SetOwner"/>
public int GetOwnerID( )
```

Using the <seealso> tag, you can reference other types, methods, properties, or fields that might be of interest to the user.

<include>. The <include> tag is different then the other primary tags because it is used to include outside XML comments, as opposed to documenting anything. The <include> tag can be useful if the XML comments in your source files are becoming increasingly large and unwieldy. To use this tag, you will need to specify the name of the file as well as the XPath expression that should be used to get to your comments. The best way to handle this is to create a file that reproduces the file generated by Visual Studio—you can even let Visual Studio create this file for you and then replace your comments with <include> statements. Here is an example of an <include> statement that would use the generated file (see the "Creating the XML File" section of this hack) for this class:

```
/// <include file='XMLLib.xml'
/// path='doc/members/member[@name="M:XMLLib.Vehicle.Start"]/*'/>
public virtual void Start( )
```

When Visual Studio compiles your code, it will use the file and the XPath expression defined in the <include> tag to retrieve the comments for this method and include them in the final XML document.

Secondary Tags

Secondary tags can be used inside of the primary tags. These tags are used to mark up and format the text that is included in the primary tags. In the last section, you saw one of these tags, <code>, but there are 11 secondary tags in all.

<c> and <code>. The <c> and <code> tags are both used to define when a piece of text is code. The only difference between the two is that <c> can be used to mark something as inline code in another sentence, whereas <code> is used to set an entire block of text as code. To put it simply, <code>

includes line breaks and <c> does not. Here is an example of using <c> when creating the summary of a method:

```
/// <summary>
/// This method closes a door of the vehicle.
/// To close the first door you can simply call <c>CloseDoor(1)</c>
/// </summary>
/// <param name="door">The number of door</param>
public void CloseDoor(int doo
```

If you wanted to provide a complete example, using the <code> tag would be appropriate:

```
/// <summary>
/// This method closes a door of the vehicle.
/// </summary>
/// <param name="door">The number of door</param>
/// <example>
/// <code>
/// //Call the CloseDoor method for the first door
/// CloseDoor(1);
/// </code>
/// </example>
public void CloseDoor(int door)
```

Both of these tags should be used whenever you include code in your comments.

<para>. The <para> tag is used to designate a paragraph in your comments. If your comments are lengthy, it is usually a good idea to break them into paragraphs to facilitate easier reading. Here is an example of using the <para> tag:

```
/// <remarks>
/// Vechicle is used as a base class for other specific classes.
/// It includes virtual methods like Start and TurnOff
/// <para>Inheriting from the Vehicle class will
/// let you take advantage of the mapping classes
/// already created for the vehicle type</para>
/// </remarks>
public class Vehicle
```

<pararef>. The <pararef> tag can be used to make a reference to a parameter. When describing a method, you will frequently refer to a parameter of the method. Using this tag, the documentation generation tool can determine which parameter you are referring to and create a link between the two in your documentation. Here is an example of using the <pararef> tag:

```
/// <summary>
/// This method closes the door specified in <pararef name="door" />
/// </summary>
```

```
/// <param name="door">The number of door</param>
public void CloseDoor(int door)
```

Note when specifying the parameter that it is case sensitive.

<see>. The <see> tag can be used much like the <seealso> tag except that you use <see> in the context of another tag. You might want to list some of the methods a class includes and use the <see> tag to refer to those methods:

```
/// <remarks>
/// Vechicle is used as a base class for other specific classes.
/// It includes virtual methods like <see cref="Start">Start</see>
/// and <see cref="TurnOff">TurnOff</see>
/// </remarks>
public class Vehicle
```

List tags. The last type of tags is the list tags. These tags are used to create lists inside your comments. The <list> tag is used to create a list and include an attribute called type. This attribute defines what kind of list you are creating; this value can be set to bullet, number, or table. The <listheader> tag is then used to define the header for your list. It can include the <term> and <description> tags, which I'll discuss in just a moment. After the <listheader> tag, your <list> tag can contain any number of <item> tags. Each <item> tag represents an item in your list and can include <term> and <description> tags. Each item should always include a <description> tag, but needs to include a <term> tag only if you are creating a definition list. (You don't have to set any properties to create a definition list; just using <terms> will tell the document generation tool that you are creating a definition list.)

Here is an example of a nondefinition list:

```
/// <remarks>
/// Vechicle is used as a base class for other specific classes.
/// It includes the following virtual methods:
/// <list>
///    <listheader><description>Methods</description></listheader>
///    <item><description>Start</description></item>
///    <item><description>TurnOff</description></item>
///    <item><description>CloseDoor</description></item>
/// </list>
/// </remarks>
public class Vehicle
```

Here is an example of a definition list:

```
/// <summary>
/// Turns the vehicle in a specific direction
/// </summary>
/// <param name="Direction">The Direction to turn.
```

```
/// <list>
///    <listheader>
///       <term>Number</term><description>Direction</description>
///    </listheader>
///    <item>
///       <term>1</term><description>North</description>
///    </item>
///    <item>
///       <term>2</term><description>South</description>
///    </item>
///    <item>
///       <term>3</term><description>East</description>
///    </item>
///    <item>
///       <term>4</term><description>West</description>
///    </item>
/// </list>
/// </param>
public void Turn(int Direction)
```

Both types of lists can be very valuable in commenting your source code.

Custom tags. I mentioned earlier that you can create your own custom tags to be used in the XML comments. Here is an example of custom tags being used:

```
/// <summary>
/// This method retrieves the owner of this vehicle
/// </summary>
/// <returns>The userID of the vehicle's owner</returns>
/// <database>
///    <sproc>usp_GetOwnerIDByVehicleID</sproc>
///    <params>
///       <param>VehicleID</param>
///    </params>
/// </database>
public int GetOwnerID( )
```

But remember that you would then need to write something to make use of these custom tags (or customize an existing tool). Although this is something that I won't be covering in this book, if you are skilled in XSLT, it is not that hard.

Creating the XML File

After marking up your code files with XML, the next step is to have Visual Studio create an XML file including all of these comments. This is easily done: right-click on your project and then click on Properties. From the property page, select the Configuration Properties folder and then the Build item—this is shown in Figure 8-1.

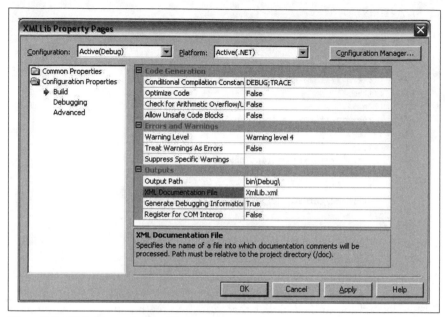

Figure 8-1. XML documentation file creation

To enable the XML documentation file creation, you simply need to enter the name of an XML file in the XML Documentation File property setting. In Figure 8-1, I have entered the name *XmlLib.xml*. When the project is built, Visual Studio will collect all of the XML comments and save them into a single file named *XmlLib.xml* in the output directory of your project.

You can then use this *.xml* file to create any different type of documentation [Hack #71].

HACK #69   Create Comments Faster

There are boring parts of the XML commenting process that you can automate to make documentation more fun (and more likely to happen).

The problem with XML documentation comments is that somebody has to write them. Even worse, often enough that someone is you. The Visual Studio IDE helps you by preparing an empty template when you type /// in front of a method, but in the end you still have to fill in the blanks.

Here's an example. Imagine a method "AppendHtmlText" that is used to append HTML text to some sort of buffer. This method has several overloads, and one of these overloads has a parameter of type "HtmlProvider". This is what Visual Studio will create when you start writing a new XML documentation comment:

```
/// <summary>
///
/// </summary>
/// <param name="htmlProvider"></param>
public void AppendHtmlText(HtmlProvider htmlProvider)
{
    ...
}
```

You would then add your text, so the XML documentation comment could, for example, look something like this:

```
/// <summary>
/// Appends the HTML text of the specified provider.
/// </summary>
/// <param name="htmlProvider">The HTML provider.</param>
public void AppendHtmlText(HtmlProvider htmlProvider)
{
    ...
}
```

This is a typical method that comes by the dozen: the method name pretty much says what it is doing and you definitely do not need much imagination to write the comment—after some time, these methods become a real drain to document. On the other hand, you simply have no choice. If you want the benefits of XML documentation comments (perhaps a nice help file generated by NDoc [Hack #71]), you have to comment *all* public (and protected) members, period.

Let's take a closer look at the earlier example. The method is written according to Microsoft's Design Guidelines for Class Library Developers; some of these rules are:

- Identifier names consisting of multiple words are written in Pascal-Casing (the method name) or camelCasing (the parameter name).
- Acronyms are treated like normal words and are formatted accordingly (for example, "Html" instead of "HTML").
- Identifier names do not contain abbreviations.
- Method names usually start with a verb.

Now when you look at this set of rules on one hand and the documentation you have written on the other, it is pretty safe to say that a large part of the documentation could have been generated automatically.

GhostDoc

GhostDoc is an add-in for Visual Studio .NET 2003 that tries to do just that. With GhostDoc installed, you move the cursor into the method or property you want to document, invoke the Document This command using either the source editor's context (right-click) menu or a hotkey, and GhostDoc will create an XML documentation comment. The result for the previous example would be:

```
/// <summary>
/// Appends the HTML text.
/// </summary>
/// <param name="htmlProvider">The HTML provider.</param>
public void AppendHtmlText(HtmlProvider htmlProvider)
{
    ...
}
```

Pretty close—but how does GhostDoc do that? First of all, it's important to note that the add-in has no idea of what the identifiers actually mean—GhostDoc simply assumes that the code is written according to the guidelines and does the following:

- It breaks up identifier names into single words by analyzing the casing.

- A word consisting of only consonants (for example, "HTML") is automatically treated as an abbreviation (other abbreviations, for example, "UML," can be specified explicitly).

- For methods, the first word is treated as a verb and thus an *s* (in some cases *es*) is added.

- A "the" is added between the first and the second word of the method name (unless the second word belongs to a configurable list of words that are never preceded by a "the").

After GhostDoc has created the XML documentation comment, the developer has to edit only a few details (for example, for the AppendHtmlText method, add "using the specified provider" to the end of the sentence) before moving on to the really interesting part of the documentation: remarks on usage, references to related methods or properties, example code—information that cannot be created automatically.

GhostDoc is driven by *generation rules*. When an XML documentation comment is about to be generated, the add-in will collect information about the code element (method, property, indexer, etc.) like name, return type, parameter names and types, and so on. This information is then compared to a set of rules, and the rule that fits best is then used to generate the documentation.

With each version of GhostDoc, the number of rules grows; the more specialized they are (for example, rules for handling Boolean properties, methods with a name consisting of only one word, etc.), the better the results.

Here are a few more examples that show only a part of what GhostDoc can automatically generate:

Documentation for an indexer. Note that the rule for indexers takes the name of the parameter into account, so it is "*at* the specified index", but "*with* the specified name":

```
/// <summary>
/// Gets the <see cref="System.String"/> at the specified index.
/// </summary>
/// <value></value>
public string this[int index]
{
    get { ... }
}
```

Boolean properties with a name consisting of only one word. If you comment Boolean properties in .NET Framework documentation style, you will definitely recognize the "Gets or sets a value indicating whether..." rule, and most likely you already have stopped counting the times you have typed this phrase:

```
/// <summary>
/// Gets or sets a value indicating whether
/// this <see cref="Demo"/> is cool.
/// </summary>
/// <value>
/// <c>true</c> if cool; otherwise, <c>false</c>.
/// </value>
public bool Cool
{
    get { return true; }
    set { ; }
}
```

A method with "of the" reordering for method and parameter names. The so-called "of the" reordering is triggered by specific words such as "size," "length," or "name" (the list of trigger words can be configured):

```
/// <summary>
/// Determines the size of the page buffer.
/// </summary>
/// <param name="initialPageBufferSize">
/// Size of the initial page buffer.</param>
/// <returns></returns>
public int DeterminePageBufferSize(int initialPageBufferSize)
```

Getting Started

First, you will need to download and run the GhostDoc installer from *http://www.roland-weigelt.de/ghostdoc*.

After running the GhostDoc installer, the next time you start Visual Studio, a couple of configuration dialogs appear to complete the setup (for example, choose a hotkey). Note that GhostDoc cannot install a hotkey if Visual Studio is not already using a custom keyboard scheme—this is a limitation of Visual Studio's extensibility model. If you are not sure, simply try to assign a hotkey; if GhostDoc setup encounters a problem, it will tell you what to do.

GhostDoc comes with a C# source file that demonstrates the features of this add-in; simply load the demo project, which can be found in a subdirectory of the folder GhostDoc was installed to. Inside Visual Studio, open the *Demo.cs* C# file, move the cursor into the body of a method, for example, and invoke the Document This command. The Document This command can be invoked using the hotkey, from the right-click menu, or from Tools → GhostDoc → DocumentThis.

After you invoke the Document This command, GhostDoc will go to work and generate as much of your XML comments as it can.

Tweaking GhostDoc

Certain aspects of GhostDoc can be configured:

- Which words are treated as acronyms
- Which words must not be preceded by "the"
- Which words trigger the "of the" reordering of an identifier name's words
- The fixed parts of the generated texts.

You can edit the configuration settings in the dialog that is opened Tools → GhostDoc → Configure GhostDoc. This dialog is shown in Figure 8-2.

In this dialog, you can also export settings to a file that can then be imported on a different computer. This is pretty handy if, for example, you want to keep the configurations at home and at work in sync.

—*Roland Weigelt*

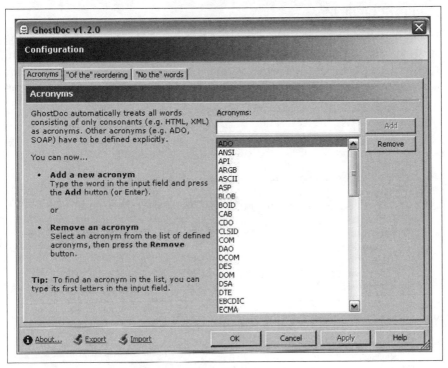

Figure 8-2. GhostDoc Configuration dialog

Create XML Comments with VB.NET

Visual Studio 2002 and 2003 won't let you use XML comments with VB.NET,
but you can use a power toy to make it possible.

XML comments are not just for C# developers any more. XML commenting is a very powerful tool—just because you happen to be developing in
VB.NET, you should not be deprived of it.

Normally in Visual Studio .NET 2002 and 2003, VB.NET developers do not
have the option of using XML comments. Thankfully, this functionality is
added in Visual Studio 2005, but what can you do before then? A power toy
called the VBCommenter adds XML commenting to VB.NET for Visual Studio .NET 2003. Using this power toy, you can add XML comments to your
VB.NET classes and functions. These XML comments will then be compiled into a single XML file, which can then be processed using any of the
available documentation creation tools (the same tools you use with C#).

Before moving on, you will need to download and install the VBCommenter
power toy from *http://workspaces.gotdotnet.com/VBCommenter*.

Using VBCommenter

Once installed, VBCommenter lets you create XML comments by using
three apostrophes, much as C# comments use three slashes for XML comments. To create a block of XML comments above a function or class, type
three apostrophes and then press Enter. Here is a sample XML section created for a generic sub:

```
'''  -----------------------------------------------------------
'''  Project     : TestXMLLib
'''  Class    : Class1
'''
'''  -----------------------------------------------------------
'''  <summary>
'''  This class contains a number of functions that we can call.
'''  </summary>
'''  <remarks>
'''  </remarks>
'''  <history>
'''      [James Avery]    10/8/2004    Created
'''  </history>
'''  -----------------------------------------------------------
```

You can also create XML comments for classes:

```
'''  -----------------------------------------------------------
'''  <summary>
'''  This sub goes and does something important.
'''  Throws CannotPerformException if an error is encountered.
'''  </summary>
'''  <remarks>
'''  </remarks>
'''  <history>
'''      [James Avery]    10/8/2004    Created
'''  </history>
'''  -----------------------------------------------------------
```

Using VBCommenter, you can create comments for any public type including functions, properties, enumerations, and so on. When you compile your
application, the VBCommenter power toy will collect all of the XML comments from your file and create a single XML file named *<YourProject>.xml*.
Here is a look at the XML created for the preceding XML comments:

```
<?xml version="1.0"?>
<doc>
  <assembly>
    <name>TestXMLLib</name>
    <version>1.0.1742.29439</version>
    <fullname>TestXMLLib, Version=1.0.1742.29439,
    Culture=neutral, PublicKeyToken=null</fullname>
  </assembly>
  <members>
```

```
    <member name="T:TestXMLLib.Class1">
        <summary>
This class contains a number of functions that we can call.
    </summary>
    <remarks>
    </remarks>
    <history>
        [James Avery]    10/8/2004    Created
    </history></member>
        <member name="M:TestXMLLib.Class1.DoSomething">
            <summary>
This sub goes and does something important.
Throws CannotPerformException if an error is encountered.
    </summary>
    <remarks>
    </remarks>
    <history>
        [James Avery]    10/8/2004    Created
    </history></member>
      </members>
    </doc>
```

From here, you can use this XML file just as it was created from C#. You can use NDoc [Hack #71] to turn this XML into some form of documentation. (You could, of course, use XSLT to transform this XML as well.)

Configuring VBCommenter

VBCommenter allows you to configure a number of settings pertaining to how the power toy operates. These options can be set from the Tools → VBCommenter Settings dialog, which is shown in Figure 8-3.

The "Create .xml files when projects are built" setting determines whether the <YourProject>.xml file will be created when the project is built. It is a good idea to uncheck this until you are actually ready to create your documentation. There is no need to create these files every time you build your solution since it slows down the build process. The "Insert XML comments in source" setting enables or disables whether XML comments are inserted when you enter the three apostrophes and press Enter—you will almost always want to leave this checked.

The last setting is the Comment Prefix, which allows you to choose between ''', ', '//, and '@ as the comment prefixes for VBCommenter. You can also specify your own custom prefix in the text box.

Hacking the Hack

One of the benefits of VBCommenter being an open source project is that you can customize the power toy to your own needs. You can download the

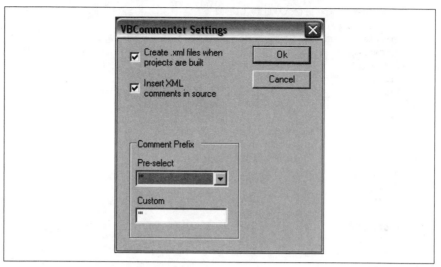

Figure 8-3. VBCommenter Settings dialog

complete source code from the GotDotNet workspace. With this code, you can modify any part of the power toy that you desire.

One of the areas of the power toy begging to be modified is the XML comments that are automatically inserted when you type three apostrophes and press Enter. All of these comments can be modified in a single file called *default-autoinsert.xsl*. This file contains an XSL stylesheet that creates the comments based on the type that is being clicked on. Here is the first part of that file:

```
<?xml version="1.0" ?>
<xsl:stylesheet xmlns:xsl="http://www.w3.org/1999/XSL/Transform"
version="1.0">
<xsl:output method="xml"/>

<xsl:template match="/xmldocinfo">
<xsl:if test="code-element-type = 'class'">
--------------------------------------------------

Project[TAB] : <xsl:value-of select="project" />
Class[TAB] : <xsl:value-of select="name" />
</xsl:if>
<xsl:if test="code-element-type = 'module'">
--------------------------------------------------
Project[TAB] : <xsl:value-of select="project" />
Module[TAB] : <xsl:value-of select="name" />
</xsl:if>
<xsl:if test="code-element-type = 'interface'">
--------------------------------------------------
Project[TAB] : <xsl:value-of select="project" />
Interface[TAB] : <xsl:value-of select="name" />
```

```
</xsl:if>
<xsl:if test="code-element-type = 'struct'">
----------------------------------------------------
Project[TAB] : <xsl:value-of select="project" />
Struct[TAB] : <xsl:value-of select="name" />
</xsl:if>

----------------------------------------------------
```

This first section of the file specifies what the header should include based on what you are commenting. You can see that there are xsl:if elements for class, module, interface, and struct types. If you want to modify the header, you can change it directly in this file. For instance, if you wanted to switch the dashes to asterisks and add a line to specify the use case that this class is part of, here is how you could change the class section of this file:

```
<xsl:if test="code-element-type = 'class'">
*********************************************************
Use Case[TAB] :
Class[TAB] : <xsl:value-of select="name" />
</xsl:if>
```

I removed the Project part and added a Use Case section. I also switched the dashes to asterisks. (You will also need to change the other side of dashes that follow the group of if elements.)

To get your changes to take effect, you need to build the VBCommenter Solution. (The *.xslt* file is an embedded resource, so it is embedded in the assembly.) After building the solution, you will need to copy the *VBCommenter.dll* file from your *bin* directory to the *C:\Program Files\ PowerToys for Visual Studio .NET 2003\VBCommenter* directory. To do this, you will need to close Visual Studio; otherwise, you will get an error stating that the file is currently in use.

After you replace the file and restart Visual Studio, the new stylesheet will be used. When typing three apostrophes and pressing Enter, you would now see the following comments:

```
''' *********************************************************
''' Use Case    :
''' Class     : Class1
'''
''' *********************************************************
''' <summary>
'''
''' </summary>
''' <remarks>
''' </remarks>
''' <history>
'''    [James Avery]    10/9/2004    Created
''' </history>
'''  -----------------------------------------------------------
```

As you can see, customizing this power toy is easy to do, and there are literally no boundaries to the customization that you can do considering that the full source code is available.

Create Documentation from XML Comments

Make all that typing and tagging pay off with an open source documentation tool that creates help documents from your XML comments.

So you have a large number of XML comments peppered throughout your application. Now what can you do with them? While Visual Studio includes some tools to work with these comments, the real benefit comes from an open source tool called NDoc. NDoc is a tool that will take your XML comments and turn them into a number of different types of documentation, including help files or MSDN-style web documentation.

The first step to creating your documentation is to generate an XML file with all of your XML comments. To do this, follow the instructions in either "Master C# XML Comments" [Hack #68] if you are using C# or "Create XML Comments with VB.NET" [Hack #70] if you are using VB.NET.

Once you have the *.xml* file, you are ready to turn it into full documentation.

Using NDoc

The next step is to download and install NDoc from *http://ndoc.sourceforge.net*. Once you have downloaded and installed NDoc, you will need to open the application, which is shown in Figure 8-4.

The next step is to create a new NDoc Project. This can be done one of two ways: you can create a new blank project and then manually select each of the assemblies that you want to document, or you can select New from Visual Studio Solution and select your solution, after which NDoc will load all of your assemblies.

After loading your assemblies, you can then configure how you want your documentation to be generated. There are way too many options to cover here, but suffice it to say you can configure just about any part of the documentation that you wish. The main choice is what type of documentation you want to generate. This is controlled by the Documentation Type dropdown. From this list you can choose any number of different types (for this example, I will leave the option set to the default, MSDN).

From this point, you simply need to click the Build button and NDoc will generate the documentation based on your XML comments. Figure 8-5 shows an example of the help file generated by NDoc.

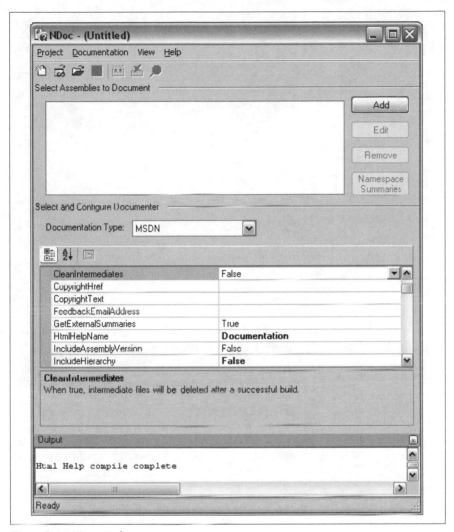

Figure 8-4. NDoc window

NDoc also generates web documentation, which can be seen in Figure 8-6.

This tool is actually that simple. In just a couple clicks, you can go from your XML comments to high-quality documentation. NDoc is a complex application with a multitude of options and different formats; I encourage you to explore the tool and its options. The tool comes with good documentation (as it should!), and you can also find lots of information at the NDoc Wiki, located at *http://ndoc.sourceforge.net/wiki*.

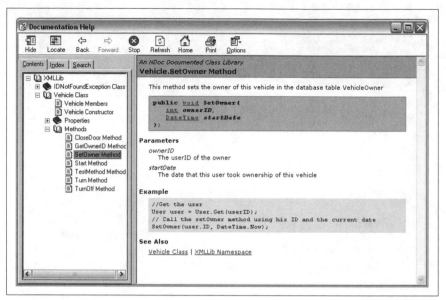

Figure 8-5. Ndoc-generated help file

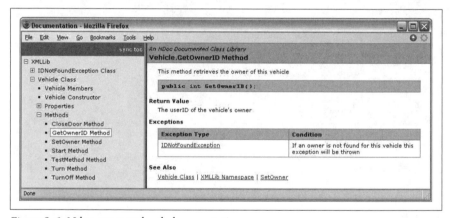

Figure 8-6. Ndoc-generated web documentation

Integrate Your Own Documentation into Visual Studio

HACK #72

Seamless integration makes for a happy world. You can take all that homegrown documentation and blend it right into the Visual Studio help system.

If you are writing a framework, control, add-in, or anything your users might use directly from Visual Studio, it can be very helpful to integrate your help documents directly into Visual Studio. Using a combination of NDoc, the Visual Studio .NET Integration Kit, and a freely available tool, you can quickly and somewhat easily integrate your documentation directly into Visual Studio.

The first step is to download the Visual Studio .NET Integration Kit. NDoc will use this kit to create your documentation in the HTML Help 2 format, the format used by Visual Studio. The Visual Studio .NET Integration Kit can be downloaded from *http://msdn.microsoft.com/library/default.asp?url=/ library/en-us/htmlhelp/html/hwmscextendingnethelp.asp*.

Create Documentation with NDoc

To integrate help documentation into Visual Studio, you have to generate your documentation a little bit differently. Instead of creating your documentation using the MSDN documentation type **[Hack #71]**, you will need to create VS.NET 2003-type documentation. This is done by simply selecting VS.NET 2003 from NDoc's list of documentation types. (This documentation type is new to NDoc 1.3, so make sure you have the latest copy of NDoc.)

You will also need to make a couple configuration changes. Under the HTML Help 2.0 Deployment section, make sure that GenerateCollection-File is set to true—you will also need to specify a CollectionNamespace. The CollectionNamespace should be a unique value similar to your project's namespace. (Don't use a URI, spaces, or special characters though.)

These settings are shown in Figure 8-7.

You will also want to make sure that you set a title for your help documents—this will be used as the top node when adding your help documents to the Visual Studio help tree. When you build your help, NDoc will do the majority of the work for you. NDoc will not only create HTML help files, but will also create the files needed to register your help files.

Registering Your Help File

The next step in this process is to register your help file. The easiest way to do this is to use a small utility called H2Reg created by the people at *helpware.NET*. This utility can be downloaded from *http://www.helpware. NET/mshelp2/h2reg.htm*.

The H2Reg utility uses an *.ini* file to specify what help files to register. NDoc is nice enough to actually generate this *.ini* file for you, and the file can be found in the same directory where NDoc put your other help files.

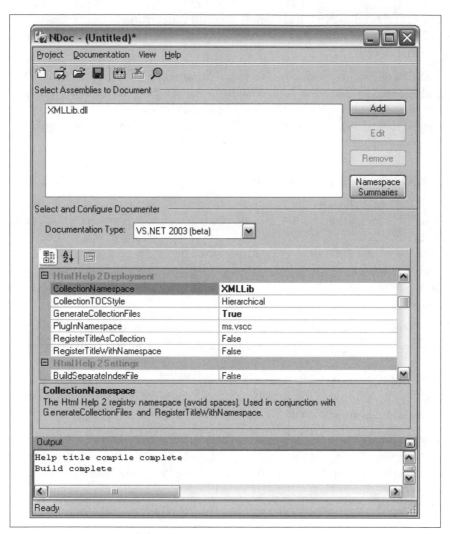

Figure 8-7. NDoc HTML help options

Once you have downloaded and installed H2Reg, you will need to run it from the command line using the -r switch and specify the name of your *.ini* file. Here is an example command that registers a help file:

```
C:\> h2reg -r CmdFile=C:\HelpDocs\DocumentationCollection.h2reg.ini
```

The H2Reg utility will then register your help documentation. This process can also easily be integrated into an installation procedure if you want to install this documentation when a user installs your add-in or control. You can include the small H2Reg executable with your installation files and simply call it from your installation and uninstallation programs. To uninstall your help documentation, you simply need to run the same command with -u instead of -r.

Include Your Help Collection

You may or may not have to perform this step. Usually the help collection is automatically added to Visual Studio, but if it does not show up, you will need to run the Help Collection Manager and add your help collection. The Help Collection Manager is easy to use and can be accessed by simply navigating to *ms-help://MS.VSCC.2003/VSCCCommon/cm/CollectionManager. htm* in Internet Explorer.

> In Windows XP SP2, you will need to make sure you give this page permission to execute its ActiveX control.

You will then see the Help Collection Manager, shown in Figure 8-8.

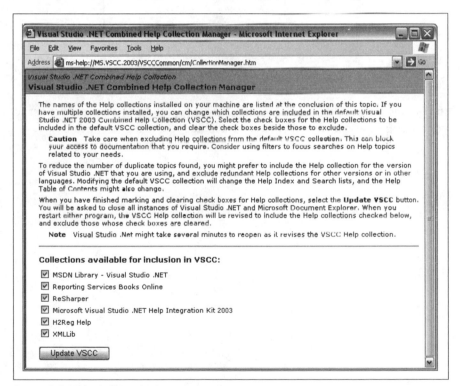

Figure 8-8. Help Collection Manager

If your help collection (XMLLib in Figure 8-8) is not already checked, you will need to check it and then click the Update VSCC button. Your help collection will now be installed and ready to use in Visual Studio.

You should now see your help documents in Visual Studio. An example of how they appear is shown in Figure 8-9.

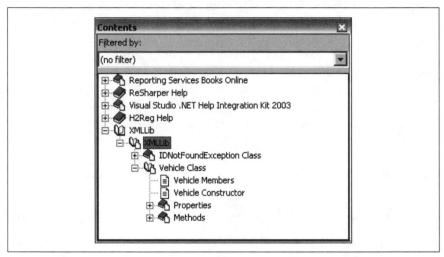

Figure 8-9. Integrated help

Integrating your help documents into Visual Studio can be a great benefit to your users—using a couple of freely available tools makes it much easier.

CHAPTER NINE

Server Explorer Hacks
Hacks 73–76

The Server Explorer is a very useful part of Visual Studio, yet it continues to be one of the more underused and underappreciated parts of the development environment. Using the Server Explorer, you can interface with databases, event logs, services, performance counters, and more.

The Server Explorer can interface with your local system as well as with remote servers and databases. To connect to a remote machine, all you need to do is click the Add Server button on the top of the Server Explorer and then enter the name or IP address of the remote server. To connect to another server or database, you must be a recognized user on that remote server or database. The type of user you are on that machine, or the local machine for that matter, will dictate what operations you are allowed to perform through the Server Explorer.

One of the best uses of the Server Explorer is being able to view a list of all the services on your local machine or any remote servers you are attached to. From the list of services, you can start or stop any services that you would normally have permission to start or stop. This is just the beginning of what can be done with the Server Explorer.

The hacks in this chapter teach you how to interface with performance counters and how to manage your database through the Server Explorer. This chapter will also look at a download from Microsoft that will allow you to access WMI through the Server Explorer.

To open the Server Explorer, click the Server Explorer tab that's next to the toolbox, or choose View → Server Explorer (Ctrl-Alt-S).

Access Performance Counters

#73   Windows' performance counters can reveal all sorts of information about the inner working of your machine. Use the Server Explorer to interact with these performance counters.

The Server Explorer provides an excellent interface to access the performance counters on your computer. Using the Server Explorer, you can drag performance counters directly from the Server Explorer to your application. In this hack, you will see how to build a simple application that reads from a performance counter and reports its value to the user.

The Server Explorer includes a node called Performance Counters, which can be seen in Figure 9-1.

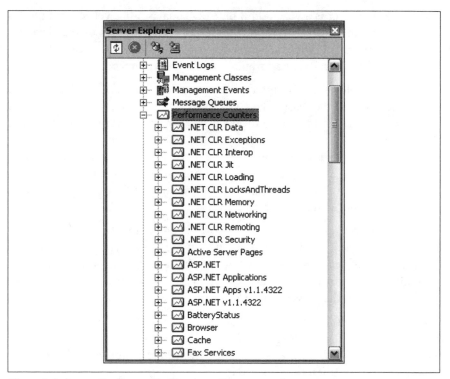

Figure 9-1. Server Explorer—Performance Counters node

Each of the nodes you see in Figure 9-1 is a category that includes a number of performance counters listed beneath it. The contents of the Memory category can be seen in Figure 9-2.

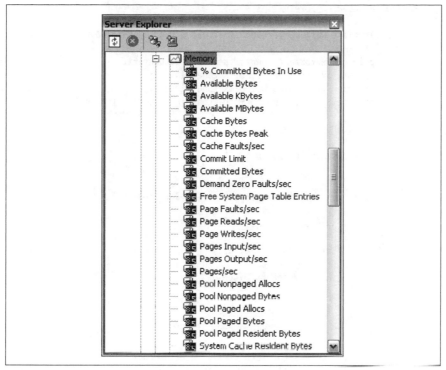

Figure 9-2. Server Explorer —Memory performance counters

From the Server Explorer, you can then drag the performance counter to your Windows Forms, and you will see the counter show up in the component section of your form, as seen in Figure 9-3.

Figure 9-3. Performance counter component

Once the performance counter object has been added to your form, you can then access the performance counter through your code. The following code is a simple example of reading from the Available MBytes performance counter:

```
using System;
using System.Drawing;
using System.Collections;
using System.ComponentModel;
using System.Windows.Forms;
using System.Diagnostics;
```

```
namespace ServerExplorerExamples
{
    public class PerfCounterExample : System.Windows.Forms.Form
    {
        private PerformanceCounter performanceCounter1;
        private System.Windows.Forms.Label label1;
        private System.Windows.Forms.Label label2;
        private System.ComponentModel.Container components = null;

        public PerfCounterExample()
        {
            InitializeComponent();
        }

        protected override void Dispose( bool disposing )
        {
            if( disposing )
            {
                if(components != null)
                {
                    components.Dispose();
                }
            }
            base.Dispose( disposing );
        }

        #region Windows Form Designer generated code
        private void InitializeComponent()
        {
        this.performanceCounter1 = new PerformanceCounter();
        this.label1 = new System.Windows.Forms.Label();
        this.label2 = new System.Windows.Forms.Label();
        ((System.ComponentModel.ISupportInitialize)
        (this.performanceCounter1)).BeginInit();
        this.SuspendLayout();

        this.performanceCounter1.CategoryName = "Memory";
        this.performanceCounter1.CounterName = "Available MBytes";
        this.performanceCounter1.MachineName = "JAMESA-TABLET";

        this.label1.Location = new System.Drawing.Point(8, 32);
        this.label1.Name = "label1";
        this.label1.Size = new System.Drawing.Size(96, 16);
        this.label1.TabIndex = 0;
        this.label1.Text = "Available MBytes:";

        this.label2.Location = new System.Drawing.Point(112, 32);
        this.label2.Name = "label2";
        this.label2.Size = new System.Drawing.Size(100, 16);
        this.label2.TabIndex = 1;

        this.AutoScaleBaseSize = new System.Drawing.Size(5, 13);
        this.ClientSize = new System.Drawing.Size(292, 266);
```

```
        this.Controls.Add(this.label2);
        this.Controls.Add(this.label1);
        this.Name = "PerfCounterExample";
        this.Text = "PerfCounterExample";
        this.Load +=
        new System.EventHandler(this.PerfCounterExample_Load);
        ((System.ComponentModel.ISupportInitialize)
        (this.performanceCounter1)).EndInit();
        this.ResumeLayout(false);

    }
    #endregion

    private void PerfCounterExample_Load(
        object sender,
        System.EventArgs e)
    {
        //Get the value of the performance counter
        label2.Text = performanceCounter1.NextValue().ToString();
    }
}
}
```

When you run this code, it will produce the form shown in Figure 9-4.

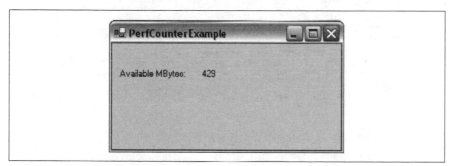

Figure 9-4. PerfCounter Example form

Counter Information

You can view additional information about counters by right-clicking on a category and clicking the View Category menu item. This will display the Performance Counter Builder form (Figure 9-5), which includes a description of the category as well as a list of all the performance counters in that category. Click on a performance counter and you will be shown a description of it. This is a great way to investigate the counters in each category and what they report on.

The Server Explorer makes it easy to browse all the performance counters on your machine and then access them in your application.

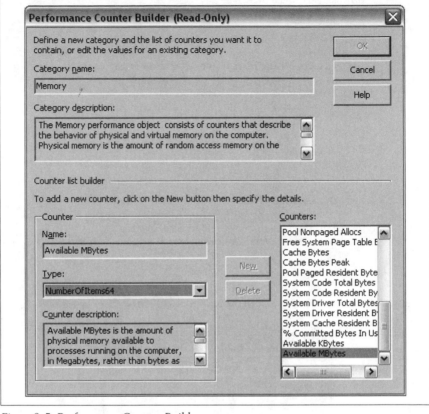

Figure 9-5. Performance Counter Builder screen

HACK #74   Diagram and Modify a Database

Why leave Visual Studio to administer your database? Use the Server Explorer
to create tables, views, stored procedures, and more.

We all love to hate SQL Server Enterprise Manager and its seemingly end-
less number of modal dialogs and nonsizable forms, but the Server Explorer
allows you to work with your database from a development perspective. It
doesn't include all the features that Enterprise Manager does, but it provides the basics needed to work with your database. Figure 9-6 shows the
basic database interface included with the Server Explorer.

> The capabilities of the data tools in Visual Studio vary based
> on the version of Visual Studio you own. For a complete list
> of capabilities, please refer to *http://msdn.microsoft.com/
> library/default.asp?url=/library/en-us/vdbt7/html/dvconvisual-
> databasetoolseditions.asp.*

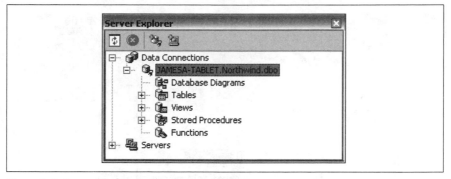

Figure 9-6. Server Explorer—database options

Database Diagrams

Database Diagrams can be used to design your database and create relationships between your tables. Using the Server Explorer, you can edit and create new database diagrams. To create a new database diagram, you simply need to right-click on the Database Diagrams node and select New Diagram. You will then see the Add Table dialog shown in Figure 9-7.

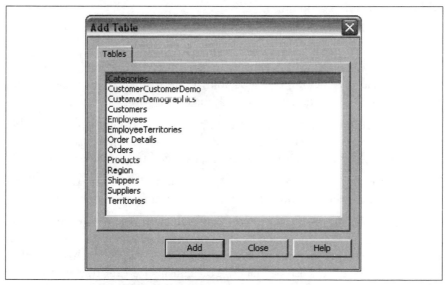

Figure 9-7. Add Table dialog

From this dialog, you can select the tables you want to work with. When you click Add, the table will be added to your diagram. If you add multiple tables, Visual Studio will automatically add primary/foreign key relationships to the diagram. Figure 9-8 shows the Database Diagrams interface.

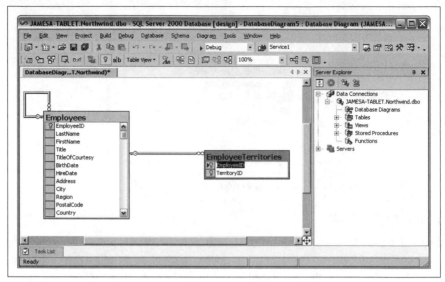

Figure 9-8. Database Diagrams interface

Using this interface, you can configure the tables, add relationships or keys, add or edit columns, and more.

Tables

Using the Server Explorer interface, you can work directly with the tables in your database. By clicking on the Tables node in the Server Explorer, you will see a list of all the tables in your database, as shown in Figure 9-9.

Use this list to perform various table functions. If you right-click on a table and click on Retrieve Data from Table, you will see a portion of the data from your table in an easy-to-view format, as seen in Figure 9-10.

You can also edit a table by right-clicking on it and choosing Design Table from the context menu. You will then see the window shown in Figure 9-11.

From the table design window, you can change and configure any of the table settings that you can change directly through Enterprise Manager. In fact, you have probably noticed that the interface is pretty much identical to the interface in Enterprise Manager. You can also create triggers for your tables by right-clicking on a table and choosing New Trigger.

Views

Using the Server Explorer, you can create and edit views much like working with tables. The Views node shows a list of all of the views in your database.

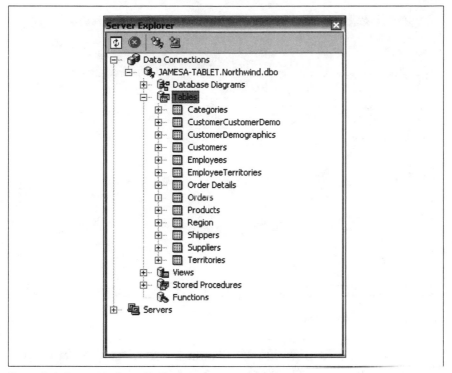

Figure 9-9. Server Explorer Tables interface

Just as with tables, you can design a view by right-clicking on it and choosing Design View. The design view is shown in Figure 9-12.

Much like the table designer, the view designer is very similar to the one in Enterprise Manager. You can also add triggers to the view by right-clicking on the view and clicking Add Trigger.

Stored Procedures

Support for stored procedures is one area in which the Server Explorer excels. The Server Explorer displays not only the name of the stored procedure, but also includes a list of the parameters and return columns from the stored procedure. This node is shown in Figure 9-13.

From the Server Explorer, you can create new stored procedures, edit stored procedures, and even run them. By right-clicking on the stored procedure and choosing Run Stored Procedure, you will then see the parameters dialog shown in Figure 9-14.

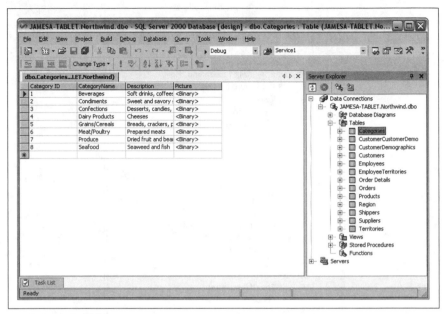

Figure 9-10. Table data view

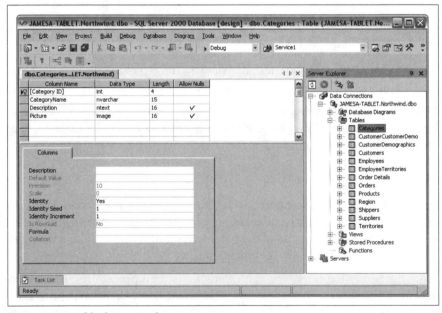

Figure 9-11. Table design window

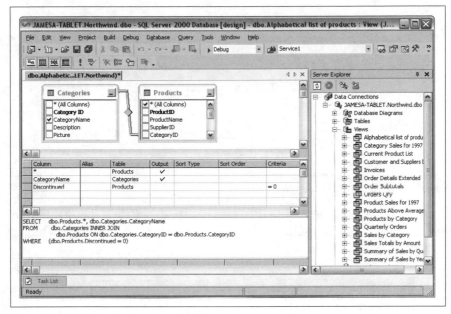

Figure 9-12. Design view

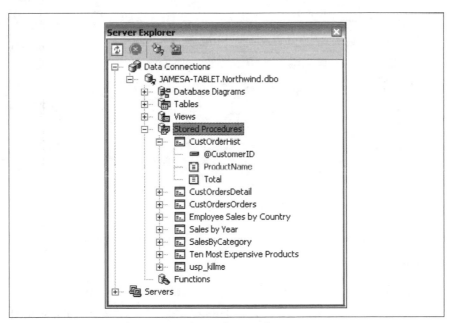

Figure 9-13. Server Explorer—Stored Procedures node

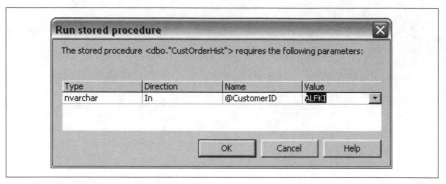

Figure 9-14. Run Stored Procedure dialog

After specifying all the required parameters, you can click the OK button and you will see the results of the stored procedure shown in the Output window, as shown in Figure 9-15.

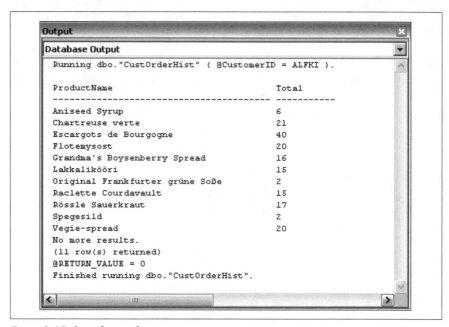

Figure 9-15. Stored procedure output

You can also step into and debug the stored procedure [Hack #40].

The Server Explorer lets you create inline, table-valued, and scalar-valued functions. After creating a function, you can then edit, run, or step into the functions in much the same way as stored procedures.

Using the Server Explorer can be a much more pleasant experience than working with the Enterprise Manager or SQL Query Analyzer.

Script Your Database

Most applications involve some sort of data, and where you have data you probably have a database. Script the creation of your database with the Database Project and the Server Explorer.

Managing databases is always a difficult task; you have to manage not only the tables but also the views, stored procedures, functions, and triggers. In an enterprise environment, you are most likely working with multiple databases. Keeping those databases synchronized with one another is a daunting task. All of this is not easy, but using the Database Project and the Server Explorer can help make these tasks much more manageable.

The Database Project

The Database Project is different than most of the projects you are used to using in Visual Studio. The project does not have an output like an executable or assembly, but instead is just something that can be used to collect and store SQL scripts. The idea behind the Database Project is that, instead of trying to use one of your many databases as the "master" database, you should instead maintain a store of *create scripts* that can be used to create your database at any time. If you need a new copy of the database, you simply run this collection of scripts, instead of trying to make a copy of the database. This has a number of benefits:

- You can ensure that all databases are using the same objects.
- You can always create a new copy of the database from scratch.
- By using scripts, you can catch any objects that might no longer be valid—for example, stored procedures that reference columns or tables that no longer exist. When a script for that stored procedure is run, it will throw an error if the referenced column or table no longer exists.
- You can control these scripts using source control.
- You can incorporate the creation of the database into the build process to catch problems quickly. (You might not want to actively create the development database, but instead create a test database.)
- You can script required data to be added to the database, such as values for metadata or lookup tables.
- You can script test data to be used for unit testing.

Maintaining a list of scripts can be a cumbersome task though; this is where the Database Project and the Server Explorer come into play.

Create a Database Project. The first step in the process is to create a Database Project. To do so, you simply need to go to File → New Project and then expand the Other Projects node and select Database Project. This dialog is shown in Figure 9-16.

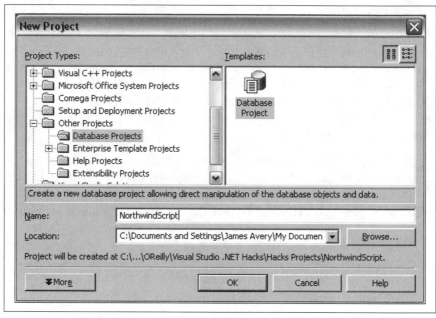

Figure 9-16. Creating a new Database Project

Next, you will be asked to pick the database that you want to manage with this project. You will see the dialog shown in Figure 9-17. (If you do not have any database references created, instead you will see the Data Link Properties dialog to choose a server and specify the login information.)

From this dialog, you can select an already configured reference or create a new reference using the Add New Reference button. After creating the project and configuring a database reference, you will see the project loaded in the Solution Explorer, as seen in Figure 9-18.

The next step is to populate your project with the scripts to build your database.

Create scripts. Creating scripts can be a tedious task. The Server Explorer makes this process a little easier. You can create your objects in the normal fashion using the Server Explorer or Enterprise Manager, then, using the Server Explorer, you can generate create scripts by simply right-clicking on

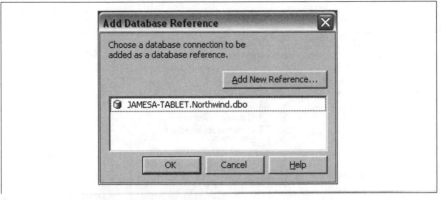

Figure 9-17. Add Database Reference dialog

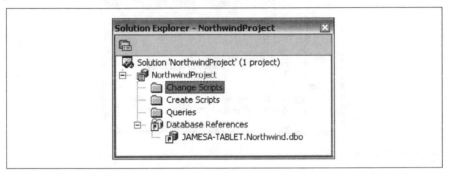

Figure 9-18. Northwind Project in the Solution Explorer

the object and choosing Generate Create Script, as shown in Figure 9-19. (You can also right-click on the entire database to script the entire database.)

 To use the Create Scripts functionality, you must be using SQL Server 7 or 2000 and have the client tools for SQL Server installed on your development machine.

After clicking Generate Create Script, you will see the dialog shown in Figure 9-20.

Using this dialog, you can use the Formatting and Options tabs to configure how the script should be created; then click OK and the script will be generated. After generating the create script, you will see a number of scripts in the Solution Explorer, as shown in Figure 9-21.

In the figure, you see four different scripts that create the table, its foreign keys, indexes, and so forth. Using the Generate Create Scripts command, you can go through your database and create scripts for every object in the

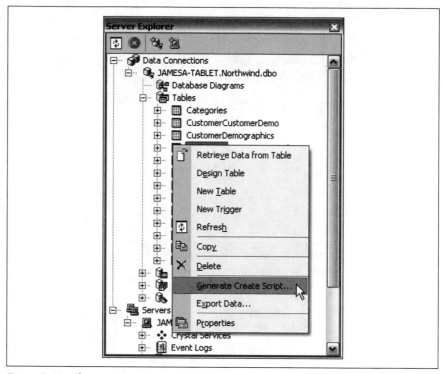

Figure 9-19. Choosing Generate Create Script

database, using the options that you prefer. You should end up with a Database Project including scripts for your entire database. (You can use folders to organize all these scripts.)

Create command file. Now that you have a project filled with the scripts for your entire database, how can you take these scripts and create a new database from it? This is where command files can be used. If you right-click on the Create Scripts folder, you will see an option for Create Command File, as shown in Figure 9-22.

You will then see the Create Command File dialog shown in Figure 9-23.

From this dialog, you can select the scripts that you would like to include in the command file; then when you click OK, the command file will be created. Here is an example command file:

```
@echo off
REM: Command File Created by Microsoft Visual Database Tools
REM: Date Generated: 10/17/2004
REM: Authentication type: Windows NT
REM: Usage: CommandFilename [Server] [Database]
```

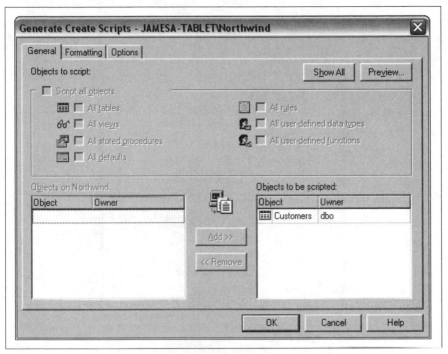

Figure 9-20. Generate Create Scripts dialog

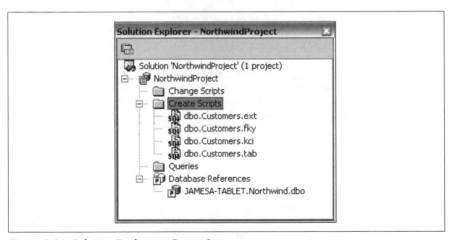

Figure 9-21. Solution Explorer—Create Scripts

```
if '%1' == '' goto usage
if '%2' == '' goto usage

if '%1' == '/?' goto usage
if '%1' == '-?' goto usage
if '%1' == '?' goto usage
```

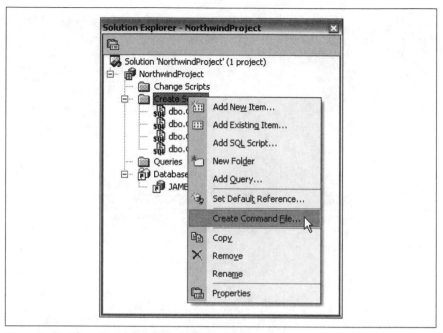

Figure 9-22. Choosing Create Command File

```
if '%1' == '/help' goto usage

osql -S %1 -d %2 -E -b -i "dbo.Customers.tab"
if %ERRORLEVEL% NEQ 0 goto errors
osql -S %1 -d %2 -E -b -i "dbo.Customers.kci"
if %ERRORLEVEL% NEQ 0 goto errors
osql -S %1 -d %2 -E -b -i "dbo.Customers.fky"
if %ERRORLEVEL% NEQ 0 goto errors
osql -S %1 -d %2 -E -b -i "dbo.Customers.ext"
if %ERRORLEVEL% NEQ 0 goto errors

goto finish

REM: How to use screen
:usage
echo.
echo Usage: MyScript Server Database
echo Server: the name of the target SQL Server
echo Database: the name of the target database
echo.
echo Example: MyScript.cmd MainServer MainDatabase
echo.
echo.
goto done

REM: error handler
```

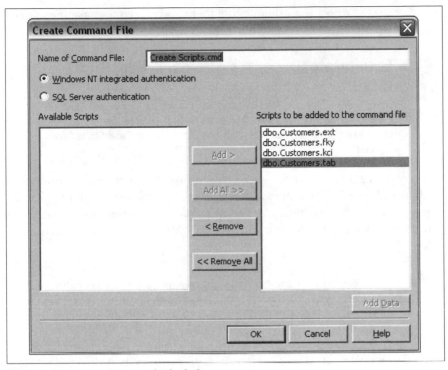

Figure 9-23. Create Command File dialog

```
:errors
echo.
echo WARNING! Error(s) were detected!
echo -------------------------------
echo Please evaluate the situation and, if needed,
echo restart this command file. You may need to
echo supply command parameters when executing
echo this command file.
echo.
pause
goto done

REM: finished execution
:finish
echo.
echo Script execution is complete!
:done
@echo on
```

If you look at the text of the command file, you can see that it uses the *osql* utility to execute each of the scripts. You can run this command file by simply right-clicking on the command file and clicking Run, or you can also incorporate this command file into your build process.

The Database Project is a valuable tool that can be used to make the managing of your databases easier and less prone to error.

HACK #76   Enumerate Processes, Drives, Shares, and More

Using WMI (Windows Management Instrumentation), you can discover information about a system's drives, processes, printers, file shares, and much more. Install and use the WMI extensions for the Visual Studio Server Explorer.

To access WMI from the Server Explorer, you will first need to download and install the WMI extensions for Server Explorer from *http://msdn.microsoft.com/library/default.asp?url=/downloads/list/wmi.asp*. Versions are currently available for Visual Studio .NET 2002 and Visual Studio .NET 2003.

> You will need to have the appropriate permission on either your local machine or the remote server to access WMI classes. The permissions you need vary based on the WMI class you are trying to access.

After you have installed these extensions, you will see two new nodes, Management Classes and Management Events, in the Server Explorer, as seen in Figure 9-24.

Adding Classes

You can also see in Figure 9-24 a long list of the things you can interface with through WMI. You can add even more classes by right-clicking on the Management Classes node and choosing Add Classes. You will see the dialog shown in Figure 9-25.

From this dialog, you can select any other classes that you want. All you have to do is select the class from the Available Classes list and then click the Add button to move it to the Selected Classes side. When you click OK, the new class will be shown in the Server Explorer.

Creating Managed Classes

The real benefit of having WMI classes in the Server Explorer is that you can then create strongly typed managed classes to interact with these WMI classes. Using WMI from .NET is not always easy or intuitive, but using a couple of functions available through the Server Explorer makes it much

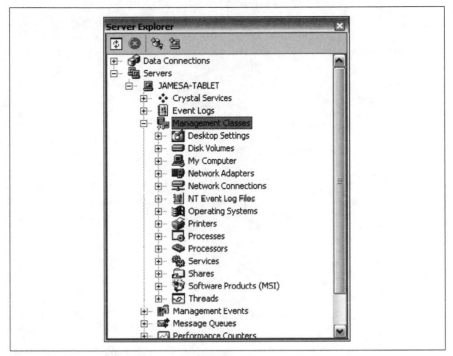

Figure 9-24. Server Explorer—WMI nodes

easier. To create a managed class for a WMI class, you simply need to right-click on the class and click Generate Managed Class, as shown in Figure 9-26.

After you click Generate Managed Class, a new class will be added to your project. In the case of processes, the name of the class will be *Win32_Process.CS*. This file is a complete managed wrapper for the Process WMI class, including all methods, properties, and even custom collections.

You can then use this class through your code to directly interface with WMI. Here is an example of getting a list of all the processes currently running on a machine:

```
using System;
using System.Drawing;
using System.Collections;
using System.ComponentModel;
using System.Windows.Forms;

//The namespace that the Server Explorer added to the project
using ServerExplorerExamples.ROOT.CIMV2;

namespace ServerExplorerExamples
```

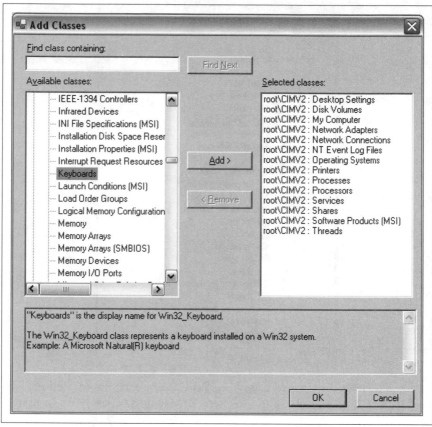

Figure 9-25. Add Classes dialog

```
{
    public class WMIExample : System.Windows.Forms.Form
    {
        private System.Windows.Forms.ListView processView;
        private System.Windows.Forms.ColumnHeader ProcessName;

        private System.ComponentModel.Container components = null;

        public WMIExample( )
        {
            InitializeComponent( );
        }

        protected override void Dispose( bool disposing )
        {
            if( disposing )
            {
                if(components != null)
                {
```

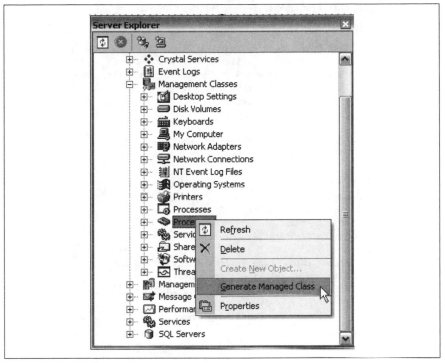

Figure 9-26. Choosing Generate Managed Class

```
            components.Dispose( );
        }
    }
    base.Dispose( disposing );
}

private void InitializeComponent( )
{
    this.processView = new System.Windows.Forms.ListView( );
    this.ProcessName =
    new System.Windows.Forms.ColumnHeader( );
    this.SuspendLayout( );

    this.processView.Columns.AddRange(
    new System.Windows.Forms.ColumnHeader[ ] {
        this.ProcessName});
    this.processView.Location =
    new System.Drawing.Point(8, 8);
    this.processView.Name = "processView";
    this.processView.Size =
    new System.Drawing.Size(240, 160);
    this.processView.TabIndex = 0;
    this.processView.View =
    System.Windows.Forms.View.Details;
```

```
            this.ProcessName.Text = "Process Name";
            this.ProcessName.Width = 236;

            this.AutoScaleBaseSize =
            new System.Drawing.Size(5, 13);
            this.ClientSize = new System.Drawing.Size(292, 266);
            this.Controls.Add(this.processView);
            this.Name = "WMIExample";
            this.Text = "WMIExample";
            this.Load +=
            new System.EventHandler(this.WMIExample_Load);
            this.ResumeLayout(false);

        }

        private void WMIExample_Load(
            object sender,
            System.EventArgs e)
        {
            //Loop through the ProcessCollection and add a row
            //to the processView listview
            foreach(Process p in Process.GetInstances())
            {
                processView.Items.Add(p.Name);
            }
        }
    }
}
```

The preceding code is a simple form that will loop through the process class and for each process add an item to the ListView. When this code is run, you will see a form like the one shown in Figure 9-27.

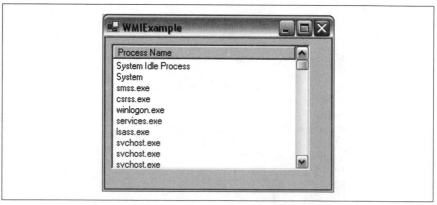

Figure 9-27. List of processes currently running

You could go on to include more information about each of the processes in the ListView or let the user select a process and see more information about that process. Using the methods available on the Process class, you could also allow the user to set the priority of the process, set the owner, or terminate the process.

 You may have noticed that there is also a set of Server Explorer extensions for Active Directory. While these extensions exist, they will work only with Visual Studio .NET 2002 and only if Visual Studio .NET 2003 is *not* installed on the same machine. For that reason they will not be covered in this book.

This is just a small sample of what can be done using WMI with the Server Explorer. If you find yourself with the need to work with WMI, you should definitely make use of the WMI extensions. They make what would otherwise be a tedious task quite easy.

Work with Visual Studio Tools
Hacks 77–82

Visual Studio includes a number of different tools that can be used both inside and outside of the IDE environment. The hacks in this chapter cover the Visual Studio command prompt and some of the tools that are easily accessible from it. You will also see how to make the Visual Studio command prompt more accessible by adding various shortcuts to it.

This chapter also includes hacks on stress testing your applications, making it harder for your code to be decompiled and understood, and generating UML from your code (and vice versa).

HACK #77 Master the Visual Studio Command Prompt

Put the mouse down for a few minutes as you learn how to do nearly everything right inside of the Visual Studio command prompt.

The Visual Studio command prompt (VSCP) is a command prompt that loads environmental settings for Visual Studio and the .NET Framework. What this means is that you can open the command prompt and type in the command for a Visual Studio or framework tool, and it will work without you having to type the full path or navigate to where that tool is located. (VSCP also sets certain environment variables, without which many of these tools would not function correctly.)

To use the VSCP, you need to navigate to Start → Program Files → Microsoft Visual Studio .NET 2003 → Visual Studio .NET Tools → Visual Studio .NET 2003 Command Prompt. (If you are using a different version of Visual Studio, this menu path will be slightly different.)

Figure 10-1 shows an example of the Visual Studio .NET 2003 Command Prompt.

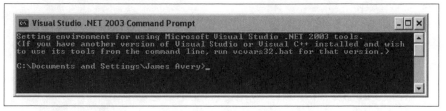

Figure 10-1. Visual Studio .NET 2003 Command Prompt

From the command prompt, you can access any of the various tools you commonly need to use from the command prompt. Some of the more common utilities that you will use while developing applications are:

sn.exe
> Used to strongly sign assemblies [Hack #54]

gacutil.exe
> Used to add assemblies to the global assembly cache

xsd.exe
> Used to generate strongly typed DataSets from XML schemas [Hack #49]

ildasm.exe
> Used to view the Intermediate Language code generated by your code [Hack #63]

wsdl.exe
> Used to generate web services code based on Web Service Description Language (WSDL) files

As you can see, a number of useful tools can be quickly accessed through the Visual Studio command prompt.

Add the Visual Studio Command Prompt as an External Tool

Because of all the helpful utilities available through the VSCP, you might frequently find yourself opening the command prompt and then navigating your way to your project or solution directory. There is a better way. You can add the VSCP to Visual Studio's Tools menu and have it automatically open to your project or solution directory:

1. Open the External Tools configuration window through Tools → External Tools.

2. Click the Add button.

3. Set the name to something like:
   ```
   Visual Studio Command Prompt
   ```

4. Set the command to:
   ```
   C:\WINDOWS\system32\cmd.exe
   ```

5. Set the arguments to:

```
\k c:\Program Files\Microsoft Visual Studio .NET 2003\Common7\Tools\
    vsvars32.bat
```

6. Set the initial directory to any of the available options. (These include $(SolutionDir) and $(ProjectDir), which would place you in the solution directory or project directory, respectively.)

7. Click OK.

Figure 10-2 shows an example of the External Tools [Hack #33] dialog with these settings entered.

Figure 10-2. External Tools dialog

The VSCP will now be added as a tool on the Tools menu. You will be able to quickly get to the tool and even have it open in the directory of your choice.

Add the Visual Studio Command Prompt to the Explorer

Another way to get the VSCP at your fingertips is through a little registry hack that will add an "Open VS command prompt here" option in the Windows Explorer. The easiest way to add these registry settings is to create a *.reg* in your favorite text editor with the following code:

```
Windows Registry Editor Version 5.00

[HKEY_LOCAL_MACHINE\SOFTWARE\Classes\Directory\shell\VSCP]
@="Open VS Command Prompt Here"

[HKEY_LOCAL_MACHINE\SOFTWARE\Classes\Directory\shell\VSCP\command]
@="cmd.exe /k \"C:\\Program Files\\Microsoft Visual Studio .NET
2003\\Common7\\Tools\\vsvars32.bat\""

[HKEY_LOCAL_MACHINE\SOFTWARE\Classes\Drive\shell\VSCP]
@="Open VS Command Prompt Here"

[HKEY_LOCAL_MACHINE\SOFTWARE\Classes\Drive\shell\VSCP\command]
@="cmd.exe /k \"C:\\Program Files\\Microsoft Visual Studio .NET
2003\\Common7\\Tools\\vsvars32.bat\""
```

You will, of course, need to modify the path to reflect the version of Visual
Studio that you are using and where you have it installed. Then save the file
with a *.reg* extension. When you double-click on the *.reg* file, you will be
asked if you want to add this information to your registry. After adding this
information to your registry, you will then see an option in Explorer like the
one shown in Figure 10-3.

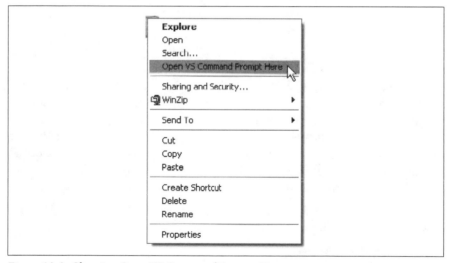

Figure 10-3. Choosing Open VS Command Prompt Here

You will now be able to right-click on a folder in the tree view of Explorer
and then choose "Open VS command prompt here" and VSCP will be
opened in that directory.

The Visual Studio command prompt is a valuable tool, and having it at your
fingertips no matter where you are is very handy.

See Also

- "Combine the Visual Studio Command Prompt and the Command Window" [Hack #98]

Launch Visual Studio from the Command Prompt

If you want to exercise obsessive control about how Visual Studio is launched, you'll be pleased to know that you can do it all from your friendly neighborhood command prompt.

The Visual Studio IDE executable is called *devenv.exe* and includes a number of command-line switches that can be very useful. Elsewhere in this book, we have looked at a couple of these switches, but in this hack, you will learn about all the switches and how they can be used.

> Typing command-line switches every time you launch an application is time consuming and just plain inefficient. Remember that you can create shortcuts that call an executable using command-line switches; you could have a number of different shortcuts for Visual Studio with different command-line switches.

Setting Fonts

One of the simplest, but very useful, things you can accomplish using command-line switches is setting the font and font size for the IDE. To specify the font, you can use the /fn switch, and to specify the size, you use /fs. It is important to note that this is not the font size of the text or contents of your files, but rather the text size of the IDE. You won't see it affect the normal menus, but the font and size of the document tabs, options dialog, and so forth will all be in the specified font type and size.

The following command line could be used to set the Visual Studio IDE font to Verdana and the size to 14:

```
C:\> devenv /fn Verdana /fs 14
```

This does not need to be set each and every time you run the IDE; these settings will be saved and used from here on out. This is the same setting you can configure under Tools → Options → Fonts and Colors, then selecting the Dialogs and Tool Windows option from the Show Settings drop-down.

Execute a Command

Using the command switch, you can launch Visual Studio and automatically call a Visual Studio command. All you need to do is specify the switch /command and then follow it with the name of the command that you want to execute. These are the same commands covered in "Master the Command Window" [Hack #46]. In this example, I will call the File.OpenSolution command—I almost always open Visual Studio with the intent of opening a solution, so this saves a couple of mouse clicks:

```
C:\> devenv /command File.OpenSolution
```

When you run this command, Visual Studio will open, and the New Solution dialog will open. You could also use /command to execute a macro you have written to perform more complex actions.

Run a Solution

You can automatically run a solution from the command line using the /run switch. The following is an example of running a solution from the command line:

```
C:\> devenv /run HacksWinSample.sln
```

When this command is run, the IDE will open and automatically jump into debug mode loading your application. You can also use the /runexit switch, which will launch your applications and minimize the IDE. When you close your application, the IDE will be closed as well.

Building Projects and Solutions

You can build your projects or solutions using command-line switches. This can be a great alternative if you don't have time to configure a build tool like NAnt, but want to create a build process using a batch file. To build a solution, you use the /build switch as well as the /project or /solution switch. Here is an example of building a solution from the command line:

```
C:\> devenv HacksWinSample.sln /build release
```

After the /build switch, you specify the solution configuration that you want to use when building this solution—in this example, I have used the release configuration. Running this will build the solution without opening the IDE, and the build results will be returned to the command prompt window. A number of other build switches are detailed in Table 10-1.

Table 10-1. Build switches

Switch	Description
/clean	Cleans the project or solution according to the configuration of that project or solution
/rebuild	Cleans and builds the project or solution
/project	Specifies the project to build
/projectconfig	Specifies the configuration to use when building the project
/deploy	Tells Visual Studio to deploy the solution after it has been built
/out	Specifies the name of a file to send any build errors to

Other Switches

A number of other command-line switches can be used to do various things with Visual Studio. These command-line switches are shown in Table 10-2.

Table 10-2. Command-line switches

Switch	Description
/lcid	Specifies the default language to use for the IDE. Example: devenv /lcid 1033
/mdi	Specifies that Visual Studio should be run in MDI mode.
/mditabs	Specifies that Visual Studio should be run in MDI mode with tabs on documents enabled.
/migratesettings	Tells Visual Studio to trigger the settings migration process, which can be used to move settings from one version of Visual Studio to another. (You usually see this screen the first time you run a new installation of Visual Studio.)
/nologo	Launches Visual Studio without the splash screen.
/noVSIP	Disables a developer's VSIP license on this workstation.
/safemode	Specifies that Visual Studio should open without loading any VSIP packages.
/setup	Resets certain parts of Visual Studio ("Manage Add-ins" [Hack #92]).
/resetskippkgs	Enables VSIP packages by clearing any SkipLoading tags. After running safe mode, this will need to be run to reenable any packages you still want to run.
/rootsuffix	Can be used to specify a registry suffix [Hack #30].
/?	You can always use this switch to view the help for *devenv.exe*.

Stress Test Web Applications

#79 You'll never be able to perform a decent test with one mouse and one keyboard. Use the Application Center Test tool to simulate legions of users.

The focus of this hack is to use ACT from within Visual Studio. In many cases, it's preferable to use the ACT tool in its standalone version, so that will be discussed toward the end of this hack.

Like all good web developers, we want to know whether our applications perform well. Does our design and implementation hold up to the expected load levels? Are we seeing the right amount of throughput? How many concurrent users can we handle? How many requests per second can the web application deliver? Will we see memory leaks after a certain amount of time?

These are all valid questions when it comes to performance testing. Of course, there are many other questions, but most of them come when the performance metrics start to get collected and analyzed. In many cases, performance testing occurs too late in the development process. This is in large part due to time constraints; performance testing is put off until toward the end of an application life cycle, when it's too late to do anything about it.

To do some performance testing on web applications early in the development cycle, developers can use the Microsoft Application Center Test (ACT) tool. This tool comes with Visual Studio Enterprise Edition and is a valuable resource in any developer's toolbox; it can be used from within Visual Studio or as a standalone tool. Although not a replacement for something like Mercury's LoadRunner suite, it is a powerful asset because it can provide developers a clear indication of how their web application will perform in the early stages of an application cycle, thus letting them iron out any major performance issues long before the application is deployed to production.

If you do not have the Enterprise Edition of Visual Studio, you can still use a free utility called the Web Application Stress Tool. This tool, while not as feature rich as ACT, will perform a lot of the same actions. The Web Application Stress Tool is a predecessor to ACT, so they have certain similarities as well. You can download the tool from *http://www.microsoft.com/downloads/details.aspx?FamilyID=e2c0585a-062a-439e-a67d-75a89aa36495&DisplayLang=en.*

Stress Testing Configurations

The ACT tool generates load by using a web browser. In all configurations, the web browser is the client. And because the client is just a web browser, it can invoke HTTP calls to any web server, local or remote. This creates a few different configurations for setting up your stress tests. A typical web application will consist of several layers that are (possibly) deployed across multiple tiers. This means that your stress test configuration will likely fall into one of the three configurations shown in Figure 10-4.

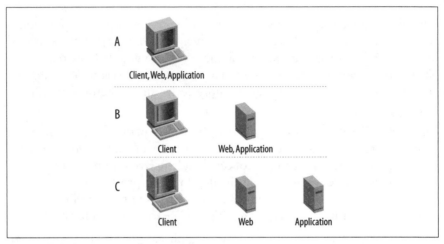

Figure 10-4. Stress test configurations

Here is an explanation of Figure 10-4:

- Configuration A shows that the client, the web server, and the application logic all run on the same machine. This will likely be a developer's workstation.

- Configuration B shows the client is now physically separated from the web server and application logic, both of which are still deployed together on the same box. This is the case in which the web application is running on a separate server and the developer is using her machine as the client.

- Configuration C shows that the client, web server, and application logic are all running on separate machines.

Also note that products such as Virtual PC or VMWare could be used to emulate any of these configurations on a single machine. In fact, it's highly suggested you use these products to create a virtual distributed environment to match the environment where your web application will live. Doing so tends to provide more realistic expectations, basic as they may be, during development.

Identifying Test Cases

Before creating your tests, you must first identify your test cases. These could range from simple web page requests to more complex tests that have user workflow with several steps, tasks, and web pages. The key thing is to identify the start and end points of the test. This will allow you to determine the scope of your test and know when to stop recording your test, as you'll see later.

Create an ACT Project

To use ACT for performance testing a web application, you'll first need to create an ASP.NET application in Visual Studio and run it to make sure it does what you want. You can then create an ACT Project by following these steps (assuming you chose to install ACT during the installation of Visual Studio .NET Enterprise Edition; it's selected by default):

1. In the Visual Studio Solution Explorer, right-click the solution, click Add, and select New Project.
2. In the Add New Project dialog box, under Project Types, expand Other Projects and click Application Center Test Projects.
3. In the Templates box, select the lone choice of ACT Project.
4. Type a name for the project, select the location, and click OK.
5. You will now see that your ACT Project has been added to your solution.

Creating a Test

Now that you've identified your test cases and created an ACT Project, you can create and add individual tests to your ACT Project by performing the following actions:

1. In the Solution Explorer, right-click your ACT Project, click Add, and select Add New Item.
2. Under Templates, select Browser Recorded Test.
3. Type a meaningful name for the test and click OK.
4. The Browser Record dialog will appear. Click the Start button.
5. A new instance of Internet Explorer will open. Note that ACT uses IE even if it is not your default browser.
6. In the browser, type the URL where your web application is running. Finish "clicking-through" your test case and then close the browser.
7. In the Browser Record dialog box, notice the Request Details text box has a list of the requests that were made. Click the Stop button, then click OK.

8. You will now see that the test script file (e.g., *TestName.vbs*) has been opened up in the editor and has been added under your ACT Project in the Solution Explorer.

> One thing to understand before creating your tests: all ACT tests are either VBScript or JScript, and you have the option of letting ACT generate the scripts for you (recommended) or writing the test scripts yourself. If you let ACT autogenerate the test scripts, they will be created using VBScript.

Test Properties

Now that you've created your ACT Project and added some tests, you need to set the properties of those tests. The Properties window is where you set your load levels, test duration, and test iterations. To view these settings, right-click on a test and select Properties. The Properties window appears, as shown in Figure 10-5.

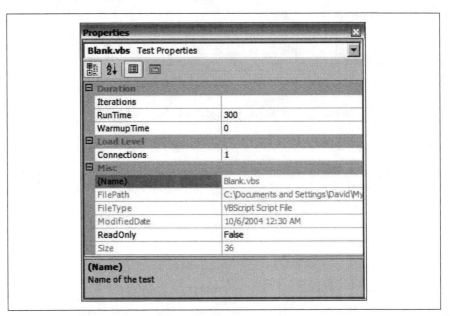

Figure 10-5. The Properties window of a test

By default, a brand-new test is set up to run one browser connection for five minutes (Connections = 1, RunTime = 300; RunTime is in seconds). This default configuration is actually a good "smoke test" to get started.

To gather a wide range of metrics, it's best to perform tests with varying load based on duration and iterations. A test based on duration will tell you

how many requests were served in the specified time. A test based on iterations will tell you how long it took to run the test the specified number of
times.

Duration example. To configure a test to run 10 connections for one hour,
enter 10 for Connections, 3,600 for the RunTime, and blank out Iterations.

Iterations example. To set up a test to run 1,000 iterations using five connections, enter 1,000 for Interations, 5 for Connections, and blank out RunTime.

Running a Test

The last thing to do at this point is run your test. To do this:

1. Right-click the test in the Solution Explorer and select Start Test.
2. The Output window now appears and displays statistics for the test as it
   is running. A sample is shown in Figure 10-6.

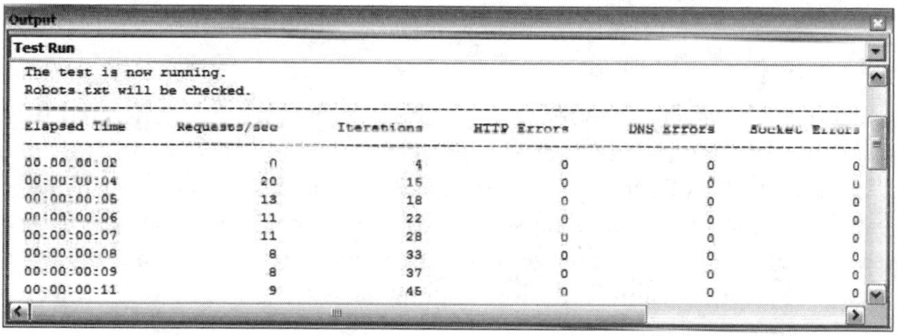

Figure 10-6. Output window when running a test

3. You now have two options: let the test run its course or stop it manually, which can be done by right-clicking on the test in the Solution
   Explorer and selecting Stop Test from the context menu that appears.

Viewing Test Results

After your test has finished running, you can view the results by right-clicking on the test and selecting View Results. A new window will appear that
resembles the one shown in Figure 10-7.

The test results window provides a quick view of the statistics for the test
run. You can see items such as total run time, total number of iterations,
and average requests per second. ACT autogenerates a report name using

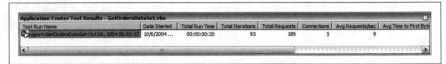

Figure 10-7. Test results window

the test name and a timestamp. Every time a test is performed, ACT generates a report, even if the test was stopped before it completed. And if you rerun the same test with the same configuration over and over, ACT will still generate separate reports for each test run.

To delete a test report, right-click on a report in the test results window and select Delete.

If you do not like ACT's report naming convention, you can rename a report by right-clicking on it, selecting Rename, and typing in a new name. For instance, you might want to name a report based on the test name and its configuration, such as Report-GetOrdersDataSet-1000Iterations or Report-GetOrdersDataSet-10Connections-1Hour.

Customizing Test Scripts

As mentioned earlier, browser recorded test scripts are autogenerated using VBScript. This has its advantages, because you can customize and/or modify the generated VBScript to better suit the specific needs of your tests. In most cases, the autogenerated script will be all you need, but it's nice to know that if you need to change it, you can very easily. You can see the generated VBScript by simply double-clicking a test in your ACT Project. A sample is shown in Figure 10-8.

The format of the script is simple and modular. For every single request in the recorded test, a SendRequest( ) method is created, each one being autonumbered starting at 1. It's important to understand that a SendRequest( ) method does not necessarily correlate to a page request. A single web page can contain several images or references to JavaScript files and CSS stylesheets. Each of these types of items is an individual request, thus ACT will generate a SendRequest( ) method for each one. Depending on how your web pages are designed, the generated VBScript could become quite large.

The good thing is everything can be found in a given SendRequest( ) method. Each SendRequest( ) method is a simple subroutine call that must be invoked by the main program. To see this, look at the bottom of your generated script. You will see something like this:

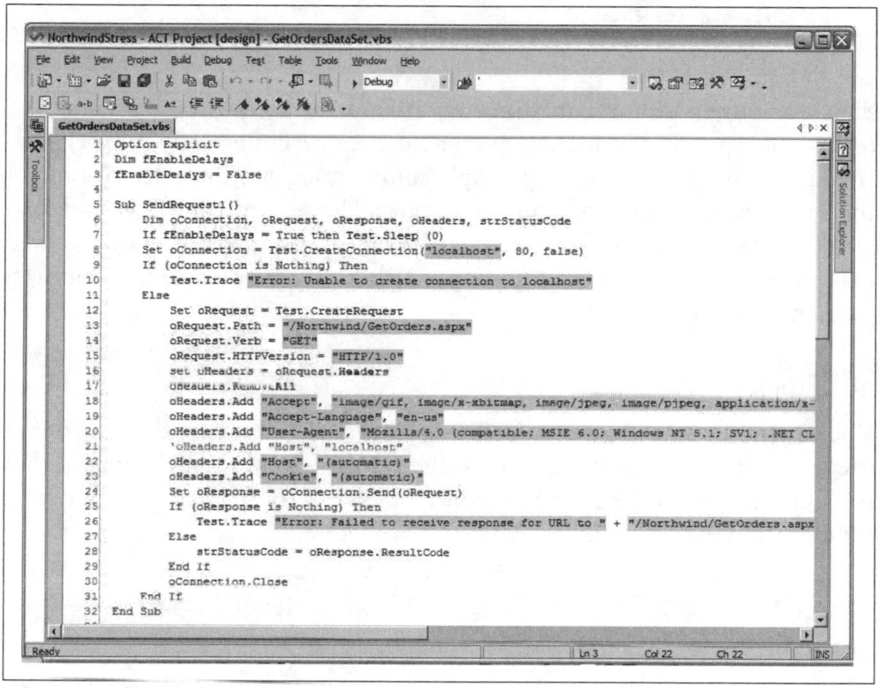

Figure 10-8. Autogenerated VBScript

```vbscript
Sub Main()
    call SendRequest1()
    call SendRequest2()
End Sub
```

The Main() subroutine is nothing more than a series of calls to the SendRequest() methods. To demonstrate how you can customize your script, let's presume your test case is a single web page that contains 10 images, and all you want to do is test the load time of that page. The ACT tool will generate 11 SendRequest() methods: SendRequest1() for the page request and SendRequest2() through SendRequest11() for each image request. Your Main() subroutine then looks like this:

```vbscript
Sub Main()
    call SendRequest1()
    call SendRequest2()
    call SendRequest3()
    call SendRequest4()
    call SendRequest5()
    call SendRequest6()
    call SendRequest7()
    call SendRequest8()
    call SendRequest9()
```

```
      call SendRequest10( )
      call SendRequest11( )
End Sub
```

Simple enough, so you run your performance tests, analyze the data, and realize the page is not loading within acceptable limits. You can begin to streamline the performance by simply commenting out the calls to some of the SendRequest( ) methods for the images. Then rerun your tests and analyze the results. This type of easy modification of the script allows you to make quick changes to your test scripts without having to redesign your web page and record a new test.

ACT Project Files

You've seen how to create an ACT Project in Visual Studio, add and configure test scripts, run tests, and view the results. Another cool thing is that ACT creates and manages all its project files in XML format. You can see a sample of these files in Figure 10-9.

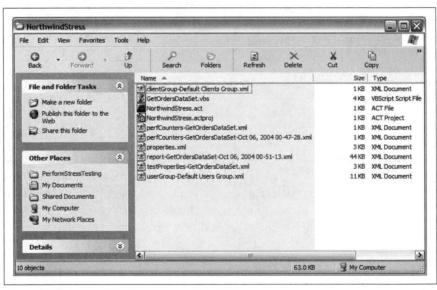

Figure 10-9. Some of the files generated by ACT

With the exception of the *.vbs* file, every file shown in Figure 10-9 is an XML file, even the *.act* and *.actproj* files. As you configure and make changes to your ACT Project and tests, the ACT tool is modifying these files behind the scenes as needed. A quick look at the *testProperties-GetOrdersDataSet.xml* file shows the following XML:

```xml
<?xml version="1.0" encoding="UTF-8" ?>
<!DOCTYPE Settings>
<DefaultValues >
    <TestProperties >
        <ControllerReportTimeout type="long" value="5"/>
        <Timeout type="long" value="120"/>
        <Duration type="long" value="300"/>
        <Warmup type="long" value="0"/>
        <UseIterations type="bool" value="False"/>
        <Iterations type="long" value="200"/>
        <UseRateControl type="bool" value="False"/>
        <TargetRPS type="long" value="40"/>
        <PerfCollectionInterval type="long" value="10"/>
        <TestType type="long" value="1"/>
        <GenerateUsers type="bool" value="True"/>
        <UsersToGenerate type="long" value="5000"/>
        <CollectPerfCounters type="bool" value="False"/>
        <CollectRuntimeHistory type="bool" value="true"/>
        <Locale type="long" value="1033"/>
        <CollectPerPageData type="bool" value="true"/>
    </TestProperties>
    <DynamicTest >
        <Language type="string" value="VBScript"/>
        <NumberOfThreads type="long" value="5"/>
        <FollowRedirects type="bool" value="False"/>
        <RedirectDepth type="long" value="15"/>
    </DynamicTest>
    <Network >
        <Enable type="bool" value="False"/>
        <NATRange type="long" value="0"/>
        <Distribution.9.6K type="long" value="1"/>
        <Distribution.14.4K type="long" value="4"/>
        <Distribution.28.8K type="long" value="5"/>
        <Distribution.56K type="long" value="20"/>
        <Distribution.128K type="long" value="15"/>
        <Distribution.512K type="long" value="15"/>
        <Distribution.T1 type="long" value="15"/>
        <Distribution.Unlimited type="long" value="15"/>
        <PropagationDelay type="long" value="200"/>
        <NATStartAddr type="string" value="10.10.1.1"/>
        <NATStopAddr type="string" value="10.10.1.255"/>
        <ClientPortStart type="long" value="1000"/>
        <ClientPortEnd type="long" value="5000"/>
    </Network>
    <StaticTest >
        <DefaultServer type="string" value="localhost"/>
        <DefaultMethod type="string" value="GET"/>
        <DefaultHTTPVer type="string" value="HTTP/1.1"/>
        <DefaultPort type="long" value="80"/>
        <SessionCount type="long" value="5"/>
        <UseRandomDelay type="bool" value="True"/>
        <MinDelay type="long" value="10"/>
        <MaxDelay type="long" value="1500"/>
```

```
        <FollowRedirects type="bool" value="True"/>
        <RedirectDepth type="long" value="15"/>
    </StaticTest>
</DefaultValues>
```

ACT: The Standalone Tool

Up to this point, you've seen how to use ACT from within Visual Studio. However, you cannot get to all of ACT's functionality from within Visual Studio itself. Other features available in the standalone tool are:

- Graphical reporting
- Report breakdown
- Additional statistics
- Defining users
- Performance counter monitoring

To see all that ACT has to offer, you must use the tool on its own. This section will highlight ACT in that way.

Create an ACT Project. To use ACT for performance testing, you'll first need to create and deploy your web application in one of the configurations mentioned earlier. Once you've done that, you can create an ACT Project by following these steps:

1. Click Start → All Programs → Visual Studio .NET 2003 → Visual Studio .NET Enterprise Features and select Microsoft Application Center Test.

2. Click File → New Project (Ctrl-N).

3. In the New Project dialog box, type a name for the project and select a location (by default, the location is in the *C:\Documents and Settings\ <username>\My Documents\ACT Projects* directory). Then click OK.

4. You can save the project any time by clicking File → Save Project (Ctrl-S).

Creating new tests. You can create and add individual tests to your ACT Project by performing the following actions:

1. In the left pane, right-click Tests and select New Test. A wizard will start; just follow the steps.

2. When prompted for a test source, select Record New Test.

3. When prompted for browser record, click the Start Recording button. This will open a new instance of Internet Explorer (note that ACT uses IE even if it is not the default browser).

4. In the browser, type the URL where your web application is running. Finish "clicking-through" your test case and then close the browser.

5. In the wizard, click the Stop Recording button and then click Next.

6. Give the test a name and click Next. Then click Finish.

7. You'll now see the test you just recorded listed in the right pane.

A sample ACT Project. To demonstrate the ACT tool, I've created a sample web application named Northwind that contains a single web page, *GetOrders.aspx*. This page is used to retrieve all the orders from the Northwind database on my local SQL Server. In ACT, I've created a project named NorthwindStress and recorded a test named GetOrdersDataSet, as shown in Figure 10-10.

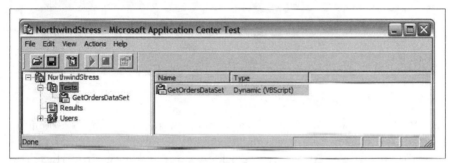

Figure 10-10. The NorthwindStress ACT Project

The GetOrdersDataSet test is quite simple: open the web page, click the Get Orders button, and display the results. Figure 10-11 shows the page when you first open it, and Figure 10-12 shows the page with the results.

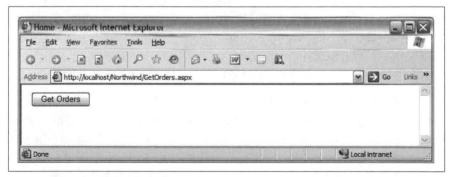

Figure 10-11. Get Orders page first time in

In fact, these two views are what was recorded when I created the GetOrdersDataSet test in ACT. The end of the test case is the results page.

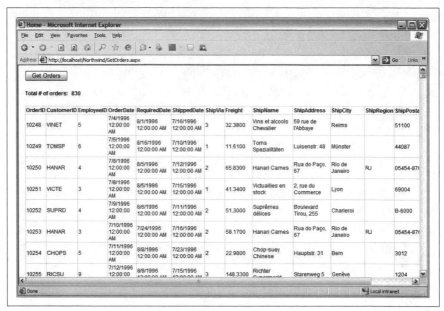

Figure 10-12. Get Orders page with results

Test properties. Each ACT test has a set of properties where you set the load levels, test duration, test iterations, users, and performance counters to capture. To view these settings, right-click on a test and select Properties. The Properties window appears and displays the General tab, as shown in Figure 10-13.

The General tab is where you set the load level and duration. By default, a brand-new test is set up to run one browser connection for five minutes. This default configuration is actually a good "smoke test" to get started. The General tab is where you'll spend most of your time when setting the properties of a test.

The Advanced button simply displays a checkbox to generate detailed test results, which is on by default. It's best to always leave this box checked.

The next tab is the Users tab, as shown in Figure 10-14.

For tests that do not need to store the HTTP cookies created and used during the test run, users can be automatically generated by ACT during the test on an as-needed basis. Automatically generating users will help to avoid potential problems that are caused when the test's population of users is too small to match the number required to create the specified load level for the test run.

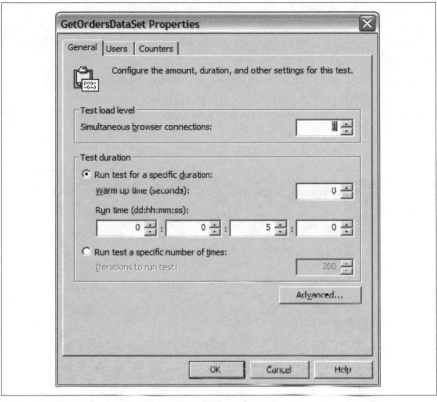

Figure 10-13. General tab in Properties window

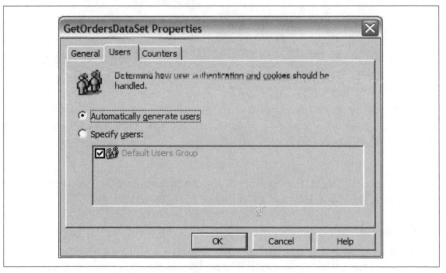

Figure 10-14. Users tab in Properties window

For tests in which authentication is required or you want to view or reuse the cookies that were created, users and user groups must be created and then selected in the Users tab. You will be able to set the name, domain, and password for each of these users.

The last tab of the Properties window is the Counters tab. This is where you add any performance counters you wish to capture, which could be for the test client and/or the web server. For this sample, I've added a few performance counters and changed the collection interval to two seconds, as shown in Figure 10-15.

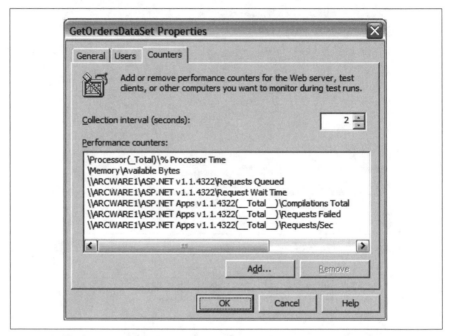

Figure 10-15. Counters tab in Properties window

You can add performance counters in this tab by clicking the Add button. A dialog then appears for you to make your selections, shown in Figure 10-16. If you've used the Performance Monitor tool at all, this dialog will look very familiar.

As you can see, using the ACT tool in standalone mode offers many more test settings than when using ACT from within Visual Studio.

Defining users. Another advantage of using ACT outside of Visual Studio is the ability to define users and groups of users for your tests. Provided for you is a group of users named Default Users Group, containing 200 users (User0-User199) with generic passwords, as shown in Figure 10-17.

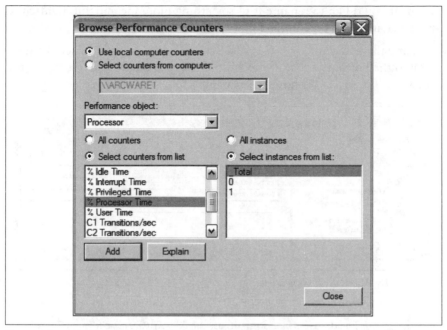

Figure 10-16. Browse Performance Counters dialog

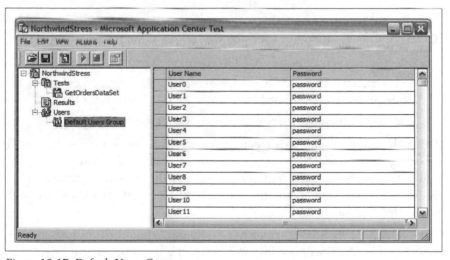

Figure 10-17. Default Users Group

To create your own groups of users, you have three options: type them in by hand, let ACT generate them for you, or import them from a comma-delimited list. Also note that all users must belong to a group.

First, to create your own users group, click on Users in the left pane, right-click and select Add. A group with the name of New Users Group will be added. If you'd like to rename it to something more meaningful, right-click, select Rename, and type in the name.

To manually add your own users, select the users group to place them in, scroll to the bottom of that group's list of users, and enter the username and password. Figure 10-18 shows an example.

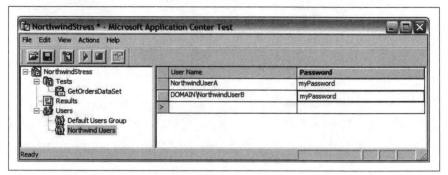

Figure 10-18. Manually adding a user

 To add users in a domain, use the DOMAIN\Username format.

To let ACT generate a set of users for you, follow these steps:

1. Select the target users group. Click Actions → Generate Users.
2. The Generate Users dialog appears. Enter the number of users, the name prefix, and password (see Figure 10-19). Then click OK.
3. The list of generated users will now appear in the right pane.

The only thing of note with generating users is the start number. ACT always generates users beginning with the number 1 (as you can see, the ability to change the start number is disabled). In the sample shown in the figure, the users created for me were *DOMAIN\NorthwindUser1* through *DOMAIN\NorthwindUser5*.

The last way of creating users in ACT is by importing them from a comma-delimited file; ACT will not import users if the file is in other formats. The file should contain usernames and corresponding passwords. To import users from a file, do the following:

1. Select the target users group. Click Actions → Import Users.
2. Browse for your file, select it, and click Open.
3. The list of imported users will now appear in the right pane.

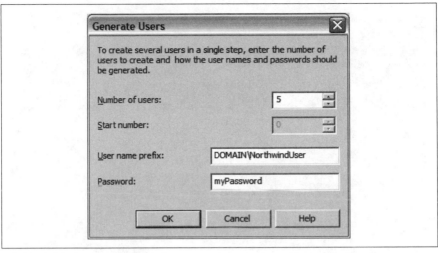

Figure 10-19. Generate Users dialog

This shows the contents of a sample file (Figure 10-20 shows the list of users after being imported from the file):

```
DOMAIN\NorthwindUserA,myPasswordA
DOMAIN\NorthwindUserB,myPasswordB
DOMAIN\NorthwindUserC,myPasswordC
DOMAIN\NorthwindUserD,myPasswordD
DOMAIN\NorthwindUserE,myPasswordE
```

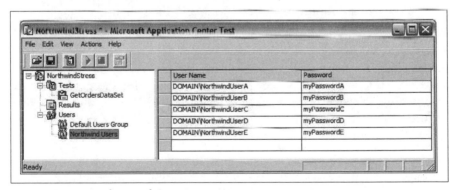

Figure 10-20. List of users after import

Running a test. Running a test in ACT outside of Visual Studio is much the same as running it within Visual Studio—right-click the test to run and select Start Test from the context menu that appears. Both methods display the statistics as the test is running, but using ACT in standalone mode allows you to see a nice graphic instead of a line of text. The graphic is shown in Figure 10-21.

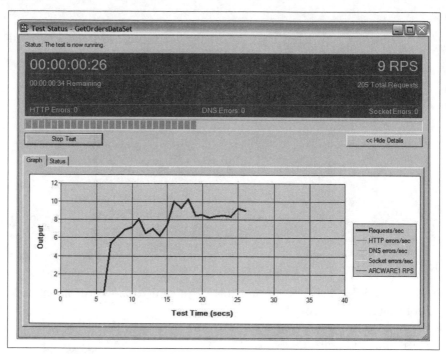

Figure 10-21. Statistics graph while test is running

Viewing the results. Once your tests have completed, you can check out the results by clicking Results in the left pane and then choosing the appropriate test report under Test Runs (top pane, left). A snapshot is shown in Figure 10-22, with more statistics shown in Figure 10-23.

Recall that I added a few performance counters to monitor for the GetOrdersDataSet test. You can view the statistics for those performance counters by selecting Performance Counters under Report (top pane, right). Figure 10-24 shows the performance counter statistics for the GetOrders-DataSet sample.

And that should about do it. You've seen how you can easily create and manage performance tests for your web applications using ACT, from both inside and outside the Visual Studio IDE. The primary reason for using ACT within Visual Studio is for the tight integration with your ASP.NET Projects, but you don't get ACT in its full capacity. The main reason for using ACT outside of Visual Studio is the better user experience, plus you can take advantage of everything ACT has to offer, such as graphical results, user groups, and performance counter monitoring.

—Dave Donaldson

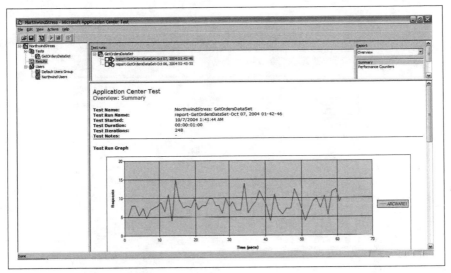

Figure 10-22. Report summary snapshot

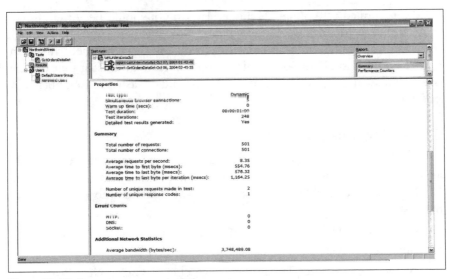

Figure 10-23. Report summary statistics

Obfuscate Your Code

HACK #80

Even if you have trouble reading your own code, you might still want to make it hard for others to decompile the assemblies you ship out the door.

As in the Java world, a number of tools are available that will easily decompile your .NET code [Hack #63]. Both the Java Virtual Machine and the .NET Common Language Runtime provide means of using reflection to "look

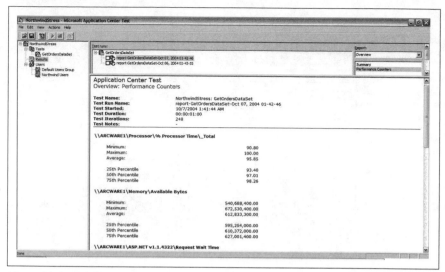

Figure 10-24. Performance counters statistics

inside" compiled assemblies. If this is alarming, it should be. After all, you may have class libraries with highly confidential business logic—if that logic were to fall into the wrong hands, you could lose your competitive advantage. Luckily, Visual Studio contains a tool named Dotfuscator that you can use to make sure that the output of a decompiler is as close to gibberish as possible.

Create a Dotfuscator Project

To use the Dotfuscator, you'll first need to create a project in Visual Studio and compile it (in this case, I've created a project with a class named Simple-Math). Then create a Dotfuscator Project for your assembly by following these steps:

1. On the Visual Studio menu, click Tools → Dotfuscator Community Edition. This will start the Dotfuscator.

2. At the Select Project Type dialog box, choose Create New Project and click OK. You'll now see a tool with several tabs along the top (Figure 10-25).

   Although several tabs and numerous options can be configured in the Dotfuscator, you need to configure two items at a minimum to create an obfuscated assembly. They are the trigger file(s) and the build destination directory. Once these two options are set, you can save the Dotfuscator Project for use later. Dotfuscator Projects are saved in XML format.

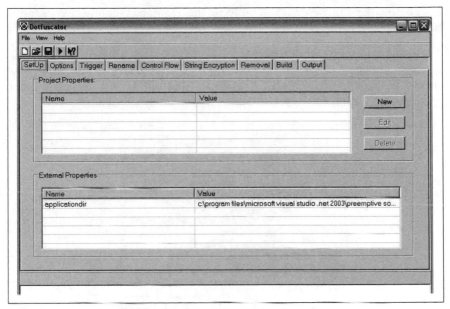

Figure 10-25. Dotfuscator window

3. Click the Trigger tab and notice that nothing is there. Now click Browse, search for your assembly, and click Open. You'll see that your assembly has been added to the Dotfuscator Project.

4. Click the Build tab. For the Destination Directory, click Browse, search for the directory where you want to place the obfuscated assembly, and click OK. Be sure this directory is not the same directory where the Debug assembly is placed.

5. Click File → Save Project (Ctrl-S). Browse to the location where you want the XML file saved, give it a name, and click Save.

Build the Dotfuscator Project

Now that you've created and saved a Dotfuscator Project, you can build it. Click File → Build (Ctrl-B). This will rebuild your assembly with the obfuscation options you specified in the Dotfuscator Project.

Now that you've got an obfuscated assembly, let's take a look at it using two well-known tools, ILDASM and Reflector.

Investigate the Results with ILDASM

As you know, ILDASM can be used to view an assembly's manifest and its IL code [Hack #63]. You can use this tool to verify the Dotfuscator did its job by comparing the obfuscated assembly to the regular assembly. My Simple-Math class will be used as the example.

So launch ILDASM and open the unobfuscated assembly. Now launch another instance of ILDASM and open the obfuscated code. In both instances, expand the class(es) listed and take a look. Figure 10-26 is the unobfuscated assembly; Figure 10-27 is the obfuscated assembly.

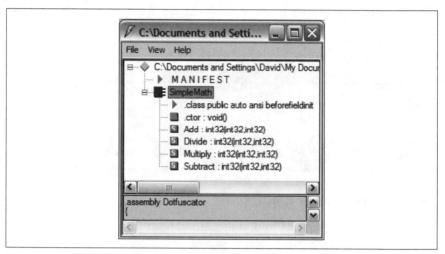

Figure 10-26. Unobfuscated assembly

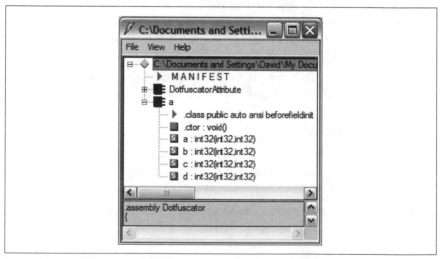

Figure 10-27. Obfuscated assembly

Notice that the class name (SimpleMath) and its methods (Add, Divide, Multiply, Subtract) are clearly visible in the unobfuscated assembly, while the obfuscated assembly does not contain any names of significant meaning. If someone were to use ILDASM on your obfuscated assembly to gain knowledge of your business code, they won't find it very useful.

Let's now take a look at the actual IL code produced. For simplicity, we'll look at just one of the methods—the Add method. Figure 10-28 is the unobfuscated IL code for the Add method; Figure 10-29 is the obfuscated version.

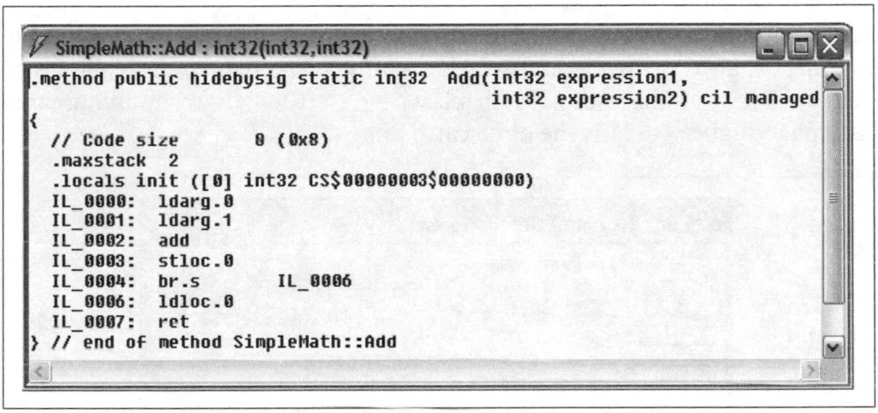

```
SimpleMath::Add : int32(int32,int32)
.method public hidebysig static int32  Add(int32 expression1,
                                           int32 expression2) cil managed
{
  // Code size       8 (0x8)
  .maxstack  2
  .locals init ([0] int32 CS$00000003$00000000)
  IL_0000:  ldarg.0
  IL_0001:  ldarg.1
  IL_0002:  add
  IL_0003:  stloc.0
  IL_0004:  br.s        IL_0006
  IL_0006:  ldloc.0
  IL_0007:  ret
} // end of method SimpleMath::Add
```

Figure 10-28. IL code for unobfuscated Add method

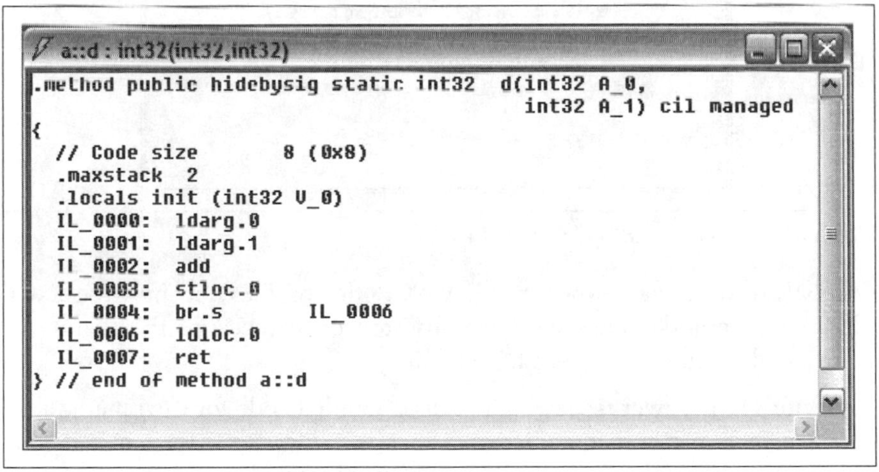

```
a::d : int32(int32,int32)
.method public hidebysig static int32  d(int32 A_0,
                                         int32 A_1) cil managed
{
  // Code size       8 (0x8)
  .maxstack  2
  .locals init (int32 V_0)
  IL_0000:  ldarg.0
  IL_0001:  ldarg.1
  IL_0002:  add
  IL_0003:  stloc.0
  IL_0004:  br.s        IL_0006
  IL_0006:  ldloc.0
  IL_0007:  ret
} // end of method a::d
```

Figure 10-29. IL code for obfuscated Add method

Notice that the only difference in the IL code is the method signature. The actual code execution path is identical, thus both assemblies will execute exactly the same. There is no performance penalty for code obfuscation.

Investigate the Results with Reflector

Reflector is a tool that can be used to "look inside" .NET assemblies and see its codepaths and logic [Hack #64]. It does not produce an exact copy of the actual code for an assembly, but that's not the point. It's used to provide insight to the logic used for the internals of an assembly. Therefore, continuing to use the SimpleMath class, we'll investigate the differences Reflector shows between unobfuscated and obfuscated assemblies.

Launch two instances of Reflector: one to open the unobfuscated assembly and the other to open the obfuscated assembly. The figures show the disassembler view of the SimpleMath class. Figure 10-30 is the unobfuscated assembly; Figure 10-31 is the obfuscated one.

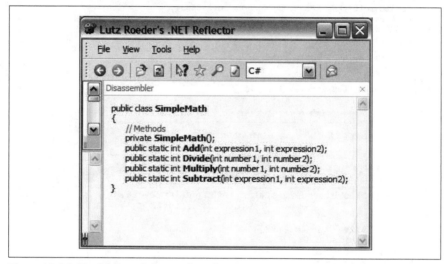

Figure 10-30. Unobfuscated class with Reflector

Similarly to what was shown in ILDASM, Reflector does not show the actual class and method names in the obfuscated code (because the IL for the obfuscated assembly does not have them).

Reflector's real power is viewing the disassembled code for each method, so using the Add method again, let's take a look. This is the disassembled code for the Add method. Figure 10-32 is the unobfuscated version; Figure 10-33 is the obfuscated one.

As you can see with this extremely simple example, the disassembled views are very similar. However, to know that the "d" method was for adding two numbers, I had to view the disassembled code for each method in the obfuscated assembly and then had to realize that the "d" method did in fact simply add two numbers together. Any .NET assembly even slightly more complex than this example will benefit from code obfuscation.

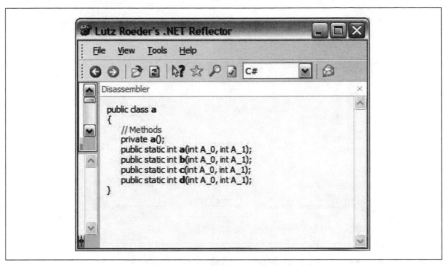

Figure 10-31. Obfuscated class with Reflector

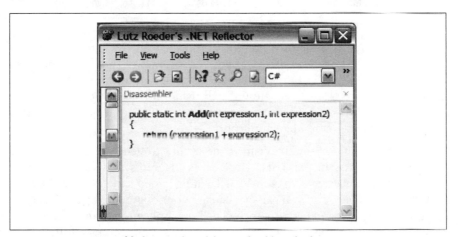

Figure 10-32. Disassembled view of unobfuscated Add method

Code obfuscation is only ever a deterrent—given enough effort and time, even the most obfuscated code could be decompiled and understood. The only guaranteed way to ensure your code will not be decompiled is to never put it on the client machine in the first place. One technique is to encapsulate your sensitive business logic in a web service and call that web service from your application. Just because obfuscation is not a guarantee does not mean it is not valuable, since it will still prevent the majority of people from being able to decompile your application.

—*Dave Donaldson*

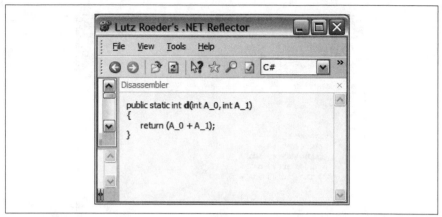

Figure 10-33. Disassembled view of obfuscated Add method

 H A C K **Generate Code from UML**

#81 Get a jump start on your coding efforts by using Visio to generate your code.

When Microsoft purchased Visio for its business productivity division in 1999, the company began working on getting it to better integrate with its Office and Visual Studio product suites. This has lead to advancements in Visio itself, especially as to the use of UML for designing applications. UML is an industry standard that allows architects and developers to produce design documents and diagrams that are commonly understood and used during the development of an application.

One of the advancements in Visio is the ability to generate code from the design documents, in particular UML class diagrams that can be used to generate code for your classes in Visual Studio. Visio can generate the code in C#, VB, or C++, and you can even create your own templates in Visio for how you want it to generate your code. For application teams that utilize design documents, this can be a nice jump start to your coding effort.

 This feature is available only in the Visio for Enterprise Architects version that comes with Visual Studio .NET 2003 Enterprise Architect Edition. No other version of Visio includes code generation.

A Simple Class Diagram

To have Visio generate code for your classes, you first need to create a UML class diagram. To create new diagrams, navigate to File → New → Software → UML Model Diagram. Then use the shapes in the UML Static Structure section to create your class diagram. Figure 10-34 shows the class diagram I have created to generate code from.

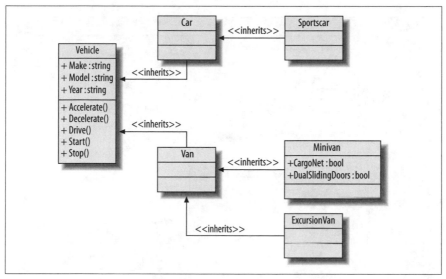

Figure 10-34. Class diagram of Vehicles class hierarchy

Figure 10-34 shows a class diagram that documents a Vehicle class hierarchy. This rather simple example shows an abstract base class named Vehicle that contains a few properties (Make, Model, Year) and methods (Accelerate, Decelerate, Drive, Start, Stop). The class diagram then shows other implementation classes and their relationships to one another.

Generate the Code

Now that you've created a class diagram in Visio, follow these steps to auto-generate the code in Visual Studio:

1. On the File menu, click UML → Code → Generate. The Generate dialog box will appear.

2. For Target Language, select C# (or C++ or Visual Basic).

3. Type a Project Name and select a Location to put it in.

4. Check the "Add classes to Visual Studio Project" checkbox.

5. Select the template to use. The template list contains several Visual Studio Project types to choose from.

6. Type a Solution Name and check the Create Directory for Solution checkbox.

7. Select all classes for which you want to generate code.

8. Click OK. A sample Generate dialog is shown in Figure 10-35.

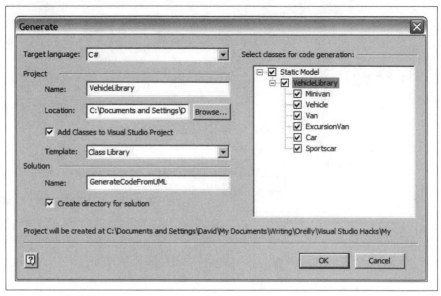

Figure 10-35. The Generate dialog

View the Code

Now that you've generated your class code from Visio, go take a look at it. Go to the location that you chose in the preceding steps. You should see a folder with the name of your solution. The solution folder will contain a Visual Studio Solution file as well as a folder with the project name you specified. For instance, in this example, the solution is named Generate-CodeFromUML and the project is named VehicleLibrary.

Double-click your generated solution file to open a new instance of Visual Studio. Chances are the IDE will show the *Class1.cs* file in the editor. But wait, you say, I didn't create a class named Class1 in Visio. Right you are. The best I can figure is that this is a small quirk with Visio's code generator. You can either ignore this file or just delete it.

The important thing is that you will see a file for each of your classes in the Solution Explorer, as shown in Figure 10-36.

At this point, you have a fully functional project in Visual Studio; you can now begin to modify it as needed. But first, take a look at the generated code. Here is the code for the abstract base class Vehicle:

```
// Static Model
public abstract class Vehicle
{
    public string Make;
    public string Model;
```

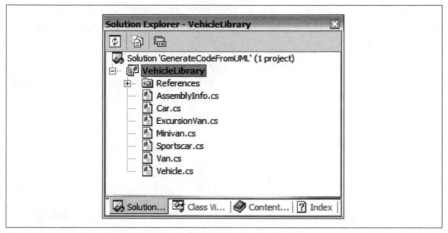

Figure 10-36. Generated class files in the Solution Explorer

```
public string Year;

public virtual void Accelerate()
{
}

public virtual void Decelerate()
{
}

public virtual void Drive()
{
}

public virtual void Start()
{
}

public virtual void Stop()
{
}

}// END CLASS DEFINITION Vehicle
```

As you can see, Visio does an adequate job of generating code for your classes and can save you an immense amount of time, especially if you have a class library with a lot of classes that contain a lot of properties.

Hacking the Hack

You've seen that Visio does a pretty decent job of generating your class code right out of the box. But what if you didn't quite like the way it generated your code? Or maybe its format is a little off from your own way of writing code. You can edit and/or create your own code generating templates so that Visio generates code that way you like it.

To get to the code template editor, click UML → Code → Preferences. This will bring up the Preferences dialog. Several options are found in this dialog, but for the purposes of this hack, I focus on creating two new templates, one for your own class template and another for your own property template.

Create a new class template. With the Preferences dialog, open, under Default, click Code Templates. This will show additional options, as shown in Figure 10-37.

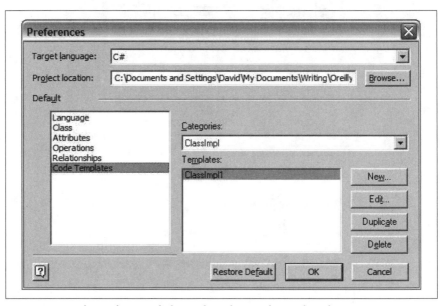

Figure 10-37. The Preferences dialog with Code Templates selected.

By default, Visio provide a class template named ClassImpl1. The safe way to create your own new template is to copy ClassImpl1 and then modify it. To do this:

1. Under Categories, select ClassImpl. A template named ClassImpl1 appears in the Templates list.

2. Click Duplicate. The Edit Template window will appear (Figure 10-38). I won't go into all the details here, but what the Edit Template really shows is a combination of normal text and Visio macros. The macros are denoted by the %macro_name% format. There are too many macros to cover here, but you can see the list by opening the Visio help and reading the help topic titled "Use built-in macros to speed up code formatting".

3. Give the new template a name and modify the template as you see fit.

4. Then click OK. Your template name will now appear in the Templates list.

5. Under Default, click Class.

6. Under Class Template, select your class template name from the Implementation list. Click OK.

7. Now every time Visio generates class files for you, it will use your new class template instead of the default one.

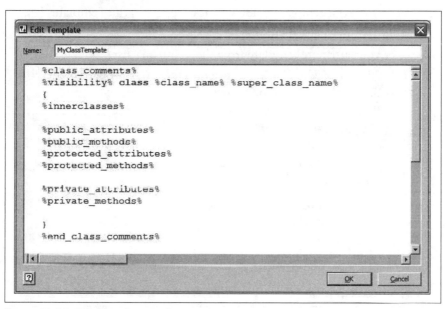

Figure 10-38. Edit Template window

Create a new property (attribute) template. By default, Visio creates code for properties in this format:

```
public bool CargoNet;
```

However, your coding style might have properties looking like this:

```
private bool m_CargoNet;
public bool CargoNet
{
    get { return m_CargoNet; }
    set { m_CargoNet = value; }
}
```

To create your own template for properties (called attributes in Visio), follow these steps:

1. With the Preferences dialog open, under Default, click Code Templates.
2. Under Categories, select Attribute.
3. A template named `Attribute1` will appear in the templates list. Click Duplicate.
4. The Edit Template window will appear again. For our example, make the template look like Figure 10-39.
5. Click OK. Your template name will now appear in the Templates list.
6. Under Default, click Attributes.
7. Select your attribute template from the Templates list.
8. Click OK. Now when Visio goes to generate your property code, it will use your template instead of the default.

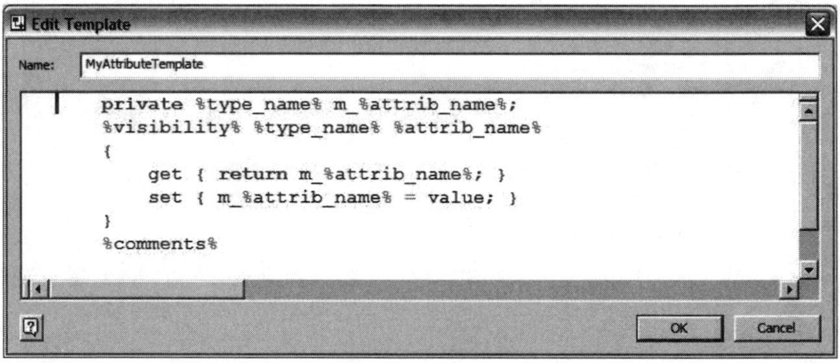

```
Edit Template                                                   ×
Name:    MyAttributeTemplate

         private %type_name% m_%attrib_name%;
         %visibility% %type_name% %attrib_name%
         {
              get { return m_%attrib_name%; }
              set { m_%attrib_name% = value; }
         }
         %comments%


                                                    OK        Cancel
```

Figure 10-39. New Visio code template for properties

Regenerate your code and view it. Now that you've created your own code templates for classes and properties, regenerate your code by following the steps just listed. Then open your generated solution and open the *Minivan.cs* file in the Visual Studio editor. Notice the format of the properties has been updated to reflect the use of your code template:

```
// Static Model

public class Minivan : Van
{
    private bool m_CargoNet;
    public bool CargoNet
    {
        get { return m_CargoNet; }
        set { m_CargoNet = value; }
```

```
    }

    private bool m_DualSlidingDoors;
    public bool DualSlidingDoors
    {
        get { return m_DualSlidingDoors; }
        set { m_DualSlidingDoors = value; }
    }
}
// END CLASS DEFINITION Minivan
```

I've demonstrated a simple example of using Visio to autogenerate your class code to get a jump start on your coding effort. However, Visio code templates can be customized much further, and I suggest you experiment with it to find the right degree of code generation you are comfortable with.

Visio has limited support for round-tripping. Visio can generate code from diagrams, but when you change the diagrams, it can't update the code based on your changes—it can only completely regenerate the code. Visio can also generate diagrams from code, but can't update those diagrams, only re-create them from scratch. Some other tools like Rational XDE provide much more complete round-tripping support.

—Dave Donaldson

HACK #82 Generate UML Design Documents from Code
Use Visual Studio to generate design documents in Visio.

Like all good developers, you keep your design documentation up-to-date, right? Most likely, that's a no. After all, who wants to constantly go back and continuously update design documents while coding? Most developers I know usually don't have the time because they are too busy trying to get the application implemented.

To help with this task, you can use Visual Studio to generate those pesky design documents, in particular the class diagrams, by having it reverse engineer your code. Although it won't replace and update all of your design documents, it can cut down on the amount of time it takes to maintain them manually. Essentially, this hack is the opposite of "Generate Code from UML" [Hack #81].

Reverse Engineer Your Code

To get started, you first need to create a Visual Studio Project. This can be any type of project, and most likely it's one that you've been working on or have already created. In this hack, I'm going to use the *VehicleLibrary* example found in "Generate Code from UML" [Hack #81]. To refresh your memory, the Solution Explorer of that project can be seen in Figure 10-40.

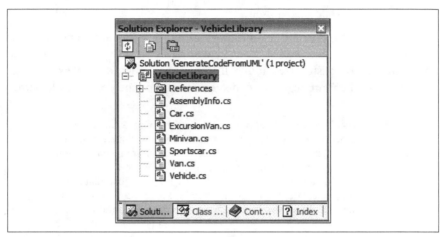

Figure 10-40. VehicleLibrary project in the Solution Explorer

To reverse engineer the code for this project, do the following:

1. Click Project → Visio UML → Reverse Engineer.
2. Browse to the location where you want your Visio file to be saved, give it a name, and click Save.
3. Depending on the size and complexity of your project, the reverse engineering process may take a moment or two.
4. Once your code has been successfully reverse engineered, an instance of Visio is automatically started. You can see in the Model Explorer that your classes have been automatically created (see Figure 10-41).
5. You can also see in your Visual Studio instance that the generated Visio file has been added to your project under the Solution Items folder.

Create Your Class Diagram

Unfortunately, that's as far as the reverse engineering will take you. You'll have to create the class diagram manually. Depending on the size of your

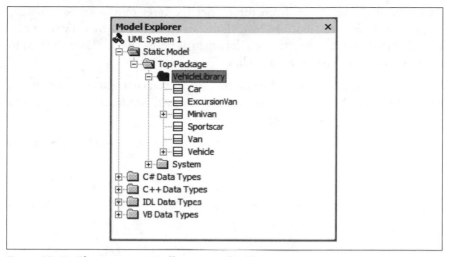

Figure 10-41. Classes automatically generated in Visio

class hierarchy, this may or may not be a big deal. The positive spin to this is that Visio is smart enough to understand the relationships between the generated classes.

For instance, when you drag your classes onto a diagram, Visio automatically determines their relationships and draws the generalization lines for you. An example is shown in Figure 10-42.

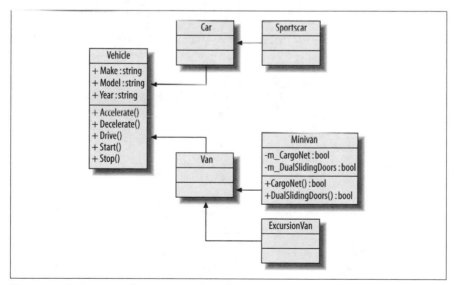

Figure 10-42. Dragging classes onto a Visio diagram

As I was dragging classes from the Model Explorer onto a static structure diagram in Visio (see Figure 10-42), all the arrowed lines were drawn for me. I didn't have to remember all the relationships between the classes, which in this case happen to be inheritance lines.

So as you can see, Visual Studio can be used to reverse engineer your classes from code into Visio for use on class diagrams, sequence diagrams, and other related design documents.

—Dave Donaldson

CHAPTER ELEVEN

Visual Studio Tools for Office
Hacks 83–85

The latest incarnation of Microsoft Office—Office System 2003—brings integration with the .NET Framework that takes developing Office-based solutions beyond Visual Basic for Applications (VBA). Additionally, Microsoft has released a toolset for Visual Studio that creates six new project templates to get developers started quickly on creating their application. Visual Studio Tools for Office 2003 (VSTO) gives developers the ability to choose C# or VB.NET to develop document-centric solutions in a managed code environment and take full advantage of the framework, including XML integration, Web Services, and Code Access Security.

—Brian Sherwin

HACK #83   Install Visual Studio Tools for Office 2003

Office is much more than a spreadsheet, word processing, database, and presentation tool. It's a complete platform for developing incredible applications.

Visual Studio Tools for Office (VSTO) is available as a download for MSDN subscribers and is also available for purchase. Starting with Visual Studio 2005, Visual Studio Tools for Office will be included with all full versions of Visual Studio (except the Express editions).

In order to get started with the VSTO, you will need to install Microsoft Office Word 2003 or Excel 2003. Now, these products are still primarily COM-based applications, so you are going to need to go beyond the standard installation and add the Primary Interop Assemblies (PIA) to the installation. The assemblies will be installed only if you chose to add the .NET programmability support to your installation choices or if you did a complete installation when you originally installed Office.

In the following steps, if you perform a custom installation, be sure to select the .NET Programmability Support under Excel and/or Word. In addition, select Microsoft Forms 2.0 .NET Programmability Support under Office Tools and select .NET Programmability Support under the Microsoft Graph component, which you will find under the Office Tools node.

If you haven't installed Office 2003 or Visual Studio 2003

Since the PIAs are installed into the Global Assembly Cache (GAC), you should install the products in the following order:

- Microsoft Visual Studio .NET 2003
- Microsoft Office System
- Visual Studio Tools for the Microsoft Office System

If you have installed Office 2003 but not VS.NET

If you have already completed the install of Office 2003, you will need to install the products in this order:

If you did not perform a complete installation for Office 2003, you can add the components noted earlier by using Add/Remove Applications from the control panel and updating your installation choices for Microsoft Office System 2003. You will need to have your installation CD available.

- Install Visual Studio .NET, including at least Visual Basic .NET or Visual C# (or both) and the MSDN product documentation.
- Install Visual Studio Tools for the Microsoft Office System.

If you have installed VS.NET but not Office 2003

- Install Microsoft Office 2003 (see the previous note if you need a custom installation).
- Install Visual Studio Tools for the Microsoft Office System.

When You Deploy

Once you have completed an application built on the Microsoft Office System, you will need to deploy the solution to an end user's computer and install the following:

- Microsoft .NET Framework 1.1
- Microsoft Office Excel 2003 and/or Microsoft Office Word 2003, including the necessary primary interop assemblies

Considerations

Keep the following in mind when developing with the VSTO.

Handling optional parameters. You may find that writing the same applications for the VSTO will take more effort to accomplish the same task depending on what language you are using. Take, for example, the following code to create a new Excel workbook in VB.NET:

```
Dim wb As Excel.Workbook = _
    ThisApplication.Workbooks.Open("C:\VSHacks\LoanCalc.xls")
```

However, to accomplish the same thing in C#, you would need to type the following:

```
Excel.Workbook wb = ThisApplication.Workbooks.Open(
    "C:\\VSHacks\\LoanCalc.xls", Type.Missing, Type.Missing,
    Type.Missing, Type.Missing, Type.Missing, Type.Missing,
    Type.Missing, Type.Missing, Type.Missing, Type.Missing,
    Type.Missing, Type.Missing, Type.Missing, Type.Missing);
```

Closing the debugger closes Office application. If you are debugging your new Office application through Visual Studio, you will find that if you close your document, you will be returned to Visual Studio to continue working with the code. However, if you close Visual Studio or stop the execution of your code (by clicking the Stop Debugging button or pressing Shift-F5), you will also close your Office application—any work that you did in your Office document will not be saved and you won't be prompted to save your work.

COM-based assemblies still return COM-based HResults. Although the .NET Framework will wrap COM-based HResult errors as an exception, you will find that sometimes the error messages aren't all that helpful. If you are having difficulty with a particular procedure, try recording an Office macro to do the same task and compare your code to the VBA that was created during the recording of the macro.

—Brian Sherwin

HACK #84 Create a Command Bar in Word 2003

How about a .NET-powered toolbar in Word? You'll want to click it for no good reason at all, just knowing how cool it is that you're calling into managed code.

In this hack, you will be creating a command bar item with a list of customers from the Northwind database.

If your installation of the Visual Studio Tools for Office is complete, you should see some additional project types in Visual Studio's New Project dialog. I'll show you how to create a new Visual C# Project for a Microsoft Word template called *CommandBar* (as shown in Figure 11-1).

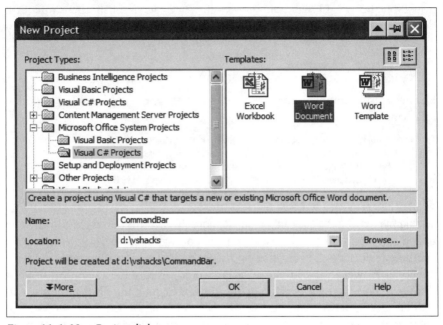

Figure 11-1. New Project dialog

Once you have selected the project template and named the project, click OK and you'll be presented with the Microsoft Office Project Wizard (Figure 11-2). Since you are going to be working with a new document template, select the option to Create a New Document. If you want to change the name or location of the document template that will be created, you can change the corresponding text box.

On the Security Settings tab, the wizard will automatically update your security settings to allow the managed code document to run. There is not space here to explain how to set all of the security settings, so until you can spend some time figuring out the Code Access Security model for the project, I suggest that you let the wizard make the necessary changes. When you click Finish, the wizard will create the required document templates and a code-behind class for the document.

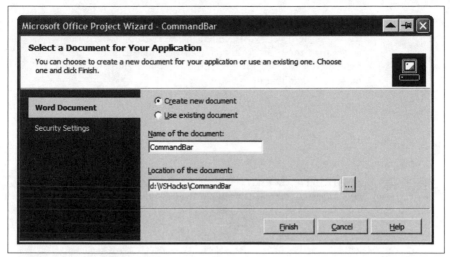

Figure 11-2. Microsoft Office Project Wizard

Create the Command Bar

When the wizard has completed, you will be placed into the main code file named *ThisDocument.cs*. Most of your code will execute when a user creates a new instance of your document. This event is handled by the following method:

```
protected void ThisDocument_New( )
{
}
```

At this point, you are going to need to create some class-level variables to work with as you build your command bar. The main class is OfficeCodeBehind, so your code should look something like this:

```
public class OfficeCodeBehind
{
    private object oMissing = System.Reflection.Missing.Value;
    private Office.CommandBar CBar;
    private Office.CommandBarComboBox CBarComboBox;
    private Office.CommandBarButton CBarButton;
    // ...
}
```

Next, you will need to write some code to create the different user interface elements that you plan to place on the command bar. In this example, you will need a combo listbox and a button. (You may need to change the connection string, highlighted in bold, to suit your SQL Server or MSDE installation.)

You will notice that in this section of code, you will be using the oMissing object you defined in the preceding code. This is because these are optional variables in the Word document and C# does not support optional variables, so you must pass in a default value.

```csharp
private bool SetupCommandBar( )
{
    try
    {
        // Create command bar for this document
        ThisApplication.CustomizationContext=ThisDocument;
        CBar = ThisApplication.CommandBars.Add("Customer Form",
            oMissing, oMissing, (object)true);

        // Add a combo box to the command bar
        object objType = Office.MsoControlType.msoControlDropdown;
        CBarComboBox = (Office.CommandBarComboBox)
            ((CBar.Controls.Add(objType, oMissing, oMissing,
            oMissing, (object)true)));
        CBarComboBox.Caption = "Select:";
        CBarComboBox.Style = Office.MsoComboStyle.msoComboLabel;
        CBarComboBox.ListIndex = 0;
        CBarComboBox.Width = 250;
        CBarComboBox.BeginGroup=true;

        //Add items to combo box from database
        SqlConnection conn =
            new SqlConnection("data source=localhost;
            initial catalog=Northwind;integrated security=true");
        SqlCommand cmd = new SqlCommand("select CustomerID,
            CompanyName from customers", conn);
        SqlDataReader dr;
        conn.Open( );
        dr = cmd.ExecuteReader( );
        int i = 0;
        while (dr.Read( ))
        {
            i += 1;
            CBarComboBox.AddItem(dr["CustomerID"].ToString( )
                + "-" + dr["CompanyName"].ToString( ), i);
        }
        dr.Close( );
        conn.Close( );

        // Add a button to the command bar to insert data
        CBarButton = (Office.CommandBarButton)
            (CBar.Controls.Add((object)1, oMissing, oMissing,
            oMissing, oMissing));
        CBarButton.Style=Office.MsoButtonStyle.msoButtonCaption;
        CBarButton.Caption = "Insert";
```

```
        // Make the new command bar visible.
        CBar.Visible=true;
        return true;
    }
    catch (Exception ex)
    {
        MessageBox.Show("Error creating CommandBar: " + ex.Message,
            "Customer Form", MessageBoxButtons.OK,
            MessageBoxIcon.Error);
        return false;
    }
}
```

In the preceding code, the first thing you need to create a command bar is a reference to the current instance of the Microsoft Word application you will be working in. Once you have this reference, you can create a new command bar by calling the Add method of the CommandBars collection.

The next step is to create the drop-down combo box (Office.MsoControlType. msoControlDropdown). Once you have created the combo box, you can set the properties for how you want the control to appear to the user.

After the combo box is created, you are ready to populate the control with values from a database. In this example, the data will be coming from the Northwind database on the SQL Server of the machine that is running the code. Since you will need only the CustomerID and CustomerName from the database, it is a good practice to select only that data. Since you will be using a SqlDataReader to get the data, you will be responsible for opening the connection in your code before executing your SqlCommand object. The ExecuteReader object will create a SqlDataReader object and pass the reference back to the variable we have declared in order to read the data. At this point, you have not read any data.

The while loop begins reading the data by grabbing the next available row. As long as the SqlDataReader successfully returns data, the code that adds the item to the combo box executes. Unfortunately, in this example, the primary key that we need to use to identify the customer is a string-based key, so you cannot use it as the index parameter of the AddItem method. For now, you will make the key part of the display text and retrieve the key value when you handle the button click later. After reading the data, you need to close the SqlDataReader and the SqlConnection.

Next, you need to create the button on the toolbar (Office.CommandBarButton) and set its display properties. Finally, show the command bar to the user with the Show method.

Now that the method to create the command bar is complete, you will need to call the method to initialize the command bar's creation when a new document is created:

```
protected void ThisDocument_New()
{
    SetupCommandBar();
}
```

Now, test your new command bar by executing the application. Visual Studio should start an instance of Word, create a new document from your blank template, and finally raise the ThisDocument_New event, which will create your command bar as shown in Figure 11-3.

Figure 11-3. Command bar in Word

Handle the Command Bar Events

Now that you have a command bar in Word, you need to listen for the events that the command bar raises. In this section, you will learn how to wire up the command bar events to your custom code.

The first order of business is to create a class-level delegate for the events you want to handle:

```
public class OfficeCodeBehind
{
    private Office._CommandBarButtonEvents_ClickEventHandler
        CBarButtonEvent;
    ...
```

Second, you will need to create a method containing the code you want to run when the command bar raises the event. In this code, you will be taking the combo box selection and looking up the customer record to type the address into the Word document:

```
private void CBarButton_Click(
    Office.CommandBarButton btn,
```

```
      ref bool Cancel)
{

    // Get Word ready to receive data
    Word.Selection sln = null;
    sln = ThisApplication.Selection;
    ThisApplication.Options.Overtype = false;

    // Get customer ID back into individual fields
    string wrkString = CBarComboBox.Text;
    string[ ] Customer = wrkString.Split('-');

    // Get customer information from database
    SqlConnection conn = new SqlConnection("data source=localhost;
        initial catalog=Northwind;integrated security=true");
    SqlCommand cmd = new SqlCommand("select * from customers
        where customerid = @CustID", conn);
    cmd.Parameters.Add("@CustID", Customer[0]);
    SqlDataReader dr;
    conn.Open( );
    dr = cmd.ExecuteReader( );

    //Output customer Address Data to Word
    while (dr.Read( ))
    {
        sln.TypeText(dr["CustomerID"].ToString( ) + "\n");
        sln.TypeText(dr["CompanyName"].ToString( ) + "\n");
        sln.TypeText(dr["ContactName"].ToString( ) + "\n");
        sln.TypeText(dr["Address"].ToString( ) + "\n");
        sln.TypeText(dr["City"].ToString( ) + ", ");
        sln.TypeText(dr["Region"].ToString( ) + "  ");
        sln.TypeText(dr["PostalCode"].ToString( ) + "\n");
        sln.TypeText(dr["Country"].ToString( ));
    }
    dr.Close( );
    conn.Close( );
}
```

In the preceding code, you first create a variable for the current selection in
Word. The next step is to take the selection from the combo box and split
the text into an array containing two items.

> In a scenario in which you are able to use an integer primary
> key, you would want to use that value as the indexer when
> calling the AddItem method as you build the command bar:
>
> ```
>     CBarComboBox.AddItem(dr["CompanyName"].ToString( ),
>         dr["CompanyID"]);
> ```
>
> If you take this approach, you would be able to query for the
> key value by using the following code:
>
> ```
>     int CustomerID = CBarComboBox.Value;
> ```

Next, you need to create a SqlConnection, SqlCommand, and SqlDataReader to retrieve the data from the database. Once you have retrieved the record, you will output the records to the Word.Selection variable that you created earlier using the TypeText method.

Now that you have created the method to output the data record to your Word document, you need to wire that code into the button by attaching the delegate to your event handler:

```
private void WireUpEvents( )
{
    // Set up the Click events for the command bar buttons.
    CBarButtonEvent =
        new Office._CommandBarButtonEvents_ClickEventHandler
        (CBarButton_Click);
    CBarButton.Click += CBarButtonEvent;
}
```

One last order of business is to finish the document initialization process by updating the ThisDocument_New method to call the event wire-up code after the command bar has been created:

```
protected void ThisDocument_New( )
{
    SetupCommandBar( );
    WireUpEvents( );
}
```

Now, build and test the application once again. This time, when you click the button on the command bar, the name and address for the customer will be typed into the Word document.

—Brian Sherwin

HACK #85 Display a Windows Form from Excel 2003

Create a graphical application to gather information for Excel.

In this hack, you'll learn how to make an Excel workbook pop up a Windows Form application to collect information and insert it into to the worksheet.

Create a Windows Form

Start by creating a new project in Visual Studio. Choose the Visual Studio Tools for Office project group and then the project type, Excel Workbook. For this example, I'm going to create a graph of orders for customers, so I'll use *CustomerOrders* for the name of the project, as shown in Figure 11-4.

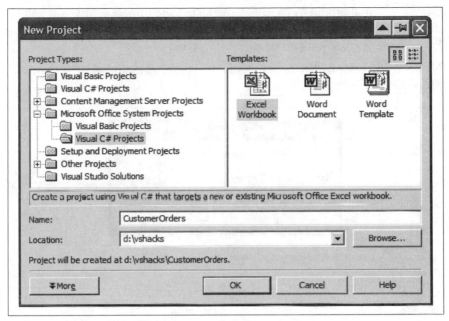

Figure 11-4. New Excel Workbook Project dialog

In the Microsoft Office Project Wizard, select the radio button to create a new document (Figure 11-5). Next, give the document a name and choose the location to store the document on your machine. At this point, you do not need to make any changes to the security tab, so click Finish to complete the wizard

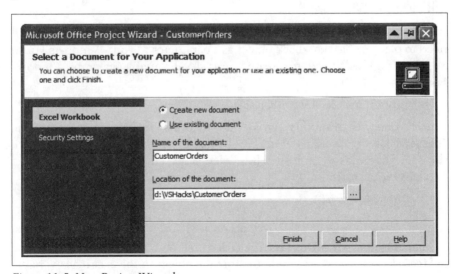

Figure 11-5. New Project Wizard

Once the Visual Studio Wizard has completed the project setup, you will be dropped into the solution. At this point, you will need to add a Windows Form to the application and name it GetCustomer.

Next, create a form that looks similar to Figure 11-6 and set the controls' properties according to Table 11-1.

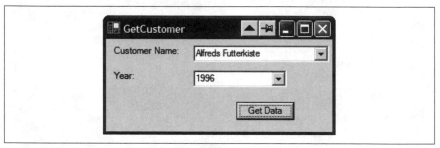

Figure 11-6. GetCustomer Windows Form

Table 11-1. Windows Form controls and properties

Required controls	Properties
Label	Text: Customer Name:
ComboBox	Name: cboCustomer
Label	Text: Year
ComboBox	Name: cboYear
Button (Get Data)	Name: cmdOK

Initialize the Windows Form

In order to communicate with the code behind the Excel document, you will need to pass the ThisWorkbook object as a parameter to your Windows Form. So, first, you will need to create a class-level variable in your Windows Form:

```
private OfficeCodeBehind excelCode;
```

The next step is to modify the Windows Forms constructor to accept the ThisWorkbook object as a parameter. In C#, the form constructor will have the same name as your form class. Here's the empty constructor for the GetConstructor form:

```
public GetCustomer( )
{
}
```

Update this constructor to take the CodeBehind object as a parameter of type OfficeCodeBehind and add code to store the object in the excelCode variable

you created for this class. This should be done after the call to Initialize-
Component (which initializes the form):

```
public GetCustomer (OfficeCodeBehind targetExcelCode)
{
    InitializeComponent();
    this.excelCode = targetExcelCode;
}
```

The next step is to create an instance of the Windows Forms class and call
the Show method. In this example, you are going to do this when the workbook first opens the new document:

```
protected void ThisWorkbook_Open()
{
    GetCustomer inputForm = new GetCustomer (this);
    inputForm.Show();
}
```

At this point, you should be able to build and test your code. Excel should
start and open your blank form. Sure, it doesn't do much yet, but you
should run it now to make sure that all of the pieces are falling together.

Gather Data with the Windows Forms

Now that you have the form opening up when the user starts a new instance
of the Excel document, you need to add code to the form's Load event to
populate the combo boxes with data from a database. First, to make life a
little easier, in your Windows Forms class, you need to add references to the
data namespaces listed here:

```
using System.Data;
using System.Data.SqlClient;
```

Next, create a method to handle the form's Load event. The easiest way to
do this is to double-click anywhere on the form (as long as it is not a control), and you'll be placed in the code editor for this method. (You may need
to change the connection string, highlighted in bold, to suit your SQL Server
or MSDE installation.)

```
private void GetCustomer_Load(object sender, System.EventArgs e)
{
    //Get the customers and order years from the database
    SqlConnection conn = new SqlConnection("data source=localhost;
        initial catalog=Northwind;integrated security=true");
    SqlDataAdapter da = new SqlDataAdapter("select CustomerID,
        CompanyName from customers", conn);
    DataSet ds = new DataSet();
    da.Fill(ds, "Customers");
    da.SelectCommand.CommandText = "select distinct
        datepart(\"Year\", orderdate) as [Year] from orders";
```

```
    da.Fill(ds, "Years");

    //Using databinding, fill the combo boxes with data
    cboCustomer.DisplayMember = "CompanyName";
    cboCustomer.ValueMember = "CustomerID";
    cboCustomer.DataSource = ds.Tables["Customers"];
    cboYear.DisplayMember = "Year";
    cboYear.ValueMember = "Year";
    cboYear.DataSource = ds.Tables["Years"];
}
```

This method connects to the SQL Server using a data adapter. In this example, a DataSet is used in order to take advantage of the .NET data-binding capabilities to fill the combo boxes. Then the control properties are set to map the data fields to show the friendly text (CompanyName) and make the CustomerID available for later.

Once the user makes a selection of the customer and a year, you will need to use the selections to query the database for the order counts by month and then output the results to the Excel workbook:

```
private void cmdOK_Click(object sender, System.EventArgs e)
{
    SqlConnection conn = new SqlConnection("data source=localhost;
        initial catalog=Northwind;integrated security=true");
    SqlCommand cmd = new SqlCommand(
        "select datepart(\"Month\", Orderdate)
        as [Month], count(orderid) as OrderCount
        from orders
        where customerid = @CustID
            and datepart(\"Year\", OrderDate) = @Year
        group by customerid, datepart(\"Month\", Orderdate)", conn);
    cmd.Parameters.Add("@CustID", cboCustomer.SelectedValue);
    cmd.Parameters.Add("@Year", cboYear.SelectedValue);
    SqlDataReader dr;
    conn.Open();
    dr = cmd.ExecuteReader();

    //initialize array
    string[,] OrderCounts = new string[12,2] {
        {"Jan", "0"},   {"Feb", "0"},{"Mar", "0"},{"Apr", "0"},
        {"May", "0"},{"Jun", "0"},{"Jul", "0"},{"Aug", "0"},
        {"Sep", "0"},{"Oct", "0"},{"Nov", "0"},{"Dec", "0"}
    };
    while (dr.Read())
    {
        //get Month number from first column
        int Month = (int)dr["Month"];
        //get OrderCount from second column and put in array
        OrderCounts[Month - 1, 1] = dr["OrderCount"].ToString();
    }
    dr.Close();
```

```
    conn.Close();

    //Output customers order data to Excel
    for (int i = 0; i != 12; i++)
    {
        for (int j = 0; j !=2; j++)
        {
            this.excelCode.EchoStringToCell(OrderCounts[i,j],
                new int[2] {i+1,j+1});
        }
    }
}
```

In the method that handles the click event of the command button, you are going to connect to the SQL server and retrieve the counts of orders for a particular client for the selected year. Notice that by using the SelectedValue property of the combo boxes, you have the CustomerID field. Later, when you are building the chart, you will use both the Text property and the SelectedValue property to label your work in the Excel sheets.

There are a couple of ways that you could have handled the output of the data for each month. Here, the use of an array, initialized to the default values, allows you to control what is displayed for the month names without writing too much Transact-SQL. Now all you need to do is get SQL Server to return the rows where data exists. The other option would be for SQL to return results for each month and then write the data directly from the data reader to the Excel worksheet.

Finally, to send the data to the Excel worksheet, you need to move through the two dimensions of the array and call the EchoStringToCell method that you will create in the next section. This function will take a string value and an array for the cell location in which to place the data. For example, int[2] {1,1} sends the data to row one, column one.

```
public void EchoStringToCell(string str, int[] cell)
{
    Excel.Worksheet sheet1 =
        (Excel.Worksheet)this.ThisApplication.Sheets.get_Item(1);
    ((Excel.Range)sheet1.Cells[cell[0],cell[1]]).Value2 = str;
}
```

At this point, compile and test your application. Excel should start and immediately display your Windows Forms. After entering data, click the OK button, and your data should populate the Excel spreadsheet.

Create a Chart in Excel

The last thing to do then is to create a chart of the data that you read in from the database. In the following code, you will pass the CustomerID,

CompanyName, and Year that the user has selected. You will be using this information to customize the layout of the chart page by labeling the items appropriately.

In order to build the chart, first get a reference to the first worksheet in the collection (where you have been putting all of the data) and create a new chart sheet following this page by calling the Add method of the Charts collection.

After you have created the chart page, call the chart wizard to build the chart for you. Don't worry if there seem to be a lot of parameters that aren't clear yet. The easiest way to get familiar with the parameter options is to use the Record Macro feature within Excel and inspect the code that is generated.

```
public void CreateChart(
    string CustomerID, string CompanyName, int Year)
{
    // Now create the chart.
    Excel.Worksheet xlSheet =
        (Excel.Worksheet)this.ThisApplication.Sheets.get_Item(1);
    Excel.Chart xlChart = (Excel.Chart)ThisWorkbook.Charts.Add
        (Type.Missing, xlSheet, Type.Missing, Type.Missing);
    Excel.Range cellRange = (Excel.Range)xlSheet.UsedRange;

    xlChart.Name = CustomerID + "-" + Year.ToString();

    xlChart.ChartWizard(cellRange.CurrentRegion,
        Excel.Constants.xl3DBar, Type.Missing,
        Excel.XlRowCol.xlColumns, 1, Type.Missing, false,
        CompanyName + " Orders for " + Year.ToString(),
        Type.Missing, Type.Missing, Type.Missing);

    // Apply some formatting to the chart title.
    xlChart.ChartTitle.Font.Size = 16;
    xlChart.ChartTitle.Shadow = true;
    xlChart.ChartTitle.Border.LineStyle = Excel.Constants.xlSolid;
}
```

Now update the method behind your Get Data button to call this new method and create the chart:

```
private void cmdOK_Click(object sender, System.EventArgs e)
{
    //Data has already been loaded to the page, now create chart
    this.excelCode.CreateChart((string)cboCustomer.SelectedValue,
        (string)cboCustomer.Text, (int)cboYear.SelectedValue);
}
```

At this point, you can build and execute your application. Now, when you click the Get Data button, the data will populate the Excel page and then immediately create a chart of the data.

These hacks introduce the capabilities of the Visual Studio Tools for Office and get you quickly up to speed with creating your own solutions based on Microsoft Office System 2003. With the integration of the .NET Framework, you can work in the language that is familiar to you, take advantage of reusable components, and build on existing Web Services to quickly build a line of business applications.

—Brian Sherwin

CHAPTER TWELVE

Extending Visual Studio
Hacks 86–91

Much of this book has been about extending Visual Studio, but this chapter specifically covers the objects and API used to directly interact with the Visual Studio environment. Visual Studio includes a rich automation object model that can be used to interact with just about every part of Visual Studio.

The hacks in this chapter cover the Visual Studio automation object model, its various classes and how they can be used, how to reference the DTE assembly from outside of Visual Studio, and how to add a new file template to Visual Studio.

This chapter also covers how to write and install Visual Studio add-ins, as well as how to find commands in Visual Studio and create a custom icon for your add-in.

HACK #86 Automate Visual Studio

Reach into Visual Studio and pull all its strings with the Visual Studio automation object model.

The Visual Studio automation object model provides an interface for you to develop macros, add-ins, and other tools that access and manipulate the Visual Studio environment. Using this object model, you can access and change just about every part of Visual Studio.

In this hack, you will learn about the object model and some of the more useful tasks that can be automated using it. In this hack, I will not be focusing on macros [Hack #51], add-ins [Hack #89], wizards [Hack #88], or any of the other ways that the object model can be accessed. Rather, I will focus on the object model itself and include small code snippets that accomplish a specific task. I will use macros as examples throughout this hack simply because they are easier for you to try out and test, but it is important to remember that these operations could be performed by anything operating against the object model.

 Using the macro recording functionality of Visual Studio [Hack #51] can be a great way to discover how to do something through the DTE (Development Tools Extensibility) object. It isn't always perfect, but it is sometimes easier than trying to find the answer in the documentation.

MSDN includes a great reference to this object model. You can access the MSDN documentation through Help → Contents → Visual Studio .NET → Developing with Visual Studio → Reference → Automation and Extensibility Reference or from MSDN Online at the following URL:

*http://msdn.microsoft.com/library/default.asp?url=/library/en-us/vsintro7/
html/vxoriExtensibilityReference.asp*

The automation object model chart is particularly useful since it shows a visual hyperlinked representation of the entire object model, and you can drill down into the documentation for each class.

At the top of the object model is the DTE object. This object contains all of the classes and collections that you will be working with to automate Visual Studio. This is the object that your macro or add-in will reference and use.

Automate Documents

Possibly the most frequently used object in the DTE is the Document object. Using the Document object, you can work with and manipulate any of the documents currently loaded in Visual Studio. You can work with two main properties on the DTE object to interface with the documents. The first is the Documents object, which is a collection of all the documents currently open in the IDE. The other property is called ActiveDocument and is a reference to the document that is currently shown in the document window.

Using just these two objects, you could write a macro to loop through the collection of documents and close all but the active document:

```
Public Sub CloseAllButActive( )
    'Declare and get an instance of the active document
    Dim active As Document = ActiveDocument

    Dim d As Document
    'Loop through each document and if it [is? NE] not
    'the active document close it
    For Each d In DTE.Documents
```

```
        If Not d Is active Then
            d.Close( )
        End If
    Next
End Sub
```

Another way to work with a document is to manipulate its actual text. Many of the macros in this book do this. To work with the text of the document, you will use the TextSelection object. The TextSelection object is a reference to the currently selected text, but it can really be used to change any of the text in the document.

The TextSelection object contains methods like StartOfDocument, EndOf-Document, StartOfLine, and EndOfLine. Something I commonly have to do is move existing text into a try...catch block—this is something you could easily automate using the TextSelection object. Here is an example of a macro that surrounds the selected text with a Try...Catch block:

```
Public Sub InsertTryCatch( )
    Dim selection As TextSelection = ActiveDocument.Selection
    Dim text As String

    text = "try" & vbCrLf & " { " & vbCrLf & _
    selection.Text & vbCrLf & "}" & vbCrLf & _
    "catch" & vbCrLf & "{" & vbCrLf & "}"

    selection.Text = text
End Sub
```

You would need to write a different macro to create a VB.NET Try...Catch block.

The Documents object is extremely valuable. When writing macros and add-ins, this will probably be one of the more frequent objects you use.

Invoke Commands

The DTE object includes a Commands collection that contains all of the commands currently in Visual Studio. Commands are normally used by wiring them to a keystroke [Hack #24] or through the command window [Hack #46], but you can also call them directly through the DTE.

To call a command directly, you simply need to call the ExecuteCommand method on the DTE object. Here is an example of calling this method:

```
DTE.ExecuteCommand("Edit.FormatSelection")
```

This code will execute the Edit.FormatSelection command, effectively the same as calling this command from the Command Window or through a shortcut key. You can get a reference to the actual command object through the DTE.Commands.Item method. Here is an example of getting a reference to this same command:

```
Dim com As Command = DTE.Commands.Item("Edit.FormatSelection")
```

Once you have the command object, you can add it to a command bar (more commonly known as a toolbar) [Hack #89] or even delete it if needed. The Commands object also includes an AddNewCommand method, which can be used to add custom commands for an add-in.

Automate Windows

Visual Studio includes a large number of different windows. So many in fact that there is a hack in this book dedicated to just knowing how to best manage all these windows [Hack #16]. The Windows collection of the DTE object allows you to access these windows and work with them. To get a reference to a window, you will need to use one of the many vsWindowKind constants. There is a constant for each of the windows that can be shown in Visual Studio. Table 12-1 shows a list of some of the more common windows and their corresponding vsWindowKind constant.

Table 12-1. Window constants

Window	Constant
Toolbox	vsWindowKindToolbox
Solution Explorer	vsWindowKindSolutionExplorer
Output window	vsWindowKindOutput
Properties window	vsWindowKindProperties
Command window	vsWindowKindCommandWindow

Here is an example of creating a reference to a window:

```
Window win = env.Windows.Item(Constants.vsWindowKindToolbox);
```

Using the Window object, you can set normal window properties, such as whether the window is visible or autohides, but more importantly, you can sometimes access more functionality. The toolbox is a great example of this. A Toolbox object can be accessed by referencing the Object property of the Window class. The following code shows how to get this object:

```
ToolBox toolBox = (ToolBox) win.Object;
```

Once you have the ToolBox object, you could then work with the toolbox [Hack #28].

In addition to the objects covered in this hack, there are also objects that can access projects, solutions, the debugger, source control, command bars, macros, and much more. For more information, refer to the excellent MSDN documentation and some of the examples throughout this book.

HACK #87 Access Visual Studio from Standalone Applications

When a macro or add-in is not what you are looking for, you can always use the automation object model from a normal Windows Forms application.

The EnvDTE assembly can be referenced by C# and VB.NET applications to directly reference the Visual Studio IDE. Using this assembly, you can modify windows, add custom toolbox items, and much more. Working with this assembly has a number of pitfalls though, and this hack shows ways to get around them.

When using the DTE object from an application. you can perform any of the same actions that you would normally do from a macro or add-in.

> You can get a reference to the currently executing instance of Visual Studio using this line of code:
>
> ```
> EnvDTE.DTE dte =
>     (DTE)Marshal.GetActiveObject("VisualStudio.DTE.
>         7.1");
> ```
>
> This will return a reference to the currently executing instance of Visual Studio as opposed to a reference to a new instance of Visual Studio.

Version Issues

After adding a reference to the EnvDTE assembly in your project, the first thing you normally will do is create an instance of the DTE object, using a line of code like this:

```
DTE env = new DTE();
```

This will work fine if you have only Visual Studio .NET 2002 installed. If you also have another version of Visual Studio installed, then no matter what assembly you reference, this call will return the DTE object for Visual Studio .NET 2002 (unless you don't have it installed).

This is because both assemblies are the exact same COM wrapper that accesses different versions of Visual Studio. To get the correct version of this class, you will need to use the ProgID of the class. This can be done using the following piece of code:

```
Type latestDTE = Type.GetTypeFromProgID("VisualStudio.DTE.7.1");
EnvDTE.DTE env = Activator.CreateInstance(latestDTE) as EnvDTE.DTE;
```

This piece of code will retrieve the object to work with Visual Studio .NET 2003. You could change the ProgID to get the object for 2002 or 2005 by simply changing the version number at the end of the ID (7.0 and 8.0, respectively).

It is a good idea to always use this method when accessing EnvDTE—while you may have only one version of Visual Studio installed on your machine, other users may have any number of versions installed.

The Notorious "Call Was Rejected by Callee" Error

While working with EnvDTE, you will most likely come across random occurrences of "Call was rejected by callee" errors. The key to avoiding this error lies in using an OLE message filter. The filter will watch all calls, and when one fails, it will wait and try again instead of throwing this error. The following OLE message filter will watch for any calls and then retry them instead of throwing an exception:

```
using System;
using System.Runtime.InteropServices;

class MessageFilter : IOleMessageFilter
{
    //
    // Public API

    public static void Register()
    {
        IOleMessageFilter newfilter = new MessageFilter();

        IOleMessageFilter oldfilter = null;
        CoRegisterMessageFilter(newfilter, out oldfilter);
    }

    public static void Revoke()
    {
        IOleMessageFilter oldfilter = null;
        CoRegisterMessageFilter(null, out oldfilter);
    }

    //
    // IOleMessageFilter impl

    int IOleMessageFilter.HandleInComingCall(int dwCallType,
            System.IntPtr hTaskCaller,
            int dwTickCount,
            System.IntPtr lpInterfaceInfo)
    {
        System.Diagnostics.Debug.WriteLine
            ("IOleMessageFilter::HandleInComingCall");
        return 0; //SERVERCALL_ISHANDLED
    }

    int IOleMessageFilter.RetryRejectedCall(
            System.IntPtr hTaskCallee,
            int dwTickCount,
```

```
                    int dwRejectType)
{
    System.Diagnostics.Debug.WriteLine
        ("IOleMessageFilter::RetryRejectedCall");

    if (dwRejectType == 2 ) //SERVERCALL_RETRYLATER
    {
        System.Diagnostics.Debug.WriteLine("Retry call later");
        return 99; //retry immediately if return >=0 & <100
    }
    return -1; //cancel call
}

int IOleMessageFilter.MessagePending(System.IntPtr hTaskCallee,
        int dwTickCount,
        int dwPendingType)
{
    System.Diagnostics.Debug.WriteLine
        ("IOleMessageFilter::MessagePending");
    return 2; //PENDINGMSG_WAITDEFPROCESS
}

//
// Implementation

[DllImport("Ole32.dll")]
private static extern int CoRegisterMessageFilter(
        IOleMessageFilter newfilter,
        out IOleMessageFilter oldfilter);
}

[ComImport( ), Guid("00000016-0000-0000-C000-000000000046")],
InterfaceTypeAttribute(ComInterfaceType.InterfaceIsIUnknown)]
interface IOleMessageFilter
// deliberately renamed to avoid confusion
// w/ System.Windows.Forms.IMessageFilter
{
    [PreserveSig]
    int HandleInComingCall(
        int dwCallType,
        IntPtr hTaskCaller,
        int dwTickCount,
        IntPtr lpInterfaceInfo);

    [PreserveSig]
    int RetryRejectedCall(
        IntPtr hTaskCallee,
        int dwTickCount,
        int dwRejectType);

    [PreserveSig]
    int MessagePending(
        IntPtr hTaskCallee,
```

```
        int dwTickCount,
        int dwPendingType);
    }
}
```

C# and VB.NET versions of this class can be downloaded from the book's web site (see *http://www.oreilly.com/catalog/visualstudiohks*).

To use this messaging class, you need to call the `Register()` method before starting to work with EnvDTE, and then call the `Revoke()` method when you are done working with the object. The following code demonstrates this usage:

```
// Register the OLE message filter
MessageFilter.Register();

Type latestDTE = Type.GetTypeFromProgID("VisualStudio.DTE.7.1");
EnvDTE.DTE env = Activator.CreateInstance(latestDTE) as EnvDTE.DTE;

// Work with the DTE object here

// Unplug the message filter
MessageFilter.Revoke();
```

This message filter should prevent any "Call was rejected by callee" exceptions from being thrown while working with EnvDTE. Thanks to Shawn A. Van Ness for posting this method and code on his web log, which can be found at *http://windojitsu.com/blog*.

HACK #88 Create a File Template

The Add New Item dialog isn't set in stone. You can extend it by adding your own item or project template.

When you create a new file in your Visual Studio Projects, you generally use the Add New Item dialog (see Figure 12-1). If you look at the categories listed on the left half of that window, you can see that the dialog box is organized according to the types of files you might need to create in a given project type.

> Visual Studio 2005 includes an enhanced and improved mechanism to create item and project templates. These enhancements were not available at the time of this writing, but stay tuned to *http://www.visualstudiohacks.com* for more information when they become available.

Visual Studio provides many different types of template files for the many different types of projects. Rather than just displaying them all in a long list,

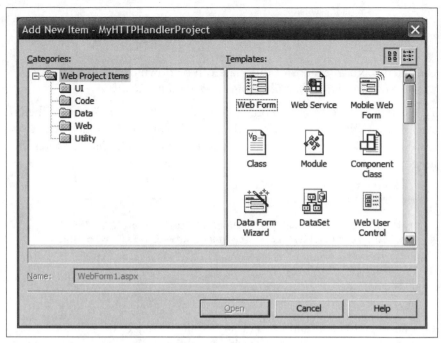

Figure 12-1. Visual Studio .NET 2003 Add New Item dialog

the Visual Studio team provided some of the gentle guidance you would expect. If you're working on a Web Project, it initially displays all the templates for the types of files that might be used in Web Projects. The most common type of file that developers create in an ASP.NET Web Project is a Web Form. Accordingly, the Web Form template is first one in the list.

Once you choose a given template, you're provided the chance to name the file that will be created from it. A fairly generic name is suggested, like *WebForm1.aspx* for those created from the Web Form template. You'll almost always change this name.

The final steps are for Visual Studio to add the new file instance, with your chosen filename, to your project and display it in the editor pane of the IDE. Depending on the template you chose, you'll see the appropriate initial content in the editor.

It's what appears in that initial content that is up for grabs in this hack. If this is a source code file, you'll see plain text. The plain text is the starter code or markup for the given file that you or another developer will expand upon. This hack shows you how to create your own template and have it produce the initial plain text you need.

Create Your Own Template

Visual Studio provides a number of built-in templates for nearly all of the file types that are involved in the different types of .NET applications. One hack opportunity is to take one of the existing templates and just modify it to your needs. The other opportunity is to create one from scratch, which is what I will be covering in this hack.

Visual Studio .NET 2003 Is Missing a Template

Actually, in this hack, I'd like to make up for a hole in Visual Studio. In addition to the Visual Studio IDE, Microsoft also offers a free tool for web development called Microsoft ASP.NET Web Matrix, or Web Matrix for short. The Web Matrix is a small tool that is not as fully featured as Visual Studio. Visual Studio is able to create many more file types than the Web Matrix. So you'd think that Visual Studio's set of templates would definitely be the superset of file types. Not quite. There's an HTTP Handler file type that appears in the Web Matrix Add New File dialog (see Figure 12-2). Strangely enough, this is missing from Visual Studio. So let's make up for this disparity.

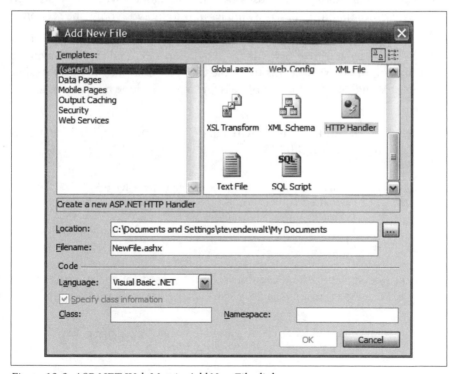

Figure 12-2. ASP.NET Web Matrix Add New File dialog

Similar to the *.aspx* extension for the Web Form templates, ASP.NET HTTP Handlers use an *.ashx* extension. We won't go into all the differences between a Web Form and an HTTP Handler in this hack. The salient difference to note is that the initial text that the HTTP Handler template uses will be different from the Web Form template. Whereas the *.aspx* file contains markup text with angle brackets, the HTTP Handler template is actually all code; in this case, it's C# or Visual Basic .NET.

Get Your Template Listed in the Add New Item Dialog

Navigate to the *C:\Program Files\Microsoft Visual Studio .NET 2003* folder. Depending on what language (for example, C# or VB), look for either the VC# or VB7 folder. Inside the given language folder, look for *CSharp-ProjectItems* or *VBProjectItems*, respectively. Compare the filenames in the folders to the templates in the Add New Item dialog. This is where Visual Studio stores templates. It uses a combination of *.vsz* files and *.vsdir* files. So to get our template display, we've got to create the appropriate *.vsz* and *.vsdir* files. The entry in the *.vsdir* file will point to our *.vsz* file.

VSZ Files. Visual Studio .NET uses *.vsz* files to launch wizards. These are simple text files that look like the *.ini* files of old, but with only one section.

To create a new VSZ file, you can copy one of the existing files or start from scratch by creating a new text file in your favorite text editor and saving it with the *.vsz* file extension. Inside of the file, you first need to specify what version of Visual Studio this template is for, which is done by specifying:

```
VSWIZARD 7.0
```

This tells Visual Studio that your template will function with Visual Studio .NET 2002 (7.0) or 2003 (7.1).

You may notice that some of the templates have VSWIZ-ARD 6.0 specified, meaning that the template was created for Visual Studio 6. Templates with this specified are still understood and work with Visual Studio .NET 2002 and 2003.

The next line specifies the class that should be used for the wizard. In this example, I use VsWizard.VsWizardEngine.7.1 (the default wizard engine).

You could write your own wizard engine by creating a class that implements the IDTWizard interface.

Next, you will need to specify any number of parameters to send to the wizard engine. This example specifies the name of the wizard, the type of project, and whether the wizard includes a UI. The complete .*vsz* file can be seen here for a C# first and then a VB.NET version of the HttpHandler:

```
VSWIZARD 7.0
Wizard=VsWizard.VsWizardEngine.7.1
Param="WIZARD_NAME = CSharpHTTPHandler"
Param="WIZARD_UI = FALSE"
Param="PROJECT_TYPE = CSPROJ"

VSWIZARD 7.0
Wizard=VsWizard.VsWizardEngine.7.1
Param="WIZARD_NAME = VBNETHTTPHandler"
Param="WIZARD_UI = FALSE"
Param="PROJECT_TYPE = VBPROJ
```

The WIZARD_NAME parameter specifies the name of the wizard, in these examples, either CSharpHTTPHandler or VBNETHTTPHandler. The WIZARD_UI parameter specifies whether this is a simple template or a complete wizard; in this example, we are just creating a template, so we will pass false. The last parameter specifies the type of project this item will be added to, CSPROJ and VBPROJ, respectively.

VSDir Files. VSDir files are simple text files that tell the Add New Item and New Project dialogs what to display, including details like the name and icon.

Just like the .*vsz* files, the .*vsdir* files are plain text files. The format is different though. There are multiple entries inside, one per line, with the pipe symbol (|) separating the different parts of the given entry.

While you can update one of the existing .*vsdir* files, it is better to create a new .*vsdir* file. If you modify one of the existing files, your changes will be overwritten if the user reinstalls or repairs his installation of Visual Studio.

First, create a new blank text file in your favorite text editor, save it with an extension of .*vsdir*, and save it in the Web Project Items subfolder. Next, you need to add a line that represents the new template. Here is the code you need to add for C# and VB.NET. (You should put all the code on a single line, rather than wrapping it as it's shown here):

C#:
```
..\CSharpHTTPHandler.vsz| |HTTP Handler
|15|VSNet Hacks HTTPHandler
|{FAE04EC1-301F-11d3-BF4B-00C04F79EFBC}|4534
|0|HTTPHandler.ashx
```
VB.NET:
```
..\VBNETHTTPHandler.vsz| |HTTP Handler
|15| VSNet Hacks HTTPHandler
```

```
|{164B10B9-B200-11D0-8C61-00A0C91E29D5}|4533
|0|HTTPHandler.ashx
```

Although it is broken up here, all code should appear on one line in the text file. These entries have up to nine parts. Let's look at the VB.NET code as an example.

The first part (`..\VBNETHTTPHandler.vsz`) is the relative path to the *.vsz* file for the template. The second part (the space between the | and |) is optional and left blank in this example.

The third part (`HTTP Handler`) contains the words that go under the icon for the template in the Add New Item dialog, so keep it short.

The fourth part (`15`) is important; it's known as the `SortPriority`. It determines the order in which the templates appear in the dialog. The ones included with Visual Studio start with 10 and continue in increments of 10. For example, the next template that normally appears is the WebService template. It has a `SortPriority` of 20. I use 15 so that this one shows up between these two.

The fifth part (`VSNet Hacks HTTPHandler`) is the description that appears in the box of the same dialog when you click on the icon. You'll have a little more room for this, but not much; it has to fit on a single line.

The sixth and seventh (`{164B10B9-B200-11D0-8C61-00A0C91E29D5}` and `4533`) parts have to do with the icon that'll be used in the dialog to represent this custom template. The sixth part is the DLL path or CLSID of a DLL that has an icon resource in it. You can just leave this the same as the one used for the default WebForm. Similar to the resource strings mentioned above, the seventh part is the resource number in that DLL that points to the particular icon in the DLL. Stick with the one from the WebForm for now. The eighth part (`0`) is a bit mask for some flags; again, you should also stick with the values for the WebForm template.

The ninth part (`HTTPHandler.ashx`) is the last one. It's the suggested filename I talked about earlier. Set it to *HTTPHandler.ashx*. Visual Studio will use this as a suggested base name and adjust it to *HTTPHandler<N>.ashx*, where *N* will get replaced with an increasing integer in that pattern with which you're familiar (*HTTPHandler1.ashx*, *HTTPHandler2.ashx*, etc.).

Wizards Directory Structure

Now that you've got the Add New Item dialog supplied with the necessary *.vsz* and *.vsdir* files, you must put the template where Visual Studio expects it to be. Look back in the VC# and VB folders for the

VC#Wizards and *VBWizards* subfolders. Inside these folders, you'll find the various wizards and templates.

Inside the wizards folders are further subfolders that contain each individual wizard. The names of these folders match the WIZARD_NAME parameter from the *.vsz* files. So you'll want to add a *CSharpHTTPHandler* and *HTTPHandler* folder to the *VC#Wizards* and *VBWizards* folders.

Inside these folders, you must follow some conventions for templates and scripts that Visual Studio will require to be able to find your files. You'll need a Templates folder and a Scripts folder. Inside each of those folders needs to be a 1033 folder. 1033 isn't really a magic number. It's a LocaleID that represents standard English. Since we're just dealing with an English installation of Visual Studio here, this is what the folder needs to be named. If you were to use an installation of a different spoken language, you should expect a different number.

HTTPHandler.ashx Template File

You now have nearly everything set up that you need to have this hack work. You've got Visual Studio acknowledging that your template exists. If you bring up the Add New Item dialog box, you'll see an entry for the HTTP Handler (see Figure 12-3). If you click the Open button, it will now try to find the *HTTPHandler.ashx* file in the *Templates/1033* folder of *VC#Wizards* or *VBWizards* folder.

Next, you need to create the actual template. Since you're going to use the HTTP Handler from Web Matrix, you can fire it up and copy the template or just use the following code:

VB.NET:

```
<%@ WebHandler language="VB" class="[!output SAFE_ITEM_NAME]" %>

Public Class [!output SAFE_ITEM_NAME] : Implements IHttpHandler

    Public Sub ProcessRequest(context As HttpContext)
        Implements IHttpHandler.ProcessRequest
        ' TODO: Write request handling code here
    End Sub

    Public ReadOnly Property IsReusable As Boolean
        Implements IHttpHandler.IsReusable
        Get
            Return True
        End Get
    End Property

End Class
```

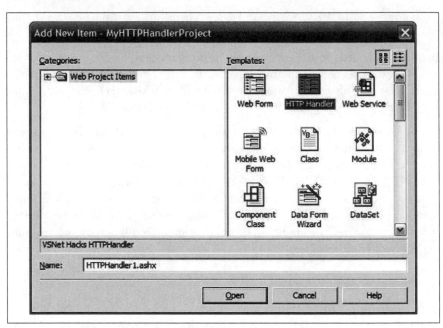

Figure 12-3. Hacked Visual Studio .NET 2003 Add New Item dialog

C#:

```
<%@ WebHandler language="C#"
class="[!output SAFE_NAMESPACE_NAME].[!output SAFE_CLASS_NAME]" %>

using System;
using System.Web;

namespace [!output SAFE_NAMESPACE_NAME] {

    public class [!output SAFE_CLASS_NAME] : IHttpHandler {

        public void ProcessRequest(HttpContext context) {
            // TODO: Write request handling code here
        }

        public bool IsReusable {
            get {
                return true;
            }
        }
    }
}
```

You will need to replace the names of the classes and namespaces with [!output SAFE_NAMESPACE_NAME] or [!output SAFE_CLASS_NAME] in C# or [!output SAFE_ITEM_NAME] for the class name in VB.NET. These will be replaced with namespace and class names by the wizard engine.

Change the name of the file to be *HTTPHandler.ashx* so that it matches the suggested base name you gave in the *.vsdir* file entry. Save the file into the *Templates/1033* folder.

If you are creating a C# wizard, you next need to create an *.inf* file that lists the files to add to your project. Create a new text file in a text editor and add the following line to that file:

```
HTTPHandler.ashx
```

Next, save the file with the name *templates.inf*.

Default.js Script

This is the final step. When Visual Studio gets to the point of adding the template file to the project, it invokes a JavaScript file. This enables anyone who wants to extend Visual Studio to be able to perform any custom steps that might be necessary. The preferred choice for providing this type of extension is scripting.

You don't need anything complicated to add the *HTTPHandler.ashx* file to the project. Create a new text file and add the following code to that text file:

C# template

```
function OnFinish(selProj, selObj)
{
    try
    {
        var strProjectName    = wizard.FindSymbol("PROJECT_NAME");
        SetTargetFullPath(selObj);
        var strProjectPath    = wizard.FindSymbol("TARGET_FULLPATH");

        var InfFile = CreateInfFile();
        AddFilesToCSharpProject(selObj, strProjectName,
                    strProjectPath, InfFile, true);
    }
    catch(e)
    {
        if( e.description.length > 0 )
            SetErrorInfo(e);
        return e.number;
    }
    finally
    {
        if( InfFile )
            InfFile.Delete();
    }
}

function SetFileProperties(oFileItem, strFileName)
```

```
    {
    }
```
VB.NET template
```
    function OnFinish(selProj, selObj)
    {
        try
        {
            var strItemName = wizard.FindSymbol("ITEM_NAME");
            var strTemplatePath = wizard.FindSymbol("TEMPLATES_PATH");
            var strTemplateFile = strTemplatePath + "\\HTTPHandler.ashx";

            var item = AddFileToVSProject(strItemName, selProj,
                               selObj, strTemplateFile, true);

            return 0;
        }
        catch(e)
        {
            if( e.description.length > 0 )
             SetErrorInfo(e);
            return e.number;
        }
    }
```

Save the file as *default.js* in the *Scripts/1033* folder of your wizard.

Try It Out

That's it. Create a Visual Studio .NET 2003 Project. Bring up the Add New Item dialog. The HTTP Handler item should appear as the second one in the dialog box. Adjust the *HTTPHandler1.aspx* name if needed and click the Open button. A new *HTTPHandler.ashx* file will appear in your project.

—Steven Dewalt

HACK #89   Writing a Visual Studio Add-in

Although the automation model can be more fun than a barrel of monkeys, add-ins let you really extend the environment.

In this book, you have learned about a large number of different add-ins that you can install to enhance the functionality of Visual Studio. In this hack, you will learn how to write one of those add-ins. The topic of writing Visual Studio add-ins can be, and has been, the topic of entire books, so needless to say, this hack will simply be an introduction to the topic.

Add-ins are installable extensions to the Visual Studio IDE. Through add-ins, you can accomplish quite a bit with the IDE. An excellent example of this is TestDriven.NET [Hack #93], an add-in that really adds significant functionality to the IDE.

I am not going to attempt anything that grandiose for this hack. Instead, you will learn how to create a simple add-in that adds an item to the Tools menu and to the right-click menu that will allow you to select text and then click the menu item to surround that code with a try...catch block.

Create the Project

To get started, you will first need to create a new add-in project by going to File → New → Project and then selecting the add-in project from Other Project → Extensibility Projects. This dialog is shown in Figure 12-4.

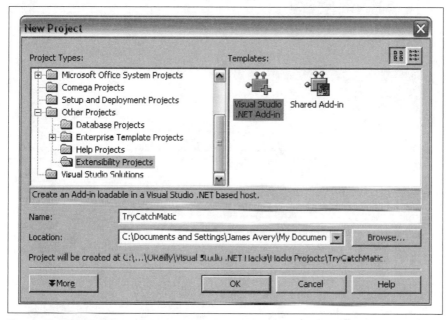

Figure 12-4. New add-in project

This launches the Extensibility Wizard shown in Figure 12-5.

Click Next to move to the first screen of the Extensibility Wizard, shown in Figure 12-6.

In the first screen of the wizard, you choose what language you want to use to create this add-in. In this example, I will use C#, but you can also use Visual Basic or Visual C++. After choosing the language, click Next and you will see the Select an Application Host screen (shown in Figure 12-7).

On the Select An Application Host screen, you choose what application hosts you want your add-in to be compatible with. The choices are the Microsoft VSMacros IDE and the regular IDE. It is a good idea to enable

Figure 12-5. Extensibility Wizard

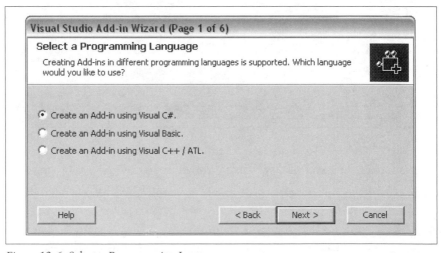

Figure 12-6. Select a Programming Language screen

your add-in for the VSMacros IDE only if you think users will really get value out of using your add-in in that IDE. In this case, the add-in could indeed be useful from the macro IDE, so I will leave both of these checked.

When you click Next, you will see the name and description screen shown in Figure 12-8.

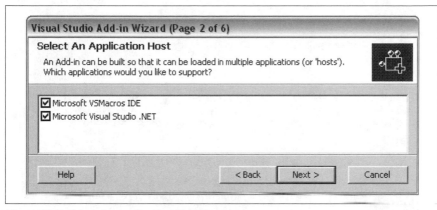

Figure 12-7. Select An Application Host screen

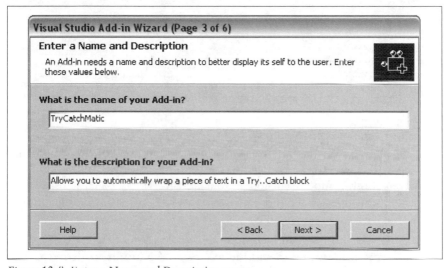

Figure 12-8. Enter a Name and Description screen

In the name and description screen, you get to name your add-in and provide a brief description of the tool. Clicking Next will show you the options screen shown in Figure 12-9.

The add-in options screen includes a number of options for how you want your add-in to work. Here are the options you must decide upon on this screen:

Would you like to create UI for the user to interact with your add-in?
This option decides whether a menu item will be added to the Tools menu. Having this button on the Tools menu does not mean that you will need to create a complex UI by any means. In this example, I am going to check this box because I want users to be able to click a button in the Tools menu to insert a try...catch block.

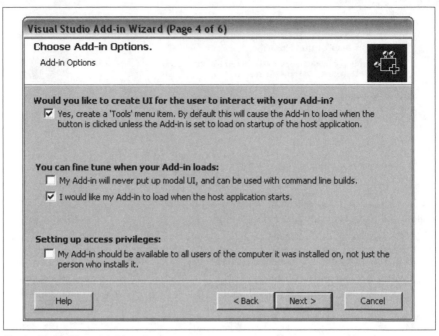

Figure 12-9. Choose Add-in Options screen

My add-in will never put up modal UI

> This option decides whether your add-in can be used during command-line builds [Hack #78]. You need to check this box only if your add-in will never show a modal UI and if your add-in would benefit from being loaded during such a build. Since this add-in is strictly a coding add-in, I will leave this box unchecked.

I would like my add-in to load when the host application starts

> This option decides if the add-in will be automatically loaded. This can always be configured and changed by the user, so I am going to uncheck it. There is no reason to force the user to load the add-in every time.

Setting up access privileges

> This option determines whether the add-in will be available to all users or just the user who installs the add-in. Unfortunately, the install program does not ask the user to make this choice during the install process so it is usually a good idea to leave this unchecked.

After you have configured the add-in options for your add-in, you can click Next to be shown the help about screen, which is shown in Figure 12-10.

The help about screen lets you configure whether an About box should be enabled for your add-in and, if so, what should be included in that box.

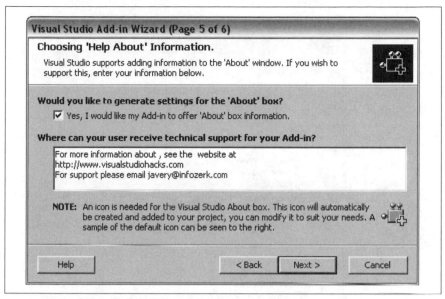

Figure 12-10. Choosing 'Help About' Information screen

When you click Next, you will see the Summary screen shown in Figure 12-11.

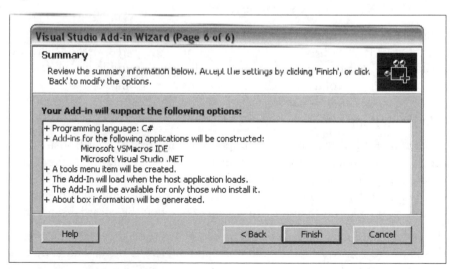

Figure 12-11. Add-in Summary screen

After completing the wizard, you will see two projects in the Solution Explorer, a class library and a setup project. You will also notice a file called *Connect.cs*, as shown in Figure 12-12.

Figure 12-12. New projects in Solution Explorer

Visual Studio also adds a great deal of the boilerplate code to the *Connect.cs* file for you. If you open it, you will see all of the required methods already created with default code. You could actually run this add-in already, and it would handle the command—it just wouldn't do anything.

Add Menu Item

Since you checked the Tools menu option in the project wizard, Visual Studio will have already added the command for your add-in to the Tools menu, but you usually want to also have a menu item somewhere else. In this example, I want to have a menu item also on the right-click menu. To do this, you will need to modify the default code that the wizard generated.

When your add-in is loaded, Visual Studio calls the OnConnection method—this is where you will need to add commands. Here is the default code created by the wizard:

```
public void OnConnection(object application,
            Extensibility.ext_ConnectMode connectMode,
            object addInInst, ref System.Array custom)
{
    applicationObject = (_DTE)application;
```

```
addInInstance = (AddIn)addInInst;
if(connectMode == Extensibility.ext_ConnectMode.ext_cm_UISetup)
{
    object [ ]contextGUIDS = new object[ ] { };
    Commands commands = applicationObject.Commands;
    _CommandBars commandBars = applicationObject.CommandBars;

try
{
Command command = commands.AddNamedCommand(addInInstance,
   "TryCatchMatic", "TryCatchMatic",
   "Executes the command for TryCatchMatic", true,
   59, ref contextGUIDS,
   (int)vsCommandStatus.vsCommandStatusSupported
      +(int)vsCommandStatus.vsCommandStatusEnabled);

CommandBar commandBar = (CommandBar)commandBars["Tools"];
CommandBarControl commandBarControl =
        command.AddControl(commandBar, 1);
}
catch(System.Exception /*e*/)
{
}
}

}
```

The boldfaced code is the section that actually creates the command and then adds it to the Tools command bar. Using the same Command object, I am also going to add it to the Code Window command bar, which represents the right-click menu when inside the code window. First, you need to create a CommandBar object and get a reference to the correct command bar, then add your command to that command bar using the AddControl method. You should insert these two lines after the last line within the try block:

```
CommandBar commandBar2 = (CommandBar)commandBars["Code Window"];
CommandBarControl commandBarControl2 =
        command.AddControl(commandBar2, 1);
```

This command will now show up on the Tools menu as well as the right-click menu in the code window after the add-in is installed. For information on how to find the various command bars in Visual Studio, please refer to "Find the Name of That Command Bar" [Hack #90].

You will most likely also want to add something to the catch block, since the code created by the wizard simply "swallows" the error. You can write the exception using Debug.WriteLine or implement some other method of handling the exception.

Write the Code

The next step is to write the code that will do the work of the add-in. In this example, I will be writing a simple piece of code that surrounds the selected text with a `try...catch` block. This code needs to be added to the Exec method that was added for you by the wizard. Here is a look at the default code:

```
public void Exec(string commandName,
        EnvDTE.vsCommandExecOption executeOption,
        ref object varIn, ref object varOut, ref bool handled)
{
    handled = false;
    if(executeOption ==
        EnvDTE.vsCommandExecOption.vsCommandExecOptionDoDefault)
    {
        if(commandName == "TryCatchMatic.Connect.TryCatchMatic")
        {
            handled = true;
            return;
        }
    }
}
```

This code first checks the executeOptions and then checks to see if the command being called is the command for this add-in. Inside the last if statement is where you will write the code for what your add-in will actually do. Here is the code I have added to get the currently selected text and then surround it with a `try...catch` block:

```
if(commandName == "TryCatchMatic.Connect.TryCatchMatic")
{

    string selectedText = textDoc.Selection.Text;

    string newText = "try\n { \n" + selectedText
                    + "\n}\ncatch\n{\n}";

    textDoc.Selection.Text = newText;
    handled = true;
    return;
}
```

In this code, I get a reference to the ActiveDocument and then get the selected text. I can then replace the selected text with the new, surrounded text.

Installation

When you are ready to install and test your add-in, it is pretty simple to do so, since the wizard automatically added an installer to the project.

Before doing anything else, it is of the utmost importance that you exclude any assemblies that are default Visual Studio assemblies. This could include *Extensibility.dll*, *Office.dll*, *VSLang.dll*, *DTE.OLB*, *EnvDTE.DLL*, *stdole.DLL*, and others. If you leave these assemblies in your installation project, then when a user uninstalls your add-in, it could remove these assemblies, thus breaking Visual Studio and requiring the user to either repair her installation or manually try to re-add the assemblies your installer removed.

Next, you will need to build the installer, as it is not built by default. You can do this by right-clicking on the project and clicking Build. After the project has been built, you can right-click on the installer and click Install. This will install your add-in on your machine. Next, you will need to close and then reopen the IDE, and you should see your menu items. If you do not see your menu items, make sure that your add-in is enabled in the add-in manager and then try running devenv /setup **[Hack #92]**.

This hack has been a quick introduction to the development of add-ins, but there is a lot more to learn. Here are some great resources to help you learn more about add-in development:

Visual Studio Extensibility Center
> *http://msdn.microsoft.com/vstudio/extend*

Visual Studio .NET Add-ins Yahoo Group
> *http://groups.yahoo.com/group/vsnetaddin*

Visual Studio 2003 Automation Samples
> *http://www.microsoft.com/downloads/details.aspx?familyid=3ff9c915-30e5-430e-95b3-621dccd25150&displaylang=en*

Craig Skibo's weblog (Developer of the Visual Studio Automation Object Model)
> *http://blogs.msdn.com/craigskibo*

Dr. Extensibility's weblog
> *http://blogs.msdn.com/dr._ex*

Find the Name of That Command Bar

#90 Use a freebie from Microsoft to discover the names of the different command bars in Visual Studio.

One of the difficult tasks when working with Visual Studio is finding out what the names of the various command bars are. Command bars are used by Visual Studio to store commands. The Tools menu is a command bar, as is the right-click menu. To create a new command and assign it to a command bar, you will use code that looks like the following:

```
Command command = commands.AddNamedCommand(addInInstance,
    "Add-IN", "Command", "Executes the command for this Add-in",
    true, 59, ref contextGUIDS,
    (int)vsCommandStatus.vsCommandStatusSupported +
    (int)vsCommandStatus.vsCommandStatusEnabled);

CommandBar commandBar = (CommandBar)commandBars["Tools"];
CommandBarControl commandBarControl =
    command.AddControl(commandBar, 1);
```

The preceding code would add a new command to the Tools menu. As you can see, there is a collection named commandBars that you use to specify which CommandBar you want to add your command to. The problem is that there is no easy way to find out what these names are in Visual Studio. Thankfully, there is a way to get a list of all these CommandBars using a free download from Microsoft.

Install the Command Browser

The add-in you can use to view the names of the different command bars is actually part of the automation samples. To download this add-in, go to:

> http://www.microsoft.com/downloads/details.aspx?familyid=3ff9c915-30e5-430e-95b3-621dccd25150&displaylang=en#filelist

Choose the Command Browser Add-in from the list of files (*CmdBrowser. exe*). Download this file and then extract its contents to a directory on your hard drive. This will put the code for this add-in on your machine. Next, you need to follow these steps to get the command browser installed:

1. Open the *CmdBrowser.sln* file in Visual Studio.
2. Build the solution in Visual Studio.
3. Close Visual Studio.
4. Run the *AddinRef.reg* file in the *CmdBrowser* directory.

This will install the Command Browser on your machine.

Run the Command Browser

When you start Visual Studio, you should see a new command on the Tools menu for the Command Browser. (If you don't, you may need to enable the add-in by using the Add-in Manager or run devenv /setup **[Hack #92]**.)

When you run the add-in, you will see the Command Browser, which is shown in Figure 12-13.

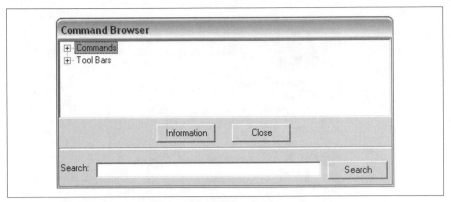

Figure 12-13. Command Browser

The node titled Commands includes a list of all the commands in Visual
Studio. If you expand the node, as shown in Figure 12-14, you can then
select a node and get more information about that node in the Command
Information dialog, shown in Figure 12-15.

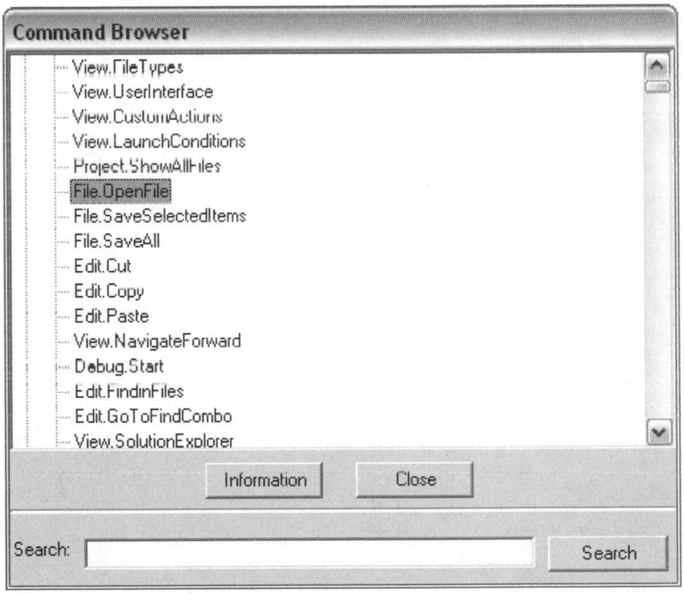

Figure 12-14. Command Browser commands

This dialog shows you the name of the command, the GUID and ID of the
command, as well as the current keystroke bindings.

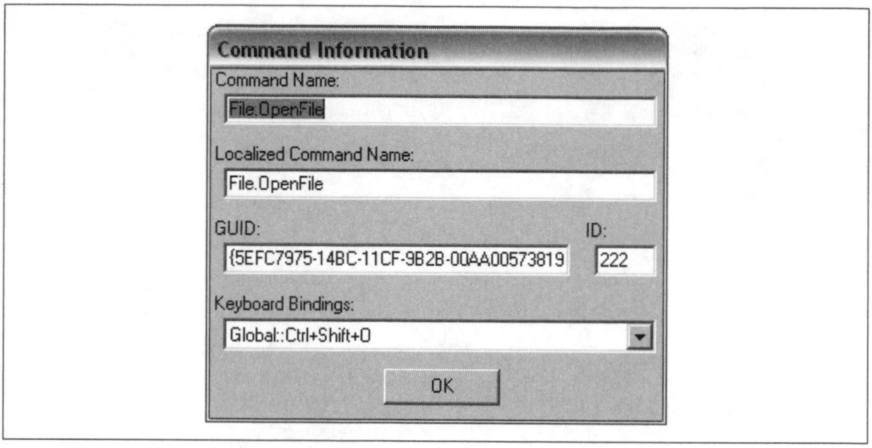

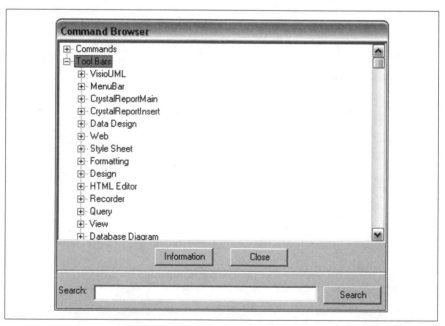

Figure 12-15. Command Information dialog

More importantly, you can also use this tool to view all the command bars
under the Tool Bars node, which is shown in Figure 12-16.

Figure 12-16. Command Browser—Tool Bars node

Under this node, you can see the names of all the command bars in Visual
Studio. If you have a hard time finding a command bar, the best way to find
it is to look at one of the items on that command bar in Visual Studio and
then search for that command in the Search box. Figure 12-17 shows how
search can be used to quickly find a command bar.

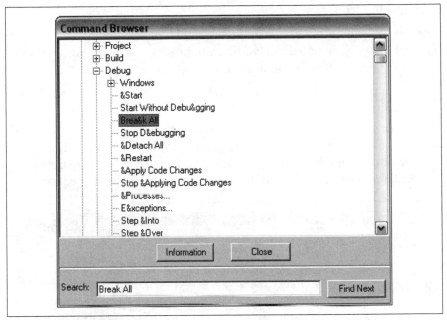

Figure 12-17. Command Browser Search

After you have found the command bar, you now have the key used with the commandBars collection. As another example, here is the code to get a reference to the Debug command bar:

```
CommandBar commandBar = (CommandBar)commandBars["Debug"];
```

The Command Browser makes it easy to find the elusive names of command bars so you can add commands from your add-ins to those command bars.

HACK #91 Change the Icon for Your Add-in

Learn how to replace that not-so-lovely smiley face of an icon for your add-in.

By default, when you create a new Visual Studio add-in, you are given a goofy smiley face icon as the icon for your add-in. If you plan on sending your add-in out to anyone, I highly recommend creating your own icon or setting it to a more appropriate built-in icon. Customizing the icon used with your add-in is not as easy as it should be. In this hack, you will learn the steps needed to create this custom icon, and then ensure that it is installed properly with your add-in.

Creating the Icon

The first step is to create a satellite assembly and embed an icon in that assembly. Yes, you actually have to create a new assembly; you can't just embed the resource in your add-in's assembly!

1. Add a new Class Library Project to your Add-in Solution (File → New → Project).

2. Add a new bitmap to your project. Using the bitmap editor (just double-click on your bitmap to open it), you can create a bitmap. The size of the bitmap should be 16 by 16, and if you want to use transparency, use Red: 0, Green: 254, Blue: 0. Figure 12-18 shows the bitmap editor.

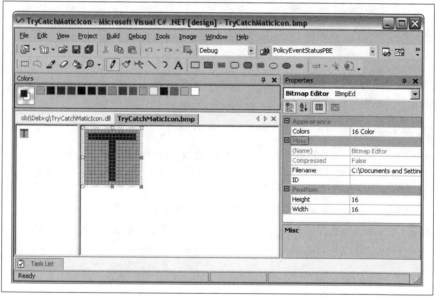

Figure 12-18. Bitmap editor

3. Compile your Class Library Project and then click the Show All Files button on the Solution Explorer.

4. Navigate to the obj → Debug folder in the Solution Explorer and then double-click on the *.dll* file.

5. Right-click on the root folder and select Add Resource as shown in Figure 12-19.

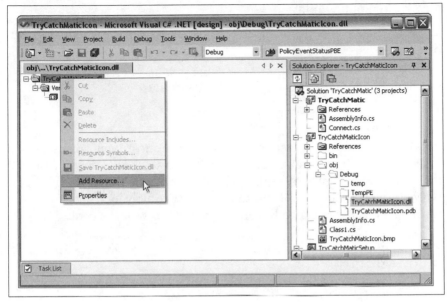

Figure 12-19. Add Resource button

6. From the Add Resource dialog, select Icon and then click on Import as shown in Figure 12-20.

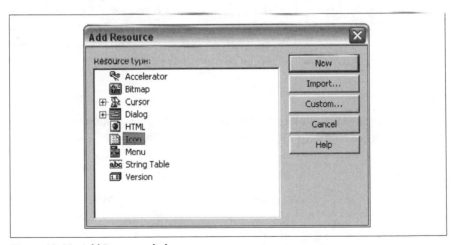

Figure 12-20. Add Resource dialog

7. Navigate to your bitmap file and click OK.

Your icon will now be embedded in the satellite assembly. After embedding the bitmap, note the ID of the bitmap since you will be using that later.

Modify Command Code

The default code to add a command created by the Add-in Wizard is shown here:

```
Command command = commands.AddNamedCommand(addInInstance,
"TryCatchMatic", "TryCatchMatic", "Surround W/ Try..Catch",
true, 59, ref contextGUIDS,
(int)vsCommandStatus.vsCommandStatusSupported
+(int)vsCommandStatus.vsCommandStatusEnabled);
```

The Boolean value here represents whether the icon you are using is a Microsoft icon or a custom icon. You will need to change this to false and then replace the number 59 with the ID of your bitmap. (This is usually 101, but you can check by double-clicking on your assembly in Visual Studio and expanding the folder named Bitmap). Here is the new line of code:

```
Command command = commands.AddNamedCommand(addInInstance,
"TryCatchMatic", "TryCatchMatic", "Surround W/ Try..Catch",
false, 101, ref contextGUIDS,
(int)vsCommandStatus.vsCommandStatusSupported
+(int)vsCommandStatus.vsCommandStatusEnabled);
```

This command will now try to use the bitmap with the ID 101 in your new assembly.

You could alternatively set the icon to another of the default icons. You could do this by leaving the Boolean value set to true and then specifying another number instead of 59. To view a list of all the available icons, you can use a small utility available from *http://www.visualstudiohacks.com/iconspy*.

Add to Installer

Finally, you need to configure the installer to include your new assembly and add a couple of new keys to the registry to tell Visual Studio where your icon is.

To add assembly:

1. Right-click on the setup project and choose View → File System.

2. Create a directory called 1033 (or your local version, if you are not using English) under the Application Folder.

3. Right-click on the 1033 folder and choose Add → Assembly.

4. This will display the Add Assembly dialog from which you can select your assembly. The final result is shown in Figure 12-21.

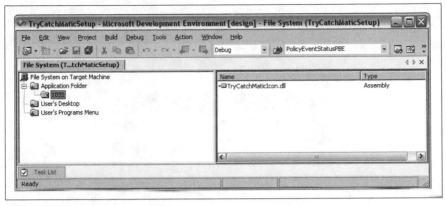

Figure 12-21. Setup project—File System

Your satellite assembly will now be installed when your add-in is installed.

To add registry keys:

1. Right-click on the setup project and choose View → Registry.
2. Navigate to HKEY_CURRENT_USER → Software → Microsoft → VisualStudio → 7.1 → AddIns → *MacroName*.
3. Add a new string value called SatelliteDllName and enter the name of your *.dll* file as the value.
4. Add a second string value called SatelliteDllPath and enter a value of [TARGETDIR]. Figure 12-22 shows the end result.

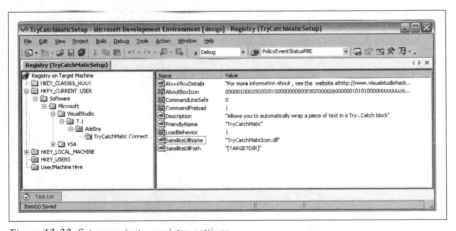

Figure 12-22. Setup project—registry settings

Next, you will need to rebuild your setup project and then reinstall your add-in. You may need to run devenv /setup for your changes to take effect **[Hack #92]**.

After reinstalling your add-in, you will now see your icon in the Tools menu, as shown in Figure 12-23.

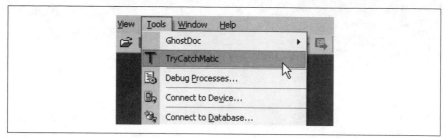

Figure 12-23. Add-in with new icon

Adding a custom icon for your add-in is not the easiest of procedures, but it is definitely a *must* if you plan on distributing your icon to other users.

Enhancing Visual Studio
Hacks 92–100

The hacks in this chapter focus on add-ins that enhance the overall functionality of Visual Studio. Previous chapters covered a lot of add-ins that help in a particular area of Visual Studio, like navigating the IDE or writing faster code, but in this chapter, the add-ins are more general enhancements to the functionality of Visual Studio.

This chapter will first look at how to best manage add-ins, including how to hack them to install for different versions of Visual Studio; how to manage installed add-ins; and how to repair add-ins that are not working properly. You'll also learn about add-ins that can spellcheck your code, test regular expressions in Visual Studio, generate better Web Services code, unit-test applications, and more.

 ## Manage Add-ins
#92 Visual Studio can do a lot on its own. You can have it do so much more if you take advantage of add-ins.

Visual Studio add-ins are an excellent way to expand on the functionality of Visual Studio. Throughout this book, we have talked about a number of different add-ins and how they can be used to make the most out of Visual Studio. We have even talked about how to write add-ins [Hack #89]. This hack explains how to best work with add-ins. They can sometimes be troublesome and hard to manage.

Installing Add-ins

All add-ins should come with an installer; if they don't, then they probably come with some sort of detailed instructions on where you should put files and how you should modify the registry to get everything working.

It is usually a good idea to close Visual Studio before running any add-in installation programs. Most installation programs won't stop you from installing with Visual Studio open, but this can lead to strange behavior, especially if you are uninstalling an old version of an add-in and installing a new version.

Each add-in has to be added to the registry for every version of Visual Studio that it will run in. Because of this, you will sometimes run across an add-in whose installer is configured to install for one version of Visual Studio, but not the version you are using. You can often duplicate the registry settings from one version and then move them to the other version, but this won't work all the time—in fact, it might not work most of the time—but sometimes it is well worth a shot.

Here is the process for moving the registry settings from one version to another:

1. Open *regedit* (Start → Run → type **regedit**).
2. Navigate to the following registry key: *HKEY_LOCAL_MACHINE\ SOFTWARE\Microsoft\VisualStudio\<7.0>\AddIns\<YourAddin>*.
3. Right-click on the key and choose Export from the context menu that appears.
4. Save the *.reg* file to your computer.
5. Open the *.reg* file in Notepad and replace all instances of \7.0\ with \7.1\. (This would move settings from Visual Studio .NET 2002 to Visual Studio .NET 2003. Use the version numbers that apply to your version of Visual Studio.)
6. Save and close the *.reg* file.
7. Double-click the *.reg* file and click OK when the dialog asks if you want to add this information to your registry.

After following this procedure, the add-in may or may not work in the new version of Visual Studio, but it is worth trying until the author comes out with a new version tailored to your version of Visual Studio.

Add-in Manager

The Add-in Manager can be found in Tools → Add-in Manager and is shown in Figure 13-1.

The Add-in Manager configures the add-ins that are installed for your version of Visual Studio. The leftmost column displays the name of the add-in

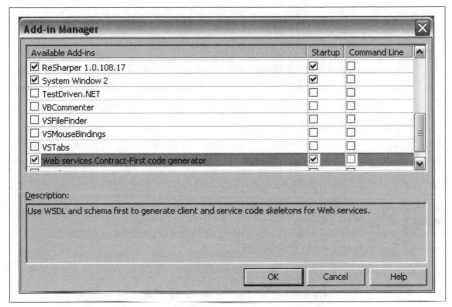

Figure 13-1. Add-in Manager

and a checkbox. If that checkbox is checked, it means that the add-in is currently loaded. You can check this checkbox and then click OK, and the add-in will be enabled for just this instance of Visual Studio; when you restart Visual Studio, the add-in will not automatically be loaded again. The checkbox in the Startup column controls whether the add-in will be automatically loaded each and every time Visual Studio is loaded. I find that, unless you use an add-in constantly, it is best to leave it unavailable until you need it. For add-ins you use constantly though, it is nice to have them automatically available when you load the IDE. The last checkbox, under the column Command Line, specifies whether this add-in should be loaded when Visual Studio is accessed for command-line operations. For instance, you can build a solution by calling the *devenv.exe* command with the /build switch, and this checkbox determines if the add-in should be loaded when Visual Studio is started this way.

Repairing Add-ins

Sometimes add-ins just don't work properly. You can try a couple things to get an add-in to work properly. Sometimes simply disabling the add-in and restarting Visual Studio will fix your problems. The next tactic should be to run the repair function of the add-in installer (if one exists; rerun the installer to see if it offers you this option), which usually does a fair job of fixing any problems. If this does not work, you can take a couple of other steps to try and get the add-in working again.

Visual Studio includes a command-line switch called /setup that will do a reset on Visual Studio, restoring it to its initial state. Using this switch will erase some of your customizations, but sometimes it is the only way to get an add-in, or even Visual Studio itself, working properly again.

There is also a /safemode command-line switch that will start Visual Studio in safe mode. Visual Studio safe mode loads only the default environment and services, which disables any VSIP add-ins (not all add-ins) that might be causing a problem.

HACK #93   Run Unit Tests Inside Visual Studio

Testing can be just a few clicks away when you use TestDriven.NET to run unit tests right inside of Visual Studio.

Test Driven Development is the practice of writing unit tests for your code before you actually write that code. By writing a test and then writing the code to make that test pass, you have a much better idea of the goal and purpose of your code. Test Driven Development also encourages complete code coverage, which not only increases the quality of your code, but also allows you to refactor the internals of a method or class and quickly and easily test the outside interface of the object.

TestDriven.NET is a unit-testing add-in for Visual Studio. It was developed for a number of years under the name NUnitAddIn. It now supports multiple unit testing frameworks and is compatible with all versions of Visual Studio .NET. It is available in free and professional versions from the TestDriven.NET web site at *http://www.testdriven.net*. Its author, Jamie Cansdale, keeps a web log charting TestDriven.NET's development at *http://www.testdriven.net/weblog*.

Installing

TestDriven.NET can be installed using an administrator or limited user account. By default, it will install for just the current user. Because limited users don't have write access to the Program Files folder, a limited user installation will install files in the user's *Application Data\TestDriven.NET* folder. An administrator installation will install files in the *Program Files\ TestDriven.NET* folder. These defaults can be changed by selecting Custom on the Choose Setup Type page.

TestDriven.NET is packaged with functional versions of the NUnit and MbUnit unit testing frameworks. It also includes an adapter for executing Visual Studio Team System unit tests when available. These will be installed to subdirectories inside the TestDriven.NET directory, as shown in Figure 13-2.

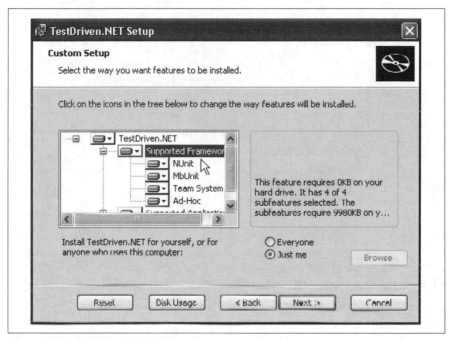

Figure 13-2. TestDriven.NET Setup

Run Test(s)

The Run Test(s) command offers a straightforward way to build and run tests. It is intended to be the default method of test execution in most contexts. It automatically detects the test framework being used and executes tests using the correct test runner. The tests are launched by a test execution engine running as an external process. This test process is kept alive in order to improve execution times on subsequent runs. Once a test process has been cached, a rocket icon will appear in the notify box.

If the code editor window is selected, the test(s) to execute will be determined by the position of the caret. Individual tests are executed by right-clicking anywhere inside a test method and selecting Run Test(s), as shown in Figure 13-3. All tests in a test fixture are executed by right-clicking inside a class (but outside of any method) and selecting Run Test(s). All tests in a namespace are executed by right-clicking inside a namespace and selecting Run Test(s).

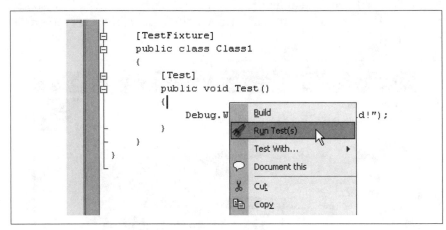

Figure 13-3. Run Test(s) menu item

The Run Test(s) option is also found on various Solution Explorer context menus. It can be used to execute all tests in a solution, project, or project item.

Ad Hoc Tests

Ad hoc tests offer a useful alternative to throwaway console applications. They should not in any way act as a substitute for real unit tests. Rather, they are intended to provide a convenient way of exploring local private methods or third-party code.

Any method that does not take parameters can be executed as an ad hoc test simply by right-clicking inside it and selecting Run Test(s). It can be a public, private, static, or instance method. In the case of an instance method, an object will be created using the default constructor of the class (providing, of course, that the class has a default constructor). The Dispose method will be called on any object that implements IDisposable, once the test has been executed.

If an ad hoc test returns an argument, the argument will be expanded to the Test output pane. Complex objects will have their fields and properties displayed. Enumerable objects will be listed. Primitive objects will be converted to strings and displayed.

Test Output and Task List

The Test output pane is the window in which all test results and warning messages appear and is shown in Figure 13-4. Trace and debug information is also sent there, along with console output and error messages. If all tests in a project or solution are being executed, the Test output pane will display only ignored or failed tests.

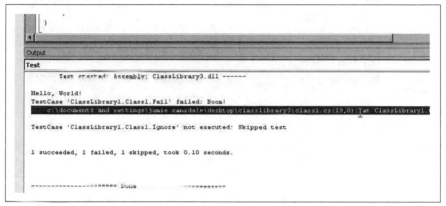

Figure 13-4. Output Test pane

When a test fails, the name of the test, together with the exception message and stack trace, is displayed. If code has been compiled with debugging information, the corresponding portions of the stack trace will contain line numbers. Double-clicking on these portions is a convenient way of navigating to the offending code.

As well as sending information to the output pane, failing tests also get added to the task list. If many tests have failed, this creates a useful summary view as shown in Figure 13-5. Generally, the further up the stack trace, the more likely the code will be of interest. Double-clicking a test in the task list is an alternative way of accessing the code in question.

Test With... Debugger

The Test With... menu offers many alternative contexts in which to run tests. Selecting the Debugger context executes test(s) with the Visual Studio debugger attached, as shown in Figure 13-6. By setting a breakpoint on a method and selecting Test With... → Debugger, it is possible to step into a unit test.

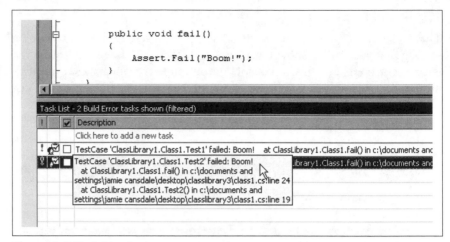

Figure 13-5. Task List view

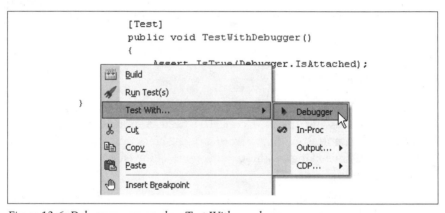

Figure 13-6. Debugger command on Test With... submenu

By default, Visual Studio will build *all* projects in a solution when executing
with the debugger. In Visual Studio .NET 2003 and Visual Studio 2005,
there is an option to "Only build startup projects and dependencies on
Run". Checking this option can significantly improve startup times when
debugging large solutions. In Visual Studio .NET 2003, this option is under
Tools → Options → Environment → Projects and Solutions. In Visual Studio
2005, it can be found under Tools → Options → Environment → Projects and
Solutions → Build and Run.

Test Projects and Solutions

By right-clicking on a project in the Solution Explorer window and selecting
Run Test(s), all tests within that project will be executed. Failed and ignored

tests are sent to the Test output pane and task list in a similar fashion to other Run Test(s) commands. Trace, debug, and console output is suppressed when executing all tests in a project or solution.

Similarly, all tests in a solution can be executed by right-clicking on the solution in the Solution Explorer window and selecting Run Test(s). For each project in the solution, the test framework being used is established and tests are executed using the correct test runner. Projects that do not contain any tests are simply ignored.

Aborting a Test Run

When a test run is in progress, an Abort Test menu item will appear on the Tools menu, as shown in Figure 13-7. Selecting this item will abort the thread the tests are executing on. When tests are aborted in this way, any cleanup logic is given a chance to run.

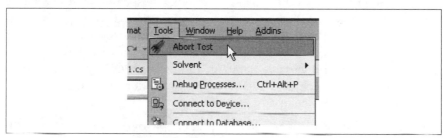

Figure 13-7. Abort Test command on Tools menu

Stopping the Test Process

You will sometimes need to stop the test process. The most common of these circumstances is when an app domain is created, but not unloaded by a test run. This can result in any assemblies loaded by the app domain being locked, which causes subsequent builds to fail. It is possible to recycle the test process by right-clicking on the rocket icon in the notify box and selecting Stop, as shown in Figure 13-8. A new test process will be launched the next time the Run Test(s) command is executed.

—Jamie Cansdale

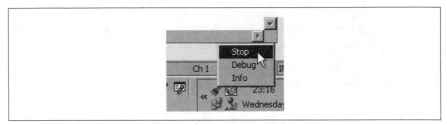

Figure 13-8. Stopping the test process

HACK

#94   Spellcheck Your Code and Comments

While there are definitely exceptions to the rule, virtually all computer programs are rife with spelling errors. Ensure that the comments and string literals in your code are free from spelling errors.

Programmers, it seems, are not the world's best spellers, in large part because compilers are kind enough to overlook any spelling snafus. While it may be hard to get worked up over source code dotted with spelling mistakes, it is important to realize that these grammatical errors can incur a real cost. When working in a team, a developer can be slowed down by misspelled comments and variable names in another's code. A spelling mistake in a string literal—such as a misspelled menu option or error message—reflects poorly on your company and software.

Spelling has become a lost art over the past couple of decades, as word processors have evolved from little to no spellchecking support to today's programs that will correct your spelling automatically as you type. While spellcheckers have become ubiquitous in word processors, email clients, and a bevy of other computer programs, they are still sorely missing from IDEs. Fortunately, Dean Giovanelli has created a free spellchecker add-in for Visual Studio .NET 2003. Armed with this spellchecker, you can quickly check the spelling of your source code, comments, and string literals, all from within Visual Studio.

Download and Install the Spellchecker Add-in

At the time of this writing, this add-in works only for Visual Studio .NET 2003 and requires that Microsoft Word 2000 or later be installed as well. Assuming your system meets these two requirements, you can get started with spellchecking your code in Visual Studio by downloading the free add-in from *http://www.devx.com/vb2themax/CodeDownload/19810*. The download contains a setup file that will install the add-in.

Once the add-in has been installed, launch Visual Studio. By default, this add-in is not loaded. To load it, go to the Tools menu and select the Add-In Manager option. This will list the add-ins currently installed on your system, which should include the Spell Checker for VS.NET 2003 Version 1.0 Add-In. To enable this add-in, check its checkbox (see Figure 13-9). You can also opt to have it loaded on each startup by checking the Startup checkbox.

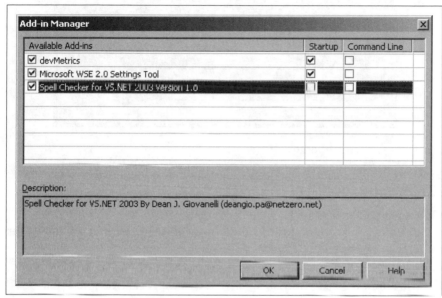

Figure 13-9. Check the Spell Checker for VS.NET 2003 Version 1.0 checkbox

Once you have checked the add-in's checkbox, click OK. You should, at this point, see a spellchecking icon in the toolbar. Additionally, there should be a new option in the Tools menu titled Spell Checker for VS.NET.

Configure the Spellchecker Options

Before you run the spellchecker for the first time, take a moment to configure the options. To configure the options, start the spellchecker add-in by clicking on the appropriate toolbar icon or menu option. Doing so will display the Spell Checker for VS.NET dialog, which contains an assortment of tabs. The first tab, Code/Text, contains the results of the spellcheck. The remaining tabs contain the assorted spellchecker options. Let's examine these tabs.

Specify what types of content to search. The first options-related tab is named, aptly enough, Options, and is shown in Figure 13-10.

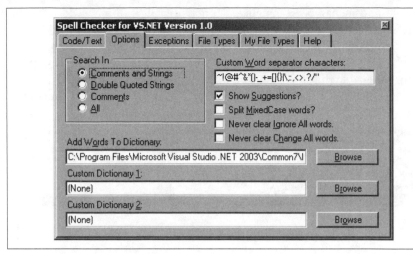

Figure 13-10. Select the portions of code to spellcheck

From the Options tab, you can indicate what content your source code should search:

Comments and Strings
Selecting this option will cause the add-in to spellcheck all comments and string literals.

Double Quoted Strings
This option causes only string literals to be spellchecked.

Comments
With this choice, only comments will be spellchecked.

All
Checks *all* content, including comments, string literals, variable names, methods—the complete source code.

From this tab, you can also specify which characters should be considered word separators. For example, the + character is, by default, added in the word separator character list. If you leave this as a word separator character, the code `salary+dividends` would be considered two words: *salary* and *dividends*. If, however, you excluded the + from the word separator character list, `salary+dividends` would be interpreted as one word.

The Show Suggestions checkbox is pretty self-explanatory. If it is checked, the spellchecker will provide suggestions for any misspelled words. Split MixedCase Words is a neat option. If checked, it will interpret mixed case words as individual words—that is, a method named `DeleteEmployee` would be spellchecked as two words: *Delete* and *Employee*. The Never Clear options, if checked, will not clear the Ignore All or Change All Word lists until the add-in is unloaded. If they are left unchecked (the default), these word lists will be cleared whenever the add-in is closed.

From the Options tab, you can also specify the location of the dictionary files to use for spellchecking with the add-in. The spellchecker uses its own dictionary file, separate from Microsoft Word's, meaning that you add commonly used variable and method names that you would not want to be considered correct spellings when using Word. Additionally, you can optionally specify up to two of your own custom dictionary files.

Indicate patterns that should be ignored or always considered misspelled. The Exceptions tab allows you to provide a list of regular expressions to indicate that certain patterns should always be ignored or should always be considered to be misspelled. From this tab, you can enter a variable number of regular expressions, one line at a time, in the text box. Prefix the regular expression pattern with an O to indicate that words that match the pattern should be ignored; use an X prefix to indicate that words that match the pattern should be marked as misspelled.

For example, imagine that you prefixed your class's member variables with the character m. Clearly, variables like mAge, mName, and so on, will trip up the spellchecker. You can opt to have the spellchecker ignore all words that begin with m, followed by a capital alphabetic character by using the following pattern in the Exceptions tab:

```
O^m[A-Z]
```

Use different spellchecking rules for different file types. Since different programming languages utilize different syntax, such as the character(s) that indicate comment regions, the spellchecker add-in utilizes different parsing rules based on the extension of the file being spellchecked. From the File Types tab shown in Figure 13-11, you can indicate how different file extensions are parsed by the spellchecker.

The add-in ships with built-in parsers for six different languages:

C#
Visual Basic
HTML/XML
C/C++
Text files
J#

These six parsers dictate how comments and string literals are parsed. Recall that from the Options tab you can specify if just comments or string literals should be spellchecked. These parsers, then, pick out the comments and

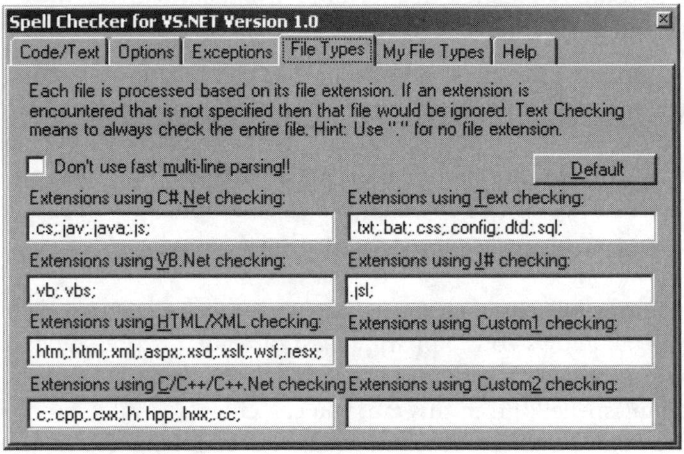

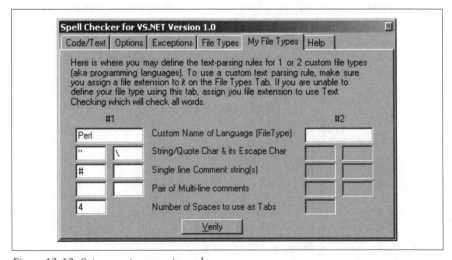

Figure 13-11. Configure how to handle various file extensions

strings for a particular language. (Unsurprisingly, the text file parser treats *all* content as content that is to be spellchecked; that is, regardless of what type of content you have opted to have spellchecked, all content in a text file will be checked.)

In addition to providing six built-in parsers, the add-in also allows you to define parsing rules for up to two custom languages. From the My File Types tab, you can specify the parsing rules, as shown in Figure 13-12. Then, from the File Types tab, you can indicate which file extensions should be mapped to which custom parsing rules.

Figure 13-12. Set up custom parsing rules.

Check for Spelling Errors

Once you have configured the add-in options, return to the Code/Text tab to begin spellchecking. As Figure 13-13 shows, from this tab you can opt to spellcheck:

- The currently selected text
- The current file
- The current line to the end of the file
- The current project

Once you have specified what to spellcheck, click the Start button to begin the spellchecking process. This will step through your code, highlighting misspelled words, prompting you to ignore the word, change it to a corrected spelling, or add it to the dictionary, as shown in Figure 13-13.

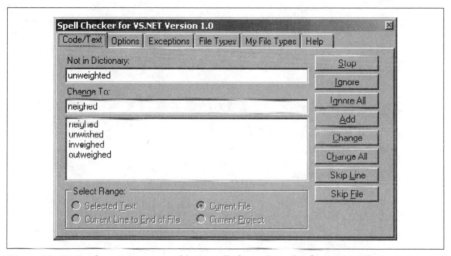

Figure 13-13. Replace, ignore, or add misspelled words to the dictionary file

Incorrect spelling in production code makes your software look unprofessional and unpolished; comments riddled with misspelled words lead to confusion and frustration for developers examining others' code. There's no reason why you shouldn't take the time to spellcheck, at minimum, your code's comments and string literals. Armed with this free add-in, such spellchecking is impressively fast and easy.

—Scott Mitchell

View an Outline of Your Controls

Drill-down, select, and drag 'n' drop all your controls, even on the most complicated forms.

In Windows Forms development, a large number of controls contain other controls. The GroupBox control can be used to group a number of controls together, particularly useful when working with radio buttons. A Panel control can be used to host controls, organize them, control their visibility, and more. One of the confusing parts of Windows Forms development is keeping track of all of these controls, where they are, and what control they are contained in.

A freely available power toy from Microsoft called the Control Outline makes this task a lot easier. You can get it from *http://www.gotdotnet.com/team/ide*.

After installing and enabling the power toy, you will have a new window that shows all of your controls in an easy-to-read and -understand outline. You can access this window from View → Other Windows → Control Outline. This window can be seen in Figure 13-14.

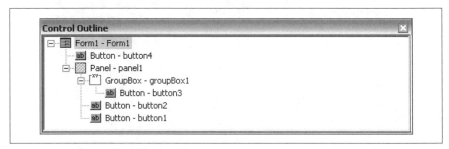

Figure 13-14. Control Outline window

As you can see, it is very easy to quickly look at the outline and determine where a control is in the container hierarchy. You can also click on a control in this outline, and it will be selected on your form, which helps when you have nested a number of controls. It is hard to select these kinds of controls in the designer.

This power toy also includes a couple of other very useful features. You can select a control in the Control Outline and click the Delete button to remove the control from the form. On top of that, you can drag and drop controls around the control outline. In the example shown in Figure 13-14, you could drag button3 outside of the groupbox1 control and drop it on the panel1 control. This would move that control, and any controls nested

---

under that control, to the new container control. Both features are timesaving and are much easier to do than trying to select and move those controls on the overly busy form designer.

The Control Outline power toy is an easy-to-install and easy-to-use feature that can be very helpful when developing Windows Forms applications.

Blog Code from Visual Studio

#96 Convert code in Visual Studio to HTML so it is easier to post that code on a web site or web log. Then, share your snippets with your adoring public.

It is easy to grab a piece of code from your project and then turn around and write about it in an article or in a post on your web log. One tricky part of the process is getting the nice code coloring that Visual Studio provides for that code. When publishing your code to an online article or weblog, you need to convert that code to HTML and hand-code all the coloring, a tedious process. A couple of hacks make it much easier to cut and paste code directly from Visual Studio and transform it into HTML so you can easily post it to your web log.

Convert to HTML with a Macro

Cory Smith (*http://addressof.com/blog*) has come up with an interesting solution to this problem. He has written a macro that will take the code you have selected, copy it to Microsoft Word, and then save it from Microsoft Word in HTML. This is possible for a couple of different reasons. This works because Visual Studio lets you copy and paste the code from Visual Studio with formatting intact. So, if you copy text from Visual Studio and simply paste it into Microsoft Word, you will notice that all of the formatting and coloring comes with the text. This gets around the funky HTML that Word typically generates because Microsoft Word now allows you to save filtered HTML, which is much cleaner than before.

> You will need Microsoft Word 2003 installed for this macro to function properly.

Following is the code for the macro. For more information on how to create and manage macros please refer to "Create a Macro" **[Hack #51]**.

```
Option Explicit On
Option Strict Off ' Using late binding.

Imports System
Imports EnvDTE
```

```
Imports System.Diagnostics

Public Module FormatCode

    Private Const wdPasteDefault As Integer = 0
    Private Const wdFormatFilteredHTML As Integer = 10
    Private Const wdWebView As Integer = 6
    Private m_text As String
    Private m_thread As System.Threading.Thread

    Sub FormatSourceCode( )

    ' Get the currently selected code snippet.
    Dim selection As TextSelection =
    CType(DTE.ActiveDocument.Selection( ), TextSelection)

    ' Check that something is selected.
    If selection.Text = "" Then
    MsgBox("No code selected!", MsgBoxStyle.Critical Or _
      MsgBoxStyle.OKOnly, "Format Code")
    Return
    End If

    ' Create a temporary file.
    Dim path As String = System.IO.Path.GetTempFileName( )

    ' Copy the selected code to clipboard (using VS.NET).
    selection.Copy( )

    ' Instantiate a new Word document to
    ' achieve HTML code formatting.
    Dim oleDocument As Type = Type.GetTypeFromProgID("Word.Document")
    Dim document As Object = Activator.CreateInstance(oleDocument)
    document.ActiveWindow.Selection.PasteAndFormat(wdPasteDefault)
    document.SaveAs(path, wdFormatFilteredHTML, False, "", True, "", _
      False, False, False, False, False)
    document.Close( )
    document = Nothing
    oleDocument = Nothing

    ' Open a new instance of Word.
    Dim oleApplication As Type = _
        Type.GetTypeFromProgID("Word.Application")
    Dim application As Object = _
        Activator.CreateInstance(oleApplication)

    ' Open the temporary document.
    document = application.Documents.Open(path)

    ' Switch to the WebView mode within Word.
    document.ActiveWindow.View.Type = wdWebView

    ' Select the whole document.
```

```
document.ActiveWindow.Selection.WholeStory( )

' Copy it to the clipboard.
document.ActiveWindow.Selection.Copy( )

' Close the document.
document.Close( )

document = Nothing
application = Nothing
oleApplication = Nothing
' Cleanup after ourselves.
IO.File.Delete(path)

        End Sub
End Module
```

After you have added and saved this macro, you can then select a piece of text in the code editor and then double-click on this macro. You will see the hourglass for a couple of moments, the macro has to open Microsoft Word, which takes a few seconds. When the hourglass goes away, you will have the formatted HTML code in your clipboard. You can then go to your favorite blogging tool and paste the HTML directly into that tool. This macro works by copying the code from Word. This means that, when you paste the code, it has to be into an application that will understand the rich formatting. For instance, pasting this into the design view of a richtextbox will work perfectly; pasting into Notepad will not work.

Convert to HTML with an Add-in

Another way to get from code to HTML is through the use of a freely available add-in called CopySourceAsHTML. First, you will need to download and install the add-in. It can be downloaded from *http://www.jtleigh.com/ CopySourceAsHTML*.

After downloading and installing the add-in, you will see a new item on the right-click menu called Copy Source as HTML. You can select text in Visual Studio and then click this item on the right-click menu. You will then see the dialog shown in Figure 13-15.

Using this dialog, you first select what type of language code you are copying, either C#, VB, or HTML/XML/ASPX. You can also configure the following options:

Line Numbers
You can set whether the HTML should include line numbers and, if so, what number the add-in should start from.

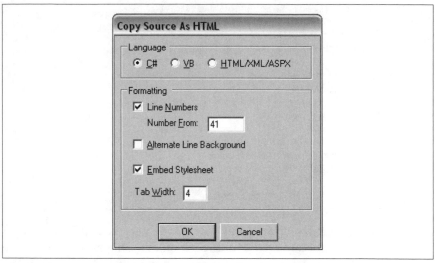

Figure 13-15. Copy Source As HTML dialog

Alternate Line Background

This option allows you to turn on line coloring, similar to what you might find in a report in which every other line is colored to make it easier to read.

Embed Stylesheet

This option determines whether the add-in will embed its stylesheet in the document or reference an external stylesheet. If you are posting a large number of snippets, it might make sense to not include the stylesheet and instead reference one copy of it.

Tab Width

Since HTML treats tabs as whitespace, the add-in has to convert all of those tabs to spaces; this option determines how many spaces should replace each tab.

After you click the OK button, the HTML formatted text will be copied to your clipboard. You can then turn around and paste it into your blogging tool.

Both of these solutions are great ways to get the color formatting of Visual Studio out of the application and onto your web log.

Collapse and Expand Your Code

Collapsing and expanding regions can be fun, but there's a free add-in that lets you do the same with If, Try, and With statements.

Classify is a Visual Studio .NET add-in that exposes a new toolbar and new context sensitive menu items when editing source code. Classify is largely compatible with C#, though some features are currently specific to Visual Basic .NET. Classify can be downloaded from *http://www.visualstudiohacks. com/classify*.

The goal of the add-in is to simplify basic coding tasks and to assist in the common aim of any good programmer, which is to make code readable and maintainable.

To assist with readability, Visual Studio .NET has a feature that enables you to collapse, or temporarily hide, sections of code. However, by default, this behavior applies only to basic code blocks like regions, subroutines, and enumeration blocks. What Classify does, for Visual Basic .NET, is take this to the next level.

Auto-Collapse and Scan-Collapse are very similar features, in that they collapse code. Auto-Collapse is invoked at will by the user in each location where code is to be hidden. Scan-Collapse automatically scans the current source file and collapses all sections of code that the programmer is likely to want to collapse.

For example, imagine that you have a subroutine containing a large Try... Catch block. Within that you have a With…End With and inside that maybe several If...End If and While...End While blocks. Having nested constructs like this often leads to having a lot of code to read, and once you've read it, you could hide it from view. When hidden, it no longer distracts the programmer or reader. So now, where you can collapse subroutines, you can additionally collapse any logical code block that has a known start and end statement, like If...End If.

With Auto-Collapse, you simply right-click the mouse over the starting statement, for example If, and Classify will collapse the code up to and including the End If.

It is important to note that collapsed regions are not persisted: each time you reload your project, your entire source code will be revealed once again. This point makes Auto-Collapse and Scan-Collapse a nondestructive activity. It also means you can freely collapse regions of code, and it will not interfere with other developers who might want the code collapsed in a different way.

In order to install Classify, simply use the Add-in Manager from the Visual Studio .NET Tools menu. Place tick boxes next to the Classify add-in in order to have it activate when Visual Studio .NET is loaded.

Once Classify is active, whenever you right-click in a source code window, you will now see additional items in the pop-up context menu as shown in Figure 13-16.

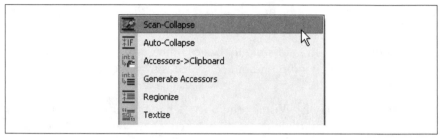

Figure 13-16. Classify right-click menu

To use Auto-Collapse, simply right-click on a line containing a start keyword, such as If, Try, and so on. The following code and Figure 13-17 show a before and after scenario for Auto-Collapse:

```
If EndLine <> 0 Then
    If EndLine > StartLine Then
        If FirstWord = "Test" Then
                DoSomething( )
        Else
            DoSomethingElse( )
        End If
    End If
End If
```

```
 8 ⊟       If EndLine <> 0 Then
 9 ⊟           If EndLine > StartLine Then...
16 ⊢       End If
```

Figure 13-17. After Auto-Collapse is applied to the first nested If

Note the trailing ..., which indicates the code can be expanded. One of the strongest ways in which you can use Auto-Collapse is to have Classify scan the entire source file and automatically choose all the code that can be collapsed. To do this, click the Scan-Collapse icon on the Classify toolbar or the Scan-Collapse item on the right-click menu.

After Scan-Collapse has been applied, as in Figure 13-18, you will see all If, Select, and Try blocks will be collapsed. Note in this example that even the Case statements within the Select Case block have been collapsed.

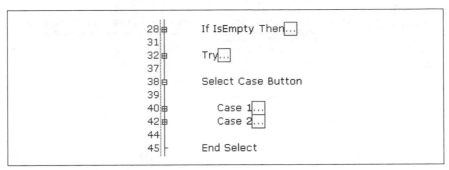

Figure 13-18. If, Select, and Try blocks collapsed

Even on a large source file, Auto-Collapse takes only a few seconds to traverse from start to end. This is a great feature to use on source code that you are not familiar with; it allows you to remove the maximum amount of code from view while still being able to peek inside blocks, all helping you to grasp the purpose of the code you are examining.

—Chris Nurse

Combine the Visual Studio Command Prompt and the Command Window
The Command Prompt and Command Window are addictive individually. Combine these two and you may never reach for the mouse again.

The VSCMDShell power toy can be used to combine two of the more valuable parts of Visual Studio, the Visual Studio Command Prompt [Hack #77] and the Command Window [Hack #46]. Since these tools are similar, someone at Microsoft had the great idea to write a window that combines the functionality of both of these tools in one place. Just having the Visual Studio Command Prompt inside the IDE is valuable—when you add the fact that you can execute Visual Studio commands, it becomes invaluable.

The first step is to download and install the VSCMDShell power toy from *http://workspaces.gotdotnet.com/VSCMDShell*.

Once you have downloaded and installed the power toy, you will find a new menu item on the Tools menu called VSCMDShell Window that will launch the window shown in Figure 13-19.

As you can see, the window looks just like the Visual Studio Command Prompt, because it is. You can do anything you can do in the normal Visual Studio Command Prompt in this window. You can run any of the utilities discussed throughout this book or even just use it as a normal command prompt.

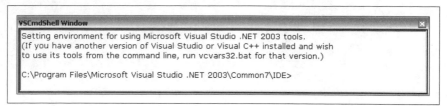

Figure 13-19. VSCMDShell Window

You can also call any Visual Studio commands from this window by simply prefacing the command with an exclamation point. Figure 13-20 shows how using an exclamation point shows the command window IntelliSense.

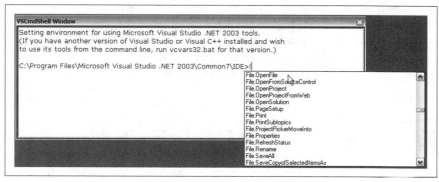

Figure 13-20. Command window IntelliSense

For instance, you could enter the following command into the VSCMDShell window:

```
>!File.OpenFile Class1.cs
```

This would call the OpenFile command and open *Class1.cs* in the development environment. For a list of helpful command window commands, please refer to "Master the Command Window" [Hack #46].

HACK #99 Generate Web Services Code

If you're a fan of contract-driven development, you can take control of the WSDL chicken-egg situation.

The .NET Framework makes it extremely easy to create and deploy Web Services; on top of that, Visual Studio makes it even easier still. You can add an *.asmx* file to your project, add a couple of methods, then build your solution, and you have just written a Web Service. This process is deceptively simple though, since a lot of things are going on in the background, including the generation of a WSDL on the server side and a client proxy on the client side. Visual Studio quietly handles all of this for you, which is not always a good thing, since Visual Studio assumes an XML-based RPC view of Web Services.

There is an idea in Web Services development called contract-first or contract-driven development. The basic idea is that, instead of letting Visual Studio generate a WSDL file for you, you should write this WSDL file by hand using a WSDL, XML, or text editor.

> WSDL stands for Web Services Description Language. It is an XML format used to describe a Web Service's interface by defining its operations and message exchange patterns. The actual messages are defined using a schema definition language like XSD.

Why would you want to write something by hand that Visual Studio will usually generate for you? Letting Visual Studio generate your WSDL is kind of like picking up a car on the lot and then letting the dealer take care of the contract for you. Sure, you get the car—but who knows what you are committed to. By writing your WSDL first, you have complete control over how your Web Service will be seen to the outside world, including its interface and data structures. This is really just a continuation of the idea of contract-driven development that has been around for years the idea of first creating a contract that your object will implement and that your clients will consume.

Writing the WSDL to your Web Services can be a task in and of itself. There are not really any great tools out there to help you along, and the format takes a little bit of getting used to. And after you have created your WSDL file, you then also need to create the client-side proxy and the server-side Web Service code. This is where the WSContractFirst add-in comes into play.

The WSContractFirst add-in was written by Christian Weyer in an effort to make contract-first development easier. Using this add-in, you can generate the code for client-side proxies and server-side Web Services based on a WSDL file right inside of Visual Studio.

First, you will need to download and install the add-in from *http://www.thinktecture.com/resources/software/wscontractfirst/default.html*.

Generate Server-Side Interface

To demonstrate this tool, I am going to start with a very simple WSDL file. This WSDL file defines a simple service called UserValidation that includes a single method, ValidateUser. This method accepts an integer as its single parameter and returns a Boolean value, specifying whether this is a valid user or not. Here is the WSDL file I have created for this simple service:

```xml
<?xml version="1.0" encoding="utf-8"?>
<definitions
xmlns:http="http://schemas.xmlsoap.org/wsdl/http/"
xmlns:soap="http://schemas.xmlsoap.org/wsdl/soap/"
xmlns:xsd="http://www.w3.org/2001/XMLSchema"
xmlns:uv="http://namespaces.infozerk.com/"
xmlns:soapenc="http://schemas.xmlsoap.org/soap/encoding/"
xmlns:tm="http://microsoft.com/wsdl/mime/textMatching/"
xmlns:mime="http://schemas.xmlsoap.org/wsdl/mime/"
targetNamespace="http://namespaces.infozerk.com/"
xmlns="http://schemas.xmlsoap.org/wsdl/">
  <types>
    <xsd:schema elementFormDefault="qualified"
        targetNamespace="http://namespaces.infozerk.com/">
      <xsd:element name="ValidateUser">
        <xsd:complexType>
          <xsd:sequence>
            <xsd:element minOccurs="1" maxOccurs="1"
                name="userID" type="xsd:int" />
          </xsd:sequence>
        </xsd:complexType>

      </xsd:element>
      <xsd:element name="ValidateUserResponse">
        <xsd:complexType>
          <xsd:sequence>
            <xsd:element minOccurs="1" maxOccurs="1"
                name="ValidateUserResult" type="xsd:boolean" />
          </xsd:sequence>
        </xsd:complexType>
      </xsd:element>
    </xsd:schema>

  </types>
  <message name="ValidateUserSoapIn">
    <part name="parameters" element="uv:ValidateUser" />
  </message>
  <message name="ValidateUserSoapOut">
    <part name="parameters" element="uv:ValidateUserResponse" />
  </message>
  <portType name="UserValidationSoap">
    <operation name="ValidateUser">

      <input message="uv:ValidateUserSoapIn" />
      <output message="uv:ValidateUserSoapOut" />
    </operation>
  </portType>
  <binding name="UserValidationSoap" type="uv:UserValidationSoap">
    <soap:binding transport="http://schemas.xmlsoap.org/soap/http"
        style="document" />
```

```
        <operation name="ValidateUser">
          <soap:operation
            soapAction="http:/namespaces.infozerk.com/ValidateUser"
            style="document" />
          <input>
            <soap:body use="literal" />
          </input>
          <output>
            <soap:body use="literal" />
          </output>
        </operation>
      </binding>
      <service name="UserValidation">
        <port name="UserValidationSoap" binding="uv:UserValidationSoap">
        <soap:address
         location="http://localhost/TestServices/UserValidation.asmx" />
        </port>
      </service>
    </definitions>
```

After creating and saving this WSDL file, you then need to add it to your project. Once it is in your project, you then simply need to right-click on the WSDL file and you will see the option shown in Figure 13-21.

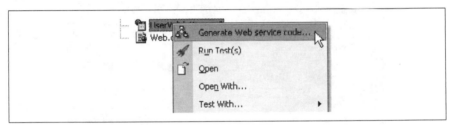

Figure 13-21. ContractFirst menu

 You could alternatively open the tool from the Tools menu and simply point the tool to your WSDL file (including a URL); it does not have to be a part of your project.

After choosing Generate Web Service Code, you will see the dialog shown in Figure 13-22.

You can configure a number of things from this dialog. In this example, I have chosen to generate a Service-Side Interface. I have also renamed the file to better match the name of my service. After you click Generate, the add-in will create two different files for you. In this example, the first is named *UserValidation.cs* and is an abstract class defining the interface for the Web Service. The code for this file can be seen here:

```
//------------------------------------------------------------
// <autogenerated code>
```

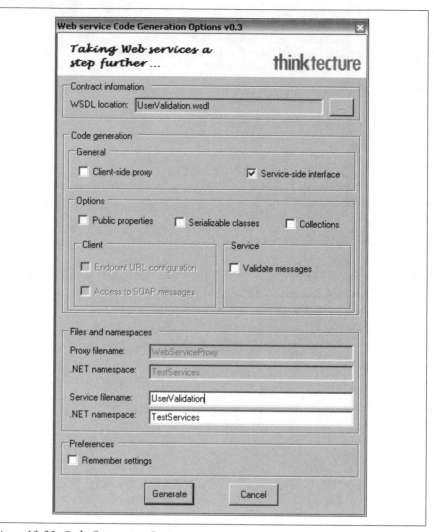

Figure 13-22. Code Generation Options

```
//      This code was generated by a tool.
//      Changes to this file may cause incorrect
//      behavior and will be lost if
//      the code is regenerated.
// </autogenerated code>
//-------------------------------------------------------------
//
// This source code was auto-generated
// by WsContractFirst, Version=0.3.1.4244


namespace TestServices
{
```

```
    using System.Diagnostics;
    using System.Xml.Serialization;
    using System;
    using System.Web.Services.Protocols;
    using System.ComponentModel;
    using System.Web.Services;


/// <remarks></remarks>
[System.Web.Services.WebServiceBindingAttribute(
    Name="UserValidationSoap",
    Namespace="http://namespaces.infozerk.com/")]
public abstract class UserValidation : System.Web.Services.WebService
{

    /// <remarks/>
    [System.Web.Services.WebMethodAttribute()]
    [System.Web.Services.Protocols.SoapDocumentMethodAttribute(
    "http:/namespaces.infozerk.com/ValidateUser",
    RequestNamespace="http://namespaces.infozerk.com/",
    ResponseNamespace="http://namespaces.infozerk.com/",
    Use=System.Web.Services.Description.SoapBindingUse.Literal,
    ParameterStyle=
    System.Web.Services.Protocols.SoapParameterStyle.Wrapped)]
    public abstract bool ValidateUser(int userID);
}
}
```

ContractFirst then also generates an *.asmx* file (including the corresponding *.cs* or *.vb* file) that inherits from this abstract class. This file can be seen here:

```
//-------------------------       ----------------------------
// <autogenerated code>
//      This code was generated by a tool.
//      Changes to this file may cause incorrect
//      behavior and will be lost if
//      the code is regenerated.
// </autogenerated code>
//------------------------------------------------------------
//
// This source code was auto-generated
// by WsContractFirst, Version=0.3.1.4244


namespace TestServices
{
    using System.Diagnostics;
    using System.Xml.Serialization;
    using System;
    using System.Web.Services.Protocols;
    using System.ComponentModel;
    using System.Web.Services;
```

```
    /// <remarks/>
    [System.Web.Services.WebServiceBindingAttribute(
        Name="UserValidationSoap",
        Namespace="http://namespaces.infozerk.com/")]
    [System.Web.Services.WebServiceAttribute(
        Namespace="http://namespaces.infozerk.com/")]
    public class UserValidationImpl : UserValidation
    {

        /// <remarks/>
        [System.Web.Services.WebMethodAttribute()]
        [System.Web.Services.Protocols.SoapDocumentMethodAttribute("
        http:/namespaces.infozerk.com/ValidateUser",
        RequestNamespace="http://namespaces.infozerk.com/",
        ResponseNamespace="http://namespaces.infozerk.com/",
    Use=System.Web.Services.Description.SoapBindingUse.Literal,
    ParameterStyle=
    System.Web.Services.Protocols.SoapParameterStyle.Wrapped)]
        public override bool ValidateUser(int userID)
        {
            return new bool();
        }
    }
}
```

Notice that the tool simply adds a stub return into the method—in this example, it will return a new bool value. From here, your job would be to implement this Web Service by writing the contents of this method, doing the actual work of determining whether this is a valid user.

Generate Client-Side Proxies

The other way that Visual Studio makes working with Web Services easy is the ability to add a web reference to a Web Service. After adding a web reference, you can then access that Web Service just as if it were a local class in your project, due to Visual Studio generating a client-side proxy for you. This proxy is simply a class that sits between your code and the actual Web Service. The ContractFirst add-in can generate client-side proxies as well, including some advanced options for code generation.

For this example, I will use the same WSDL file used for the server-side example. After right-clicking on the WSDL file and choosing Generate Web Service Code, you will now need to choose Client-Side Proxy and specify a name of the proxy, as shown in Figure 13-23.

After you click Generate, the following code will be added to your project as *UserValidationProxy.cs*:

```
//------------------------------------------------------------
// <autogenerated code>
//     This code was generated by a tool.
```

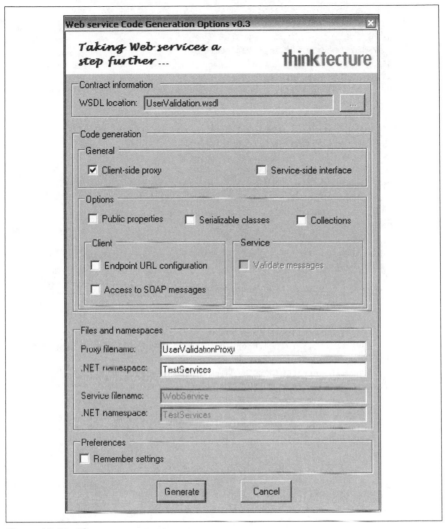

Figure 13-23. Client proxy creation

```
//      Changes to this file may cause incorrect
//      behavior and will be lost if
//      the code is regenerated.
// </autogenerated code>
//------------------------------------------------------------
//
// This source code was auto-generated
// by WsContractFirst, Version=0.3.1.4244


namespace TestServices
{
```

```
using System.Diagnostics;
using System.Xml.Serialization;
using System;
using System.Web.Services.Protocols;
using System.ComponentModel;
using System.Web.Services;


/// <remarks></remarks>
[System.Diagnostics.DebuggerStepThroughAttribute()]
[System.ComponentModel.DesignerCategoryAttribute("code")]
[System.Web.Services.WebServiceBindingAttribute(
    Name="UserValidationSoap",
    Namespace="http://namespaces.infozerk.com/")]
public class UserValidation :
        System.Web.Services.Protocols.SoapHttpClientProtocol
{

  /// <remarks/>
  public UserValidation()
  {
  this.Url = "http://localhost/TestServices/UserValidation.asmx";
  }

  /// <remark></remarks>
  [System.Web.Services.Protocols.SoapDocumentMethodAttribute("
  http:/namespaces.infozerk.com/ValidateUser",
  RequestNamespace="http://namespaces.infozerk.com/",
  ResponseNamespace="http://namespaces.infozerk.com/",
  Use=System.Web.Services.Description.SoapBindingUse.Literal,
  ParameterStyle=
  System.Web.Services.Protocols.SoapParameterStyle.Wrapped)]
  public bool ValidateUser(int userID)
  {
      object[] results =
      this.Invoke("ValidateUser", new object[] {userID});
      return ((bool)(results[0]));
  }

  /// <remarks/>
  public System.IAsyncResult BeginValidateUser(
      int userID,
      System.AsyncCallback callback,
      object asyncState)
  {
      return this.BeginInvoke("ValidateUser", new object[] {
                userID}, callback, asyncState);
  }

  /// <remarks/>
  public bool EndValidateUser(System.IAsyncResult asyncResult)
  {
      object[] results = this.EndInvoke(asyncResult);
```

```
            return ((bool)(results[0]));
        }
    }
}
```

You will then be able to use this class from your project to interface with the UserValidation Web Service.

ContractFirst Options

The ContractFirst add-in also contains a number of options and properties that can be used to customize the code that is generated by the tool. These options are shown in Table 13-1.

Table 13-1. ContractFirst add-in options

Name	Description
Public properties	If checked, the add-in will use public properties instead of using public fields.
Serializable classes	If checked, the add-in will create serializable data classes.
Collection	If checked, the add-in will generate collections to use instead of arrays.
Endpoint URL configuration	If checked, endpoint configuration in the *.config* file will be enabled.
Access to SOAP messages	If checked, read-only access to the SOAP messages will be added.
Validate messages	If checked, the add-in will enable XSD-based validation on the incoming SOAP messages.

The ContractFirst add-in is a great tool if you have subscribed to the idea of contract-first Web Service development. There are also plans in the future to add a wizard that would help you create WSDL files starting with an XSD file so you don't have to worry about all the clumsy WSDL details. Instead, ContractFirst will present you with a simple but powerful abstraction of it. Look for a lot more from this tool in the future.

HACK
#100

Test Regular Expressions in Visual Studio

Regular expressions can be much trickier than the rest of your code. Break the edit-compile-debug-shriek cycle with a free add-in that tests regular expressions right inside Visual Studio.

Regular expressions are strings of symbols and characters that are used to identify a part or parts of strings. Regular expressions are a very powerful and flexible technology, but they are also a very challenging technology. The easiest way to more efficiently work with regular expressions is to find a utility that allows you to quickly write and evaluate them. Some wonderful Windows utilities, including Regulator (*http://royo.is-a-geek.com/iserializable/regulator*) and Expresso (*http://www.codeproject.com/dotnet/expresso.asp*), are available. But both of these tools require you to run a separate application, and a free add-in called RegExinator lets you write regular expressions and then run them against the current document in Visual Studio. The add-in is not as full featured as the standalone Windows utilities, but it can be more convenient since it is built directly into Visual Studio.

> I have a small personal interest in this add-in, as I helped Peter Wright in the development of this tool.

First, you will need to download and install the add-in from *http://www.visualstudiohacks.com/regexinator*.

Evaluate Regular Expressions

The main use for the RegExinator is to evaluate regular expressions directly inside of Visual Studio. To show an example, let's say that you have a text file with names and phone numbers, and you need to retrieve a list of all the area codes from this text file. This is a perfect example of how to apply regular expressions. Here is a sample of this file:

```
James Avery, (513) 555-1212
Tammy Avery, (513) 555-1212
Louisa Avery, (615) 555-1212
```

To use RegExinator, you will need to load this file into Visual Studio and then open the RegExinator window, which is shown in Figure 13-24.

Once you have the file loaded and the tool window open, you can enter a regular expression. For this example, if you wanted to get all of the area codes, you could use a regular expression that looks something like this:

```
(\([0-9]{3}\))
```

The first (is the opening of the regular expression. The \(is an escape character for the first parenthesis of the area code. The [0-9] specifies any number between 0 and 9, and the {3} states that you want three instances of this number. The \) is the closing parenthesis of the area code, and finally) is the end of the regular expression.

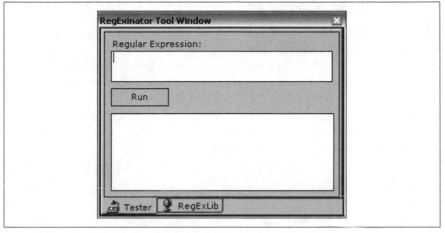

Figure 13-24. RegExinator Tool Window

You can enter this regular expression into the tool and then click the Run button. RegExinator will then process the current document using the regular expression and show the results, as shown in Figure 13-25.

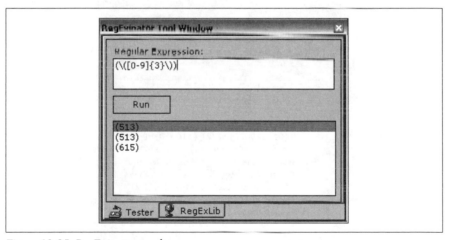

Figure 13-25. RegExinator results

You can select any of the matches, and that line will be highlighted in the document. You can also search only a selection in your document by selecting that section of the document and then running the tool. RegExinator will then look for matches only in the part of the document you have selected.

Find More Regular Expressions

The other functionality built into RegExinator is the ability to search the Regular Expressions Library from right inside Visual Studio. The Regular Expression Library (*http://www.regexlib.com*) is a web site that contains a plethora of extremely useful regular expressions cataloged by their use. It is a great resource to know about when trying to figure out a complicated regular expression. If you wanted to find a regular expression that would match both United States and European style phone numbers, you would have no problem finding one in the library. RegExLib also exposes a great set of Web Services that can be used to search the library; these services are what makes integration with RegExinator possible.

To search the library using RegExinator, you simply need to click the RegExLib tab and you will see a simple text box labeled Search. Enter your search criteria in this text box and click the Run button, and you will then see the results as shown in Figure 13-26.

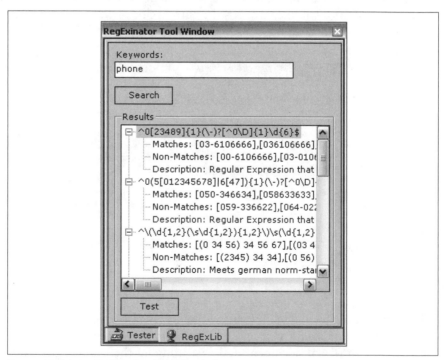

Figure 13-26. RegExLib search results

Each node in the window is a regular expression that was found in RegEx-Lib. Below each node are examples of what the regular expression will match, what it won't match, and a brief description of the expression. When you have found a regular expression that you want to test, you simply need to select the expression and then click the Test button. This will copy the expression to the Tester window where you can then run it against your document.

RegExinator is a simple but useful tool for evaluating regular expressions and searching for expressions from inside Visual Studio. For more information on regular expressions, the authoritative text on the subject is *Mastering Regular Expressions* (O'Reilly)

Index

Symbols

[ ] (brackets)
    character class in regular
        expressions, 85
    GoToBrace command, 90
{ } (curly braces), in regular expression
        replacements, 86
#{ and }#, enclosing code
        snippets, 222
<% and %>, enclosing code template
        keywords, 224
' (apostrophe)
    ''', preceding VB.NET XML
        comments, 286
    VB.NET line comments, 271
* (asterisk), in regular expression
        matching, 86
\ (backslash), escaping characters in
        regular expressions, 88
^ (caret), in regular expression
        matching, 86
? (question mark), reading variable
        values, 180
" (quotes), enclosing variables and
        commands, 134
/ (slash)
    //, C# line comments, 271
    ///, preceding XML comments, 272
/? switch (VSEdit), 177
| (vertical bar), in code templates, 222

Numbers

1033 folder, 395

A

abbreviations, identifier names and, 281
acronyms, treatment of (class library
        design), 281
ACT (see Application Center Test tool)
active code generation, 197
Add New Item dialog box, extending by
        adding file template, 389–398
Add Reference dialog, 11
AddDirective macro, 216
Add-in Manager, 418
add-ins
    changing icon for, 411–416
        adding to installer, 414
        creating the icon, 412–413
        modifying command code, 414
    classes, coloring in code, 56
    Code<Template>.NET, 221–224
    Command Browser, 408–411
    CopySourceCodeAsHTML, 435
    devMetrics, 262–265
    GhostDoc, 281–285
    managing, 417–420
        Add-in Manager, 418
        installing, 417
        repairing add-ins, 419
    PInvoke.NET, for Visual Studio, 241
    Reflector tool, 252
    RegExinator, 450

We'd like to hear your suggestions for improving our indexes. Send email to *index@oreilly.com*.

R

Colophon

Our look is the result of reader comments, our own experimentation, and feedback from distribution channels. Distinctive covers complement our distinctive approach to technical topics, breathing personality and life into potentially dry subjects.

The tool on the cover of *Visual Studio Hacks* is a voltmeter. Voltmeters, which were originally produced in 1888, are instruments used to measure differences of electric potential, commonly called voltage. An ideal voltmeter is an open circuit and therefore has infinite resistance. Although it is not actually possible to make a physical voltmeter with infinite resistance, a well-designed voltmeter has a very high resistance so that it does not have an appreciable affect on the current or voltage it is measuring. To accomplish this, a large resistor is placed in series with the galvanometer. The resistor controls the current produced by the galvanometer, which is quite small to begin with.

Most voltmeters are based on the d'Arsonval galvanometer and are of the analog type, meaning they use moving coils to give voltage readings that can vary over a continuous range as indicated by a scale and pointer. Modern digital mechanisms give readings as numerical displays and generally have a higher order of accuracy than analog instruments. This type of voltmeter provides outputs that can be transmitted over distance, can activate printers or typewriters, and can feed into computers.

Mary Brady was the production editor, and Norma Emory was the copyeditor for *Visual Studio Hacks*. Katherine T. Pinard was the proofreader. Matt Hutchinson and Mary Anne Weeks Mayo provided quality control. Ellen Troutman-Zaig wrote the index. Lydia Onofrei provided production assistance.

Hanna Dyer designed the cover of this book, based on a series design by Edie Freedman. The cover image is an original photograph by DJ Soft Tools V39 CD. Karen Montgomery produced the cover layout with InDesign CS using Adobe's Helvetica Neue and ITC Garamond fonts.

David Futato designed the interior layout. This book was converted by Joe Wizda to FrameMaker 5.5.6 with a format conversion tool created by Erik Ray, Jason McIntosh, Neil Walls, and Mike Sierra that uses Perl and XML technologies. The text font is Linotype Birka; the heading font is Adobe Helvetica Neue Condensed; and the code font is LucasFont's TheSans Mono Condensed. The illustrations that appear in the book were produced by Robert Romano, Jessamyn Read, and Lesley Borash using Macromedia MX and Adobe Photoshop CS. This colophon was written by Lydia Onofrei.

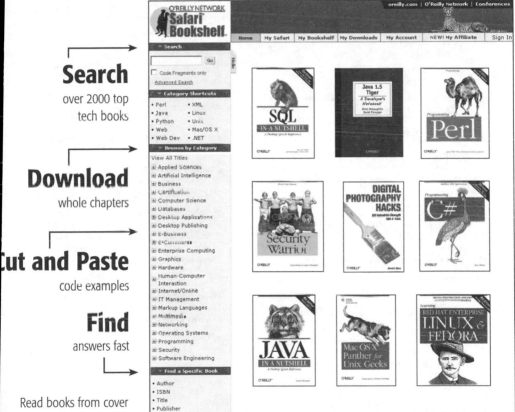

Keep in touch with O'Reilly

1. Download examples from our books

To find example files for a book, go to:

www.oreilly.com/catalog

select the book, and follow the "Examples" link.

2. Register your O'Reilly books

Register your book at *register.oreilly.com*

Why register your books? Once you've registered your O'Reilly books you can:

- Win O'Reilly books, T-shirts or discount coupons in our monthly drawing.
- Get special offers available only to registered O'Reilly customers.
- Get catalogs announcing new books (US and UK only).
- Get email notification of new editions of the O'Reilly books you own.

3. Join our email lists

Sign up to get topic-specific email announcements of new books and conferences, special offers, and O'Reilly Network technology newsletters at:

elists.oreilly.com

It's easy to customize your free elists subscription so you'll get exactly the O'Reilly news you want.

4. Get the latest news, tips, and tools

http://www.oreilly.com

- "Top 100 Sites on the Web"—PC Magazine
- CIO Magazine's Web Business 50 Awards

Our web site contains a library of comprehensive product information (including book excerpts and tables of contents), downloadable software, background articles, interviews with technology leaders, links to relevant sites, book cover art, and more.

5. Work for O'Reilly

Check out our web site for current employment opportunities:

jobs.oreilly.com

6. Contact us

O'Reilly & Associates
1005 Gravenstein Hwy North
Sebastopol, CA 95472 USA

TEL: 707-827-7000 or 800-998-9938
(6am to 5pm PST)

FAX: 707-829-0104

order@oreilly.com
For answers to problems regarding your order or our products.
To place a book order online, visit:

www.oreilly.com/order_new

catalog@oreilly.com
To request a copy of our latest catalog.

booktech@oreilly.com
For book content technical questions or corrections.

corporate@oreilly.com
For educational, library, government, and corporate sales.

proposals@oreilly.com
To submit new book proposals to our editors and product managers.

international@oreilly.com
For information about our international distributors or translation queries. For a list of our distributors outside of North America check out:

international.oreilly.com/distributors.html

adoption@oreilly.com
For information about academic use of O'Reilly books, visit:

academic.oreilly.com

Related Titles Available from O'Reilly

Hacks

Amazon Hacks

BSD Hacks

Digital Photography Hacks

eBay Hacks

Excel hacks

Flash Hacks

Gaming Hacks

Google Hacks

Harware Hacking Projects for Geeks

Home Theater Hacks

iPod & iTunes Hacks

Knoppix Hacks

Linux Desktop Hacks

Linux Server Hacks

Mac OS X Hacks

Mac OS X Panther Hacks

Network Security Hacks

PayPal Hacks

PDF Hacks

PC Hacks

Smart Home Hacks

Spidering Hacks

TiVo Hacks

Windows Server Hacks

Windows XP Hacks

Wireless Hacks

Word Hacks

O'REILLY®

Our books are available at most retail and online bookstores.
To order direct: 1-800-998-9938 • *order@oreilly.com* • *www.oreilly.com*
Online editions of most O'Reilly titles are available by subscription at *safari.oreilly.com*